# Faraday as a natural Philosopher

Joseph Agassi

# Faraday
## *as a natural Philosopher*

The University of Chicago Press, Chicago & London

The University of Chicago Press, Chicago 60637
The University of Chicago Press, Ltd., London

© 1971 by The University of Chicago
All rights reserved. Published 1971
Printed in the United States of America

International Standard Book Number: 0–226–01046-5
Library of Congress Catalog Card Number: 73–151130

# Contents

# Preface

Faraday has more biographies than even Newton and Einstein.[1] The chief reason for his popularity among biographers is that they view him as the Cinderella of science. That, at least at first, is eminently obvious: he was born the son of a poor blacksmith in a London slum and rose to great fame—the greatest experimental physicist of his time and the popular director of the Royal Institution. For my part, I view him as an ugly duckling, not an experimenter but a highly speculative and bold thinker. Though as an experimenter he was highly respected, he was deeply disappointed to find that as a thinker he was ostracized by the scientific community of his day. Now we can see how important his ideas were.

With the exception of *Michael Faraday: A Biography*, by L. Pearce Williams (1965), all works on Faraday, long and short, follow the first one, *Faraday as a Discoverer* (1868). Its author, John Tyndall, was one of the handful of close personal friends Faraday had, the only man who came close to qualifying as a pupil and as a successor to Faraday. Tyndall's thesis, as the title of his book indicates, is that Faraday was great as, and rose from rags to fame as, a discoverer of important facts of nature. This thesis is uncontestable. Faraday himself had great respect for empirical discovery and was very proud to be a discoverer; he cherished the many acknowledgments that the commonwealth of learning bestowed on him. Yet he would have been greatly disturbed by Tyndall's book. He viewed himself not as a discoverer but as a theoretician as well as an experimenter—he wanted to be known as a philosopher; success or failure was for him the success or failure of his speculations about the nature

1. For a list of Faraday's main biographies see Alan E. Jeffreys, *Michael Faraday, A List of His Lectures and Published Writings*, London and New York, 1960, pp. xxv–xxvi.

of things physical—success or failure to attain the critical notice of his colleagues. When he died, there was still no decision on the question, had he been successful in drawing his colleagues' attention to his speculations or not? Tyndall still pooh-poohed them. Spectacular success came soon after.

By now most of Faraday's ideas are commonplace in physics; he has achieved his aim, even though posthumously. Yet most of his ideas are still not attributed to him. Most scientists who happen to take any interest in history think of him as one whose researches are closely linked with intuitive models of the aether; they are very surprised to hear that so early in the history of electromagnetism, in the 1830s indeed, Faraday denied that the aether exists. In the present study I shall show in detail how most of his discoveries are related to his idea of matter as fields of forces and of fields of forces as polarizations of empty space. There were many reasons to consider all this outlandish. Thinkers from Euclid to Newton had viewed space as homogenous and isotropic—i.e., as having no preferred locations and no preferred directions. This was well in accord with all factual evidence, as much as with all philosophy and logic: the nothing has no properties; to view matter as a property of empty space sounds absurd. There was no evidence to support Faraday's fantasy; in science, it was claimed, facts must come before the theories that they back, and then these theories should be further confirmed; hence science should ignore Faraday's fantasy.

Faraday's speculations were subsequently ignored, and at times even rudely ignored. In his preface to the German translation of Tyndall's biography, Hermann von Helmholtz says Faraday used his speculations "for want of mathematical culture." A review of Faraday's *Experimental Researches in Electricity* published in the *Philosophical Magazine* (1855) at least acknowledged that Faraday was guided in his research by his speculations; even earlier writers who engaged in public debate with Faraday acknowledged that much. One of them (Riess) even met his challenge to do likewise: it is all right for Faraday to employ Faraday's speculations, the critic conceded, but anyone else who does so runs the risk of becoming prejudiced in favor of these speculations. And, need one say, prejudiced people cannot be good scientists. Let me outline here Faraday's response.

In his lecture "On Mental Education," with which Faraday more or less closed his career, he answered thus. He fully accepted the idea that scientists should beware of prejudices; indeed, this was very important to him. Anyone can be as great a scientist as I am, said Faraday, if only one gets rid of one's prejudices. In the essay he does not specify which prejudices he thought were plaguing the scientific world; but in his manifesto-like lecture "On the Conservation of Force," he says there are two competing speculations, Newton's and mine; and everyone blindly follows Newton's and ignores mine—even though Newton himself was no Newtonian! The implication was all too clear: it was not the fear of prejudice that led scientists to ignore Faraday—it was plain prejudice. All his life Faraday thought that by keeping his temper and by working hard he would finally gain attention. Only toward the end of his life did he express both his high hopes and his deep despair. He died with the conflict still unresolved.

Faraday's speculations have been rediscovered by historians of science in recent decades. They are discussed in L. Pearce Williams's scholarly, detailed, and reasonably comprehensive biography. Williams does not speak of the unorthodoxy of Faraday's speculations, or of Faraday's struggle against the orthodoxy of his colleagues, against their dogmatism and harsh indifference. Williams overlooks Faraday's struggles and does not describe the interaction between Faraday's personal struggle and his intellectual one. And so I find it possible to offer the present study, though it claims much less completeness and scholarship than his, as the more realistic of the two. Williams still beautifies both Faraday and the scientific world. He claims for Faraday more than Tyndall, and I do endorse his claim, namely that Faraday was significant as a thinker. Yet Williams's achievement is both a gain and a loss: Tyndall expresses in his volume some discontent (he is somewhat displeased with Faraday's speculations); Williams expresses none. His picture of Faraday and his environment is too unrealistically smooth, with nothing objectionable or regrettable to report.

My ambition is not to add the warts and the wrinkles to Williams's portrait. My ambition is not even to draw a portrait; it is to consider and compare two portraits of Faraday—one may be called the private, personal, or psychological, and the other may be called the public or scientific; in particular, it is my aim to integrate the two as much as possible. Let me add some general remarks on this kind of duality.

Attempts to integrate a private and a public portrait are always problematic and can never be entirely successful; what a given public hero has done might have been accomplished by a man of a different personal character; the public hero might have achieved the same thing regardless of certain private events in his life, had he married or not, had he two children or six. In his obituary notice of Faraday, his closest friend, Auguste de la Rive, says Faraday was fortunately childless and could devote himself wholly to research. This is a cruel observation—Faraday viewed his being childless as the greatest misfortune next to his having no pupils—and quite false. But perhaps the life of an artist may be linked with his art. Even if this were so, the link would be ad hoc; and hence, even when true, the theory linking his private and public life would not be intellectually satisfactory: happy and triumphant art may accompany a happy life (Rubens, Haydn) or a miserable and unhappy life (Pergolesi, Beethoven). And yet linking the two is usually expected of a biographer or historian. A politician may be a man of peace who wages war or a man of peace who makes peace; he may be a monstrous combination of a man of peace in his private life and a warmonger abroad—every case is found in history. In each case the biographer or historian faces a clear and simple challenge, though it be too difficult, and he executes it badly or well, but never well enough.

In this respect, men of science stand out: we do not expect any attempt at integrating their private and public portraits. Writing about men of science, most biographers simply refuse to take up the challenge; thus far, of the very few who have done so, few have been successful to even a humble measure. (The exceptions are Jones on Freud and Manuel on Newton.) This has led to a new type of biography—*scientific* biography and *scientific* autobiography— where the unwillingness to take up the challenge is honestly confessed. Nevertheless, there is little doubt that the scientific autobiographies of Einstein and of Planck are the only ones that have attained any measure of success in presenting a combination of private portraits—not biographies—and scientific portraits (as well as biographies).

Both Einstein and Planck were dissenters from quantum indeterminacy and believers in a sort of unified world view, simple, solid, all-embracing. Einstein combined his Spinoza-like philosophy with a Spinoza-like character— deep and quiet, above normal strife, and serenely yearning for utter simplicity. Planck combined with the same philosophy as much of the contrary character as compatible with his great spirit—irritability and displeasure, and an almost contemptuous attitude toward his colleagues for their inability to live up to the scientific ideals of utter openmindedness and constant struggle for improvement.

The present study, similarly, is a partial portrait, not a biography, civil or intellectual. I had no qualms about ignoring almost entirely Faraday's close ties with his wife, for example, though one or two of the many tender letters he wrote her have even found their way into some anthologies of English prose. Similarly, I intentionally ignore in this volume much of his scientific work, in chemistry, metallurgy, optics, and mechanics, regardless of its importance. I have tried to describe Faraday, or rather the growth of his personality, in a manner that will defy classification as either civil or intellectual. This is the intended bias of this study. Because of it, I fear you may find reading this volume rather irritating and displeasing. If so, I wish you would try to make light of it and read it as a new kind of historical novel, parallel to today's semidocumentaries, and take my documentation less as a tool of scholarship and more as an attempt to create an air of verisimilitude. This is not to say that knowingly I have forged data or even overlooked discrepancies out of little consideration for truth. Rather, it is to say that I knowingly use my study of Faraday to illustrate a philosophy, and I hope you find this philosophy thought-provoking—perhaps provoking those thoughts that may show me in error and thus enlighten me. For, the main maxim I tried to follow in my writing is, better an interesting error, which may be read and rectified, than a dull truth that will stay put like a heavy tombstone in a forgotten graveyard. I hope I have some measure of success in entertaining my reader.

Some historians of science consider the attitude just expressed—study only for (intellectual) pleasure—either facetious or dangerous. They feel that important records would be lost if we did not pay respect to facts as facts. But they have no empirical basis for this feeling. The present study contains a discussion of this view, not because I respect those who promulgate it today, but because I deeply respect the tradition of the Royal Society, now dead, that advocated it as an article of faith, to which tradition Faraday himself belonged and which tradition he began to destroy. The worst aspect of this tradition is that in the name of facts it appeals to experimentalism and in the name of facts it demands that we stick to solid facts and eschew all experimentalism.

An appreciative publisher's editor who is a respectable historian of science made some strong comments about the present study. He greatly disapproved of my poor method of documentation and of the liberty I take in italicizing and capitalizing quotations. I have tried to make some amends, especially by way of adding a bibliographic note. Let me add here that I make no claim to be an authority. The same editor complained about the absence of continuity and the difficulty he had in extracting a biography of Faraday from the present study. To remedy this I have added a brief biographical chapter that also summarizes the whole volume.

Finally, a word of thanks. It was in Spring 1956 that I finished the first draft of, and most of the research work for, the present study while a graduate student of Professor Karl Popper in the London School of Economics. I am greatly indebted to him in many ways. I did most of my research in the

**Preface**

libraries of the British Museum and the Royal Institution. I received permission to quote from manuscripts from librarians and secretaries of the Royal Institution of Great Britain, the Royal Society of London, the Institute of Electrical Engineers, London, and the Institutt for Teoretisk Astrofysikk, Oslo University. The Graduate School of Boston University supported the final preparation of the typescript. William K. Berkson, Robert S. Cohen, Daniel A. Greenberg, and Ann Moyal spent much time and effort reading and correcting the final type-script that Priscilla Parris prepared with much care. My gratitude to them all.

Sudbury, Massachusetts
Winter 1970

Faraday as a natural Philosopher

# 1　Introduction

## A Personal Biography

Michael Faraday was born in 1791 in a London slum and died in Hampton Court in 1867 as a pensioner of the Queen. Most pensioners there were high civil servants and military personnel. Perhaps he was the only scientist who ever lived there as a pensioner of the Crown. Men of science of earlier times were, at least supposedly, gentlemen of independent means, or at least people whose employment offered them sufficient leisure and money. Those who were the exception, like James Watt or Humphry Davy, had to be catered to individually. Men of science later on were professional scientists, and often academics, whose research was their means of livelihood. Faraday was employed by the Royal Institution, which hardly supported him, and which he had at times to rescue from financial ruin by very hard work. Also, true to the older tradition that he tried to follow as much as he could, he took no patent on principle and most of his public service was given free of charge. In many respects Faraday refused to move with the times and was old-fashioned and thus fairly vulnerable.

Faraday's early years were very hard; he was often hungry and had almost no schooling. He was physically too weak to follow his father's trade (that of blacksmith) and was thus assigned as an apprentice to a bookbinder. His master happened to be a Frenchman and a refugee from the French Revolution. He encouraged the youngster to study, and he probably instilled in him a measure of the political conservatism that Faraday always adhered to. When he was about twenty years old he joined the Royal Institution as a test-tube washer and as a personal assistant to Sir Humphry Davy. Though he made an impression in his various social and intellectual circles and on various important scientists, though he even started making scientific contributions, he was small fry before he invented the electric motor in 1821 at the age of thirty.

## Introduction

Just before that Faraday married and received permission to bring his bride to his attic in the Royal Institution, where they stayed (except for small excursions and for vacations prescribed by doctors) until he retired from the institution as its resident professor and director. Faraday belonged to a very small and low church—run by a rotating circle of elders—and his wife was a member of the same denomination and the sister of a close friend of his. Though he often served as an elder, he seldom talked about his religion, and though he was a master lecturer of the first order in the Royal Institution, he seemed deliberately drab as a preacher.

The years between 1821, when he discovered the electric motor, and 1831, when he discovered the electric dynamo, his thirties, were those of his rise to position and fame but at the high cost of being accused of plagiarism and of quarrels with Davy whom he had loved and admired and to whom he always remained grateful. There is no doubt that, in part, his troubles arose from his social situation. They also stemmed from a personal peculiarity, namely an unusual certain rigidity, which caused him trouble years later with his own people. One Sunday he missed church service because he had been invited to lunch with the Queen. He was told to repent and refused, and was expelled from his church for some time.

From the year 1831 what characterized his life was his intense work in his research and his progressive illness. He produced work, regularly and systematically, of high caliber and great unity of thought and style, to the year 1839, which saw the publication of the first volume of his *Experimental Researches in Electricity* as well as his first nervous breakdown. The illness was depression, the symptoms were giddiness, forgetfulness, and great aversion to all company. All in all, he published three volumes of his *Experimental Researches in Electricity* and the beginning of a fourth; he published a volume of *Experimental Researches in Chemistry* and *Physics*, and he published science books for children—childless, he had great affection for all children. Also during the same period his illness grew worse and became increasingly frequent and in longer fits. He finally had to resign his job. Before he died he was utterly senile; he had lost his speech almost entirely, and of his enthusiasm for the large-scale scenes of nature all that remained was his pleasure at observing the sunset.

From the age of fifty, however, he had been the grand old man of British science, even of science in general. He declined a British knighthood and the presidency of the Royal Society and similar honors but graciously accepted other honors and titles. He exchanged letters with many leading scientists and was consulted personally by many more. Yet he was at odds with the world of science. He was admired as a discoverer, as a physicist; he hated the word "physicist" and even the word "scientist"; he viewed himself as a philosopher and wished to be considered one; and he felt his contemporaries unjustly and rather dogmatically ignored his theories.

Though a very colorful personality, Faraday did not lead a colorful life. His few extrascientific interests suffered from his increasing scientific activity. In his youth he played the flute and sang bass and loved conversation most; he was associated with the Royal Academy of Arts, with poets and painters and groups of spirited free souls. In his middle age he had no time to enjoy his free ticket to the opera. His closest friend from adolescence came to see him once when he was a professor; after that the friend came to see him only while he was lecturing—in order not to take his time. His services to society he discharged in long hours of tedious paper work and innumerable drab committee meetings.[1] He was not active either politically or in the scientific society. His letter to *The Times*, of 1853, against spiritualism, caused quite a stir. And the one, of 1855, concerning the pollution of the river Thames was quite an event, which the satirical *Punch* noticed properly.[2] This hardly compares with Einstein's rich and varied political career. He barely accepted invitations, whether to parties or to dinners, or to any other kind of activity; he hated even to sit for a portrait—to be painted or photographed. He was at his colorful best when lecturing, especially to children. His lectures on the chemical history of a candle and on the forces of nature are milestones in the history of science literature for children and adolescents. But he had no pupils and hardly a disciple. His voluminous correspondence is either familial or scientific. In the scientific correspondence he sometimes expressed himself strongly—and his writing talent was no mean one—on friendship and other extrascientific values. But these expressions are more of regret than of fulfillment. The nearest to a personal correspondence past his adolescence are his letters to Tyndall who, though a reputed scientist, came to Faraday as a sort of pupil or disciple; he was neither. In his letters to Tyndall, Faraday expresses his feelings with less reserve than usual, both about his desire not to let his own hopes die and about Tyndall's extrascientific exploits.

1. "The bare record of Faraday's writings year by year is fascinating," says Sir Lawrence Bragg in his foreword to Alan E. Jeffrey's bibliography of Faraday, *Michael Faraday, A List of His Lectures and Published Writings*. "It shows the breadth of his interest in a vast number of scientific subjects, and the many public services he performed as a scientific expert." See also Jeffreys' own comments, pp. xix and xx, and below, pp. 169–72.

2. See Jeffreys, items 407 and 426.

## Introduction

The impact of Faraday's behavior and attitudes on society, particularly on the society of physicists and chemists, was tremendous, both because of his views about nature and because of his views about the commonwealth of learning. This takes us away from the biographical sketch, so I shall only mention one detail. Though he and Tyndall lived in the same house and were known both privately and publicly as close friends, they published in the scientific press letters to each other in which they aired their disagreements amiably. This heralded a new era in science, when criticism ceased to be a mark of hostility and could bespeak esteem.

## A Scientific Biography

Einstein begins his scientific autobiography with a description of the immense success of the Newtonian physics that he was destined to overthrow. The whole tension of the story of the overthrow is lost on those unable to appreciate the force of the establishment before the upset took place. Flavius Josephus starts *The Jewish War* by observing that those who belittle the Jewish soldiers thereby unwittingly belittle the vast Roman legions that took so many years to destroy the small forces of the Jews. In a way the establishment that Einstein overthrew was much stronger than the one Faraday opposed: statistical mechanics, for example, was a whole new field whose success was unquestionable and that looked fairly well in conformity with Newtonianism. On the other hand, as Einstein has observed, the traditional Newtonians' wall of resistance to newer ideas was cracking. The cracks were not exactly created by Faraday, but he was the person who did his best to widen them, and he had a number of first-rate disciples who have all influenced the young Einstein in one way or another.

The opposition to Newtonianism probably never died, and P. G. Tait observed (*Nature*, 1876, p. 459) that Leibniz's rather confused theory of force, devised in direct opposition to Newton's, probably had influence in the mid-nineteenth century. Whatever the exact lineage between Leibniz and Faraday, I wish to show now that both Boscovich and Kant were links. Before doing this, let me say that if we can assess at all the period when Newtonianism faced the smallest and the weakest opposition, perhaps the year 1800 would best qualify. At that period Newtonianism was taken for granted by most physicists. Newtonianism describes the world as a variety of particles each associated with its own force, attraction or repulsion. Each force was described by Newton's three laws plus one more law describing the exact dependence of that specific force on the distance. Thus, heavy matter or gross matter followed the attractive inverse square law; electric and magnetic matter followed both attractive and repulsive inverse square laws. Heat-matter, however, followed a different law. Light, too, was a different matter. And so it went. When light was proven to consist of waves rather than particles, the waves had to be properties of some sort of vibrating or elastic matter, and this vibrating matter had to fill space between the stars and the eye. That is to say, it had to fill all space, terrestrial and interstellar alike. It had to be thin enough to penetrate air and glass, it had to be thin enough to enable planets to whisk through it frictionless. Yet it had to be hard enough to vibrate thousands of times per second. There is little doubt that this strange matter—the aether—was troublesome from its very inception. There were attempts to dismiss it, for instance the idea that interstellar space is not quite empty and so it can vibrate. But this would not do: no one believed a thin gas could vibrate in such high frequencies.

Faraday's boldest idea was to allow for vibrations without a vibrating matter, for a property and a motion without a substance to have the property and to move around. When Einstein said so the public was merely puzzled; when Faraday said so the public was deeply shocked and incredulous. But let us backtrack. Let us return to Newtonianism and its assumption of the existence of empty space housed with particles of various matters and their associated forces. Let us see how difficulties in this view gave way to a newer view.

A fundamental difficulty of this theory lies in the fact that each kind of matter is associated with its own kind of force, so that different kinds of matter seem to be unable to interact except by collision. If we take two kinds of matter, say heavy and electric, and assume only the forces of gravity and electric forces, then there is no force binding the two kinds of matter to each other. Let us endow heavy matter with additional force then, whether acting on heavy matter or on electric matter. If the additional force acts on heavy matter, then it combines with the force of gravity into a resultant force. If the additional force acts on electricity, then two heavy particles interact with the additional force in the presence of an electric particle. In either case the law of gravity does not strictly hold. Moreover, we need additional forces to act between material (heavy) particles, at least in order to account for elasticity. For, if collision is inelastic it is tantamount to infinite instantaneous force.

Boscovich had a theory of matter that resolves this difficulty in one way, and Kant had later a theory that resolves this difficulty even more radically, on more Leibnizian lines. It views materiality not as something fundamental and unalterable, but rather as a flexible property of things. There is no doubt that this theory was confusing and hard to grasp, and that Faraday was familiar with it. In a series of lectures that he delivered in his twenties to a small scientific society to which he belonged he uses both the language of the Kantian hypothesis (of materiality as a property) and shows a remarkable familiarity with all the difficulties that beset Newtonianism. But he kept an open mind.

Meanwhile Hans Christian Oersted, a Kantian, discovered electromagnetism. The most remarkable and significant fact about this discovery is that the electric current seemingly neither attracts nor repels the magnet it affects: it tends to rotate it. Immediately upon the widespread dissemination of the news, men of science tried to show that the electromagnetic force was not circular. By assuming that all magnets are electromagnets and by discovering the electromagnet itself, André-Marie Ampère succeeded in explaining the action of currents on magnets as actions of currents on currents. These actions, he claimed, were either attractions or repulsions, as they should be (according to Newton's theory, that is).

Faraday opposed Ampère. Rather than explain all rotations as compound attractions or repulsions, he tried to explain all attractions and repulsions, especially between two magnets, as compound rotations. To prove his point, he made a magnet rotate endlessly around a wire, and vice versa. This was his first great discovery, and it put him on the map at the age of thirty.

When, about ten years later, Faraday discovered how a moving magnet can create a current (just as a current can move a magnet), he broke entirely away from Newtonianism. The electricity created, he claimed, was proportional to the number of lines of magnetic force that the wire cuts. The magnetic lines of force are visible if and when iron filings are spread around a magnet, and the lines are supposedly denser where the filings are thicker. But no one had assumed that the lines of force are there, in reality, even when the iron filings are removed. Faraday now did: we can cut these lines and get a real effect—hence they are real. He now believed that force is real and hence indestructible, that all forces are forces of matter—not that each force has one kind of matter all to itself—and that every force can convert to every other force.

In a Newtonian system a force can cause motion, and motion can then convert back to force—perhaps to another force. But for one force to change to another without the intermediacy of motion meant that a particle of one kind of matter can change into another. And if we want materiality to be something real or fundamental, rather than a property dependent on something more fundamental, we must assume the conservation of matter of each kind. Faraday followed Oersted here and tried throughout his life to convert one force to another. That meant, in particular, that he wanted to convert gravity to electricity, and vice versa. He tried this toward the end of his life and failed. His belief in electrogravity was revived generations later in Einstein's general relativity, and more so in his unified field theory.

As a first step toward establishing empirically an electrogravitational effect, Faraday tried to show the conservation of each force in isolation and the proportional conversion of one force to another when it took place. He particularly wished to show that electricity was a property of ordinary matter, not of any hypothetical electric matter. To speak in modern idiom, he tried to show that matter possesses both gravity and electricity, both (heavy) mass and charge. This idea was, of course, incorporated in the theory of the electron at the end of the century. His theory of electrochemistry, of ionization, and so on, served to illustrate his views. This is why he encountered so much silent opposition about his views—although he was compensated by high public acclaim for his discoveries.

Faraday's theory of electrolysis came to show that the forces in the electric pile do not act at a distance but through the medium, the electrolytic solution. He then tried to show that electrostatic forces likewise act through the medium and not at a distance. He thus discovered the dielectric, that is the role played by insulators like glass and sulphur in the distribution of force in electrostatic configurations such as condensers. In both these cases the medium was material, but to Faraday there was no essential difference between empty and full space: this is why he used the term "the medium." Indeed, he tried to discover the dielectric effect even in empty space, now known as Maxwell's displacement vector. But he could not.

The dielectric properties of the medium showed Faraday that matter has electric properties. Unlike his contemporaries, he denied that insulators are nonelectric. Indeed, he denied the categorical division of materials into insulators and conductors—seeing conductivity as a matter of degree. (This idea he shared with Georg Simon Ohm, whose views were earlier and also ignored; and yet they gained currency before those of Faraday.) Faraday was extremely ambitious. Is empty space, he asked, a conductor or an insulator? This did not make sense to his contemporaries. But to him matter of different kinds was merely different states of empty space.

Similarly with magnetism; hence all matter is related to magnetism.

Though this was observed before Faraday put his mind to it, it was practically overlooked until Faraday pressed the point: all matter is magnetic to some extent, paramagnetic or diamagnetic (like dielectric), and intervenes in the action between two magnets when placed between them.

Similarly Faraday tried to find the interaction between electricity and light, but failed. It was discovered by John Kerr about a decade after Faraday's death. Similarly he tried to find the interaction between magnetism and light. This he succeeded in finding, and it is now known as the Faraday effect. Similarly he tried to find the effect of magnetism on the color of a flame (flames are strongly diamagnetic); he failed, but under his inspiration Pieter Zeeman succeeded around the turn of the century, thirty years after Faraday's death. Similarly he tried to discover the interaction between electricity and gravity. Einstein and Eddington discovered it in 1917–19.

This does not exhaust the list of Faraday's inspiring ideas. At least one more must be mentioned, his idea of electric current, not as a flow of a special matter—electric matter—but as the collapse of the field of force—an idea worked out by Henry Poynting and by Oliver Heaviside. But, of course, the most important inspiration was Faraday's theory of electromagnetic fields of force as crystallized to the various versions of Maxwell's equations.

Faraday's theory of the world as comprised of fields of force in empty space was so revolutionary that even his disciples rejected it—at least in the first instance. Einstein made it respectable. The greatest difficulty about it is philosophical: it does not assume that space houses matter, and thus it looks idealistic; and idealism is traditionally hostile to science. Faraday, thus, was considered great but dangerous.

There is no room here to speak of Faraday's discoveries in chemistry and in physics outside electromagnetism. His scientific biography is too rich for that. Similarly, his development as a thinker is much wider than that as a scientist, but this development cannot be summarized in this section.


## A Bibliographic Note

The amount of writing by and about Faraday is enormous. It is hard to complain that there are no collected works of Faraday when there are no collected works of Newton either. Let me mention, however, various source references and their general characteristics.

Faraday's most important writings are published in his own books, chiefly his three volumes of *Experimental Researches in Electricity* (1839, 1844, and 1855) and his volume of *Experimental Researches In Chemistry and Physics* (1859). Next come his already published private papers, chiefly the seven volumes of his *Diary* (1932–36). Both the *Diary* and most of the electrical *Researches* have their paragraphs numbered. The numbering is partly an expression of Faraday's obsessive nature, partly an expression of his sense of mission. His early electrical research is not numbered in the printed version; when he began his electric research in 1831 he started numbering the paragraphs in his *Diary* and in his *Experimental Researches in Electricity*. The *Diary* is not a book in which he scribbled laboratory notes, but one into which he neatly copied his notes. Some pages of the *Diary* are copied almost verbatim in the version he sent to the printer.

The first volume of the *Researches*, from 1831 to 1839, has all paragraphs numbered consecutively from 1 to 1,748; its chapters were individual papers—series, he called them—submitted to the Royal Society, read at the society's meetings, and published in its *Philosophical Transactions*. His reading of these papers went on to the end—another old-fashioned custom that he insisted on keeping alive.

The volume is indeed astounding in its unity of both idea and style. It was written with a sleepwalker's assuredness, to use Arthur Koestler's expression. Here is one striking example: he announces his laws of electrochemistry (§ 504) and adds (§ 505), "I have this investigation in hand, with several others, and shall be prepared to give it in the next series but one of these Researches," thus referring, on 18 June 1833, and probably before, to work that, according to his *Diary*, he performed during the period 17–20 September 1833 (the next series), and in the period beginning 21 September 1833 (the next series but one)! That even he was surprised, in retrospect, is very understandable indeed.

This could not go on for long. The enormously high standard he imposed on himself, and the lack of proper recognition, soon led to his sickness. Yet, in 1844 a second volume followed. Though much more exciting, it is uneven and lacks the external unity of volume 1: the first volume contained fourteen series from *Philosophical Transactions*; the second contained only four more series, a few older papers from the early 1820s, a few papers concerning controversies, and his early papers on his speculations, reprinted from the *Philosophical Magazine* and not numbered. Volume 3 is longer but more like volume 2 than 1, and contains the material of his second period; it appeared in 1855. He was then in his early sixties; he evidently did not know whether to hope for a fourth volume or not. He published one more series, submitted one paper by a young experimenter to *Philosophical Transactions*, perhaps with some vain hopes. He then published his *Experimental Researches in Chemistry and Physics* in 1859 as if it were his last volume. In that volume he published some chemical discoveries, those on benzene and chloroform being the most important, and some physical discoveries pertaining chiefly to the liquefaction of gases. Of these discoveries, some had been made before he embarked on research aimed at his "grand generalization"; others he performed either as a public service or as relaxation while too ill to work on more important things but well enough to do some work. The exception is his paper on gold, which is an odd one, does not fit comfortably in any of Faraday's frameworks, and is well-discussed in Williams's life of Faraday (see below). To return to the volume in which this paper was published, it concludes with a reprint of what, evidently, Faraday considered his last will and testament, his paper "On the Conservation of Force" and his paper "On Mental Education" (see p. 159 and p. 127, below). Clearly he was unwilling, after this publication, to view his career as closed; but in effect it was.

Apart from the four volumes of experimental researches, there is one book of his on *Chemical Manipulations* (1827), a laboratory manual following a lecture series that—as late as 1827, when he was about thirty-six years old—he was obliged to deliver on the subject, and three volumes based on shorthand lecture notes taken when he was a grand old man and a world-famous lecturer. Two of these, edited by William Crookes, who later became a scientist of great renown, were series of lectures for children given at the close of his career. They became classic works of great fame, largely influenced public opinion in favor of science and of Faraday's ideas in particular, and in favor of his strong conviction that children are serious consumers of high quality scientific literature. They are his *The Forces of Nature* (1859) and *The Chemical History of a Candle* (1860). The remaining volume, *The Non-Metallic Elements* (1853), edited by J. Scoffern, is of little interest except that in it Faraday views allotropy (the existence of different materials made of the same substances, such as oxygen and ozone) as a consolation price for our as-yet-inability to transmute matter as the alchemists had dreamed.

Of Faraday's many posthumous publications, three are of major significance. First, his already mentioned *Diary*. Second, Henry Bence Jones's *The Life and Letters of Faraday* (London, 1870) containing bits of journals, letters, and related material. There are two editions of the same year; the first contains about fifty more pages than the other. I have used the longer one. Third, *The*

*Letters of Faraday and Schoenbein*, 1836–62, edited by George W. A. Kahlbaum and Francis V. Darbishire (Bâle and London, 1899). Other primary sources on Faraday that must be mentioned are the obituary notice by Auguste de la Rive, and the biographies by Tyndall, Gladstone, and S. P. Thompson, to be discussed at some length in chapter 6 below. To this one must add the biography by L. Pearce Williams (1965) that contains much new material, many references, and a fairly comprehensive list of existing manuscript sources. Let me close this bibliographical note by reference to Faraday's bibliographies. There are very few of these, and all one really needs to consult, in addition to Williams's biography, are two: Alan E. Jeffrey, *Michael Faraday*, *A List of His Lectures and Published Writings* (London and New York, 1960) and William T. Scott, "A Bibliographical Reference Table for Faraday's Papers on Electricity," *The Natural Philosopher*, 3, London and New York, 1964.

(I shall use the title *"Life and Letters"* to designate Bence Jones's work, *"Discoverer"* to designate Tyndall's work (all references to the 2d edition), and *"Correspondence"* to designate the volume of his correspondence with Schoenbein.)

# 2    The Formative Years

### A Young Philosopher in Search of a Life Worth Living

Faraday had no scientific education apart from his attendance at a dozen lectures by Mr. John Tatum and four lectures by Sir Humphry Davy. This evidence is misleading. Hearing sixteen lectures would make him one of the most fully trained scientists of the time. Before the foundation of the Royal Institution in England,[1] or previously the Ecole Polytechnique in France, one could attend such lectures nowhere but in one's local philosophical society, which one usually joined only after becoming a philosopher, and even a relatively important one. Besides, Faraday heard many lectures in the Royal Institution after he joined it at the age of twenty-one, and there he received excellent laboratory training in one of the only two public laboratories that then existed in England.

What was peculiar about Michael Faraday (as with Davy, Franklin, and a few others) was not that in his youth he had no scientific education, but rather that he had so little formal education. Usually, those who became philosophers had no scientific training either, but they were formally educated people; they had received a liberal education of some sort. Liberal education included then no trace of experimental science, but it did include languages and literature, moral philosophy, a little mathematics, and in college perhaps a little natural philosophy as well, though only bits of the theoretical parts of it. Faraday had none of these advantages. "My education," he later said (*Life and Letters*, 1:9), "was of the most ordinary description consisting of little more than the rudiments of reading, writing, and arithmetic at a common day school. My hours out of school were passed at home and in the street."

Before the world considered Faraday a qualified bookbinder, he considered himself a philosopher (*Life and Letters*, 1:41). Nothing could make one a

1. Gresham College was intended to be such an institution, but it was a failure.

qualified philosopher but one's own conduct: if one philosophized (which also meant that he experimented), then one was a philosopher: being a philosopher in the old sense is not much different in this respect from being a chess-player or, nowadays, being a cinema-goer.

We know very little about the way the ignorant young lad of thirteen turned into an enlightened and energetic philosopher of twenty. As Bence Jones tells us (*Life and Letters*, 1:11), "he told a friend [Bence Jones] that Watts' *On the Improvement of the Mind* first made him think, and that his attention was turned to science by the article 'Electricity' in an encyclopaedia [*Britannica*, 3d edition, 1797] he was employed to bind."

This quotation shows how much the world had changed between the days of Faraday and of Bence Jones. In the former's youth, there was no science and enlightened people philosophized; in Bence Jones's youth a young thinking man could, but not necessarily, get interested in science: Faraday's youth, but not that of Bence Jones, was spent before the split known nowadays as "the two cultures"; and so Bence Jones explains two facts that, for Faraday, were one. This unity is forcefully expressed in a letter to his closest friend, Auguste de la Rive, who once intended to write a short biography of Mrs. Jane Marcet, and who on that occasion asked him if it was true that he was inspired by her *Conversations on Chemistry*. Here is part of what Faraday, as an old man, said on that occasion about his early days (*Life and Letters*, 2:401; *Discoverer*, 7):

> Your subject interested me deeply every way, for Mrs. Marcet was a good friend to me, as she must have been to many of the human race. I entered the shop of a bookseller and bookbinder at the age of 13, in the year 1804, remained there eight years, and during the chief part of the time bound books. Now it was in those books, in the hours after work, that I found the beginning of my philosophy. There were two that especially helped me, the "Encyclopaedia Britannica," from which I gained my first notions of electricity, and Mrs. Marcet's "Conversations on Chemistry," which gave me my foundation in that science.
>
> Do not suppose that I was a very deep thinker, or was marked as a precocious person. I was a very lively, imaginative person, and could believe in the "Arabian Nights" as easily as in the "Encyclopaedia"; but facts were important to me, and saved me. I could trust a fact, and always cross-examined an assertion.

> So when I questioned Mrs. Marcet's book by such little
> experiments as I could find means to perform, and found it
> true to the facts as I could understand them, I felt that I had
> got hold of an anchor in chemical knowledge, and clung fast to
> it. Thence my deep veneration for Mrs. Marcet: first, as one
> who had conferred great personal good and pleasure on me . . .

Faraday's self-image is clear: in his youth, chemistry and electricity were the beginning of a young man's introduction to philosophy; he himself was at the time neither a deep thinker nor a precocious person—not a born philosopher. But Mrs. Marcet's work induced him to make small and inexpensive experiments to check her contentions. Faraday thus learned by his own experience the difference between the *Arabian Nights* and the *Encyclopaedia Britannica*. As we should put it today, both had inspired his powerful imagination; as he has put it, he had been credulous and then Mrs. Marcet gave him a technique to overcome credulity.

A letter to his master, George Riebau, to whom Faraday expressed his gratitude for the interest Riebau had taken in his self-education, written not long after he ceased to be an apprentice, is preserved—a token of Riebau's affection. Here is Riebau's pen-portrait of the young philosopher diligently improving his mind (Martin, *Faraday* [London, 1934], p. 13):

> After the regular hours of business, he was chiefly employed in
> drawing and copying from the *"Artists Repository"* . . . At
> other times he would make the Philosophers Tree [an amalgam
> of mercury in a large vial, with zinc and sugar of lead]—then
> turn to the blowpipe and would meal [grind] or melt glass to
> any form he wanted for his purpose . . . . Dr. Watts's *Improve-
> ment of the Mind* was then read and frequently took in his
> pocket, when he went on an early walk in the morning, visiting
> always some works of art or searching for some mineral or
> vegetable curiosity . . . his mind ever engaged, besides attending
> to bookbinding which he executed in a proper manner. . . . when
> done his day's work, would set himself down the workshop . . . If
> I had any curious book . . . to bind, with plates, he would copy
> such as he thought singular or clever . . .

It is not necessary to comment on this simple and nostalgic image of an industrious young student working hard in isolation and under disadvantageous conditions. One may notice, only, that the writer of this letter, Faraday's employer, was both a kind fatherly figure and a concealed philosopher himself —evidently somewhat responsible for the development of Faraday (as well as other of his apprentices; this point deserves further research). Perhaps I should mention that Dr. Isaac Watts, now scarcely remembered, and then as a pompous eighteenth-century hymn-writer, was once the authority on self-improvement, on studying hard, on keeping the mind open and free of prejudice, of learning from experience, and so on. Faraday's earliest publication is a small lecture he gave in his twenties, exclusively based on Watts, about means of learning: from observation, from reading, from conversations with people— about their own knowledge, about commonly interesting topics, and so on. Watts was the champion of the self-made-through-hard-work.

From his own letters we learn that Faraday read many of the books he bound and borrowed from friends more books that he also bound as an expression of gratitude and in respect for the author. (He bound very neatly books that he valued even late in life.) He experimented now and then, when he had the pennies to buy the necessary materials. His formal training in science took place in 1810, when he was eighteen or nineteen years old. It consisted of three items: he joined a class on perspective (*Life and Letters*, 1:12), and he listened to two series of lectures on chemistry, by Tatum and by Davy. When he was eighteen, he learned perspective—he never had geometry—and it was probably of little or no use to him. When he was nineteen, he saw a note in a shop-window about philosophical lectures given by one Mr. John Tatum. His eldest brother paid the fee of one shilling, and he attended the lectures; there he had the first chance to add to his chemical knowledge some elementary physics (*Life and Letters*, 1:12). Through these lectures he made contact with other young and poor students of philosophy, especially one Benjamin Abbott, really his only adolescent friend, whom we shall presently meet. One of the customers of his master encouraged him to listen to Davy's last four lectures in a series. He then decided to become a professional philosopher as soon as he had finished his apprenticeship. His letters to his first serious friend, Abbott, show his state of mind at the end of his apprenticeship. The first letter expresses his wish to progress and his admiration of Dr. Watts. Then comes an enthusiastic description of his pocket battery and of the surprising fact that such a small instrument would be able to effect chemical decomposition. And so it goes.

The style of Faraday's letters to Abbott is very charming; although, characteristically of the age, it refers chiefly to facts, it is in a peculiar free style in which Faraday reported his conjectures and mentioned his methodological principles. Of course, his notes on Tatum's and Davy's lectures, as well as his early publications, were all in the strict inductive style of the age, where facts are allowed to speak for themselves and conjecture suppressed; but it was never demanded that letters should be confined to the strict inductive style. That so many private letters were written with an eye on publication (and indeed often published[2]) may explain people's use of, even excessive use of, the inductive style. But Faraday was not taught how to write letters.

Faraday's letters to Abbott reflect more and more his failure to become a philosopher. The following extract, from Faraday's sixth letter to Abbott in 1812 at the age of twenty should be indicative enough (*Life and Letters*, 1:41):

> Time, Sir, is all I require, and for time will I cry out most heartily. Oh that I could purchase at a cheap rate some of our modern gents' spare hours, nay, days; I think it would be a good bargain both for them and me. As for subjects, there is no want of them. I could converse with you, I will not say for ever, but for any finite length of time.

2. Benjamin Franklin's communications were letters in the typical mode of their age. They have been studied in detail due to their great historical importance (see I. Bernard Cohen, *Franklin and Newton* [Philadelphia, 1956], chap. 10). The letters were obviously meant to be communications submitted for publications. "Throughout his whole life [says Cohen, p. 76, relying chiefly on Franklin's *Autobiography*, I suppose] Franklin resented the fact that his earliest communications," which were letters, "however applauded by the Royal Society, were not fully printed in the Society's *Philosophical Transactions*." Faraday's request, at the end of his 1820 letter on metal alloys to Gaspard de la Rive (Auguste's father) to have the letter published—as he did—was much in the tradition (see *Life and Letters*, 1:336, and Jeffreys' bibliography, item 73). Similarly, Auguste de la Rive published two letters by Faraday—in 1846 on diamagnetism, and in 1854 on electrodynamics of currents in fluids, a topic that concerned de la Rive since he considered it to be a crucial aspect of Ampère's theory, which he supported (see *Life and Letters*, 2:211 and 330, and Jeffreys' bibliography, items 342 and 414). Faraday himself published letters from Schoenbein with his own comments (Jeffreys' bibliography, items 257 and 265). These letters started their lifelong friendship.

For what reason I do not know, the tradition died out, though till the end of the century scientific communications in Great Britain were often submitted to editors not by the author but by some (better-known) individual who acted as voluntary referee and sponsor (as to this day do some members of advisory editorial boards). These, however, were no longer letters. (Bose's famous letter to Einstein that Einstein published with his own comments is unusual, merely an echo of what is by now quite a lost tradition.)

"Our modern gent" with much "spare time" on his hands can study; this is the eighteenth-century image of itself. Of course, some writers could live by their pens, some thinkers were university people, some were clergymen, some had small lucrative jobs such as diplomacy or private secretaryship; others, whether artists or philosophers, had patrons who supported them regularly—with moderate stipends or in other ways; nevertheless, the image of the man of culture, writer or philosopher, was that of a man of leisure—of independent means, that is. "A philosopher," said Boyle in 1661, echoed by Priestley in 1774, "a philosopher must have a purse as well as a brain."

Struggle was Faraday's chief characteristic. What personal factors contributed to this I do not know; socially, the very idea of becoming a philosopher was for a poor man an ambition that could only become feasible by immense luck or immense struggle. Davy had the luck; Faraday had the struggle. In 1842, the biographer of Davy in the *Britannica* mentions the fact that Davy had come from "a humble walk of life"; even then it was unusual for a son of a country carpenter, even a relatively well-off one, to become an intellectual. Faraday's origins were much humbler—his father was a blacksmith in the slums of London—he was hungry as a child, and he had to struggle in his teens to read in his spare time; he had to struggle as a young worker to keep his interests afloat. At that later time his earlier employer, Riebau, could not help him; Tatum did. All his early career was related to three people—Riebau, Tatum, and Davy. The latter two were merely public lecturers, and all he could do to create two-way traffic with them was to take notes on their lectures and bind them with tender love. He must have seemed a strong mixture of the pathetic and the incredible—each of his three contacts did something most extraordinary to help him.

What Davy did was to hire him in 1813 as an assistant in the Royal Institution. What Tatum did was to perform a small miracle as if for Faraday but actually for a few bright young people: he organized, in 1808, the poor man's philosophical society—and poor is what its members chiefly were—poor and young.[3] It was called the City Philosophical Society and its members met—all forty of them—for all sorts of purposes of self-improvement. After Faraday joined them, the more ambitious also met privately—especially after Faraday got his job from Davy in the Royal Institution and could play host in his attic there—to improve their speech, their pronunciation, their punctuation.

3. S. P. Thompson (*Michael Faraday*, p. 14n.) outlines the transition of the society, through varied steps, into its present form as Birkbeck College, a night school in the University of London, for young working people.

During that period—in his twenties—Faraday made enormous progress. He kept writing to Abbott, lectured to the City Philosophical Society on physics and chemistry, became a member of the Royal Institution, and worked with especially conscientious members of the City Philosophical Society. In 1813, he is twenty-one years old, struggling, shy, gentle, sensitive, and extremely conscientious; in 1821 he is a thirty-year-old philosopher of standing, with an astounding discovery (the electric motor) to his name. Let us trace then, with a little more detail, how he passed the period from 1812, when he left Riebau's shop at the age of twenty, to 1821, when he became a well-known figure.

Lack of time, we remember, was Faraday's chief complaint. For example (*Life and Letters*, 1:52):

> With respect to the progress of the sciences I know but little, and am now likely to know still less; indeed, as long as I stop in my present situation (and I see no chance of getting out of it just yet), I must resign philosophy entirely to those who are more fortunate in the possession of time and means. . . . I am at present in very low spirits . . .

In this desperate situation, Faraday took the "bold and simple step" of applying to Davy for "scientific employment," and Davy responded most favorably. Again we are fortunate that a biographer, this time of Davy, asked him for information: again it turns out to be not less enlightening for Faraday's own biography (*Life and Letters*, 1:54):

> My desire to escape from trade, which I thought vicious and selfish, and to enter into the service of Science, which I imagined made its pursuers amiable and liberal, induced me at last to take the bold and simple step of writing to Sir H. Davy, expressing my wishes, and hope that . . . he would favour my views . . . At the same time that he . . . gratified my desires as to scientific employment, he still advised me [to remain a book-binder] . . . telling me that Science was a harsh mistress,[4] and in a pecuniary

4. Newton had said that philosophy was a harsh mistress, and this became a well-known cliché. In the 1810s both Davy and Faraday would use the word "philosophy," not "science" as Faraday uses here—one of the rare occasions he used this word. Perhaps the reason is that the change from "philosophy" to "science" was just being made, and Faraday conformed before he developed a dislike for the neologism. Note his "philosophic men" rather than "scientists" in the last sentence quoted here.

point of view but poorly rewarding those who devoted themselves
to her service. He smiled at my notion of the *superior moral
feelings of the philosophic men*, and said he would leave me to
the experience of a few years to set me right on that matter . . .

We shall not be able to receive a proper impression from this letter unless
we take notice of the fact that Faraday was assured of a reasonably good—even
prosperous—career as a bookbinder (*Life and Letters*, 1:46). He speaks here
of his desire to escape from trade, which he thought vicious and selfish, and to
enter the service of science; it may be understood as a form of florid speech,
and it may be understood as a response to a calling. Going to Davy was, as he
says, a bold and simple step, only because he had a calling—just as for the
Maid of Orleans, but not for any other peasant girl, going to the Dauphin and
all that was a bold and simple step.

Simple and straightforward acceptance of a calling is the unusual—the
calling itself seldom is. In Faraday's case, the calling was not voices from within
but from Watts's *Logic* and *The Improvement of the Mind*, the best-selling
books that broadcast the same message to thousands and thousands. Although
historians of traditional philosophy do not mention Watts's system, because
it is so naïve and unoriginal, there is something inspiring in such a system—the
naïve view of the unity of moral philosophy and scientific method—something
that was a constant source of inspiration to Faraday. Davy was right, of course,
when he smiled at the naïveté of Faraday. He gave him a few years to get
over this naïveté, a few years in which they both experienced some bitter and
painful disappointments. But Faraday was the more obstinate; his naïve
belief only turned into a tough ideal of a powerful person of a "most inflexible
integrity," who seriously looked for a way of bringing about the ideal state of
affairs in which "philosophic men" would have "superior moral feelings," be
"amiable and liberal," calm, and lofty.

The hypersensitive struggling youth, as we shall see, became only more
tormented and more struggling as the years went by. His image, which became
the ideal, was moral and psychological; every philosopher, in his vision, was a
Boyle, a Spinoza, no less.

## A Quiet Period of Progress

Bence Jones divides Faraday's life into two periods—before and after the grand
discovery of magnetoelectricity in 1831, when he was nearly forty years of

age. The second period is almost entirely devoted to his monumental *Experimental Researches in Electricity*. The first period, although blessed with some valuable discoveries, is in comparison (at least to Bence Jones) merely the period of self-education. He subdivides this period into three: first, the initial stage of apprenticeship, the formation of the City Philosophical Society, and the correspondence with Abbott; second, early stages in the Royal Institution, from 1813 to 1820, as Davy's private assistant; and third, from 1820 to 1831, employed by the Royal Institution in his own right, a star but still not the great luminary. His second stage, of 1813–20, was peaceful and happy, at least in comparison to any other period of his life.

In 1813 Faraday became Davy's assistant. The job was not[5] a philosophical one, but he could learn and progress. As Bence Jones puts it in so very Victorian a manner, he started at the very bottom and with the best master. When he went with Davy to the Continent, Davy tried to make him act as a valet, while, back in London, his job was taken over by an assistant porter; when he returned, after almost two years, his deputy returned to his previous job.[6] This was, no doubt, the very bottom of the ladder.

Faraday's progress in that period was remarkable. He learned much from helping his master in his research, and Davy seems to have preferred him from the very first to any other assistant because of his devotion, courage (in dealing with explosives), and over-all ability—both technical and philosophical. He also learned the art of lecturing, and in 1816 resumed a series of lectures to the City Philosophical Society. His tour of the Continent was a great lesson to him. There he met leading philosophers, two of whom, Ampère in Paris and Gaspard de la Rive in Geneva, he very much impressed. There he learned French and a bit of Italian. There he also followed research into modern problems, since Davy was consulted by various authorities.

5. Biographers usually think that Faraday's job was scientific from the start, and they often quote as evidence Davy's conversation with a friend concerning Faraday. The friend said "put him to wash bottles; if he is good for anything, he will do it directly; if he refuses, he is good for nothing." "No, no," replied Davy, "we must try him with something better than that." See next note.

6. This story is usually told as evidence of Davy's kindness. The fact is, however, that Faraday was left to wash bottles for well over ten years. He was very ready to wash bottles, but when he was forced, contrary to Davy's express promise, to clean Davy's boots, he rebelled. This is what marred their European tour. A decade after Faraday had joined Davy, in 1823, Dr. Paris, Davy's friend and biographer, came to stay overnight in the Royal Institution; he found one glass phial to be oily and scolded Faraday for it. This nasty story would have been forgotten but for the fact that the oil was a discovery of some importance (see chap. 4, below, p. 121, and R. A. Hadfield, *Faraday's Metallurgical Researches* [London, 1931], p. 20).

So much for learning. With it came deep feelings of disappointment concerning the value of his learning, the moral value, the "superior moral feelings of the philosophic men." Faraday saw philosophic men in their work and in their social life; he saw their intrigues and their lust for fame. Presumably, like all disappointed young idealists, he exaggerated: his moral standards were too high and unrealistic, and he did not notice that a part of the evil was a direct result of the high moral standard that he—and even those philosophers—accepted quite uncritically. But he felt very strongly about it.

Even the admired Sir Humphry Davy was unfair and humiliating.[7] Faraday's feelings are expressed in various letters. Here is one quotation (*Life and Letters*, 1:170):

> Alas! how foolish perhaps was I to leave home, to leave those whom I loved, and who loved me.... And what are the boasted advantages to be gained? Knowledge. Knowledge of the world, of men, of manners, of books, and of languages—things in themselves valuable above all praise, but which every day shows me prostituted to the basest purposes. Alas! how degrading it is to be learned when it places us on a level with rogues and scoundrels! How disgusting, when it serves but to show us the artifices and deceits of all around! How can it be compared with the virtue and integrity of those who, taught by nature alone, pass through life contented, happy, their honour unsullied, their minds uncontaminated, their thoughts virtuous—ever striving to do good, shunning evil, and doing to others as they would be done by? Were I by this long probation to acquire some of this vaunted knowledge, in what should I be wiser? Knowledge of the world opens the eyes to the deceit ... and corruption of mankind.

In 1815 Faraday returned to the Royal Institution, and his interest in learning absorbed him entirely. "Understand me," he wrote in 1816 (*Life and Letters*, 1:230), "I am not complaining; the more I have to do the more I learn ...." He is already a work-maniac by then. And in 1818 (p. 286):

7. The story is somewhat complicated with annoying details of Davy's domestic troubles: a honeymoon with a rich widow, a scientific journey in enemy territory, and so on. The chief source of the story are letters from Faraday; but we have ample corroboration of it, especially in a famous letter from Auguste de la Rive to Tyndall (see Tyndall's review of Bence Jones's biography in his *New Fragments of Science*).

". . . my slight attempts to add to the general stock of chemical knowledge have been received with favourable expressions by those around me; but I have, on reflexion, perceived that those arose from kindness on their part, and the wish to incite me on to better things. I have always, therefore, been fearful of advancing on what has been said [by others], lest I should assume more than was intended . . . ." Like all work-maniacs, he twists, as he describes here, every attempt to encourage and comfort him into the "wish to incite me on to better things"—into the pressure to work even harder.

There is no law, moral or social, against compulsive hard work. For the work-maniac himself, hard work is often his only means of keeping alive—regardless of what exactly are the painful thoughts he so painfully suppresses in this manner. But this must be observed, in justice to those of Faraday's associates with whom he did not strike it well, including Davy the renowned playboy and Wollaston the celebrated leisured gentleman. Life with a work-maniac is no bliss—especially for those disposed to encourage and relax him. A work-maniac with self-control—as Faraday was—may appear a marvel to all but those who know him intimately, and then the world may well wonder why, of all people, only his intimates fail to get along with him.

When Davy was first mean to Faraday, it was merely the insensitivity of a person with a bit too much on his hands (a bitchy wife whom he had married for status and money, the loss of a valet); when he was last mean to Faraday it was with a vengeance. The vengeance is linked to a frustrated good will turned into envy. Here, first, is the good will. To begin with, Davy expresses himself in public, in a paper on his safety lamp, "indebted to Mr. Michael Faraday for much able assistance." Later his acknowledgment became warmer and much stronger (see L. Pearce Williams, *Michael Faraday*, p. 45). Since there were hardly any assistants in the philosophical world at the time, much less paid ones, Davy's acknowledgment must be considered utterly voluntary and the inauguration of a lovely tradition. Davy then encourages Faraday to publish a variety of notes of his own (*Life and Letters*, 1:224). Even in 1821 when Davy sides with those who claim Faraday was unjust to Wollaston, the matter is not of personal animosity but of a complex issue to which I have to devote a separate discussion. After some harsh words, they made it up,[8] and yet, finally, Davy became a bitter enemy. Certainly envy, being put in Faraday's shade, had much to do with this. But also frustrated friendship and good will, the inability to share Faraday's successes in a more relaxed, comradely, working relation.

8. See letter to Herschel, 1826, n. 13, p. 36, below.

In the middle of the 1810s Faraday's character becomes definite, at his mid-twenties. A poem about him is published in 1816, written by a friend from the City Philosophical Society. It is a somewhat idealized image, but I think Faraday did appear somewhat idealized to all but his closest associates. Here is a small excerpt from the poem (*Life and Letters*, 1:223):

> Neat was the youth in dress, in person plain;
> His eye read thus, Philosopher in grain;
> . . . . . . . . . . . . . . . . . .
> Warmth in his heart, good humour in his face,
> A friend to mirth, but foe to vile grimace;
> A temper candid, manners unassuming,
> Always correct, yet always unpresuming.
> Such was the youth, the chief of all the band;
> His name well known, Sir Humphry's right hand.
> With manly ease towards the chair he bends,
> With Watts's logic at his finger-ends.

Here is, finally, how Faraday himself viewed this period of his life, his twenties, which he spent as an assistant at the Royal Institution (*Life and Letters*, 2:440):

> I could not imagine much progress by reading only, without experimental facts and trials which could be suggested by the reading. I was never able to make a fact my own without seeing it . . . However, what we call [*sic*] accident has in my life had much to do with the matter, for I had to work and prepare for others before I had earned the privilege of working for myself, and I have no doubt that was my great instruction and introduction into physical science.

## An Early Attitude Toward Problems and Controversies

The old Faraday wanted his views to be noted; every other wish was secondary to this one. He did not wish people to believe him—he was equally happy to see his views criticized: what he could not take was the ignoring of his views. This is a rather normal attitude. Martin Buber, in his *I and Thou*, suggests that criticism is less of a rejection than willfully ignoring the other altogether. But this view clashes violently with Faraday's image of the philosopher who, "taught by nature alone, pass through life contented," whom science makes "amiable and liberal." Can criticism be amiable and liberal? Is criticism essential to science? Must there be controversy and heartbreak in science?

The question is still open today. Recently an influential philosopher wrote in a very influential volume impressive words on these matters. In his *Personal Knowledge* (1958), Michael Polanyi says (pp. 159–60): "I am not applauding the outbreak of such passions. I do not like to see a scientist trying to bring an opponent into intellectual contempt, or to silence him in order to gain attention for himself; but I acknowledge that such means of controversy may be tragically inevitable."

Controversy, says Polanyi, is tragic but all too often inevitable in science. This, I should say, is a rather common attitude in the twentieth century. When C. P. Snow presents in his *Variety of Men* the story of the most celebrated scientific controversy of the century, that between Albert Einstein and Niels Bohr, he says these two men, the whole incident, rather, had an aura of saintliness about it—in that no personal feelings were hurt—and of tragedy—in that it was not resolved and thus raised a screen, however thin, between these two great friends. Controversy is something our culture is still unadjusted to.

In 1913 Sir Oliver Lodge declared in his presidential address to the British Association for the Advancement of Science that science equals controversy. In recent years this idea has come to be associated with the philosophy of Karl Popper. He says that the tradition of science is the peak of the Western traditions and institutions that safeguard the critic's rights to criticize and that even encourage criticism. This is not true. When Davy criticized Lavoisier and tried to publish his criticism in the leading French journals, he could not do so. But political freedom of the press existed, and a lesser known periodical was opened to Davy. The leading French scientists threatened to call the police. The police would not come, of course. (In his article on Russian linguistics, Joseph Stalin described a different situation in Stalinist Russia.) In France the political institutions safeguarding freedom of criticism won out over the scientists' attempt at suppression. All this is well in accord with Popper's view of the rise of science—which is impossible without criticism—as deeply linked with the rise of democratic institutions. But it does not square with the details of Popper's theory of scientific institutions as the pinnacle of encouragement for criticism.

The story, incidentally, of Davy's clash with Lavoisier's greatest disciples was not mentioned in the two biographies of Davy, much to the surprise of Gerrit Moll, a friend of both Davy and Faraday, who wrote about it all to Faraday. When I went through the Faraday manuscripts in London, I bumped into this letter and later published it together with a paper "On Argument" written by Faraday in 1818 and also previously unpublished.

Bacon viewed criticism as a part of an intellectual battle. And intellectual battles seemed to him to be more ambitious than physical ones—aimed at conquering kingdoms of the mind (end of *Sylva Sylvarum*). The conqueror is one who spreads a dogma. All schools offer dogmas. The truth needs no school to advocate it. Once one puts forward a conjecture, however tentatively, one soon feels one's honor involved and is obliged to defend one's conjecture as best one can. And one can best defend one's conjecture by becoming dogmatic and refusing to see the evidence against it. Criticism is ridicule, and nobody wishes to be ridiculed; so everyone rejects criticism, no matter how just and obvious. Tentativity is the beginning of dogmatism.

Watts was a Baconian, and he devoted much space to the espousal of Bacon's doctrine of prejudice. He did not advocate the suppression of all controversy, but he expressly recommended paying attention only to the first two or three rounds of a controversy since, he said, later rounds are apt to generate more heat than light.

Such were the ideas that impressed the young Faraday. In his early correspondence with Abbott, we find him engaged in current controversy. Abbott followed Lavoisier, as almost everyone did; Faraday was more up-to-date, and he followed Davy. But what worried him was not whether Davy or Lavoisier was right—rather, whether Abbott would feel rejected. In 1812 he writes (*Life and Letters*, 1:31),

> You wrong me, dear A., if you suppose I think you obstinate for not coinciding in my opinion immediately . . . It is not for me to affirm that I am right and you wrong . . . [possibly] we are both wrong, and a third right. I am very open to conviction, but . . . I must be convinced before I renounce.

and further on (p. 34), he affirms that by means of experiment

> our dispute—no, not dispute, friendly controversy—will end . . . .
> . . . I accept of your offer to fight it out with joy, and shall in the battle experience and cause, not pain but I hope pleasure . . . .

Both Faraday and Abbott, then, at about twenty years of age, expect friendly debates, but both are apprehensive. As well they might be. Before Faraday's letter was sent he received another from Abbott, and in it Abbott requests that the controversial subject be dropped altogether. Faraday commented in a postscript (p. 40), in which he speaks of "petty passions," of his own lack of self-control, of "those humiliating, and to a philosopher disgraceful, feelings." He thought he should not send the letter, but having invested so much in it, and it being such a masterpiece, he could not resist his urge to send it, but felt ashamed. Abbott dropped chemistry and started studying electricity. Faraday "rejoiced" (p. 44); himself, he dropped chemistry and tried astronomy, but soon his apprenticeship was over and with it his independent studies. When he finally entered the Royal Institution, it was back to chemistry, of course. As to Abbott, he soon dropped studies altogether, much to Faraday's chagrin.

In 1816 Faraday gave a series of lectures to the City Philosophical Society, and the bitterness with which he spoke in his lecture on chlorine—the subject of Davy's criticism of Lavoisier—must have reflected bitter memories of the first cloud over a cooled friendship four years earlier. He explicitly declared the French chemists prejudiced, adding as evidence that they refused to call the combustion of sulphur and iron by the name of combustion since it involved no oxygen. He blames the French chemists (in a Baconian fashion) for ever having put forward a false hypothesis (*Life and Letters*, 1:219): "by adherence to a favourite theory, many errors have at times been introduced into general science which have required much labour for their removal."

The labors complained about may be Davy's, or Faraday's, or others'; the bitterness is Faraday's. He rejects now both Lavoisier's and Davy's theories, because it is no use rejecting one view and making a fetish of another; and caution against fetishism by pointing out others' fetishes, as well as one's own old fetishes, does not help much—it is only in matters of degree. "We avoid those faults which we perceive, but we still fall into others. To guard against these requires a large proportion of mental humility, submission, and independence."

I do not think Faraday had before him his letter to Abbott in which he tried hard to impose humility on himself, yet the stress on humility in both places, both of which touch upon the chlorine controversy, can hardly be viewed as accidental.

No matter. Faraday appears here antitheoretical in the strictest Baconian tradition, and, quite unusually for that tradition, very pessimistic. Yet he sticks grimly to his ideal (*Life and Letters*, 1:220):

> The philosopher should be a man willing to listen to every
> suggestion, but determined to judge for himself. He should not
> be biassed by appearances; have no favourite hypothesis; be of no
> school; and in doctrine have no master . . . . If to these qualities
> be added industry, he may indeed hope to walk within the veil
> of the temple of nature.

However religious and high-flown this rhetoric is, if Faraday were not such a sincere person there would be little point in quoting it. In 1816 he spoke thus; in 1820 he became a heretic when he saw clearly that almost all of his colleagues belonged to a school—the Newtonian school. But let me take this more slowly. In 1812 he has a clash with Abbott, and in 1813–15 he has his share of excitement and disappointment in Europe; in 1816 he lectures to the City Philosophical Society on physics and chemistry and sounds the bitter note with the hopeful cadence quoted above.

In 1817 his work progresses, he publishes some short notes on his scientific activities, lectures to the City Philosophical Society "On Some Observations on the Means of Obtaining Knowledge and on the Facilities Afforded by the Constitution of the City Philosophical Society," later published by the society. It is a rehash of Bacon's and Watts's doctrines and is optimistic again, spoken warmly and advocating warmth. He says he finds conversations, especially good ones, such as the City Philosophical Society conducts, most enjoyable and most effective as a means of obtaining knowledge.

One has to remember that Faraday was once a gregarious man when one reads that later in life he had no time for company. He had a free ticket to the opera but could not go; he used to play the flute and sing (bass), but he quit this too; he enjoyed the annual banquets of the Royal Academy of Arts, sometimes he went to parties of Lady Davy's to show no hard feelings, and he accepted invitations to parties given by Judge Grove, where they woke up the children for him to say hello to and let him vanish almost as soon as he arrived. Apart from a few dinners with leading politicians such as Bertrand Russell's grandfather, this seems to be all. One morning Abbott came to the Royal Institution. He was told that in the mornings the professor was in his laboratory and was not to be disturbed. The laboratory was in the basement and Faraday's apartment on the top floor. Abbott patiently waited at the entrance, near the doorman. When Faraday passed the marble foyer on his way to lunch he saw Abbott, embraced him, and took him to lunch. Abbott came many times afterward, but to the lecture theater and in the evenings: he did not want to disturb the professor. But all this when they were in their fifties, when Faraday was "the professor." In their twenties, when Faraday was "Mike," they met everywhere, in Faraday's attic in the Royal Institution, on outings, and at the City Philosophical Society, where Faraday confessed he loved conversation and still believed that he could acquire more knowledge by conversation than by any other means.

The lectures on science of 1816 are of little value; his lectures of 1817 on the means of obtaining knowledge and of mental inertia (i.e., prejudice rooted in laziness) are even rather silly in their Wattsian naïveté; they are, at most, of some biographical value. In 1818, for the select group of the City Philosophical Society that met for extra exercises, he writes a little sermonette about fair and honest and respectful disagreement; Watts's influence is still noticeable, but a new note emerges—of dignity, through independence of mind, through disagreement.

Think of it: the dignity of mature, respectful disagreement. Quite a reversal, this. Even today, respectful disagreement is a rather rare commodity; in Faraday's time it was hardly known.

And, finally, Faraday's lectures to the City Philosophical Society of 1818 and 1819, which show an unusually frank attitude toward problems and a strangely philosophical or broad attitude toward science.

Indeed, in the very beginning of his lectures to the City Philosophical Society, Faraday combines his stress on problems with his broad philosophical concern. He openly declares (p. 7) the question still open, whether forces are essential to matter or not, and he even complains (p. 6) that it is generally neglected. This may hint at a heresy. In another place (p. 112) he says it will hardly admit of doubt that the properties of bodies are really given to them by the matter that composes them, and he speaks (p. 113) of materiality as a property, thus showing familiarity with both Boscovich and Kant. The allusion to Kant is intriguing, especially in view of the fact that, unable to read German, Faraday probably received his ideas at second hand. The existence of a Kantian movement in physics is an intriguing modern topic—as is the existence of underground movements in science generally. It can only be studied by the examination of allusions, however casual, such as Faraday's to Kant.[9]

9. Williams has drawn attention to a remarkable paper by J. C. Delametherie, *J. de Physique*, 7, and *Philosophical Magazine*, 2 (1798), 277–82, where Kantianism is presented as a forceful and growing movement. Delametherie published a paper by Davy against Lavoisier a decade later, in the face of threats from the scientific establishment (see above, p. 24).

At the time, however, Faraday was more concerned with problems surrounding Newton's theory of light than general theories of matter—Kant's or others'—perhaps because of the then-general worry about Newton's theory of light (exhibited by Laplace's emphatic declaration that Newton's theory of light had been doubly and trebly demonstrated), perhaps because Thomas Young, the reviver of the wave theory of light, had been a lecturer at the Royal Institution and retained a distinguished membership in it till the end of his career. Anyway, Faraday expressed (p. 127) the feeling of unease at the fact that the speed of radiant heat was unknown (was radiant heat light?). Newton's theory of light, he notes (p. 67), "appearing to present a more perfect account of things and to be more refined, was hastily received," which makes it unclear whether he accepted it or not. And his assertion that "the conclusion that is now generally received appears to be that light consists of minute atoms of matter of an octahedral form, possessing polarity, and varying to size and

---

Whether this indicates that Davy was in the Kantian movement or on its fringe I cannot say. For the available evidence on this question see T. H. Levere, "Faraday, Matter, and Natural Theology—Reflections on an Unpublished Manuscript," *Brit. J. Hist. Sci.*, 4 (1968). Levere, however, quotes as rather original ideas publicly known to have been held by Robert Boyle and Joseph Priestley, and he views every manuscript as an expression of a definite opinion, not asking why it had failed to be sent to the press.

Williams quotes (*Michael Faraday*, p. 125), from a lecture of Davy of 1812 as taken down by Faraday, the unmistakenly Kantian idea that the four states of matter (light being the fourth) represent different balances between attraction and repulsion. This, however, is less explicit and bold than Faraday's 1817 (Kantian) idea of materiality as a property of things— also expressed in the 1842 manuscript reproduced by Levere and boldly published by Faraday only in 1844 and later.

Samuel Taylor Coleridge viewed Davy as a *Naturphilosoph* proper. See, for example, his letter to Dorothy Wordsworth of 24 November 1807 (quoted also in Anne Treneer, *The Mercurial Chemist, A Life of Sir Humphry Davy*, London, 1963, p. 104): "Davy supposes that there is only one power in the world of the senses; which in particles acts as chemical attractions, in specific masses as electricity, and on matter in general, as planetary gravitation. . . . When this has been proved, it will then only remain to resolve this into some Law of vital Intellect—and all human knowledge will be Science and Metaphysics the only Science." This is not to say that I challenge the generally practiced skepticism about Coleridge's evidence. Indeed, I endorse it. We know that Davy had to be under the influence of laughing gas before he could endorse idealism. Yet Coleridge read him as an idealist, as de la Rive read Faraday as an idealist (see p. 174 below)—for more or less the same heresy. I conjecture that Faraday absorbed some information about Kantianism and about *Naturphilosophie* in the Royal Institution, that he rejected only a part of what he learned, and decided to be cautious in endorsing publicly what he did not reject. Yet it cannot be said that all the Kantian and Boscovichian background that Faraday had, had come personally from Davy, as the following facts indicate. Davy responded to Oersted's paper with incomprehension and with an effort to show that the new force was central. Wollaston and more so, Faraday, responded in a more open-mined way, as described in detail below.

polarity" seems to be an expression of some displeasure at the degree of arbitrariness of "the conclusion that is now received."

All this shows how up-to-date, as usual, Faraday was concerning the goings-on within scientific research. His methodological position was still Baconian: the less one theorizes, the less one comes up with prejudices and controversies. But his imagination would not remain idle. And so, somehow, Faraday manages to twist the most antimetaphysical position into a recommendation to theorize—as little as possible, and only when it cannot be avoided—in the most metaphysical manner! I ask the reader's indulgence for the length of the following quotation, for it is crucial for its insight into Faraday. I ask the specialized reader's indulgence for the choppiness of the following quotation: he can find a more detailed one in *Life and Letters*, 1:303–11, and the (still unpublished) original in the Faraday collection in the library of the Institute of Electrical Engineers, London.

> . . . it not unfrequently happens, that the man [Newton] who is the most successful in his pursuit of one branch of philosophy thereby raises up difficulties to his advancement in another . . .
>
> The evil of method in philosophical pursuits is . . . only apparent, and has no real existence but in the abuse. But the system-maker is unwilling to believe that his explanations are not perfect, the theorist to allow that incertitude hovers about him. Each condemns what does not agree with his method, and consequently each departs from nature . . .
>
> The disagreeable and uneasy sensation produced by incertitude will always induce a man to sacrifice a slight degree of probability to the pleasure and ease of resting on a decided opinion; and where the evidence of a thing is not quite perfect, the deficiency will be easily supplied by desire and imagination. The efforts a man makes to obtain a knowledge of nature's secrets merit, he thinks, their object for their reward; and though he may, and in many cases must, fail of obtaining his desire, he seldom thinks himself unsuccessful, but substitutes the whisperings of his own fancy for the revelations of the goddess . . .
>
> Ultimately, however, facts are the only things which we are sure are worthy of trust. All our theories and explanations of the laws which govern them, whether particular or general, are necessarily deduced from insufficient data. They are probably

most correct when they agree with the greatest number of phenomena, and when they do not appear incompatible with each other. The test of an opinion is its agreement in association with others, and we associate most when we generalize.

Hence I should recommend the practice of generalizing as a sort of parsing in philosophy. It occasions a review of single opinions, requires a distinct impression of each, and ascertains their connection and government. And it is on this idea of the important use that may be made of generalization, that I venture to propose for this evening a lecture on the general states of matter.

Faraday says we all have methods, and this leads us to dogmatism. This is inevitable but can be minimized—by a method. What is evil is not method but the abuse of method—yet also, the abuse is to some measure inevitable. View only facts as certain; and if you must generalize, he adds, then generalize as widely or as broadly as possible because only very broad agreements with facts give any degree of probability. This is a most unusual view in that in the name of inductive caution it recommends boldness. Only one contemporary philosopher advocated a similar view—it was William Whewell, then a young man in Cambridge and soon to become a friend of sorts. Yet even Whewell thought that theoretical certitude in science was possible; not so Faraday, who thought only facts were certain. Anyway, the very idea that generalizations are most parsimonious is a bit misleading, to say the least, since the context suggests clearly that Faraday means generalities or broad speculations, not universalized observations such as "all swans are white." It is incredible that such a sharp person as the young Faraday should resolve his philosophical difficulty with a mere pun; but there he goes, deep in his generalities which he calls generalizations:

Matter classed into four states—solid, liquid, gaseous, and radiant—which depend upon differences in the essential properties.
Radiant state.—Purely hypothetical. Distinctions.
Reasons for belief in its existence. Experimental evidence. Kinds of radiant matter admitted.
Such are the four states of matter most generally admitted.

> They do not belong to particular and separate sets of bodies,
> but are taken by most kinds of matter; and it will now be
> found necessary, to a clear comprehension of their nature, to
> notice the phenomena which cause and accompany their
> transition into each other.

Faraday's acceptance of light as a state of matter, strangely enough, is
not as anchored in the Newtonian corpuscularian theory of light as usual; this
had an astounding consequence for his metaphysics. One of the ideas that
impressed him most in his adolescence was a brief suggestion he had read in
the third edition of the *Encyclopaedia Britannica* (1797, 4:460, Art. Electricity)
to the effect that electricity may constitute neither one fluid, nor two, but
perhaps mere vibrations. The author of the article, evidently a follower of
Boscovich with a touch of Kant's later philosophy, declared heat, light, and
electricity mere variants of the same substance (see Williams, *Michael Faraday*,
p. 14). This thought—electricity as vibrations—occurs again and again in
Faraday's speculative papers as well as in his private papers. When light,
supposedly a matter, appeared to be vibrations, most philosophers corrected
themselves and viewed light not as matter but as vibrations of matter. Not so
Faraday: for Faraday, to the end of his days, it became increasingly clear that
matter has electric properties, i.e., electric forces, i.e., that matter may be
vibrations in space—hence vibrations in empty space. And so, to him, light as
matter may indeed vibrate! But all this is sheer hindsight. In 1819, just prior
to his leap into fame, he spoke of radiant matter, of the transition of matter
from the solid, liquid, and gaseous state to the radiant state, and tried to keep
this somewhat aloof from the corpuscularian theory of light. This sounds intriguing, to be sure, but we have no evidence that he could develop these ideas
further and keep his reader intrigued. He was reluctant to theorize and to
dogmatize, and so he kept his views vague and fluid. Here is an expression of
this state of mind in Faraday's own words (*Life and Letters*, 1:310):

> Nothing is more difficult and requires more care than
> philosophical deduction, nor is there anything more adverse to
> its accuracy than fixidity of opinion. The man who is certain he
> is right is almost sure to be wrong, and he has the additional
> misfortune of inevitably remaining so. All our theories are
> fixed upon uncertain data, and all of them want alteration

and support. Ever since the world began, opinion has changed with the progress of things; and it is something more than absurd to suppose . . . that we are in possession of the highest stretch of intellect which has or can result from human thought. Why our successors should not displace us in our opinions, as well as in our persons, it is difficult to say: it ever has been so, and from analogy would be supposed to continue so; and yet, with all this practical evidence of the fallibility of our opinions, all, and none more than philosophers, are ready to assert the real truth of their opinions.

So close Faraday's lectures that sum up his period of apprenticeship. At the age of twenty-eight or twenty-nine he came closest to being happy. He became engaged and got married and was permitted to bring his wife to the institution. He started lecturing there. Again he started at the bottom of the ladder: his topic was nothing more exciting than how to organize one's laboratory; he disliked it yet it became an almost standard topic with him, and he made it into a book (*Chemical Manipulations*, London, 1827) on the topic that went through three editions and even an American edition (Thompson, *Michael Faraday*, pp. 233–34).

He published a few minor papers reporting the liquefaction of a few gases, the first of which (on chlorine) seemed to Davy so important that he claimed a share in the discovery. He embarked on metallurgical researches with an older colleague; they led to no spectacular results, but in this century they seemed to one writer, R. A. Hadfield, significant enough as pioneering work to deserve a whole monograph.[10] At the time they brought him a few papers and his first scientific friendship—with de la Rive's father, whom he had first met on the European tour with Davy.

In 1821 Faraday was assigned to write a history of electromagnetism. The subject was new but explosive. In 1819 Oersted had discovered that a conducting wire, namely a current, deflects the needle of a compass, thus inaugurating the

10. Hadfield is recognized as the father of alloy metallurgy, which was mainly that of steel alloys. The later development of tough steel rendered steel alloys less important. Yet the field of alloy metallurgy kept developing, for both practical and theoretical reasons. When Hadfield learned about Faraday's pioneering work, he was astonished by his daring and by how little he had missed success. It is heartwarming that Hadfield was anxious to pay his predecessor all the tribute he could.

field. Within a year there was a literature on it too large to survey. Faraday published his survey anonymously—he had no claim to priority, and so he did not sign it. A tradition beginning with Boyle required that one not report in print an experiment, however well known, without repeating it oneself. This had made Joseph Priestley, the educator who wrote a science textbook, into a scientist. This made the genteel Mrs. Jane Marcet describe experiments that even untrained and isolated people could repeat. This made Faraday into an expert in electromagnetics. His scientific education was complete, and he came back to his first love, electricity. Like Mozart whose mature works reflect his London notebooks of childhood, like Beethoven who almost lost his identity under the influence of Haydn and Mozart until he returned with more vigor to the style of his earliest sonatinas and bagatelles, like Van Gogh who with much labor emerged from the styles of the Paris impressionists to a heightened level of his old crude carbon sketches, so Faraday, through chemistry, some general science, philosophy, the arts, and even locution,[11] finally returned to electricity.

One day in 1821 he discovered the electric motor. Exhilarated, he went to a show; he stood in line and soon found himself in a fistfight with a big bully (he was small and painfully aware of it). He went back to work at once and issued a brilliant paper, filled with scintillating ideas and reporting hundreds of beautiful experiments; he must have worked like a slave. When he returned from his euphoria to the real world, a charge of plagiarism awaited him. Nothing could hurt him more—except perhaps the loss of Davy's friendship. No matter: the one thing soon led to the other.

## The Sad Incident

In 1821 Faraday, age about thirty, made his first outstanding discovery and at once was declared a plagiarist. The matter was settled within two years, and in 1824 the matter was closed when Faraday was elected a Fellow of the Royal Society. The cost of the incident, however, was not assessed. In my own assessment, this is one of the most important events in Faraday's life. It had two results. First, it estranged him from society. For the rest of his life he had a handful of very close scientific friends and very close relatives, one laboratory assistant, and a lot of admirers—no casual acquaintances, no associates in any sense except a few people (such as William Whewell) whom he appreciated and

11. Faraday took lessons in locution, i.e., speech, like Shaw's Eliza Doolittle: he was a Cockney, and in order to lecture he too had to learn to say "The rain in Spain," etc.

with whom he exchanged a few letters, and no lukewarm friends except perhaps a few scientists in London.[12] The society that rejected him on the pretext of a plagiarism charge, but really as a stranger and an upstart—that same society warmly welcomed him a few years later. But he was too proud to accept. (Faraday was so touchy he refused to accept knighthood even after the prime minister had apologized for having used the word "humbug"; clearly, the prime minister only withdrew his impolite expression, not the view that science is too worthless to bring its promoters titles of nobility.) He became more and more devoted to his studies and had less and less time for any other activities. But devotion to science and very hard work did not lead to the expected contentment and tranquillity. Davy had predicted a disappointment and then caused it by severing his ties with his young and devoted admirer.

Most biographers of Faraday blame an amorphous crowd for the rumors of plagiarism and Davy for his envy. This is all true, but hardly satisfactory as a complete picture. Even Davy's—culpable perhaps—envy is at the very least more complicated than his biographers and Faraday's think.

Faraday adopted Davy for a father figure, as we would say today. Due to his diffidence he was always distant, and so, against all his fervent wishes, he seemed to Davy somewhat aloof. And he coldly rejected (*Life and Letters*, 1:379) an attempt at a rapprochement that indeed was clumsy: Davy asked Faraday to remove his candidacy to the Royal Society on the ground that he was not yet ready to join the society. When Faraday refused, Davy, as president, blocked the election for about half a year, moving all the time toward and away from friendship with Faraday (*Life and Letters*, 1:380); when Faraday was elected fellow, the friendship was dead: with all the tensions and agonies, at

12. The correspondence that Faraday conducted shows clearly that in London he hardly had any intermediary between brief businesslike contacts and very close friendships or close family relationships. The exceptions are his correspondence with Charles Babbage, who pestered him, and with Sir John Herschel and Judge Sir William Grove, who were friends though not close ones. To this one has to add three. First, Sir William Snow Harris, one of the first to report Faraday's ideas in print. It seems that he was so poor a thinker that Faraday did not take him seriously though they rather enjoyed each other's company. Second and third, Sir Charles Wheatstone and John Gassiot. He met both of them fairly frequently, and he conducted his last experiments—on the cathode tube—with Gassiot's aid. But evidently they were not friends, not even as much as some of the lesser foreign correspondents Faraday had. As close friends one could, perhaps, count a few older members of the Royal Institution, such as Stodart with whom he published on metallurgy, Davy, and Wollaston. And as close friends of his own age group we can count Richard Phillips, the editor of the *Philosophical Magazine*, who published all that Faraday sent him, Edward Magrath, and almost no one else; both were from the City Philosophical Society (see Williams, *Michael Faraday*, p. 15).

least Faraday saw the relationship as a friendship until then and as estrangement from then on (*Life and Letters*, 1:359).[13]

The relation of ambivalence, of annoyance as an expression of inner restlessness and of the lack of peace with oneself, these characterize the actions of both Davy and Faraday. That Davy feared and envied Faraday the biographers of both have noticed. That he wished to resolve the ambivalence by patronizing Faraday, by being allowed to decide when Faraday was ripe for fellowship, and then to make the proposal to invite Faraday and, as president of the society, to make real song and dance about it—this is how I like to see the mass of tortured and unpleasant evidence. As for other writers on the topic, they know little of ambivalence and of the harshness that comes from a heart full of love that cannot be channeled in the usual manner.

So much for Davy. Faraday, then, was at least not very cooperative. Of course, the questions are, was he in his right? Was he wise? Was he less magnanimous to the object of his worship than he could afford to be? I doubt it. On the contrary, he was only too correct for the situation. Desperately correct, of course, and desperately trying his hardest and working hard at the same time—and thus frightfully aloof, and thus self-defeating. What George Bernard Shaw says in his preface to *Saint Joan* about there being objectively understandable reasons for offering Socrates the hemlock and crucifying Jesus is somewhat applicable here too. Perhaps Faraday was not so much of a saint to be utterly intolerable, especially since in his middle age he could not conceal the fact that he was always full of irritability up to the very lid of the pleasant and patient and good-humored demeanor with which he covered it all. But, at least in his late twenties and early thirties, he was too good and honest and loyal and dedicated and composed not to get occasionally on someone's nerves —especially on Davy's nerves, the vain and declining Davy, who was convinced that deep down in his heart he only wanted the best for Faraday but was utterly misunderstood by the whole world, even by Faraday himself.

There were also social factors, of course, both broad and narrow. The broad factors are of general interest in social history, especially of the place of men of science in society. There is too little written on this topic as yet, and most of

---

13. The following excerpt from a letter to Sir John Herschel indicates most clearly that Faraday and Davy worked together closely till they broke away from each other, regardless of the enormous emotional upheavals (Faraday to Herschel, R.S., ms, 26 May 1826): "My Dear Sir, I believe yours are the hands into which I should put a paper intended for the Royal Society. I have shown it to Sir Humphry Davy who thinks pretty well of it but does not seem quite satisfied with the argument. I cannot however alter my view and for my comfort and more my fullest confidence Dr. Wollaston is quite satisfied with it. . . ."

it is vulgar-Marxist. The locus classicus is Charles Babbage's *Reflections on the Decline of Science in England* of 1830 and the reply to it by Gerritt Moll, *On the Alleged Decline* etc., of 1831, published anonymously under the name of A. Foreigner and brought to the press by his friend Faraday. Babbage was an unreliable sourpuss, but he must have been right in the main or Faraday would not have sided with him openly. And he did, to the point of boycotting the Royal Society altogether because of its class discrimination and to the point of showing interest and sympathy toward the rise of the British Association for the Advancement of Science that Babbage had created expressly to serve as a poor man's Royal Society. The controversy that Babbage started came into the open, as I said, in 1830; the sad story of Faraday's disappointment took place in 1821 to 1823, at the time when, according to Babbage, class discrimination was already in full practice. A gentleman as Faraday always tried so hard to be, he neither knew etiquette as well as those who were born into the right society nor did he ever get the right connections. And so in his troubles he was severely handicapped.

Of course, the chief dramatis personae were not all snobs. Davy was, and large portions of the crowds that came in droves to hear his brilliant lectures in the Royal Institution[14] were—the ladies often coming to exhibit a new hat,

14. Bence Jones has written a very interesting history of the Royal Institution, but a new appraisal should prove rewarding. Count Rumford had conceived of the institution as as adult education center for the poor and was soon disappointed by its snobbery. But it always did perform valuable educational services, even though not to the egalitarian Rumford's satisfaction. Indeed, it even influenced the development of adult education in other countries, partly because its illustrious members have impressed people like Oersted and Humboldt who had great influence in their own countries. Thomas Young did a better academic job than Davy, though a much too academic job to be called popular, and Davy dismissed him. Faraday and Tyndall certainly catered for varieties of tastes, and so did the various lecturers of the Friday Evening Discourses, from the early days to date. But the general atmosphere was always rather on the snobbish side, never more so than under Davy, the playboy of London high society.

For Davy as a lecturer with snob value see W. E. Johnston, *England As It Is* (London, 1851) and T. E. Thorpe, *Humphry Davy, Poet and Philosopher* (London, 1896). Notice, however, Dalton's letter on Davy's lesson to Dalton in lecturing, published by Bence Jones, which clearly shows that he was indeed a gifted lecturer and a conscientious one. Faraday the lecturer is described by his niece (*Life and Letters*, 2:113: ". . . he would tell me my remarks helped him to make things clear to the young ones") and in some length also by Gladstone. Williams (*Michael Faraday*, p. 333) quotes a German writer telling the world about the greatness of Faraday the lecturer: Frederick von Raumer, *England in 1835* (Philadelphia, 1836), p. 230. The chapter on Tyndall as a lecturer and writer in his official biography is singularly uninformative, but see Denis Meadows, *Obedient Men* (Longmans, 1954), for a story of a well-rehearsed "accident" during a lecture by Tyndall (in which fire broke out and Tyndall displayed self-control). This is what Faraday called "Alehouse tricks" when describing to Abbott his views on the subject of lecturing (*Life and Letters*, 1:78).

as if the occasion were a new opera or some such. William Hyde Wollaston, in particular, from whom Faraday was alleged to have plagiarized, was the most impeccable gentleman the scientific world ever knew, and a very magnanimous person. Nevertheless, one cannot overlook the fact that the Royal Society was a society, as Babbage tells us, that a gentleman could join as easily as he could join any other club, and much in the same way, whereas a poor person had to prove his scientific worth before he was invited to join—much as scientists are invited to join the Royal Society in this day and age. This is not simply a generality; it was ruthlessly applied in Faraday's case. He was told clearly what was expected from a person in point of character before qualifying for a fellowship in the Royal Society. He humbly accepted the sermon (*Life and Letters*, 1:348), and was proposed as a fellow, with Wollaston as first signatory. Davy did not sign, and it took six months more for the election to go through; finally the vote took place, and there was only one blackball—everybody thinks it was Davy's.

What is the point of a secret ballot if everyone knows who has put the blackball? Evidently, Davy could not take a defeat gracefully—he was the only one on the committee who was not a gentleman. Perhaps this is what gave away the secret of the owner of the blackball, not the balloting system. As biographers amply demonstrate, Davy, unlike Faraday, was extremely well assimilated into high society. This phenomenon is, regrettably, not uncommon: many assimilated German and Austrian Jews of the early twentieth century, for example, were particularly irritated by the Jewish appearance of Eastern European Jews. Perhaps Davy was not so vulgar as some of those well-bred gentlefolk, but the unpleasant similarity is not easy to shake off.

There is, further, a more narrow sociological factor involved in our story, this time of the strict etiquette of the scientific world. Just as Faraday was caught in the transition from the high class society of science to the more classless or middle-class or technocratic society of science, so was he caught in the transition between the Baconian canons of priority and the later and more lax canons. This takes some explanation, which I now wish to offer. Perhaps I should say first, however, that to speak of Faraday as caught in a transition of scientific conduct is not altogether fair, considering the fact that he was one of the chief engineers of that transition. But this is not strictly relevant right now. Let me, then, explain the change in standards of priority and how Faraday was caught in them. I shall dwell on the story very briefly—it will come up again later—and discuss its methodological implications then and now, the ways to look at it from different viewpoints on scientific etiquette. (The story was told by Bence Jones, but with no comment.)

Briefly, the story is this. Faraday had made a prediction, and Wollaston had made a prediction. Each worked on his own; both were true. Faraday confirmed his prediction almost at once, Wollaston's prediction was confirmed only half a century later, by George Core (S. P. Thompson, *Michael Faraday*, p. 84). Faraday put much stress, during the unpleasant period, on the fact that the predictions were different. And, no doubt, by the strict empiricist, or inductivist, or Baconian, canons of the day, every fact different from any other fact, however minute, deserves praise as a discovery. But, clearly, no one adhered closely to this canon, and people used theory, common sense, and intuition in order to evaluate and differentiate new facts. Faraday said his anticipated fact had differed from Wollaston's, Davy said no. The code was on Faraday's side; but at its weakest. Davy first said bluntly, but without stating his conclusion, what the facts were:

> I cannot with propriety conclude without mentioning a circumstance in the history of the progress of electromagnetism, which, though well known to many Fellows of this Society, has, I believe, never been made public; namely that we owe to the sagacity of Dr. Wollaston the first idea of the possibility of the rotation of the electro-magnetic wire round its axis by the approach of a magnet; and I witnessed, early in 1821, an unsuccessful experiment which he made to produce the effect.

This is from Davy's published paper; it is correct but has no reference either to Faraday or to the confirmation of Wollaston's prediction. It was reported by others that when he read the paper in public he also said,

> Had not an experiment on the subject made by Dr. W. in the laboratory of the Royal Institution, and witnessed by Sir Humphry, failed merely through an accident which happened to the apparatus, he would have been the discoverer of that phenomenon.

Davy was forced to deny he had ever said this: Dr. Wollaston's experiment was not identical with Faraday's. Notice that the statement that Davy withdrew identifies the two experiments, but it does not contest Faraday's priority and it does not accuse Faraday explicitly. The accusation may, however, be implicit:

when Wollaston failed to confirm his theory, mainly because friction prevented the conducting wire from rotating around its axis in the vicinity of a magnet, Faraday was consulted. But Faraday later succeeded in convincing Wollaston and his friends that this in no way interfered with research Faraday was conducting independently at the same time concerning a wire rotating around a magnet, not around its own axis near a magnet. Implications aside, is the statement that Davy withdrew true? Are the two experiments, Wollaston's rotation of a wire around itself in the vicinity of a magnet, and Faraday's rotation of a wire round a magnet, identical? Are they not mere variants of Oersted's discovery—his deflection of a compass needle by a conducting wire? Or on the variant of Oersted's variant—the deflection of a compass needle by a conducting coil? (This variant is known as the galvanometer.) Or on the variant on Oersted by Gaspard de la Rive, Chevalier Yelin, and others (there was a priority dispute on that case too) where a light battery floating on water and discharging electricity acts like a compass?

Suppose for a minute that Faraday's and Wollaston's experiments are identical. Wollaston lost to nimble Faraday. What of it? In a recent volume on scientific standards, Robert Merton of Columbia University says that severe competition is part and parcel of scientific endeavor. He quotes Arago—an elder contemporary of Faraday, incidentally—as saying that one hour's delay may cost a scientist his chance for immortality. Now, were Wollaston and his associates so competitive, they would not have acted as they did. But Wollaston was the perfect gentleman and, though not reputed as a great scientist, he was reputed as the perfect scientist. He took his time and did not jump to conclusions or wish to publish inconclusive demonstrations of rash speculations. The timely gentleman was outsmarted by a pushy young upstart: the battle that Babbage was fighting in the open in the 1830s was raging underground in the 1820s—and Faraday was the victim.

Since that time we have learned to grant priority to ideas in order to render Merton's hypercompetitive view of science obsolete. Thus, von Laue's discovery of X-ray crystallography, deBroglie's discovery of electron waves, Yukawa's discovery of the meson, Lee's and Yang's discovery of cases where parity is not conserved, and hosts of other instances are cases where we—society—award priority for unperformed experiments. In the eighteenth century the opposite still was the case, as a matter of course. Priestley offered the inverse square law of electricity first (*History of Electricity*, *Hints*), if not Benjamin Franklin; and priority goes to Coulomb who performed the experiment.

In his important paper on his discovery Faraday engaged in a subtle and ingenious theoretical debate with Ampère. No doubt, his views are elaborations on Wollaston's, and yet largely original. In his discussion, however, he speaks as if he has no views of his own—that he only supports the ideas of Wollaston. When we discuss all this, the reader will no doubt think more highly of Wollaston's pioneering heretic ideas than of the experiment he designed; but in 1820 the code of recognition was very different—and much inferior. Faraday's generous acknowledgments of ideas to Wollaston could not matter then in comparison with the question of an experimental priority.

Boyle, who had instituted the practice of priority for facts, noted the defect of this practice. He suggested that an unconfirmed idea should be sealed and placed in a learned society's hand. So he did; so did Lavoisier; so did Faraday, in 1832[15]. In 1821 Wollaston could do this, but instead he kept the idea secret. He might indeed have felt harmed when a person he had taken into his confidence published first. But such matters can be settled; what must be dealt with publicly is the inadequacy of the rules that impose secrecy.

At the time Faraday accepted the idea that Wollaston's study was his own, and those whom he took into his confidence should have left the field alone. He said, however, he had his own idea before he had heard of Wollaston's design of an experiment, he wanted to make an acknowledgment, and so on.[16] Wollaston preferred to believe Faraday's sincerity and forget and forgive. Davy remained adamant. The question, can one own a field, is still open, and Jacques Hadamard confessed that in order to circumvent it he always dropped a topic upon hearing that he was not the only one to study it (*The Psychology of Invention in the Mathematical Field*, 1954, p. 132). But World War II and American competitiveness somehow led to the wide acceptance of Merton's conclusions. The result is that many bitter and gossipy comments are made

15. For the case of Faraday see below, pp. 106–7. The case of Lavoisier's sealed note of 1 November 1772 is well known. See, for example, Denis I. Duveen and Herbert S. Klickstein, *A Bibliography of the Works of Antoine Laurent Lavoisier, 1743–1794*, London, 1954, p. 97. I am not familiar with references to Boyle's case, though it is of exactly the same nature. See his letters to Oldenburg of 17 October 1667 and 26 October 1667 and of 29 December 1667. It seems to me that the whole matter deserves further study.

16. Faraday claimed (*Experimental Researches in Electricity*, 2:160) that Wollaston wished not to be referred to in the second of Faraday's publications on the subject. Later Wollaston said that he thought he should not have demanded such a reference, but that nevertheless Faraday should have made the reference. Faraday's view concerning the conversation that took place between them was different. This misunderstanding was corrected in a special note where Faraday made a proper acknowledgment that satisfied Wollaston as well as his friends. But the slander continued. Thus, Faraday and Wollaston had differed in point of etiquette—in which, doubtless, Wollaston was the greater expert of the two.

about Professor X who stole a dissertation topic from Professor Y so that the work of slow graduate student B went down the drain when student A graduated. Things can always get sillier and pettier.

Even if we suppose Faraday's and Wollaston's experimental ideas to be not identical, we may say, had Wollaston been the sole student of the field he might have come upon Faraday's idea sooner or later. Now, doubtless, it is not acceptable to leave an important field to one man. Hence we force any discoverer of a field—as Wollaston in a small way was—into secrecy. This may cause heartbreaking duplicities: if many work in secret, there must be what the self-same Robert Merton terms "multiple-discovery," namely a high rate of inefficiency. Also, who needs to be told that secrecy and even merely poor communications may easily breed suspicion? (Here even Wollaston was forced to compromise his conduct as a gentleman!) We must change our code of acknowledgment. But for that we must find the source of the defect.

The source is as old as our practice of acknowledgment. Bacon said, facts are prior to theories, and in the absence of theory all facts are equally different from each other. Boyle denied that facts always precede theorizing, but in order to encourage gentlemen to experiment he was ready to acknowledge the slightest variant on an old discovery as a new discovery. He even extended this to theorizing. But this does not change the fact that we sometimes acknowledge variants on important experiments as discoveries—e.g., we recognize Bragg's method of X-ray crystallography on top of von Laue's, though the one is a variant of the other; but we disregard later and quite ingenious variants as mere patents, not as discoveries. There is much to be clarified here.

Etiquette aside, the question everyone was asking is, were Wollaston's and Faraday's experiments identical or not? If this question were answerable in a clear-cut fashion, then the incident could be easily cleared. But this was not the case. Whereas Davy had reason to identify the two experiments, we have good reason to view them as different: Wollaston's wire is rotated by spiraling electrons that zoom through it, and Faraday's wire is rotated because it is a magnet with circular forces, as we shall soon see. The forces aiding Wollaston (Lorentz forces acting on the current and the collisions between the current and the wire) are much smaller than those aiding Faraday.

From our viewpoint, then, the two experiments are different, and Wollaston's is the harder to perform. From Davy's viewpoint, they are more or less the same. Let us, then, inspect the views of Wollaston and Faraday themselves.

# 3    Prelude to the Field Theory

The way to people's thoughts is through the problems that engage them. The problem of the day lay in Oersted's experiment; also, perhaps, in his explanation of it. This explanation is still in limbo, ever since Sir Humphry Davy declared that it was hard to understand. Oersted spoke of an electric conflict that leaves the wire and goes to rotate the magnet. The word "conflict" is somewhat obscure; it comes from a book by Immanuel Kant and so we may assume it was unclear to the general scientific public; we may even assume it was unclear to Davy, who was a bit of a Kantian himself (see n. 13, p. 29 above). Yet this is not the crux of the matter. The crux of the matter is that the conflict was supposed to move in empty space.

   Imagine a political conflict; it is associated in your mind with people—directly or through political force; imagine political forces in conflict but without people. If you can, you have no trouble understanding Oersted or any other field theorist; but you cannot. The difficulty is the same in Einstein's theory where an electromagnetic disturbance can travel in empty space: if the disturbance is in empty space, what is being disturbed? We must take this question slowly and see the boldness of all field theories.

### Kant and Oersted

Theories of space prior to the one proposed by Kant divide into two wide categories, plenism and vacuism. Briefly, one might say, for the vacuist most space is empty but parts of it are non-empty, where the empty parts are penetrable by matter, matter occupies the non-empty parts, and the non-empty parts are impenetrable by more matter. For the plenist this division does not hold. This exposition is not highly satisfactory. Boscovich, for example, was a vacuist, but he shrunk matter to point-masses and abolished impenetrability altogether. He assumed, instead, that forces of repulsion would keep the point atoms apart, thus giving matter its observed bulk.

Another important characterization of empty space, then, must be added: ever since the ancient debate concerning the void—of Parmenides and Democritus—it has been agreed by all parties that empty space has no properties, that the nothing has no qualities, that empty space is homogenous (each two parts of it are identical) and isotropic (in each point all directions are identical). A piece of matter may have different properties at different parts—e.g., different densities, or different tensions—and a piece of matter may have an axis of symmetry, an axis of rotation, and other kinds of preferred direction (axis of gyration, of force, of force configuration symmetry, of vibration symmetry, etc.). This was almost universally taken for granted. Therefore, if light is a wave phenomenon, then space is occupied by an aether. For waves are vibrations, and in order to have vibrations we must have something vibrate— the nothing (empty space) cannot vibrate. Of course, the aetherists can be vacuists—viewing the aether as atoms in the void—or plenists—viewing the aether as continuous and filling all space. But the wave theory of light necessitated a vibrator—a medium—an aether—for vacuist and plenist alike.

Considering all this, since Boscovich's space was homogenous and isotropic, we can say that he was a vacuist. However empty his space was, he placed the properties of matter not in space but in (pointlike) atoms. We can also clearly see why it makes no sense to speak of partly full space: if space is empty, it must have no properties; otherwise it is full—there are no middle positions possible between emptiness and non-emptiness.

There are further complications, to be sure. Descartes saw all matter as essentially extension or filling all space, and Leibniz, finding Descartes's view unsatisfactory, saw space as a property of matter. Since Newton endorsed Boyle's view, assuming both matter and empty space (adding forces to the picture), the controversy was relinquished under Newton's authority. But then things started moving slowly. Boscovich claimed that Newtonian atoms need not be extended. Kant had a similar view in his early period and a more sophisticated view in his later period. He said,[1] as a general rule of interpolation, whatever is observed to have the values O and I is possible to interpolate

1. In his *Metaphysical Foundation of Natural Science*, especially book iv. Notice that the rule of interpolation mentioned here is already in the *Critique of Pure Reason*.

theoretically as having all intermediate values. To show that he meant it, he claimed that this applies both to empty and full space. There are two kinds of forces, attraction and repulsion, and fullness is the outcome of the conflict between the two. This is far from being clear, and especially the idea of a conflict between forces is somewhat puzzling.

Oersted's work[2] was entirely unknown to the philosophical public, at least in England, until 1819. Following Kant and Schelling, he speculated that all forces of nature are manifestations of one "primordial" force, and under different circumstances the same force has different manifestations. This was in sharp conflict with the accepted Newtonian views according to which different forces are properties of different kinds of atoms: atoms are indestructible and invariant. Oersted viewed matter as conflicts of forces, following Kant; it is not clear what he meant by it, and his contemporaries only found it confusing that he talked of the electric conflict where they should talk of the electric forces. But he was even more baffling than that.

Oersted's famous paper on electromagnetics is the only paper of his which had truly wide circulation. Essentially, he describes the phenomenon and relates it briefly to his theory. The phenomenon is this: put a wire in the south-north direction over a compass and pass a current through it; the needle will be deflected; reverse the current and the deflection will go the other way. This is the whole of the discovery.

For traditional philosophers, this deflection, this rotation, is puzzling; not so for Oersted, who can easily imagine the conflict emanating from the wire and deflecting the needle of the compass.

Here is the whole of Oersted's original theory[3] (Thomson's *Annals* [1820], 15:276):

> . . . The electric conflict is not confined to the conductor, but disperses pretty widely in the circumjacent space . . . This conflict performs in circles . . . [We assume] that negative electricity moves in a spiral line bent towards the right and propels the north pole . . . The effects on the south pole are explained

2. For more detail see my *Towards an Historiography of Science*, 1963, reprinted, Wesleyan University Press, 1967.

3. Oersted's original paper was privately published in Latin and republished in his *Skrifter* (Copenhagen, 1920), edited by Kirstine Meyer, and in a special edition in various languages (Copenhagen, 1920), preface by A. Larsen. The English translation was published also in Bern Dibner, *Oersted etc.*, New York, 1962. The word "conflict" occurs in the Latin title but not in the English title, then or later on.

in a similar manner, if we ascribe to positive electricity contrary motion etc . . .

I shall merely add . . . that I have demonstrated [*sic!*] in a book published five years ago that heat and light consist of the conflict of electricities. From the observations now stated we may conclude that a circular motion likewise occurs in these effects . . .

Whatever Oersted meant by "conflict," clearly he accepted the bi-fluid theory of electricity, and he figured to himself some sort of action, perhaps a *clash* or *collision* between the two streams moving in opposite directions. But how can a conflict "disperse widely in space"? We can see, if we wish, the circular motions of "electric conflicts in circumjacent space" as vague adumbrations of highly heretic ideas. But these heretic ideas are hard to grasp even today, when they are clear and widely circulated. So let us follow the history of the process of clarification.

To complicate matters, every piece of research may be a wild goose chase. The research whose development I am going to describe was conducted with a profound sense of urgency due to the feeling that a hole had been pierced in the wall of Newtonianism. This could be an illusion. Ampère had, indeed, shown this almost at once to be but an illusion. He took it for granted that Oersted's rotation was not due to such an impossible entity as circular forces, but due to couples of Newtonian forces of pull and push. He also concluded from the electromagnetic interaction that either electricity was a magnetic phenomenon or that magnetism was an electric phenomenon. He opted for the second choice. He declared all magnets to be conglomerations of small currents; he declared any two elements of current to attract or repel each other depending on whether they run parallel or contrary to each other, and he built his electromagnet—a helix that, when conducting, acts like a magnet in all respects—and other marvelous proofs of his theory. Had Ampère been right, Faraday's story would have been very different; he was mistaken, we know, but for generations he did have more followers than Faraday; Faraday could not diminish his influence, at least in part because his theory had great merit, but also in part because he had Newton's authority to back him.

### Wollaston

The point in the sad incident that we have left open was, were Wollaston's and Faraday's predicted experiments identical or not? Davy said yes, and, in accord with the inductive code of the day, was soon forced to deny he had ever said yes. But, unbounded by this code, we may re-raise the question. Intuitively, both experiments come from the same stock: Oersted said all forces can be converted to each other. Thus, Seebeck, for instance, under Oersted's influence, tried to convert heat to electricity (Oersted viewed the heat caused by electric currents as electric forces converted to heat forces). Now we may try to reverse Oersted's experiment in varied ways. Since an electric current moves a magnet, we may try to make a magnet move a current. Oersted did this in one way; but there were other ways. Ampère did this by creating an electromagnet. Since a current rotates a magnet, we may make a magnet rotate a conducting wire—around its axis (Wollaston) or around a magnet (Faraday). Since electricity produces magnetism, we may try to make magnetism produce electricity. Many attempts at this were made in the 1820s, many variants; all failed. This was Faraday's great discovery of 1831, his greatest single discovery.

Had Faraday known in 1821 to what he was destined, had he been more self-confident, probably he would have acted differently and with much more confidence. Following the line of presentation of the previous paragraph, it is not difficult to sympathize with the view that Ampère's discovery, Wollaston's, Faraday's of 1821, and Faraday's of 1831, are all variants of Oersted's. This shows how great Oersted was, but when these three were told they were "merely" performing variants on Oersted's experiments, they were hurt and felt slighted. I have discussed Ampère's contribution elsewhere.[4] Here let me say only that the harder it is to produce a variant, the more we may appreciate it. What were Wollaston's difficulties, then?

Wollaston explained his failure to rotate a conducting wire on its axis as caused by friction (and we all agree with him to this day). He asked Faraday to help on this technical matter of reducing friction. Faraday suggested that he take for a conducting wire a magnetic needle and suspend the needle under a magnet. It did not work, and Faraday soon viewed his proposal as "hasty and useless" (*Experimental Researches in Electricity*, 2:159). Ampère later found the same solution very useful, but that is another story. Since the needle had to be connected to the battery, this connection caused enough friction to prevent success at that time. Wollaston tried to rotate a piece of wire on two metal blocks with minimal friction, and Faraday was again consulted. Again, no result. We now can easily calculate the force of rotation

4. See my *Towards an Historiography of Science*, sect. 5.

in Wollaston's experiment and explain his failure in spite of his—and Faraday's —proverbial manual dexterity. But this is hindsight.

Faraday's experiment encountered both the problem of friction and the problem of keeping the current moving while the wire that conducts it moves as well. He had a joint hung above the center of a metal ring, each connected to a pole of the battery, and a wire loosely in contact with both; now the wire could move and conduct; put a magnetic pole in the center of the ring and the wire should rotate. Friction would prevent this, but Faraday replaced the ring with a cup of mercury and poured on top of it a drop of a lubricant of his own invention.

Faraday's historical statement about himself and Wollaston was corrected with a pencil by Wollaston prior to its publication, and the alteration was chiefly an attempt to emphasize the fact that Wollaston's prediction was based on some hypothesis of Wollaston's. Faraday's evidence on this issue (*Experimental Researches in Electricity*, 2:233) makes one point clear: whereas Faraday was still thinking of electromagnetism in terms of attraction and repulsion between electric currents and magnets, Wollaston was thinking of forces going on and on in circles around the electric currents: Wollaston thought that the force acting in Oersted's experiment was *transversal* or "*vertiginous*" or "*circumferential*," when Faraday was still convinced that the force was *central* (i.e., pull or push, attraction or repulsion). From his own theory, each of them claimed, somehow he deduced some experimental expectations. This sounds perverse: it is Faraday's experiment that uses transversal forces, not Wollaston's. It was Wollaston's theory, not Faraday's that was right.

What was Wollaston's line of reasoning? Can we mobilize Newtonian mechanics to calculate the motions caused by circular forces? This seems not easy at all. Newton's theory is contradicted, at least seemingly, by the assumption of transversal forces, since according to the theory for each force there exists an opposite force and both lie on one and the same line, so that the sum of the rotation that they tend to produce is nil. When one puts a pencil on a table and tries to rotate it by *pushing* it with his two hands in opposite directions, the two forces exerted by the two hands cause a rotation, even though they may be equal in magnitude and act in exactly opposite directions. As Newton's third law demands that for each force there exists another that is not only equal in magnitude and opposite or antiparallel in direction but also lies on the same line, it follows that, when one rotates a pencil, four, not two, forces are active— two forces of the hands and two of the pencil. The question that every student has when first realizing the consequence of Newton's third law is why the experimenter's hands rotate the pencil and not the reverse, the pencil rotating the experimenter? or, perhaps, why is the system not in equilibrium, since the forces are equal and opposite? Taking the experimenter and the pencil in isolation, Newton's theory tells us that the pencil does in fact rotate the experimenter, just as the pencil lifts the whole earth when it falls toward it, although one action is very small in relation to the other action (since one force has to act on a much more massive body). Taking all three—the pencil, the experimenter, and the earth (as an isolated system)—we can say that (due to friction) the pencil rotates—ever so slightly—not only the experimenter but the entire earth.

This point is of supreme importance in Newton's mechanics. In an isolated system, if there is one rotation created in one direction, there is another in the opposite direction. The forces creating them are equal and opposite, but one force may work on a massive part of the system and cause less rotation (angular motion) than the other. The dynamical measure of the rotation (angular motion) is the so-called momentum of momentum, and is equal in both directions. According to Newton's theory, the total change of rotation of any closed system is nil.

Now let us take the theory according to which a moving electric particle and a magnetic particle cause transversal forces on each other. Quite intuitively we notice that in such an isolated system there can be an increase of momentum of momentum, say, by sticking to two ends of a moving stick the two particles in question, thus making it rotate with an ever-increasing velocity, say around a fixed point on which it may hang. Something somewhere went wrong, the moment we deviated from the assumption that all forces are central.

To locate the something that went wrong in Oersted's experiment took about eighty-five years. The presently accepted explanation of Oersted's effect (as well as of Wollaston's and of Faraday's) is the so-called *Lorentz electron theory*. It is well known that in a Newtonian system the Lorentz forces fail to obey Newton's third law. Perhaps one may declare then that Newton's third law is false; but the result of this is easily refutable. As Maxwell showed (*Scientific Papers*) even before Lorentz developed his theory, the laws of conservation of momentum and of energy may be violated if we reject Newton's third law. One can see the result in the example presented in the previous paragraph, based on Maxwell's example. There was, therefore (since perpetual motion machines were ruled out), a need to locate the error elsewhere. Maxwell suggested the adoption of an aether theory which, we can now say, amounted to giving up the law of inertia, Newton's first law, at least as far as electricity was concerned. For, according to his suggestion, the mechanical character of an isolated system is different in one case, when it is at rest relative to the aether (absolute rest), than in another, when it is in fixed velocity relative to the aether. It was exactly this hypothesis that Michelson and Morley refuted —by an experiment envisaged earlier by Maxwell. The next attempt to locate the something that went wrong in Oersted's experiment is known as the theory of relativity (both because it rendered time relative and because it reinstated[5] Newton's first law, the law of inertia, or the principle of relativity of constant motion).

Back to 1820. We do not quite know how conscious Oersted was of his violation of Newton's program, but he does say something to that effect, however vaguely. Faraday tried to explain Oersted's experiment mechanically, but instead of the presentation of an explicit Newtonian hypothesis, all he had to offer was an illustration. Imagine a compass laid horizontally and a vertical conducting wire brought near it. If the wire is on one side, it will attract it; if it is on another, it will repel it; while in the middle it will be neutral to it.

WIRES
○ Attraction
○ Neutral
○ Repulsion

MAGNET

The general fact is that when the wire is on one side the needle moves away from it, and it is not much of a hypothesis to say that the moving away is repulsion—a Newtonian may assert it unnoticingly. But this hypothesis of Faraday's can be refuted, and he did refute it and then adopt Wollaston's hypothesis. And yet, this hypothesis is what led him to think of a rotation: keep the wire on the same side of a magnet while it moves, and it will keep moving—either by making the magnet chase the wire or, as Faraday conceived the case, have only one pole act and have the current run parallel to the magnet's axis. This is not a clear idea—but nothing then was clear.

While Faraday was engaged in his Newtonian explanation of Oersted's experiment and in designing his own experiment, Wollaston was developing his anti-Newtonian theory to explain it and designing his experiment. Here

5. The title of Einstein's original paper of 1905, "On the Electrodynamics of Moving Bodies," shows that he consciously contrasted the law of inertia with the medium hypothesis.

is an anonymous[6] statement of Wollaston's theory, published in January 1821, over half a year before Faraday adopted it (*Quarterly Journal of Science* 10 [1821], 363):

> The phenomena exhibited by the electromagnetic or conjunctive wire may be explained upon the supposition of an electromagnetic current passing round the axis of the conjunctive wire, its direction depending upon that of the electric current . . .

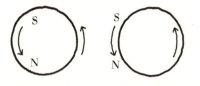

> In the above figures, such a current is represented in two sections at right angles to the axis of the wire, when similarly electrified, from which it will be apparent that the north and south powers meeting, will attract each other.
> In the following figure,

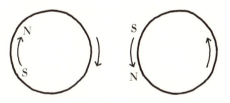

> the sections of the wire are shown dissimilarly electrified, by which similar magnetic powers meet, and consequently occasion a repulsion.

It is clear that Wollaston considered every segment of a circle around a wire to behave like a small magnet. In Poisson's theory of magnetism, any small segment of a magnet is itself a magnet; Wollaston conceived such a

6. The report was not written by Dr. Wollaston. According to Faraday's later evidence, it was written by a professor of the Royal Institution (*Experimental Researches in Electricity*, 2:231). Since it is the only source of information at hand, and since Faraday could rely on it, we may rely on it too.

closed magnet to exist around the conducting wire. Such an assumption, it is true, explains both Oersted's and Ampère's discoveries. The task, of course, was to test it independently. We may conceive of the following experiment: Since in Oersted's experiment the magnet rotates in one direction and then stays in an equilibrium, one would expect, quite intuitively (not on the basis of Newton's third law), that the wire would tend to rotate in the opposite direction when allowed to move freely. But this is not an independent test. Indeed, Oersted had tried to perform it: he mounted the wire together with the zinc and copper plates to which it is connected on a cork that was allowed to float in the acid solution. Oersted himself, it is true, failed to make the cork rotate; but the problem he had to overcome was minor, and soon others (there is a problem of priority here) succeeded in making the cork rotate. This rotation is not that of Faraday, nor that of Wollaston. Furthermore, Ampère's theory, which employs Newton's third law, explains this rotation.

Since this rotation is not in conflict with Newton's third law, perhaps when Wollaston searched for a new rotation he was consciously looking for a violation of Newton's third law. The violation is already there, of course, in Wollaston's assumption of the transversal or the circumferential force. It is there, also, in the prediction that the wire would rotate around its axis. The question is, was Wollaston aware of it? Was he offering an intuitive analogue to Newton's third law, saying that when the wire rotates magnets in a ring around it in one direction, the ring rotates it in the opposite direction? Let us make this assumption for the time being.

All this is highly conjectural—and it does not solve the loose ends of the mystery. Consider the following facts.

(a) The rotary theory on which Wollaston claimed to have based his expectation was published in January 1821 and quoted in Faraday's "Historical Sketch" (which led Faraday into his own researches), published in February 1822 (Thomson's *Annals* 3 [1822], 110).

(b) Faraday claimed in his "Historical Statement" of 1823 (in which he narrates his story of the discovery in order to clear his name of the charge of plagiarism) that his "Historical Sketch" was written between July and September in 1821.

(c) In that part of the "Sketch" Faraday commits himself to Ampère's views. "Indeed," he writes, "it is these alone among all those who have been given in public, which deserve, if any do, the title of '*A Theory*' [i.e., demonstrated theory]." (The "Sketch" was published together with the editor's sketch of Faraday's breakaway from this view.)

(d) In his "Historical Statement" (of 1823), Faraday claims that his "Historical Sketch" (1821–22) provides "proofs of my ignorance of Dr. Wollaston's views."

There is an apparent contradiction here. Wollaston claimed that he based his anticipation on a view that Faraday quotes in a paper, and Faraday later claims that this paper is a proof that even after he heard of Wollaston's anticipation he remained ignorant of the latter's *views*. And as Wollaston's view is published in the same "Historical Statement" of Faraday of 1823, in which he claims past ignorance, the "Historical Statement" of Faraday is self-contradictory, unless Wollaston's theory contained more than the idea of circumferential forces. Now, this may be shown differently too. The accusation was that in his paper on electromagnetic rotations Faraday did not make the proper acknowledgment. Faraday later admitted that there was room in that paper for some mention of Wollaston's anticipation, but that he mentioned all that he knew of it, which was less than he knew later. Faraday's paper on electromagnetic rotations does contain both Wollaston's theory of circumferential forces and the anticipation of rotation around the axis. This anticipation, Faraday claims, he failed to perform, and he therefore considered it false. For the same reason, he did not want to associate it with Wollaston's name (especially since Wollaston agreed with him; but it later turned out that Wollaston's agreement was halfhearted and that Faraday should have sensed it to be so. Oh, to live in such a difficult world!).

Thus Wollaston's theory is not merely the circumferential forces hypothesis but contains some more specific statements (as also hinted in Ampère's letter to Faraday, mentioned in note 7, p. 58, below). Perhaps some of Faraday's readers were supposed to know what Wollaston's theory was, perhaps after Faraday's success Wollaston's theory became publicly known even though a part of it remained unpublished. Faraday speaks as if he had heard about that part only after the publication of his own paper—and therefore long after he attempted to help rotate the wire. It may seem very strange to us, but not to contemporaries of Wollaston, that he was ready to ask for the aid of Faraday the technician, the assistant, but not of Faraday the experimenter, the philosopher. He told Faraday of his experiment, but not of the development of his theory—not before Fararaday became a success.

My attempted reconstruction of the situation, assuming that Wollaston's theory has an unpublished (and forgotten) part, again rests on a scientific code that is now defunct. Wollaston demanded, I assume, in accord with the practices of the time, priority only for that part of his theory that was incorporated in Faraday's theory and that Faraday originally acknowledged. He could not properly claim priority for the part of his theory that was different from Faraday's, and therefore people cannot sharply distinguish between his own and Faraday's experiments. From the point of view of accepted theories of the time, it was difficult to ascertain the difference between the two experiments; but if each of these experiments was a test of a different theory, then the difference might become clearer. But then, we do not know the different theories. Science moved rapidly even at that time, and theorists preferred not to publish their intermediate steps. When the old quantum theory was developed, it was equally rapid, or more so; but it was viewed as intermediary, and many intermediate steps were published for the record. E. T. Whittaker, in a report on quantum theory to the British Association (1927, p. 26), mentions the claim that "anything printed is *ipso facto* out of date." He expressed a sense of exhilaration at being superseded so rapidly, quite unlike the Baconian spirit in which Wollaston and Faraday grew. It is no puzzle, then, that what happened around 1820 will, in part, remain a mystery. Faraday is the first man after Kepler to freely publish his own ideas together with his own refutations of them. Wollaston, in contrast, was pre-Faradayan.

## Faraday's Earliest Theory

Faraday's "On Electro-Magnetic Rotations" takes up Wollaston's idea of rotational forces around a conducting wire and performs miracles with it. It has often been said, how important is mathematics for science, how Faraday was ignorant of mathematics, and how he miraculously overcame this serious defect. Here we have an occasion to follow Faraday's close reasoning. We must notice, first, that traditional modes of reasoning, whether more mathematical or less mathematical, simply fail to apply (since rotational forces are not Newtonian). But this is precisely why his paper is so often ignored: Faraday the heretic is still scarcely known. There are exceptions, to be sure, but they are scarce and dispersed. The only comment on Faraday's heresy of 1821 that I was able to find is contained in de la Rive's obituary notice on Faraday (*Philosophical Magazine*, 34 [1867], 424):

> Struck by the experiments of [Ampère] . . . Faraday was led, by
> theoretical ideas which were rather disputable [*sic!*] and not
> very conformable to the principles of [Newtonian] mechanics,
> to assume [his famous rotations].

He verified this . . . result by experiment; and Ampère soon
showed its accordance with his theory, adding to it other facts
of the same nature. It is not less true that the discovery [of
Faraday] . . . was quite unforeseen, and at the same time very
important; for up to that time there was no [known] example
of any such action in physics.

De la Rive's argument is enlightening. Ampère later showed that Faraday's
facts follow from his own theory. Still they were quite unforeseen and very
important. Or, to put it more dialectically, the first statement raises a problem
that the second answers. The problem is this: if Faraday's facts follow from a
known theory, are they really new? The disputable theoretical idea that de la
Rive says Faraday discovered for himself is of course Wollaston's theory of
circumferential forces; as de la Rive admits, it is "not very conformable to
the principles of [Newtonian] mechanics." Whether Ampère could answer
Faraday's objections to Newton's principles may be left as an open question:
even if he could, one must admit that Faraday originated not only experiments
but also a theory that claimed to compete with Ampère's theory. This is only
alluded to in the last sentence of the above quotation from de la Rive. Even
he could not be entirely open about Faraday's early heresy.

Faraday presented his theory of 1821 in the inductive style of his day:
some of his assertions are cryptic and come after the experiments that substan-
tiate them, some are merely hinted at; and the whole paper is filled with a
barrage of experiments. A part of his theory was repeated more explicitly in
a paper published three months later. (It was the usual inductive method of
sending a feeler before stating a theory explicitly.) I quote this part now because
it is the clearest exposition of any part of the theory of 1821 (*Experimental
Researches in Electricity*, 2:151):

Considering the magnetic pole as a mere centre of action,
the existence and position of which may be determined by
well-known means, it was shown by many experiments . . . that
the electro-magnetic wire would rotate round the pole, without
any reference to the position of the axis joining it with the
opposite pole in the same bar: for sometimes the axis was
horizontal, at other times vertical, whilst the rotation continued

the same. It was also shown that the wire, when influenced by the pole, moved laterally, its parts describing circles in planes perpendicular nearly to the wire itself.

The vague phrase "centres of action," by which Faraday characterizes poles, begins to signify the fact that he was rejecting the Newtonian view according to which a magnetic pole was the place to which the (resultant) magnetic force was bound; he was beginning to reject the entire Newtonian view of forces.

We assume now with Faraday the first hypothesis, that wires and poles tend to rotate around each other in circles perpendicular to the wire. The second hypothesis that includes a more fundamental revolution is presented in a very queer manner (p. 136): "It has been allowed, I believe, by all who have experimented on these phenomena, that the similar powers repel and the dissimilar powers attract each other; and that, whether they exist in the poles of the magnets or in the opposite sides of conducting wires."

I do not know if it is humility or generosity or a wish not to appear too bold that made Faraday offer such a new idea as if it were public knowledge. No philosopher, before Faraday, spoke clearly of *forces acting on forces*, save perhaps Wollaston (and then not in print). Forces, says the Newtonian, act only on bodies, and belong to bodies. Certainly Faraday's "Historical Sketch of Electrodynamics" does not indicate that the idea that forces can act on forces was "allowed by all who have experimented on these phenomena"!

Assume now with Faraday that (1) around a magnet and a conducting wire there is a field of forces arranged tangentially to circles and that (2) *two* forces attract or repel each other if they are opposite or parallel (otherwise the projection of one on another would cause the action). We can now explain both the interaction of magnetic poles and that of conducting wires. There are altogether four possibilities, attraction and repulsion between wires and between poles, and they are explained by two hypotheses. Additionally, one of these two hypotheses, the one concerning circumferential forces, explains the four tendencies of wires and poles to rotate in either direction around each other.

One might raise a query here: it is true that the two hypotheses explain magnetic interactions and currents interaction, and it is also true that one of the two hypotheses explains the pole-current interaction; but what happens if we try to apply both hypotheses to the pole-current case? We know that a pole possesses forces that act on a current and that a current possesses forces that act on a pole. How would these two forces act on each other?

Faraday made the situation tougher for himself when he adapted Ampère's hypothesis and asserted (with the usual diffidence) that magnets and electromagnets are identical. At first glance, this move seems to destroy the whole theory. If a magnet is merely a current, why speak of magnet-magnet interaction? So many objections to Faraday's theory can be raised in this manner.

Faraday's assumption that circumferential forces act between a current and a magnet now becomes, it seems, the assumption that circumferential forces act between two currents, of which one is straight and the other circular. But Ampère's theory of interaction between two currents is in a (mathematical) sense much simpler, much more tenable, and explains as much. It seems that Faraday's theory now collapses.

Faraday's solution is that the pole has the properties of one side of a wire. Any one side of the wire, Faraday claims, has the following properties: (a) it acts on a magnet and (b) it rotates around another wire. Now it follows immediately that any electromagnetic force has *two* properties: (a) it attracts or repels parallel or antiparallel electromagnetic forces (like Ampère's current), and (b) it tends to rotate clockwise or counterclockwise, perpendicular or antiperpendicular electromagnetic forces. This, I believe, was tested by Faraday's experiment described in the figure here. A bent wire is shown to behave like a magnet, because a side of it is exposed to action of magnets and wires.

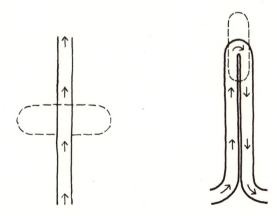

The two dotted lines of electromagnetic force act on each other circumferentially since they are perpendicular to each other.

It should be noted, however, that the assumption that one force tends to rotate another when perpendicular to it is not made explicit by Faraday. It is cryptically[7] introduced, mainly by emphasizing the *fact* that an electromagnet rotates around a wire like a magnet, as if to claim that facts enforce such a hypothesis.

Ampère viewed all magnetism as due to electric forces. He concluded from this that all magnets are electromagnets. Faraday rejected Ampère's view and endorsed the conclusion from it. This he did by ignoring the view, by praising the conclusion drawn from it, and by calling the conclusion "Ampère's hypothesis." To Faraday's readers this was quite easy to fol ow. To modern readers this may cause confusion; my own experience at least was such.

Faraday assumed, then, the existence of four kinds of forces between current elements, electric (parallel and antiparallel in the plane) and magnetic (clockwise and anticlockwise in perpendicular). He also assumed Ampère's hypothesis. He also used an intuitive law of composition of forces. These, he showed, suffice to explain all the known phenomena in a simple and straightforward manner. In addition, they explain other innumerable phenomena that Faraday described. I shall not dwell on the immense problems of carrying out all the experiments that Faraday describes. It should suffice to mention that in the rather short biography of Faraday in the *Encyclopaedia Britannica* his disciple Maxwell found space to express his admiration at the ingenuity exhibited in this fine piece of work of 1821. The upshot is simple: attraction and repulsion between wires and magnets take place in *triads*, two poles and a wire or two wires and a pole: central forces are the results of compositions of noncentral forces.

The problem remains: what do forces act upon? The answer should inevitably be that they act only on the circular forces that belong to other bodies, and thereby on the bodies to which they belong. Thus one body (say, a wire) acts and is acted upon by another (say, a magnet) by its relation to its own circular forces, by the relation of these circular forces to the circular forces of the other body, and by other bodies in relation to its own circular forces. A body—it seems—is thus moved *not* by the forces exerted by another body, but by its queer bonds with its own forces (i.e., its being their center) that are

7. I do not know where one could expect to find evidence bearing any relevance to the problem save the mentioned papers and the notes in his *Diary*. The notes, however, are very sketchy and contain nothing that is not in the published papers. Perhaps Ampère's letters, especially that of 10 July 1822, may help (see *Correspondence du Grand Ampère*, vol. 2).

acted upon by the forces of the other wire. However, I do not think that in 1821 Faraday had this clearly in mind. It took him twenty years to express with clarity the idea presented here, together with some of its far-reaching implications (namely, that the wire too is merely the center of action—all matter is but centers of forces). Meanwhile, he stopped at the assessment that one hypothesis, circumferential electromagnetic forces and their properties, can already explain everything electromagnetic. The way in which he attributed this program, which he so admirably fulfilled, to Dr. Wollaston (*Experimental Researches in Electricity*, 2:145) shows how far he was from belittling him. Indeed, he presents the whole matter as a controversy between Ampère and Wollaston (pp. 131 ff.) and he himself merely as one who sides with Wollaston.

Faraday prepared his paper on rotations, and the hundreds of experiments on which he reported in it, over the course of a month or so (the "Sketch" was finished in September and "Rotations" published in October). Besides, he was frightfully busy with many other affairs. This astonishing output, as well as the method by which the work was produced, were to become very characteristic of the man. The first idea he had was probably to vary the position of the wire in the vicinity of a compass. (Oersted already used the perpendicular position of the wire, but Faraday had a theory to test by this method.) He then came to the idea of rotary forces. He had hardly developed the theory when he devised a test for it. The number of tests of the theory is really surprising, while the theory itself, perhaps because it breaks so widely from the conventional, is very sketchy, or at least very sketchily and cryptically presented. This reminds one of Faraday's idea of the importance of facts and the advisability of talking in utter generality, which he made public two years earlier.

The most unconventional item in Faraday's view, of course, is the assumption that space is filled with forces that are not bound to particles, at least not as yet, and that have some properties that usually only bodies have. In classical theory, a body acts on another body, either by impact or by force. Here a force acts on a force. How, according to what laws, and to what effect—all these questions are answered, but not by a theory. They are answered by a strong intuition that is conveyed to the reader easily, surprisingly easily, by vague notions, a general discussion, and mainly by beautiful illustrations galore.

Theoretically this is evidently insufficient. As a start it is brilliant. I must admit, with all my rejection of Baconian inductivism, of the classical emphasis on fact, and of the reluctance to theorize clearly, that Faraday could advantageously use any theory, even this very inductivism. (That is, by the way, also because he took his inductivism seriously, and also because he bravely theorized on all occasions.)

In 1821 Faraday occupied a minor post in the Royal Institution, although his colleagues esteemed him highly. He had published works that gave him the position of a leading chemist and metallurgist. The first electromagnetic paper is practically[8] his first attempt in physics. Overnight he became a leading physicist. At home the waves of slander and accusation shaded his success. Abroad he became known as one of the foremost British physicists and the leading figure in electromagnetics. A discussion of whether he was a physicist or a chemist is not very much to my taste. But I am quite willing to emphasize that although Faraday's interest was always universal, his chemical knowledge was much more accurate and extended than his physical knowledge. His knowledge of physics was much more restricted to first principles and general ideas and important phenomena. His lack of mathematical facility was always an impediment to his career as a physicist. But mathematics is not everything —not even in physics. His first physical paper shows this not because it is full of experiments but because it is a closely reasoned theoretical debate too fluid for useful mathematical explorations.

### Faraday versus Ampère

Electrostatic and magnetostatic induction were well known phenomena. Oersted found a kind of electromagnetic induction: electricity causes magnetism. The inverse problem was now to find magnetoelectric induction—magnetic influence on electricity. The idea was that perhaps currents are caused by magnets. Since magnets are, according to Ampère's hypothesis, nothing but currents, the problem was equivalent to finding electrodynamic induction, currents that somehow cause or affect other currents.

This was a wrong approach. For all we know, electricity, strictly speaking, cannot evolve from magnetism. But prior to 1831 the common problem was to evolve electricity from magnetism; Ampère made a hypothesis concerning this and so did Faraday.

Since Faraday did not record his hypothesis, it is difficult to ascertain how

8. He previously (1818) refuted the theory of de la Rive's father Gaspard concerning "sounding flames." See *Discoverer*, pp. 11–12.

different his and Ampère's views are in this respect. I suppose he had one: he
first tested his own prediction and later he tested Ampère's predictions.

Faraday always admired Ampère. In the very letter to Gaspard de la Rive
(*Life and Letters*, 1:355) in which he expressed sharp disagreement with
Ampère, claiming that his new rotations support his views but disagree with
Ampère's, he still expresses his respect:

> . . . M. Ampère's experiments are excellent, and his theory
> ingenious; and, for myself, I had thought very little about it
> before your letter came, simply because, being naturally
> skeptical on philosophical theories, I thought there was a great
> want of experimental evidence. Since then, however, I have
> engaged on the subject.

The question whether Ampère could or could not explain the new rotation
by his own theory is a difficult one. De la Rive, we remember (p. 55), said
that Ampère did so successfully. He also presented this view in his famous
*Treatize on Electricity* (London [1853], 1:239 and 251, cp. 2:2). Maxwell
also rather agreed with de la Rive on this point, at least when he wrote his
first paper (1856) "On Faraday's Lines of Force." From our vantage point
we can say, at least, that Ampère's attempt to save the theory was far from
fruitful, and probably unsuccessful as well. E. T. Whittaker, who was the best
mathematical physicist among the historians who dealt with the problem and
who sympathized with the Ampère school, somehow admitted that Ampère
could not explain the rotation. "The weakness of Ampère's work," he said (*A
History of Theories of the Aether and Electricity*, 2d ed., p. 86), "evidently
lies in the [i.e., Newton's] assumption that the force is directed along the line
joining the two elements; for in the analogous case of the action between two
magnetic molecules, the force is *not* directed along the line joining the molecules." Ampère, however, being convinced that his own and Faraday's theory
were equivalent, preferred to employ Faraday's theory in order to deduce
further testable statements from it and to test them. Faraday obviously tried
to intensify the difference. It seems clear that the structuralist character of
Faraday's theory fascinated both of them, although they tried to employ the
same kind of thought in opposite directions. In his diary (1:71; *Life and Letters*,
1:362) in the entry for 10 September 1822, Faraday reports an attempt to
detect with the aid of polarized light some structure in the voltaic pile. This

experiment and variants of it he repeated later again and again throughout his life, always unsuccessfully. In 1822 Faraday reports that "no particular arrangement of particles could be ascertained in this way." But on what he had based his expectation I do not know.

Toward the end of 1824, he tried to find magnetism in ordinary crystals (*Life and Letters*, 1:382). He gives no explanation; in his speculations of later years his structural ideas led him to suppose that matter is nothing but structures of the electromagnetic field. His 1824 experiment shows that he at least made some attempts to develop his theory in this heretic direction.

In the entry for 21 January 1823, he reports on a series of electromagnetic experiments. One of them is a test of Newton's third law. Here it is (p. 93):

> Tried to make Magnet revolve in a circle of wires . . . would not do—no tendency to motion.
>
> It appears the action does not regard the material substance at the centre but simply the current of electricity or the magnetic pole, *the substance merely giving locality to the power*. In that case, when the current or the pole is not in the centre of motion, it in acting by producing rotation must carry the material with it; but when in the centre it produces all its effect without affecting the substance or making it revolve. Hence a wire placed to revolve round a magnetic pole has *no tendency in the way of reaction to make the pole or magnet revolve on its axis. . . .*
>
> If this be true, then in my rotation apparatus the wire ought to move equally well though the magnet turned with it . . .

Again Faraday comes to the revolutionary conjecture that it is the tendency of the current or the pole to rotate, which in turn rotates the wire or the magnet; and that if the wire or pole is in the center of symmetry it would not tend to move. This explanation, as we know today, is false; but the conclusion is true. The magnet around which the wire rotates would not, according to Faraday, tend to rotate in the opposite direction. According to Newton, it would; and when it is fixed, it transmits the rotation, or momentum of momentum, to the earth. The last lines of the above quotation describe a crucial experiment between Newton and Faraday—and Faraday had the upper hand. By connecting the revolving wire to the magnet, we should stop the revolution according to

Newton (in order not to violate the law of momentum of momentum), while according to Faraday the wire would only drag the magnet along (and therefore revolve more slowly).

Perhaps it is an error to ascribe to Newton the view that Faraday here refuted. Whether Newton's third law holds in relativity theory is hard to say, and whether it is true or not is even harder to say. Perhaps we should say that Faraday was merely refuting a naïve application of the law to a new field. Be it so. It is established, nonetheless, that Faraday was a conscious heretic as early as January 1823, less than a year and a half after his first electromagnetic discovery.

Why Faraday never published this experiment I cannot say. There was nothing in the inductive code to stop Faraday publishing merely the fact, the new fact, that a wire would revolve around a magnet also when it is rigidly connected to the magnet, provided that the magnet is not held up by excessive friction. This might not have caused a revolution, but just as Faraday did not fail to notice the significance of the fact, others might not too. I cannot think that he feared any kind of terror. I have only one explanation: he was collecting material; he tried to solve the major problem of his theory and publish all the material together. But not until 1831 could he do this. On 28 December 1824 he made an entry in his diary stating that he had failed to solve this problem— he had failed to find the inverse to Oersted's effect.

The entry to his diary was published[9] in July 1825, republished in his *Experimental Researches in Electricity* (2:162) and again in Bence Jones's biography (1:382); he speaks there of an "expectation . . . for various reasons" that magnets produce electric currents. They do not—"a fact which, though of a negative kind, appears to me of some importance."

In a note of less than a page, from which the above is quoted, at least six hundred different variations are recorded (which is not less than one week's work, and judging from other evidences probably much more). Had Boyle's orthodox style been used, the note would be extended into a book. Instead, the

---

9. Ostwald has claimed (*Grosse Männer*) that because of his weak memory Faraday got into the habit of writing down everything. This is mixing three unrelated details. First, Bacon's and Hooke's inductivist advice to keep a commonplace book or a diary, since every memory is weak and every circumstance important; second, the fact that Faraday lost his memory completely in his old age; and third, the fact that he kept accurate diaries and journals. Faraday had an unusual memory even after his first nervous breakdown. And his diary was no commonplace book: he never made an entry without having first carefully drafted it. The entry in the text above, for example, he found sufficiently polished to be published as it stood. (He did keep a commonplace book in his early days.)

anticipation is mentioned first, although without any reference to the theory on which it was based. The publication of "negative results" was in this case *not* contrary to the inductive tradition since it was a refutation of a widely received opinion. Even today, inductive journals (of experimental biology and of psychology, for instance) are reluctant to publish theories, and refuse to publish refutations: yet they make an exception and expressly allow refutations of popularly accepted errors. As Tyndall has noted, Faraday based his anticipation on a different theory than the received view, to wit, Ampère's theory; but the anticipation was nearly the same, or at least both Ampère's and Faraday's anticipations were refuted in the same series of six hundred or so experiments.

What was the basis of Faraday's anticipation? I do not know. All he said was that as "a reaction" to his rotation he expected the current to *diminish*. Why, I do not know. Ampère, on the contrary, expected the current to *increase*, and the reason is evident: it was to explain magnetostatic induction, namely why a magnet causes an iron bar in its vicinity to behave like a magnet. This defect can be amended by adding an obvious assumption: currents induce currents. This addition to the theory can be tested by Faraday's experiment, and the results, we saw, are negative. The current was neither increased nor decreased—at least not visibly so—by the presence of a magnet, or of a current and so on. Faraday decided to devise a more decisive test of Ampère's addition to the theory. In an entry for 28 November 1825 (*Life and Letters*, 1:383), he records a much more sensitive experiment in the same vein. Again, negative results. He tried a variant, with currents perpendicular rather than parallel to wires that should develop currents: again they do not. Faraday still did not exclude the possibility that electrodynamic induction still exists, only in a still much weaker form.

From 1824 to 1831 we find Faraday trying again and again to confirm Ampère's hypothesis concerning induction. This in itself raises my suspicion that he gave up his own revolutionary theory and seriously considered Ampère's views.

## Energy and Mechanism

A great discovery is so difficult to make because it is a refutation of a great principle, an important theory, or an accepted mode of thinking that is deeply seated in people's minds and is, therefore, accepted uncritically.[10] That Fara-

10. See my *Towards an Historiography of Science*, final sections.

day's discovery of 1831 was a great discovery there is no doubt. Why? Usually people point out that it is technically of supreme importance. This is true but irrelevant. Bragg (in his centenary lecture of 1931 to the Royal Institution) was the only one who explicitly discussed the theoretical significance of Faraday's discovery. He claimed that it led to Einstein's relativity since it was a discovery that it was not the magnet that causes currents, but the motion of a magnet relative to the conductor. This is unsatisfactory: many effects discovered before 1831, and especially Oersted's experiment, had to do with relative motion, and anyhow, the greatness of Faraday should not depend on Einstein.

What was new in Faraday's discovery was not so much the phenomena of transversal action—this was not so new after 1820—but his new concept of energy or power. The mistake Faraday corrected in 1831 pertained to motion: not the presence of a magnet caused a current in a wire but the motion of a magnet caused current in a wire. Energetic considerations clash with the error and agree with the correct result. But in the 1820s, when Faraday was making ever more sensitive measurements, it did not occur to him that the magnitude of the reverse Oersted effect must be commensurable with Oersted's effect. Energetic considerations, conservation laws—all these come in the 1830s.

The problem of the day, we remember, was to find the "inverse" of Oersted's effect. What exactly is "inverse" is never clear. The "inverse" of, say, the steam engine effect is the conversion of work into heat, e.g., by friction. The "inverse" of the chemical production of electricity, namely of the voltaic pile, is the chemical decomposition caused by the electric current, namely electrolysis. Strictly speaking, the "inverse" of Oersted's experiment, the wire's action on a magnet, is very easily obtained by using a fixed magnet and a movable wire in order to enable the wire to rotate. But the problem was not to accept the "inverse" of the motion but the "inverse" of the effect itself, of the magnetization by electricity; to wit, electrification caused by magnetism, or electrification caused by a magnet.

In 1820 the first experiment of this kind was recorded: Fresnel declared that he observed magnetolysis—a chemical decomposition caused by magnets. Soon, Fresnel declared his own experiment to be unsuccessful, unrepeatable, null and void. After 1831, it became part and parcel of all electromagnetic[11]

11. In his *Correlation of Forces* (1846), Judge Sir William Grove argued that the idea of converting magnetism into electricity (in contradistinction to Faraday's conversion of motion of a magnet into electricity) is not only in opposition to electromagnetic theory but also counter to the laws of conservation. This is untrue. The law of conservation only demands that

theories that there is no magnetic charge and that therefore magnetolysis is impossible; magnetism cannot be converted into an electric current (and electrolysis is an electric current). But as early as 1822, Ampère tried a different way of obtaining current from a magnet. The story of this event is very complicated (see S. P. Thompson's *Faraday*, pp. 105–6). In 1831 Faraday declared that Ampère's experiment too was unsuccessful.

In 1824 a successful experiment was made by Arago. To detect magnetism in copper he made a suspended magnet oscillate above a copper sheet. The oscillations were clamped. No trace of iron was found in the copper. He conjectured that the copper, if rotated, would set in motion the suspended needle, somehow in accord with Ampère's speculation concerning the relations between electric currents (and therefore magnets) and the aether. This is so (and not due to any friction with the air, since the needle can hang within an air-tight box, and still rotate). Later it was found that the inverse also occurs: a rotating magnet causes the copper plate in the vicinity to rotate.

Since it is natural to explain such actions as aether drift, and since according to Ampère's speculation electric currents are the sources of these drifts, it is odd, perhaps, that presumably prior to 1831 no one tried—or else he might have succeeded—to detect the currents that evolve on the rotating plate in the presence of a magnet, even though it was known that the better the conductivity of the rotating plate the bigger the effect discovered by Arago. Of course people did not know how to measure currents in a rotating plate (rather than a long wire), but this they could have learned how to do with little effort.

It may sound strange that prior to 1831 Faraday did not suspect that Arago's effect is a variant of his own rotation of 1821 on the assumption that currents evolve in the rotating plate. But this can only show us, prior to 1831, how far people were from considering energy as real. Prior to 1831, even though the old axioms that there can be no perpetual motion machine was quite widely

---

magnetolysis, if possible, should cause demagnetization of the magnets employed in the process, or some other loss of energy to compensate for the gain of energy through decomposition.

Faraday, it seems, understood this better than Grove. In his diary he says, "Made Arago's expt. with the earth magnet, only no magnet used, but the plate put horizontal and rotated. The effect at the needle was slight but very distinct . . . . Hence Arago's plate a new electrical machine."

Although the experiment with the earth magnet leads to weaker results, only thus, and not in using ordinary magnets, is the idea established that Arago's plate is a new electrical machine since, even if magnets are exhausted by the process, the earth's magnet is a sufficient source of magnetism.

accepted (as part and parcel of Newtonianism), it never occurred to people to think in terms of energy. True, heat and work were converted into each other, but according to accepted views (as in detail Carnot showed) it is the transition of the fluid of heat, not its annihilation, that caused work. The thermodynamic theory of heat, it is true, already existed then; it was then the only example of thinking in energetic terms. In 1820 Dr. Hare of Philadelphia—a follower of Ben Franklin—refuted Davy's thermodynamic theory of heat and insisted on assuming the existence of a fluid of heat. One of his central arguments against Davy was that in his theory energy did not conserve! The French philosophers were developing the theory of caloric to such an extent that soon Whewell, for one, considered it as proved. The only one who clung to thermodynamics was the Cartesian Herapath, the reviver of statistical mechanics, and he was treated very intolerantly by the Royal Society and was very unsuccessful in his campaign (see *Dictionary of National Biography* and references there). It may sound odd that, prior to 1842, no one inquired into the qualitative aspects of the phenomena of heat evolving from electricity or other energetic sources; such as problems involved in thermoelectricity, piezoelectricity, physical chemistry, and so on. Ampère had a theory of electrodynamics, but he was interested in the problems of force, not of work or energy. Energy was never a part of Newtonianism. The law of conservation of energy was merely a consequence of Newtonian mechanics, and, prior to 1831, it was of some mathematical but of little experimental interest. In 1800 Volta mentioned only in passing that his pile is a perpetual motion machine, and Roget, also in passing, declared this to be an argument against Volta's theory—not even bothering to make some experiments in this direction. The only one who was keenly interested in the problem was M. H. Jacobi (not to be confused with his brother, Karl Gustav, the famous mathematician) who hoped to utilize the discovery of Oersted in order to build a perpetual motion machine. Here is Sir David Brewster's comment on his story (*Encyclopaedia Britannica*, 8th ed., 21:645–46):

> The great discovery of magneto-electricity by Dr. Faraday led M. Jacobi of St. Petersburg to abandon the theoretical view which induced him to apply electromagnetism as a locomotive power. His machines, the electromotive force of which he had supposed to be independent of time, produced but very restricted effects, in place of being the source of a force [i.e., energy] infinitely great. The principal cause of this limitation was the formation

> of magneto-electric counter-currents generated by the very
> motion of the machine. In his conversations with Bessel, M.
> Jacobi had often told him that if magneto-electricity obliged him
> to abandon his theoretical views, M. Bessel would be compelled
> one day to take an account of it in his theory of the pendulum,
> and perhaps even in his calculations on planetary bodies. M.
> Jacobi has no scruple in placing the discovery of magneto-
> electricity on a level in point of importance with that of
> gravitation.

Had Jacobi accepted the law of conservation of energy perhaps he might have been able to predict Faraday's discovery. But he did not accept it, and those who did accept it cared too little about the problems that Oersted's experiment has created for them.

This is not to say that what was overlooked is the obvious. Even after Faraday made the discovery and after he explained it, a lot remained for his followers to notice before they accepted it. Here is the telling passage from Maxwell, who was usually all too anxious to ascribe an idea to Faraday, even when he himself was the co-author of it (*Treatise*, § 543, 2:190):

> A step of still greater scientific importance was soon after made
> by Helmholtz in his *Essay on the Conservation of Force*, and by
> Sir W. Thomson [Kelvin], working somewhat later, but
> independently of Helmholtz. They shewed that the induction
> of electric currents could be mathematically deduced from the
> electromagnetic actions discovered by Oersted and Ampère
> by the application of the principle of the Conservation of
> Energy.

The validity of the deduction, incidentally, was questioned by Hertz (see his *Miscellaneous Papers*, 1896, p. 289 n.), and notice that Faraday noticed the possible alternatives that Hertz claimed could have balanced the energy loss in Oersted's effect and tested them empirically very early in the day!

All this may provide a measure of the revolutionism of Faraday.[12] The

12. Brewster, it may be noticed, views Faraday's and Jacobi's work as the stimulus leading to the mathematical astronomers' employment of the energy theorems in their practical work. For Kelvin's debt to Jacobi see his life by Thompson, pp. 198, 397.

experiment of 1831 was surprisingly revolutionary and Faraday was not slow to realize this. But the discovery itself was hardly a consequence of his thoughts—rather of his perseverance. Arago's experiment did not lead him to think in terms of work or power, as he did soon after his discovery of 1831. The idea that not only electricity can be converted to motion, or heat to electricity, or electricity to chemical affinity, but also that *force*, that *power* can be converted into electricity—this occurred neither to Faraday nor to anybody else prior to 1831.[13]

On the contrary it seems that Faraday seriously tended to accept the Newtonian explanations of Arago's experiment in terms of pull and push. To which I pass now.

### Back to Ampère?

Arago had no explanation of his effect, and he refused to commit himself to a theory proposed by Poisson. "I have always admired the prudence and philosophic reserve shown by M. Arago," exclaimed Faraday in 1832 (*Experimental Researches in Electricity*, 2:182) in resisting the temptation to offer an explanation of his own effect and in refusing his assent to the imperfect theories of the others [Ampère?]—waiting for one that was perfect in its application. "Admiring his reserve I adopted it in this respect, and perhaps for this reason had my eyes open to recognize the truth when it was presented." This was written in 1832. In 1831 Faraday had shown that Arago's experiment consists of *two* general facts, the fact that a rotating metal creates current (*Experimental Researches in Electricity*, 2:85), and Faraday's old magnetoelectric rotation of 1821. Having explained the mystery of Arago's experiment so successfully, he could speak more easily about it and commend Arago for suspension of judgment. But before that, Arago's suspension of judgment offered him little consolation. He was under a strong inner pressure to submit and accept Arago's mechanistic explanation in spite of, or perhaps more so because of, Arago's prudence. In a private letter of 1831 he gives a full expression to his sense of relief (*Life and Letters*, 2:9 italics in the original):

> You will think I am hoaxing you, or else in your
> compassion you may conclude I am deceiving myself. However,

13. The law of conservation of force is an immediate corollary to Oersted's theory; yet he had a complex view of rates of conversion. See my *Towards an Historiography of Science*, sect. 17, esp. p. 72.

you need do neither, but had better laugh, as I did most heartily when I found that it was neither attraction nor repulsion, but just one of my *old rotations* in a new form. . . . Hence is also explained the effect which Arago observed, . . . It is quite comfortable to me to find that experiment need not quail before mathematics, but is quite competent to rival it in discovery; and I am amazed to find what the high mathematicians have announced . . . has so little foundation . . . .

This letter is one big sigh of relief. Three mathematicians said the Arago forces are central (Arago, Babbage, Herschel); Faraday's suspension of judgment was the rejection of Newtonianism; Arago's suspension of judgment was the adherence to it pro tem; who knows who is right? The code of scientific attitudes is so vague on beliefs that it is hard to say who adheres to it and who violates it. Did he adhere to it or was he a dogmatist? But then he laughs in relief; the mathematicians were in error, and he with experimental power came up the winner! The sense of relief is tremendous—Faraday dared celebrate a victory again for a while.

I do not know if Faraday ever gave up his 1821 theory. There is a passage he wrote in 1825 which is Ampèrian (*Life and Letters*, 1:384), but one can easily explain this away. The available evidence is altogether too scanty. The only published electric work of Faraday between his great discoveries of 1821–22 and of 1831 is the note of December 1824 in which he merely reports a failure. Faraday never said how much his own refutation of his own anticipation was relevant to his 1821 theory and how much Arago's theory had influenced him. If we remember how seriously he took the doctrine of prejudice, the idea that suspension of judgment is essential for the conduct of fruitful research, how ready he was to abandon the whole of Newton's mechanics, we cannot rule out a priori that a single refutation set him back to central forces and made him consider his deviations as "folly of the youth" and "self-love."

Faraday returned to his attempts to confirm Ampère's theory in 1828 and again in 1831 (*Life and Letters*, 2:2); his discovery of 1831 was such a shock to him, and he then appeared boldly with a full-fledged field theory; from then on he devoted almost the whole of his research time to electricity with a genuine sense of the mission he had to convey. He had devoted relatively little time to electricity before 1831. In 1827 he was primarily a chemist. He had published then his bulky laboratory handbook of *Chemical Manipulations*.

There is no indication that prior to 1831 Faraday did see his electrical research as his central activity. His presentation of the 1821 theory in a cryptic language shows his usual diffidence, and his subsequent experiments hint at the possibility that between 1821 and 1831 he seriously, though ruefully, considered the whole episode rather futile.

Tyndall has suggested that Faraday "was at this time [prior to 1831] full of the theory of Ampère, and it cannot be doubted that numbers of his experiments were executed merely to test his deductions from that theory" (*Discoverer*, p. 28). Tyndall even describes the 1831 discovery as a refutation of his earlier views (*Discoverer*, p. 26).

Perhaps Faraday seriously considered following Ampère, but could not make up his mind—especially as he was not fully competent to judge Ampère's and Arago's mathematical theories.[14]

14. Faraday's notes to his lectures of 1827 (R.I., MS) may supply further evidence that he did not decide between the two theories. In the beginning the word "attractive" appears and is deleted in pencil. As Faraday used to mark in pencil (with the sign X) all the experiments as he performed them during the lectures, it is quite possible that he deleted the word during or soon after the lecture. The very fact that he intended to perform some experiments and then did not perform them is very interesting. I here quote the relevant passages from this lecture. "Magnetism, principally as evolved from electricity," Friday evening lectures, 2 June 1827.

(p. 51) Magnetism is so striking an illustration of attractive forces as to draw the attention of all who have the opportunity of observing its phenomena and is the more impressive as being exerted only by a few particular kinds of matter which may be made permanent residence of this power.

(p. 54) Peculiar arrangement of the magnetism in the connecting wire—unlike any thing observed in magnets—not in poles but in every part of the wire—wrapped as it were round it in opposite directions—in tangents—Dr. Wollaston's term vertigenous or circumferential magnetism.

(p. 55) Now proceed to some experiments—due to M. Ampère, and highly important to the theory of this branch of science.

(p. 56) The effect of curving the wire into a helix is to produce a polar arrangement which in the large way exhibits M. Ampère's views of ordinary magnets—his views simply stated—*all effects found to be accordant as far as they have yet been traced*—a helix has poles and a helix will point like a needle when influenced by the earth

(Exp.) Pointing of a ring

—————————————————helix

[The following is deleted in pencil]

M. Ampère finds that besides the virtigenous power of the current of electricity it tends to elongate itself [Not performed] (*Exp.* ) Ampère's of elongated current . . . due to a similar cause as in fact the same effect. [Not performed] (exp)

The effect altogether is apparently the same as that usually called the repulsion of similarly electrified particles.

## Ampère's Theory Refuted

In 1828 Faraday tested again the hypothesis of current induction, and again he left the problem unsolved. In 1831 he learned of a means to produce extraordinarily strong electromagnetic forces and he then used this to repeat the experiment. He still thought that current induction exists but that its magnitude is very, very minute.[15] The new method of obtaining stronger currents excited again an idea to try again; perhaps the current induced by the new strong current would be detectable.

The new means of obtaining strong electromagnets from strong currents was discovered by Faraday's friend Gerrit Moll. (It was mentioned in *Experimental Researches in Electricity*, § 57.) He described it in a letter to Faraday dated June 1831 and in periodical publications. In August 1831, Faraday tried again the experiments of 1825 and 1828. This time he did not put two wires near each other but rather coiled two long wires on the two sides of a wooden ring.[16] The experiment was thus repeated, again with negative

---

Effect of current on neighbouring plate of copper [Not performed] (exp.) Ampère's may be compound to the effect of one magnet over another but is by no means striking or satisfying

[in pencil] Expts. were wanted here.

[End of deleted passage.]

(p. 57) Arago's last researches—entirely distinct from any that have yet been noticed so far as we perceive or understand the phenomena.

(p. 58) The action is reciprocal for the magnet in motion will carry metals forward or the metals in motion will carry magnets forward and on the contrary a magnet in motion is retarded by a quiescent metal placed near it and metal in motion is retarded by a quiescent magnet near at hand.
. . . Causes—Herschel, Babbage and others—Arago's objections—power a repulsive one—not yet thoroughly examined.
Ampère's second experiment is the unsuccessful experiment discussed by Faraday (*Experimental Researches in Electricity*, 1, see index there, Art. "Ampère").

15. In this he was following Oersted's mode of thought. See my *Towards an Historiography of Science*, sect. 17.

16. It has been stated by some recent authors that Faraday was here guided by mere intuition, that it is impossible to find the reason for his construction of a ring. In Tyndall's opinion, however, it cannot be doubted that Faraday was testing Ampère's theory. He hoped that a really strong magnet might cause some effect that he might accumulate. Hence the coiling of each of the wires. According to the theory tested, it would be even better to lay the two wires in parallel and in great proximity, no matter in which form. This is true according to the theory that he later developed and also, for that matter, according to any up-to-date theory. Thus the coiling of the wires was merely a matter of technical facility; the main factors were the intensity of the currents and the length of the wires. The benefit of arrangements like that of Faraday

results (*Experimental Researches in Electricity*, § 7.) The experiment was repeated again with still longer coiled wires, with an iron instead of a wooden core, and with increased currents. Still no results. "Many similar experiments" (§ 9) led to the same negative result. Still longer wires were employed, the isolation of the wires was better secured. Success at last!

When the contact was made, there was a sudden and very slight effect at the galvanometer, and there was also a similar slight effect when the contact with the battery was broken. But while the voltaic current was continuing to pass through one helix, no galvanometrical appearances or any effect like induction could be perceived upon the other helix, although the active power of the battery was proved to be great.

The effect was found to be not as anticipated—not as a result of the current but as a result of the *variation* of its strength. Faraday used stronger and stronger tools to detect an effect producible by much weaker means, not only because he could not know the magnitude of the desired effect, but because he misplaced it: the effect he was searching was there in each of his previous experiments, and yet he regularly missed it; or rather he looked in the wrong direction: he did not look at the galvanometer while he was making contact. Perhaps he was then anxious to secure good contacts. What made the change in 1831? Possibly he noticed the momentary change only by accident. In this case, although what he saw was refutation of the view that he was testing, he might have noticed it not solely because his eyes fell upon it. There may be another explanation, however: perhaps he thought that the effect on the galvanometer existed but was so small, its needle moved so slightly, that the difference between the old and the new position of the needle was not noticeable. He might then have looked at the galvanometer while making the contacts, thinking that although the new position of the needle was scarcely to be distinguished from the old one, the motion, the displacement itself, might be observed. Instead, he saw a great displacement and an immediate return to the old position. The return was thus a refutation of his earlier expectations.

The discovery was made on the second day of the last trial. In his diary

---

is that a long wire and a short one can thus be placed in proximity, an impossibility with the alternative arrangement. The result is that by shortening the induced wire the induced tension increases and vice versa. This apparatus is called a *transformer*. Faraday's apparatus can hardly be said to have been a real transformer since the length of the induced wire was equal to the length of the inducing wire.

Thus the accepted views that Faraday's instrument was the best and that he was guided by mere intuition are both false.

he wrote (*Life and Letters*, 2:3) that he might have discovered the cause of Arago's effect. He stopped the experiments and sat thinking. In a letter written over three weeks later (*Life and Letters*, 2:3, and S. P. Thompson's *Faraday*, p. 110) he said:

> . . . I am busy just now again on electro-magnetism, and think I have got hold of a good thing, but can't say. It may be a weed instead of a fish that, after all my labour, I may at last pull up. I think I know why metals are magnetic when in motion though not [generally] when at rest.

This is the famous timetable: the last two days of August 1831 ended with the discovery, then over three weeks of intense thinking, then another eight days of tests of his field interpretation of the first experiment: currents are induced in conductors when these cut lines of magnetic force. According to the field interpretation, all the experiments on induction that are reported in the first two papers are merely variations of one and the same experiment. The eight days of tests end in the beginning of November, and he starts writing the first series of his *Experimental Researches in Electricity*, which he read on 24 November. Five days later he writes from a holiday resort (*Life and Letters*, 2:6):

> . . . as to news, I have none, for I withdraw more and more from society . . .
> . . . I have been working and writing a paper that always knocks me up in health, but now I feel well again, and able to pursue the subject . . .

In the next week he continues the experiments. The sense of mission is evident here. Faraday believed that he was embarking on an entirely new way. So he was, but he had no idea of its character. The paper was written in the inductive style. Facts were mainly presented, and the theory of lines of force that, when cut by a conductor, create a current in it, is very briefly stated. Ampère's and Arago's theories are not declared false—they are not even mentioned. Ampère's hypothesis of molecular currents in magnets is supported and praised, and the false impression is created that this is the whole of Ampère's theory.
One "unsuccessful experiment" by Ampère (mentioned in a note on

page 72, above) is "reconciled," and in a note Fresnel is praised for having declared in public his unsuccessful experiment (see p. 65) to be unsuccessful. An indirect but very clear challenge is thus made to all the brave philosophers to publicly admit past errors.

Evidently Faraday believed that he gained a complete victory and that past errors that he now refuted could, as was usual in the inductive tradition, be forgotten and buried. Every article of the inductive code spoke for him. But Newtonian mechanism was more deeply rooted than inductivism. The errors he refuted were, to a large extent, corrected. But the isolation started immediately. At first people only refrained from passing judgment on his view; but when he insisted, he was more and more often ignored as a theoretician.

It was his mistake not to attack Ampère's theory explicitly. Even now, in the "enlightened" age of open criticism, hardly anyone mentions that Faraday refuted Ampère's theory. In all my search I found only one such assertion. It was made by one of the last great amateurs, Justice W. Grove, professor at the London Institution and one of the earliest writers on the laws of conservation.

Grove was one of the many nineteenth-century thinkers who tried to abandon Newtonian mechanism. Yet he was the most unsuccessful; he was always a Newtonian mechanist. With every blow that Newtonian mechanism received, the view that only facts have room in science gained new adherents. This antimechanistic, inductive approach, which is usually known as Mach's functionalism, is common to all who rejected mechanism, Newtonian or otherwise, but had nothing to replace it with. The first of them was Berkeley;[17] another was Grove. Although he was an inductivist, he explicitly attacked Bacon's essentialism. And not hoping to find theories hidden in facts, he demanded that we confine our research to facts, or "facts and relations" as he put it. Here is a quotation from a lecture at his institution that he read and published in 1842 in which he propagated the law of conservation of power as a sort of confined program of search for laws of transformation of power from one form to another (*Correlation of Forces*, 1846, pp. 5, 7):

> Instead of regarding the proper object of physical science as a search after *essential causes*, I believe it ought to be a search after facts and relations . . .

> Electricity and Magnetism afford us a very instructive example of the belief in secondary causation. Subsequent to the discovery

17. For Berkeley as a precursor of Mach see K. R. Popper, *Conjectures and Refutations*, 1963.

by Oersted of Electro-Magnetism, and prior to that by Faraday of Magneto-Electricity, Electricity and Magnetism were believed by the highest authorities to stand in the relations of cause and effect, i.e., electricity was regarded as the cause, and magnetism as the effect, and where magnets existed without any apparent electrical currents to cause their magnetism, hypothetical currents have been supposed for the purpose of carrying out the causative view; but magnetism may now be said with equal truth to be the cause of electricity, and electric currents may be referred to hypothetical magnetic lines; again, if electricity is the cause of magnetism, and magnetism cause electricity, why then electricity causes electricity, which is absurd.

Grove does not seem to have taken Faraday's "hypothetical magnetic lines" more seriously than Ampère's "hypothetical currents." He could say that now we know that the electromagnetism is reducible not to electricity but to the "hypothetical" fields. But like others he wanted to have either some demonstrable theory or else no theory at all. And, he showed, no authority secures a theory like Ampère's from refutation. Therefore he demanded that scientists stick to facts. No philosopher in his senses could accept such advice, not even Grove and Mach themselves. They were simply inconsistent; they were good scientists and bad methodologists. Additionally they were not enough antimechanists to seriously consider the field theory. Others preferred a dogmatic adherence to Newton's mechanics to inconsistency. And this meant in the accepted framework that mechanics was to be accepted as essentially true, though capable of small corrections here and there. And for the sake of the preservation of Newton's mechanics, Faraday's theory was partly ignored, partly regarded as unripe—and as such dangerous to discuss in public too soon.

A philosophical vacuum was created. Ampère's theory was accepted with some qualifications by some philosophers, and others preferred some theory that assumes transversal forces linked to particles and acting at a distance. But a state of confusion started to develop. Until the end of November 1831, Ampère's theory was often highly praised and discussed in public. Then comes a period in which there is no mention of any electromagnetic theory.

Such a state can continue for some years; but, no doubt at least at first, Faraday was content to disturb the mechanists and hoped to overcome sooner or later the diffidence toward his own theory. His next attack (on Volta's contact theory) was more open. But only in 1842, after slow recovery from his nervous breakdown, did he boldly adopt the critical or argumentative style. He never had occasion to return to argue against Ampère's theory: rather, he argued then against Ampère's successor, Weber.

Since Faraday explicitly attacked Volta's contact theory of the pile, many historians report that he refuted it. Since he never explicitly attacked Ampère's electrodynamic theory, none dare to draw the inference that his magneto-electric effect contradicts this theory,[18] especially as Maxwell allegedly saved it. Yet, without realizing the fact that Faraday (rightly) felt that he had won a glorious triumph over Ampère, who, as a mathematician, was by far superior to Faraday—without realizing this fact, it is impossible to understand the effect of Faraday's discovery on his quasireligious conversion and on his later progress.

One need not quote Grove to prove that Faraday refuted Ampère's views. What the quotation shows is that, in spite of their reticence, people were indeed aware of the fact. And the most aware of them was Faraday, who late in his life wrote to encourage heresy (*Life and Letters*, 2:389):

> If you would even get them to say yes or no to your conclusions, it would help to clear the future progress. I believe some hesitate because they do not like to have their thoughts disturbed. When Davy discovered potassium it annoyed[19] persons who had just made their view of chemical science perfect; and when I discovered the magneto-electric spark, distaste of a like kind was felt towards it, even in high places. Still science must proceed . . .

18. A similar difficulty occurred in the controversy over electrochemistry. Faraday gave the impression (§§ 1797 and 1958) that he was in full agreement with de la Rive, though he was careful to outline only broad agreement. A letter to Schoenbein (*Correspondence*, p. 51, also quoted in Williams' *Michael Faraday*, p. 403, with no comment) tells of the confusion of a leading Continental scientist and how it was cleared up in a personal conversation with Faraday: "when he learned from me that I by no means go the length of De la Rive . . . he seemed to think that [certain] objections were rather against De la Rive than against me . . ."
   Here we see a double standard practiced in the name of good manners in spite of resulting communication difficulties. Faraday was the first to deviate from the custom, but not always (see also note, p. 258, about the same confusion).
19. The word "annoyed" is a euphemism for the state in which one threatens to call the police and close down a journal. The story was discussed above. Faraday's story of what annoyance occurred in 1831 is very cryptic, and I found no way of illuminating it. He does not refer to it anywhere else, as far as I know.

## Prelude to the Field Theory

Faraday's *Experimental Researches in Electricity* had its paragraphs numbered consecutively and appeared in series—for a period of well over twenty years. No doubt, when he began the second series he knew his project might take time, but he was distressed when marks of recognition failed to appear before his patience had run out. He told himself again and again to be a little more patient and he worked harder and harder, breaking more and more inductive taboos and thus becoming more and more remote from the ideal community of philosophers whose chief concern is the truth and whose chief reward is peace of mind. Though he did not know it in 1831, in 1856 he knew it all too clearly: some scientists wish for the illusion of perfection, some for progress; and the latter must declare war on the former, knowingly or not. Planck discovered this around 1900, and Einstein around 1930. Some historians think it is now a thing of the past and may be forgotten.

# 4    The First Vintage

This is the chronology of the growth of the field idea. In the year 1821 Faraday employed a theory that was, rudimentarily and in retrospect, a field theory. In 1831 he employed a field theory proper. For a while he did not know the force of his own idea; in a definite sense he was even unaware of it. He simply felt that he had found a new mode of expression and he employed it freely—like a bird that enjoys the cushion of air beneath it, hardly noticing its own flight. It all started with Faraday's small attempt to describe his discovery accurately. One fact could be better expressed in field language. Soon things got out of his control; Faraday found himself speculating. Even wildly. His first wild speculation dates from March 1832. It is inferior, no doubt, to his 1844 speculations, but it is based on lines that he pursued systematically and consistently from then on. He changed his views on various matters; but he developed all his ideas in one single direction. The chief developments in Faraday's career as a speculative thinker, as a natural philosopher, are two—one methodological, one scientific. Methodologically, he gave up his reluctance to speculate though not his critical suspicion of all speculation, his own in particular. Scientifically, he developed his theory of electrodynamics in order to force his peers to recognize his own speculations.

There is, I think, something deceptive about all this. The ease with which Faraday began clashes too violently with the efforts he had to invest in later years. It is not that I believe in hard work but I do usually look for the investor: I cannot assume without examination the existence of so much good luck in one stroke. I think Faraday's early luck was in part thanks to other people's contributions (as is true of others too). This is not to belittle Faraday:

on the contrary, observing his predecessors' contributions we can more clearly appreciate his own. When we see how much he owes to Boscovich and to Kant we are in position to see (*pace* L. Pearce Williams) how much more we owe to him than to his predecessors.

## Boscovich's Program

Boscovich's ideas never gained a fair treatment in public because he interpreted Newton's theory of gravity as only approximately true. When Boscovich's ideas could be of any use, the generality of scientists were reluctant to doubt the absolute certitude of Newton's theory. Nowadays we do not seem to appreciate the force of the view that Newton's theory of gravity is absolutely certain. People generally feel that we saved it sufficiently well by claiming that it is a first approximation to an accepted theory; people are also content with some sort of near-certainty as a substitute for the old absolute certainty. These two changes are obviously correlated. But by now Boscovich's program is obsolete.[1]

1. The last word on the subject of Boscovich's influence seems to me to be in Emile Meyerson's *Identity and Reality* (London, 1930; Dover reprint, 1962, pp. 74–75): "Boscovich's system has rarely been applied in its entirety by scientists. We hear very little said of his unique curve of force. In the nineteenth century Saint Venant resuscitated and simplified his hypothesis . . . However . . . [he] has not had much success. And yet Boscovich's ideas have had considerable influence upon science because he was the first resolutely to strip the atom of extension." He sees the merit of Boscovich's system in the way it solves the problem of elastic collisions, but considers it too artificial. "And so it is not surprising," he says quite surprisingly, "that the dynamicists [?] have generally [?] preferred to surround their point-atoms with many forces, varying accordingly to different laws. Such amongst others was Kant's views."

Though I endorse this verdict, it needs a few detailed corrections. As far as Kant is concerned, he is treated fully enough in the next section. As far as point atomism is concerned, let me quote J. L. Synge in his review of C. Truesdell's *Essays in the History of Mechanics* (which contains an incredible essay on Saint Venant's principle) published in *Science* 168 (17 April 1970), 354: "For some years I have been spreading it around that it was Boscovich who was responsible for introducing the concept of the point-particle . . . Not so, says Truesdell (p. 107); the credit should go to Euler, and he dismisses 'the learned Slovenian Jesuit' in a disparaging footnote (p. 282). My only excuse is incredible credulity. I believed what I read in L. L. Whyte's *Roger Joseph Boscovich* (Humanities Press, 1961, p. 121): according to him Faraday, Maxwell, Kelvin . . . saluted Boscovich as the originator of this concept, which, when you come to think of it, is a very queer concept indeed."

I find this passage rather amusing. Truesdell dismisses Boscovich because he hates speculations. Point atoms as such belong, not to Boscovich, not to Euler either, but simply to Newton. No one will deny that. The point atom that is Boscovichian is the one that possesses short-range (attractive and respulsive) forces in addition to gravity; these were used in Faraday's

In point of principle near-certainty is no better than certainty. In addition, near-certainty is of much less interest: it bears no relevance to science and has no interest either to the scientist or to the historian of science. In contradistinction, the alleged certitude of Newtonianism, the view that Newton's mechanics is absolutely true, had surprising implications and provided in itself a *program*; it turns out to be an *interpretation* of other theories besides the theory of gravity.

It is a well-known though amazing fact that the aim of many Newtonians was to base all physics and chemistry on Newton's theory of gravity. They intended not only to harmonize but even to deduce all physics from Newtonian gravity! Why? The answer that seems the most obvious is this: Newton, knowing *how* to make induction, made the widest generalization possible. This answer is a sufficient explanation, but it is open to some objections. One objection is that Newton's own program was wider, including not only attractions but also repulsions, and forces like cohesion, electricity, and others. We need stronger arguments to narrow down Newton's program.

The answer to my problem is to be found in the argument of P. M. Roget (of the famed Roget's *Thesaurus*), who in 1832 opposed the program I am now discussing:[2]

study of catalysis and adhesion (see chap. 8, below) as well as in Maxwell's statistical mechanics; Maxwell's use of Boscovich's idea was pointed out repeatedly in Kelvin's *Baltimore Lectures*. And so Whyte corrects Meyerson on this point. But Whyte, like Williams and almost everyone else, is mistaken about Faraday in general: only Meyerson noted (*Identity and Reality*, p. 79) that Faraday was "pretending to follow in theory the ideas of Boscovich [since he] felt a great repugnance to the conception of forces acting [at a distance]"; others lost sight of the wood for the trees.

For the latest concerning Boscovich's influence, see Richard Olson, "The Reception of Boscovich's Ideas in Scotland," *Isis* 60 (1969), 91–103, for the recent literature on the topic. Olson opens his paper by explaining the current interest in Boscovich as due to his alleged influence on Faraday and others. Olson is noncommittal on this point; he is only interested in the lines of transmission of Boscovich's influence, particularly on the reasons for his influence in Scotland. Olson also presents briefly Boscovich's ideas, but his presentation is not sufficiently problem-oriented.

2. P. M. Roget, *Treatize on Electricity* (1832, p. 64, § 239; quoted in Taylor's *Scientific Memoirs*, 1 (1837), 469, where the editor has added: "the following passage . . . was noticed . . . by Prof. Faraday in his lecture at the Royal Institution."

Solomon Maimon, by contradistinction, rejected the program not because it was based on a logical error, as Roget says, but because it cannot be executed. Hence Newton's theory is imperfect. See, for example, Maimon's *Autobiography* (1793), II, chap. 6 ( my translation): "Even Newton's excellent world-system has many defects [as] . . . many phenomena are not explicable by the laws of universal attraction, which proves that there exist still other universal laws, which can be added to the rest of the laws and bring them into one unity. . ."

> It is a great though a *common* error to imagine, that the condition assumed by Aepinus, namely that the particles of matter when devoid of electricity repel one another, *is in opposition* to the law of universal gravitation established by the researches of Newton; for this law applies, in every instance to which inquiry has extended, to matter in its ordinary state, that is, combined with a certain proportion of electric fluid. By supposing, indeed, that the mutual repulsive action between the particles of matter is, by a very small quantity, less than that between the particles of the electric fluid, a small balance would be left in favour of the attraction of neutral bodies for one another, which might constitute the very force which operates under the name of gravitation; and thus both classes of phenomena may be included in the same law.

Two views are here offered. The first is this. Aepinus's theory is here reconciled with Newton's theory of gravity, both by claiming that the additional forces are small and by the assertion that every celestial body, taken as a whole, is electrically neutral. This amounts to the assertion that Newton's gravity is only approximately true, though it is an excellent approximation, and only under a given condition, though one which usually exists in nature. Further, it is asserted, gravity may be explicable as the result of slight deviations of celestial bodies from the state of electrical neutrality. This is a fascinating idea which was tossed out by Father Beccaria in the mid-eighteenth century. It was returned to regularly; the last respectable exponent of it was Ritz in 1905. In the early nineteenth century, P. M. Roget and O. F. Mossotti advocated it; and Mossotti claimed to have given it a mathematical expression using a variant of Poission's theory.

As Williams shows (*Michael Faraday*, pp. 294–95), Faraday was very excited about Mossotti's paper. As we shall notice later repeatedly, Faraday admired Poisson's mathematical theory, though it assumed action at a distance, which Faraday rejected; he thought it would be easily adapted to his own physical view. And so, naturally, he might have seen in the idea of gravity as an electric phenomenon a way of eliminating gravitational action at a distance too. In any case, he mentioned to Whewell ". . . my notion which I think I mentioned to you that Universal Gravitation is a mere residual phenomenon of Electrical attraction and repulsion." Faraday wanted Whewell to check

Mossotti's mathematics. I do not know the end of the story (Williams does not say), but, clearly, the mathematics did leave much to be desired.

Williams notices (*Michael Faraday*, pp. 295–96) a puzzling fact on which I wish to comment: Although Mossotti's theory was quite unlike that of Boscovich, enthusiasm for it was whipped up in Britain at the same time that a revival of Boscovichianism began and references to works by Boscovich and his early disciples were published in the *Philosophical Magazine* (10 [1837], 357). The most important similarity between Boscovich and Mossotti, Williams says in solving this puzzle, "was the association of both attractive and repulsive forces with 'matter.'" To this I do not agree, because "matter" signified for these two theorists quite different abstractions. What, the literature clearly shows, really excited people about Boscovich was his promise to retain Newtonian mechanics as precisely true in the large but not true at all in the small. This was the first view of Newtonian mechanics as an approximation.

The same concern is shown in the above quoted passage from P. M. Roget, in his contrast between his own extremely radical views and the most conservative ones (this is a common mode of arguing). He did not conceal his view that Newton's theory is absolutely true in the large only—though he was not too clear about it either (Mossotti was). What he considered to be a "common error" is the view that Aepinus's theory excludes the view of Newton's theory of gravity as in the large absolutely true. If this were so, then any confirmation of Newton's theory would, by itself, be a refutation of Aepinus's theory. Roget pushed this view to the extreme. If we wish Newtonian mechanics to remain absolutely true in absolutely all cases, we arrive at a surprising conclusion, but one that is at least consistent. It seems to be this: if any theory be proved to be independent of Newton's theory of gravity, then there may exist some cause for some planetary motion that is not Newtonian gravitational force. If so, then Newtonian gravity cannot be claimed to be the true *cause*, the *essence*, of planetary motion. Therefore, for the sake of certitude, to secure one field of science, great adventures were demanded in all other fields. Certitude based on inductive arguments demanded formidable theories and wild speculations to base all physics on gravity.

That such strong forces as electric forces can be explained by assuming such a weak force as gravity, and that dual forces like electricity and magnetism can be esplained by it, is hardly credible at first sight, as Faraday has often stressed. The conclusion could have been very revolutionary had the problem been subject to a public discussion—as Boscovich had desired it to be. He was the first to consider Newton's theory of gravity not to be the peak of perfection, a consideration that not even Faraday and Maxwell dared to present to the public. Boscovich was the first courageous Newtonian to *interpret* Newton's theory of gravity as only *approximately* true: absolutely true only in the large but false in the small. His *program* is a wonderful example for the theory of interpretation; it is also the link or the transition between Newton's and Kant's programs.

Boscovich's researches grew out of a study of a small *problem*. His problem was that of *collisions*. If two absolutely rigid bodies collide, then at the moment of contact, their momenta change *instantaneously* with the instantaneous change of the *direction* of their motion. According to Newton's theory of force, such changes are caused by forces of unlimited magnitudes, which is absurd. To claim that the colliding bodies, say billiard balls, are elastic is an evasive answer, since we want to *explain* elasticity. If *atoms* are absolutely rigid, then the problem is only shifted from billiard balls to atoms. And Newton did consider atoms to be absolutely rigid. Boscovich had a better theory. When he tried to present the idea more fully, he was surprised to find himself writing a bulky (and a very beautiful and argumentative) book that includes a new interpretation and a program for future research (*A Theory of Natural Philosophy*, 1759; English trans., Chicago, 1922).

The mere idea that we have to employ attractive as well as repulsive forces in physics is of course Newton's. But he implied—or seemed to imply—the view that every force, attractive or repulsive, is attached to a *different* matter (or "fluid"). This became the standard doctrine of Newtonianism (see I. B. Cohen, *Newton and Franklin*). Boscovich denied the existence of any fluid save gross or imponderable matter (p. 87). He insisted that attached to each particle were both attractive and repulsive forces.

To explain collision without admitting the *discontinuity* of change of momentum, Boscovich denied that bodies can ever come into *contact*. He assumed that two bodies attract each other unless they approach each other more closely than a given interval, where attraction ceases and repulsion starts. More precisely, he permitted the force to change from attraction to repulsion and back a few times. (The view employed by nuclear physicists, incidentally, is this: two protons repel each other unless they are thrust against each other to approach each other to nuclear distances [$10^{-13}$ cm], in which case they attract each other to form a nucleus. But they also have to assume that the attraction diminishes when the protons come still closer to each other, to prevent the protons from attracting each other until they become one. All this is not so much hypothesis as interpretation, of course.)

Boscovich discovered, or stressed, a major problem in Newtonianism: if all material particles attract each other (according to Newton's law), then quite independently of the behavior of imponderable matter (electric, magnetic, and other fluids), the size of all ponderable matter should have diminished, at least on one planet or star, to the minimum. And if the same argument is applied to the atom itself, then the atom, too, being composed of matter, should shrink —the minimum, said Boscovich, would be a geometrical point (p. 291). The earth should shrink to a point, which is not the case.

Hence, Boscovich argued, the assumption of short-range repulsive forces is a solution both to the problem of collision and to the problem of the extension of matter and its seeming permanence. But he tried to do more with his theory. He suggested solving the problem of density by assuming the mass of a body to represent the *number* of atoms in it. He suggested solving many problems, concerning viscosity, cohesion, elasticity, and so on, by assuming that such forces are alternately attractive and repulsive.

Boscovich did not explain all these phenomena—he had hardly any new explanation of the facts; he only interpreted them; he showed how a few explanations of them may be worked out along the lines of his solution of the problem of collision. He thus had a program and, he argued, a better one than the accepted program.

Boscovich's program is, in the final analysis, quite unsatisfactory. I shall not discuss the defects in it, since it is by now superseded. It was never seriously considered before Faraday because it interpreted Newton's theory of gravity as imperfect (pp. 109, 121) (and also because Dalton opposed it).

In order to contrast Boscovich with Kant or with Faraday, two points should be stressed. The first is the view concerning space. For Boscovich, as for Newton, space is still empty space; it is still only the stage on which the atomic drama is played, to use the metaphor most favored by Einstein. Although the drama is more geometrical, and although Boscovich had intended to be more Leibnizian and allow space to come into the play as an actor, not merely as the stage, he is still essentially in the tradition. For, while in the theory of Boscovich, forces are concentrated in the atom, they are *central* forces, properties of the atom, in the theories of Kant and of Faraday the properties of particles of matter are properties of space, or rather independent entities filling space—they *are* matter, they constitute *relations* between space and forces. (This view that force is a *property* is especially manifest in Boscovich's argument against Leibniz's animism: though atoms are endowed with forces, they are still inanimate, since they are deprived of other mental properties [p. 123].)

I know of no exposition of Boscovich's program as a program save that of Boscovich himself. He exposed his idea in the first part of his book. He developed it mathematically and showed what it can explain in the second part. And he extended it into a program in the third part. Boscovich made an important contribution to science; his general idea is speculative or meta-physical—nonscientific—which is very evident from his treatment of the various problems he handles in his third part. To enlist support he had to argue—as he did—that our theories are not perfect; that even if they are the best, Nature may choose the second-best (p. 109); that it is enough if we develop imperfect theories and try to improve upon them (p. 107).

It seems clear that Boscovich's program goes deeper than Newton's—it aims at a deeper picture of the universe. Newton tried to explain matter and its behavior by assuming matter and laws of force. Boscovich claimed that here too much is assumed. Extension can be explained, he showed, not only by endowing atoms with extension. Moreover, he added, when that explanation is used, then the problem is thereby merely shifted; what keeps the size of the atom is not explained by Newton or within Newton's program. Boscovich still assumes matter—the material point; but it is already less material than Newton's matter. Nevertheless, it is still, counter to his claim (p. 87), not entirely a nonmaterial point, since it is endowed not only with force but also with inertia. He thus did not fully explain matter by force, or even offer a mere interpretation on these lines. (This criticism is due to Whewell, who was a Kantian.)

## Kant's Program

I shall now present a brief summary of salient points from Kant's *Metaphysical Foundation of Natural Science*. This work marks a high point in his philosophical development. It was published in 1786 between the two editions of his *Critique of Pure Reason* (1781 and 1787). The *Critique* was, and still is, considered his magnum opus because it allegedly contains his metaphysics. Not so, said Kant: it only contained the conditions necessary for a valid metaphysics. When his *Critique of Pure Reason* was misunderstood, he wrote a popular version of it— with the omission of the parts that cannot be popularized, as indicated carefully in the body of the popular version. The popular version of the *Critique of Pure Reason* Kant entitled *Prolegomena* (i.e., prefaces) *to Any Metaphysics Which in Future May Claim Scientific Status*. The next step in that direction was his *Metaphysical Foundations of Natural Science*.

In the preface Kant complains that chemistry is merely empirical and hence uncertain and hence unscientific. To be scientific it must be founded on firm metaphysical foundations *and* be mathematical. We need principles to deduce from them, for example, the laws of chemical interactions and the relative densities of the elements. The principles must be those of matter in general, not of this element or that (which is an empirical affair altogether); such a principle is "a real *metaphysics of corporeal matter*." Metaphysics, says Kant, deals with possible experience, and the sceme of all possible experiences is the table of categories. Kant considered this table charming: it presents a complete and watertight division of the sciences; to this end his book is divided into four parts, each exhibiting three principles—thus filling all his twelve categories. Nowadays, all philosophers who ally themselves with reason in one way or another, even to some degree, find any doctrine of *"the"* categories rather incomprehensible and quite repulsive. No matter. In accord with his table of categories, Kant divides natural science into kinematics (quantity), dynamics (quality), mechanics (relations), and phenomenology (modality). The connection with *"the"* categories is rather loose, but the division is quite interesting.

The significance of Kant's division of mechanics to kinematics and dynamics is not related sufficiently to the present study to go into detail. Before the spread of the influence of Thomson (later Lord Kelvin) and Tait, it was obligatory to present physics by beginning with space, time, and force, as Newton did it. Thomson and Tait, like Kant before them, began with space, time, and motion. Another innovation by Kant is his willingness to assume absolute space while denying it any empirical content. I have discussed this point in another place.[3] I shall therefore leave Kant's kinematic and discuss his dynamics.

The very beginning of Kant's dynamics is heretical. His kinematics naturally applies to mass-points. (This makes kinematics include not only motions but also quantities of motion, which is not as charming as Kant hoped.) In dynamics we have not only forces but also bulky bodies: matter fills space, not primarily (as in Descartes and in Newton) but in virtue of its being endowed by forces (as in Leibniz and Boscovich). Bulk, solidity, or impenetrability is derivative—from the forces of matter. These are only two primary or primordial or original forces, attraction and repulsion; but only repulsion is what gives matter its bulk, and repulsion is the same as elasticity.

Kant introduces the dynamic particle not as a point atom but as a particle

3. "Leibniz's Place in the History of Physics," *J. Hist. Ideas*, 30 (1969).

that fills space, and it fills space by virtue of a finite force of any given magnitude. This, the reader realizes at once, leads to one of two possible corollaries. Take a particle that is endowed with a large elastic force and, second, one endowed with a small elastic force. The first occupies a larger portion of space than the second, or the first is denser than the second. Or a combination of these two possibilities may occur. Indeed, Kant notes at once that an attraction stronger than a repulsion may increase the density of a particle by decreasing its bulk; he hastens to add, however, that no pressure, however large, can cause compression to be complete. Incompressibility, or bulk, or impenetrability, or occupying space, or filling space, is thus relative: matter can shrink, but not to a point.

Substance, then, is that which occupies space by virtue of possessing force, i.e., by virtue of being movable; mass, therefore, is a property of force. This may sound like a surprising result, but presumably Kant had intended to attain it; we know that Leibniz had been criticized for his inability to explain inertial mass. It is no accident, either, that the distinguished nineteenth-century Kantian, William Whewell, criticized Boscovich for his assumption—rather than deduction from other principles—that the mass-points are endowed with inertia. Nor is it so surprising, come to think of it, that Faraday in his later years (see below, p. 230) required inertial mass to be explained by the theory of fields of force. Now the question one might ask at once is, how does Kant introduce inertia into his kinematic theory if inertia, as we saw, is the result of bodies possessing forces and if kinematics assumes no forces? The answer is that Kant assumes in kinematics the principle of equivalence of all inertial systems, to use modern parlance. At what point did the equivalence of inertial systems, or the principle of Galilean transformations, become prominent is a very difficult problem—after all, clearly, Newton presented and employed that principle—and not much studied. No doubt, a few reasons led to the prominence of the principle, including the replacement of Galilean inertial systems with Lorentzian ones in 1905. Yet Kant's division of mechanics into kinematics and dynamics also has something to do with it. Kant insisted in his kinematics, that, kinematically speaking, velocity is but a ratio of distance to time intervals. Yet he endowed relative frames of reference with constant velocities relative to each other. Einstein, in contrast, deduced (*The Meaning of Relativity*) the principle of Galilean transformation from Newton's dynamics.

Back to dynamics. Since a particle occupies space in varying degrees of density, since the density is of forces occupying space, matter is divisible—not atomic.

Whereas repulsive force is necessary to give matter its bulk and inertia, attractive force is necessary to give matter its boundaries. Materiality is thus the result of the combined presence of repulsion (elasticity) and attraction (gravity). Attraction without repulsion leads to the collapse of the system to a point, and repulsion without attraction to the expansion of the system endlessly; in either case space is empty; hence matter is the interplay of both forces; the result of the conflict between them. Similarly, Kant proves that repulsion is action by contact and attraction is action at a distance. This is a fine compromise between Newton and Leibniz, indeed a synthesis or a combination of the two.

Kant makes it abundantly clear that in his view any particle of matter whatsoever is a combination of two, and only two, primary or original forces, that one of these, attraction, is what causes gravitation, so that all varieties of matter are ultimately due the variability of the force of repulsion, or original elasticity. He goes further and declares that just as attraction varies at large distances as the inverse square of the distance, so the repulsive force acts at vanishing distances as the inverse cube of the distance. So even the magnitudes of the forces are fixed. What, then, can vary to account for the observed variety of things? Kant's answer is, the "degree of filling of space."

The central thesis of Kant is that matter is composed of three qualities, attraction and repulsion as the two primary qualities, and the resultant one of the degree of filling of space. Here is what seems to me to be Kant's central point (part II, Prop. 8, note 2, my translation):

> As all given matter must fill its space with a definite degree of repulsive force, in order to constitute a definite material thing, only an original attraction in CONFLICT with the original repulsion can make possible a definite degree of the filling of space, WHICH IS matter . . .

Matter, then, is a conflict of forces. I have already mentioned Oersted's acceptance of this quaint idea. No doubt, even when Kant presented it, as an a priori truth, no less, he was aware of its shortcomings and of its unorthodoxy. Indeed, he soon admits both points.

Kant frankly admits that his idea is but a program, and he proceeds to outline the way he thinks the variety of the observed forces of nature might be derived from his two primary forces. Elasticity, for example, is the resultant of the mixture, say, of air and the matter of heat, and is partly primary or original, partly derivative. He similarly talks of cohesion, solidity, friction, and chemical forces. He is fascinated by the fact that a chemical solution does not necessarily conserve the combined volume of solvent and solute: the solution constitutes *"an elastic medium*. This *alone* will afford a sufficient reason..." (italics in the original).

Kant seems to be reassured now. He contrasts his view with the mechanical view that was most popular "with little change from old Democritus to Descartes, and even our own times"—this may be the understatement of the eighteenth century. Kant's dispute with the mechanists ends with an admission of his own weakness: his metaphysics, as metaphysics, is not an explanation but merely the ground for explanation, a suggestion of possibilities —a program for explanations.

The third part of Kant's book concerns mechanics—the quantity of motion, mass (= quantity of motion/velocity), conservation of matter, inertia, equality of action and reaction. This is all proven, and thus covers the full extent of Newtonian mechanics. I dare say I find this quite heavy going. What one must notice is that whereas Newton starts with his three laws and then specifies the special nature of gravity, elasticity, and perhaps other forces, Kant starts with these two only and proceeds to Newton's three laws later on. The fourth part, phenomenology, is even harder to follow. It returns both to questions of relative and absolute space and to Kant's own theory of knowledge and the place of his theory of space in it.

Throughout my presentation I have overlooked Kant's theory of knowledge and its import; it is far too complex a matter, and I have dealt with it elsewhere (see n. 3, p. 87, above). It is no accident that Delametherie's report on this book (see note 9, p. 28, above), for example, entirely centers on Kant's dynamics, and even then without mentioning its most revolutionary part—the idea of partial emptiness or partial fullness. The reduction of all forces, especially chemical, to the two primary ones is evidently what caught people's fancy.

Kant influenced a generation of investigators. His views were soon confused with those of Schelling and Hegel under the umbrella title *Naturphilosophie*. Oersted, who mentions his debt to Schelling, his friend, in the opening of his doctoral dissertation, certainly was a prominent Kantian. (The word "conflict" occurs in the title of his original paper on the discovery of electromagnetism, but not in the title of the English translation.) Other leading chemists of the day, Ritter, Davy, and Berzelius, were also influenced by Kant. To what extent Schelling and others also influenced them, and to what effect, I cannot say. I suppose Schelling's influence was marginal to

Kant's. But even the value of Kant's influence on anyone but Oersted is hard to pin down. Anyway, when Oersted came up with circular forces, it was a violent break away from orthodox Kantianism. Without summing up Kant's influence before his program's demise, let me point out that chemistry was prominent at the period, that all chemists, Kantians or Lavoisierians, hoped to explain the properties of matter (i.e., solidity, fluidity, etc.), that Kant gave chemistry the hope of no less than mathematical respectability. When Davy first met Laplace, he tells his brother during his last illness, he expressed his hope of seeing "mathematical laws" of chemistry and of "the mechanical properties of matter"—thus incurring Laplace's anger. What a telling story, this. (See his *Collected Works*, 1:168.)

## The Field Concept in Physics and in Mathematics

In Oersted's theory we have the conflict moving in space; in Wollaston's theory we have magnetic fluids around wires. Let us consider these two ideas closely.

Wollaston's idea may be presented thus: The lines of force or the magnetic curves around the conducting wire are circular; iron filings will order themselves around it in circles. Each piece of iron, we know, is temporarily magnetized. We can imagine that it is attracted to an invisible magnet that has the opposite polarities, just as two magnets will attract each other if they are put together in opposite directions. Now we remove the filings. But we have not removed the many invisible magnets unless we break the electric current. We now ask, what can be the size of this invisible magnet? In Wollaston's theory, the size of the small invisible magnet is the size of a magnetic molecule, or a molecule of the magnetic fluid, or an "elementary dipole." (We must remember that no one assumed the existence of isolated magnetic atoms at the time molecules of north and south polarity were postulated.) In order to retain Wollaston's idea without space filled with magnetic molecules we may consider the following. Imagine one such circle of magnetic molecules; make the molecules decrease in size and increase in number while keeping the appearances (the iron filings' behavior, the deflection of the compass, etc.) unchanged; let their number increase indefinitely and the size of each of them shrinks to a point. We now have a magnetic field as envisaged by Faraday.

Faraday's idea of *polarization of space* is not easy to grasp. Let us consider the difficulty concerning the transition to a point size dipole. Assume, with Faraday, that space around the conducting wire behaves as if each point in it is a magnetic dipole, which has *no* size but that otherwise is no different than an ordinary dipole, i.e., a dipole according to the accepted theory. An ordinary dipole normally acts on a third pole at a distance thus: each of the two poles exerts at a distance a force on the third pole; the two forces are opposite, and usually almost equal. Usually the distance of the third pole from one of the poles of the dipole is almost equal to its distance from the other and, therefore, one pole acts slightly more strongly than the other. At a great distance the slight difference becomes so very small that it may be ignored for all practical purposes. When the dipole shrinks to a point, its two poles exert exactly the same forces in opposite directions on the third pole and therefore the two actions cancel each other. A point dipole *cannot act at a distance*; it cannot act at all.

We see, in this discussion, how one might strain one's imagination, while holding received opinions about forces, and come closer and closer to Faraday's notion of fields of forces—without being able to go all the way. For, the smaller the imagined dipole, the closer a holder of the received notions will come to Faraday's view; but he will be unable to make the dipole pointlike and still conclude that there is any polarization in the field. Once the two poles collapse to one there is no action at a distance, no axis of symmetry, no polarization, no field. Faraday had no difficulty here: he postulated that the axis of symmetry that we can imagine while reducing the size of the dipole remains even after the dipole's size shrinks to zero. This axis of symmetry is now known as the line of gradient, or the normal to equipotential surfaces, and in other terms; it is the perpendicular to the line of force. Actually, we do not need this axis of symmetry that is perpendicular to the directions of polarization; we need the directions of polarization themselves—the lines of force. And in just the way the axis of symmetry disappears when the two poles become one, in the same way the direction of polarization, the line connecting the two poles, collapses when the two unite. Faraday identified it nonetheless with the line of force as manifested in the iron-filings arrangement; to a Newtonian this is impossible.

Mathematically, then, the axis of symmetry of the dipole and the line connecting the two points, being perpendicular, are equally handy for the description of the fields; when dipoles collapse into points, they become lines of force. Alternatively, we may describe equipotential lines—or surfaces, speaking about three-dimensional fields—and the lines of force become gradients to the equipotential surfaces. It is agreed among historians of science that the mathematical theory dealing with potential surfaces and gradients was, in the period of about 1830–60, fairly novel and revolutionary. It is agreed among historians of science that it is appropriate to gasp at the genius of Faraday who, not knowing even the rudiments of that theory as it was being developed in his day, not even in possession of rudimentary mathematical training of any sort, was able to apply in his research potential theory as it was later developed by his disciples, from Maxwell to Poynting. This bewildered idolatry—which began with Faraday's contemporary, the great philosopher William Whewell —is both an expression of dogmatism and a fear of coping with the problems that Faraday imposed on his dogmatic opponents.

What is novel in potential theory? This question historians of physics delegate to historians of mathematics; and thus they manage to evade the problems at hand by separating the history of mathematics from that of physics (the division between the two fields is valid, between their histories it is not). Potential theory was invented by the greatest eighteenth-century Newtonian mathematical physicists; it was in accord with Newtonian theories of action at a distance. In Faraday's own time potential theory was developed as an instrument for the study of elasticity, again in accord with Newtonianism. When Faraday's disciples, Kelvin and Maxwell, transferred ideas of potential theory from elasticity to electromagnetics, the dogmatic Newtonians hoped that they were also transferring Newtonian physical ideas of action at a distance. Far from being shocked, as they would be were the novelty mathematical, they were pleased and hopeful.

Thus, potential theory was no heresy. Much as one might gasp at Faraday's incredible mathematical intuitions, one must notice this. His mathematical intuitions belong to the later stages of his career when he was struggling to improve the precision and explanatory power of his field theories. His very first idea of the field is not a mathematical novelty—mathematically it is not sophisticated—but a physical novelty. It is breathtaking not in its sophistication, not even physical sophistication, but in its daring and revolutionary character. It raises all questions afresh. It declares many solutions, accepted at the time as quite satisfactory, to be merely transitional and fundamentally unsatisfactory; it took physics three or four generations to cope with the upheaval caused by Faraday's collapse of a magnetic dipole into a point of polarization axis.

In closing this section I should like to point out that Maxwell found the full correlation of the potential theory with the field theory a sufficiently striking novelty; he wrote about it in a fan latter addressed to Faraday and dated 9 November 1857 (Williams, *Michael Faraday*, p. 513). Far from being shocked by Faraday's efforts to develop the theory of gravitational fields (an effort that only Einstein brought to fruition), Maxwell encouraged Faraday— first on philosophical grounds (quoted below, p. 318), and second on the grounds that Faraday's method applied to gravitation is the *"embodiment* of the same ideas which are expressed *mathematically* in the functions of Laplace and of Sir W. R. Hamilton in Planetary Theory" (italics Maxwell's). It is a pity that such an idea, a bold conjecture in 1857, is considered by most historians of mathematics and of physics as obvious in the 1830s.

## Magnetic Fields and Ampère's Hypothesis

The picture Faraday had in mind, of collapsed dipoles, is only an attempt to make Wollaston's idea work. The problem of how small molecules or dipoles can act upon a magnet's pole is answered in detail by Coulomb and Poisson: if many small molecules or dipoles are arranged in the same direction, they act as a big magnet. An ordinary magnet, further, is nothing more than an ordered aggregate of small but finite dipoles. Now, if we imagine these dipoles in rings around conducting wires, as Wollaston did, it is quite evident that this will not do: a ring would not act on an additional pole for reasons of symmetry. Faraday's rings are fundamentally different; an element of a ring does not act like ordinary magnets at a distance; its action is localized in space. Additionally, Faraday alluded to the theory that all magnetic action is made in this way. The action is localized by the polarized state of space. Space is polarized not in the ordinary sense of the polarization of a magnet but in the new sense that though it is empty it tends to move a pole that occupies it in one direction and an opposite pole in the opposite direction. It is thus a *dual force*, as Faraday called it. We can well describe the polarized point as possessing one force, provided that we denote opposite magnetic poles (or charges) with the signs + and − to designate that the same force would act on them in opposite directions. The difference between the two descriptions is merely verbal.

If we now try to compare the field view with the magnetic matter view, we see that the field view is superior not only because it works better but also because it is less puzzling that space is affected (polarized) by electric currents than that it is suddenly filled with a (magnetic) fluid when the electric current is made to flow. Also the problem of the viscosity of the fluid does not arise. Still the problem of the creation of the field (or the polarization of space) is not thus solved.

Here we may employ Oersted's theory. Oersted sees the conflict, which if we wish we may identify with the state of polarization in question, in a state of permanent flux. In Oersted's theory the state of affair is sustained because the source—the conducting wire—goes on and on emitting the conflict.

Possibly the conflict flows away rapidly but in each point of space there is the conflict because the flow is even. But what happens when we vary the intensity of the current?

All this shows how many problems occur with the introduction of a new idea. And I have not yet mentioned the major problem, which is, how does the field act on a pole if the pole is not a center of the magnetic charge, if there is no magnetic fluid? No answer—at least, not yet.

The direction of Faraday's answer, however, is clear in advance. Ampère, who held a Newtonian theory of action at a distance, declared that magnetic poles do not exist in order to conclude that magnetic forces do not exist. Faraday favored the idea that magnetic poles do not exist, but tried to retain the idea of magnetic forces.

The literature is not clear on this point, and we have Faraday to blame for the confusion. He endorsed Ampère's hypothesis and rejected Ampère's electrodynamic theory; but in courtesy to Ampère he allowed people to confuse the two. In order to clarify the situation we must very clearly and methodically detach Ampère's hypothesis from Ampère's electrodynamic theory. Only then the hypothesis may change its meaning or at least its significance by having it incorporated in different theories. Ampère's hypothesis is that ordinary magnets are electromagnets, that a magnet possesses no magnetic fluid. But in Ampère's electrodynamic theory it had a greater significance than that. In Ampère's electrodynamic theory not only do magnetic fluids not exist, for Ampère no other source of magnetism exists: there exists no magnetic force, he said. Faraday's magnetic field, although it is not a fluid, is magnetism of a different kind. A magnetic fluid is the source of the magnetic force. Ampère abolished the magnetic atoms, and the magnetic force vanished too—according to Newtonian mechanics. Faraday, like Oersted, did assume the existence of magnetic forces, even though he denied the existence of magnetic atoms. For Faraday, but not for Newtonians, (magnetic) forces could float in empty space. The idea of a field of magnetic force, then, is contrary to Ampère's idea of abolishing magnetism; it contrasts with Ampère's electrodynamics though it embraces Ampère's hypothesis of the electric origin of all magnets.

## Magnetoelectric Induction

This section will be devoted to the ideas of the first two series of Faraday's *Experimental Researches in Electricity*, the First Series of November 1831 and the Second Series of January 1832.

In the first paper Faraday discusses three theoretical points: first, the strangest of all of Faraday's ideas—his electrotonic state; second, his theory of magnetoelectric induction; and third, his explanation of Arago's experiment. I shall not discuss the third point. Enough to say concerning it that it satisfactorily explains Arago's experiment. A simple theory explains magnetoelectric induction: a conductor is charged when it cuts magnetic curves or magnetic lines of force. Let us skip for a while Faraday's puzzling theory of the electrotonic state. The second paper contains one purely experimental point (induction from the earth's magnetic field) and one theoretical point that is the rejection of that puzzling theory of the first paper, the theory of the electrotonic state. Since this theory was rejected by Faraday a few months after he suggested it, no one (to my knowledge) except Williams ever took the trouble to present the theory, even though the same story was repeated in 1834. It is all the more peculiar that Faraday published the theory in the first place, in spite of all the negative results of his attempts to confirm it, as reported in his first paper. Maxwell, for one, noted that Faraday had a fixed idea of the electrotonic state that he tried to introduce into theory in the first *Experimental Researches in Electricity*. This, obviously, is quite different from the instances in which Faraday did introduce some theory of the electrotonic state—in each case concrete evidence forced Faraday to withdraw. What I wish to describe here is the concrete reason that forced Faraday to reject in his Second Series the idea he introduced in the First. Unfortunately, Williams explains this rejection (*Michael Faraday*, p. 205) by the claim that lines of force were more tangible than the electrotonic state—thus mixing the general case, in which Faraday was adamant, with the specific case, in which Faraday had to give way for specific reasons. The specific reasons turn out to be quite interesting.

Faraday discovered two modes of induction for which he supplied two explanations. The first induction is attained by varying a current: this he called volta-electric induction. The second is the induction attained by moving a conducting wire relative to a magnet; this he called magnetoelectric induction. The second effect is explained by the wire's cutting of the magnetic lines of force. The explanation of the first effect, the volta-electric induction is the troublesome point.

Again, for the best presentation of the theory, we must turn to the already quoted private letter. Faraday had already deviated from the inductive style (*Experimental Researches in Electricity*, § 5): "These results I purpose describing, not as they were obtained, but in such a manner as to give the most concise view of the whole"; but he did not as yet give an explicit public statement of his view. And so we have to use his correspondence. Here then is Faraday's experiment with his private explanation (*Life and Letters*, 2:7):

> . . . Electricity in currents therefore exerts an inductive action like ordinary electricity, but subject to peculiar laws. The effects are a current in the same direction when the induction is established; a reverse current when the induction ceases, and a *peculiar state* in the interim. Common electricity probably does the same thing; but as it is at present impossible to separate the beginning and the end of a spark or discharge from each other, all the effects are simultaneous and neutralise each other.

The induced current, we see, is a *transition* from the ordinary state of relaxation to the electrotonic state of tension, or the transition back. Between the moments of creating a current and of breaking it, an adjacent wire is in the electrotonic state. All electrostatic tension, he suggests, is the same electrotonic state! Faraday does not yet declare, at least not in his published paper, that the electrotonic state is electric polarity, though he soon makes such a conjecture which he intends to test (*Life and Letters*, 2:8; italics in the original):

> The new electrical condition which intervenes by induction between the beginning and end of the inducing current gives rise to some very curious results. It explains why chemical action or other results of electricity have never been as yet obtained in trials with the magnet. In fact, the currents have no sensible duration. I believe it will explain perfectly the *transference of elements* between the poles of the pile in decomposition. But this part of the subject I have reserved until the present experiments are completed; and it is so analogous, in some of its effects, to . . . peculiar properties [the existence of tension even prior to the creation of the current] of the poles of a voltaic pile, that I should not wonder if they all proved to depend on this state.

So now the electrotonic state is assumed to be tension created by *polarity*, a peculiar arrangement of the molecules in the wire. The assumption is soon altogether abandoned—because the field theory is more forceful, has more explanatory power, then even Faraday at first notices. There is a problem involved here that no one but Faraday ever mentioned, and the solution rendered the theory of the electrotonic state redundant. At first Faraday did not entirely reject Ampère's conjecture (currents induce currents in the vicinity) that he had refuted, but only tried to modify it; this seems to be the source of his theory of the electrotonic state (*Experimental Researches in Electricity*, § 60):

> Whilst the wire is subject to either volta-electric or magneto-
> electric induction, it appears to be in a peculiar state; for it
> resists the formation of an electrical current in it, whereas, if
> in its common condition, such a current would be produced;
> and when left uninfluenced it has the power of originating a
> current, a power which the wire does not possess under common
> circumstances.

In other words, one current still tends to cause a current in an adjacent wire, as Ampère had predicted; but while the adjacent wire is in an ordinary state, it does not resist this tendency, and while it is in the electrotonic state, it does resist it. This explains the momentariness of the induced current: soon the wire changes states and stops the current.[4] This transition is possibly the induced current itself. Why Faraday assumed it is clear: it explains the *direction* of the induced current, the fact that when the inducing current breaks the induced current is the reverse of the current induced by creating the contact. Moreover, the electrotonic state may be detectable by some tests, and one of the means of its detection may be a peculiar effect discovered by Ampère. This makes the hypothesis of Faraday seem to have a high explanatory power. But Faraday fails to detect any effect of the state, and he proves Ampère's effect to be unrepeatable, unsuccessful. The attempt to save Ampère's conjecture entirely fails: a current tends to cause on an adjacent wire no detectable effect whatsoever; only variations of its strength evolve a current in the latter. Nonetheless, Faraday does not yet give up his theory of electrotonic state and even publishes it together with a surprising amount of "negative results"! Why? Such a breach of tradition is not made unthoughtfully. And surely the function of the hypothesis was not merely to save Ampère. What were Faraday's reasons?

4. The (still current, accepted) theory of electric heat is similar: the cold wire is an excellent conductor; while conducting it heats up and thereby loses conductivity.

The answer to this question is not clearly given even in the second series of Faraday's *Researches*. Let us postpone discussion for a while. The problem that Faraday presents is a different one, the discrepancy between previously obtained results as to the *magnitude* of the forces obtained in Arago's effect (§ 193). He first conjectures that the different results are due to employing different metals. He finds out that the only difference resulting from employing different metals is proportional to their different conducting power and no more (§§ 212, 213). In other words the conjecture that different matter is induced to different degrees is rejected and past observed results are considered as observational errors (due to Newtonian explanations of the phenomena). This forces Faraday to reconsider more carefully his theory of magnetoelectric induction; in magnetoelectric induction, is the induced current simply due to cutting lines of force or due to the transition from being situated in a field of magnetic forces of one strength to a field of a different strength (§ 217)? (Although usually the change of field is involved with cutting lines of force during the transition, a wire can cut lines of force without passing to a place where the field is stronger.) Previous experiments indicate that only the cutting causes induction, not the change of the field's strength. But this has to be tested. An ingenious test[5] is to rotate a cylindrical magnet around its axis of symmetry near a wire. This leads to no sensible induction (§ 218), which seems to indicate that only the variation of strength counts. This experiment is explicable, however, by assuming that the lines of magnetic force are independent of the magnet; that they do not rotate with it (§ 220). But, if so, then the magnet itself, when it rotates, cuts its own lines of force, which do not rotate with it, and therefore should itself be induced. This was confirmed (§ 222); a rotating magnet is electrified. This experiment is evidently a decision for the hypothesis that the mere cutting of lines of force is the cause of induction and against the hypothesis that the transition from a strong to a weak field is the cause of induction.

5. E. T. Whittaker (*A History of the Theories of Aether and Electricity*, revised edition, 1951, 1:173) says that this is a "curious problem." He does not explain *why* Faraday was interested in it. Weber tried to refute Faraday's experiment but could not. He claimed then, according to Whittaker, that the lines of an ordinary magnet are derivable from a potential, and therefore if they revolve they would exert no influence. I do not know how Whittaker could accept such an argument or even report on it without comment, without even mentioning the experiments of Faraday and Weber and without discussing Weber's own attempt to solve the mystery, which does relate to a potential. Weber's difficulty relates, indeed, to the fact that only outside a magnet can a potential describe the magnetic forces, not inside it; which is a trivial corollary to Ampère's hypothesis.

In the First Series (§ 114), then, a theory was proposed according to which cutting lines of magnetic force induces electric currents. In the Second Series this theory is given two interpretations. And although one interpretation seems to be refuted by many previous experiments, many new ingenious experiments (only a few of which are mentioned here) were devised in order to ascertain that only the one interpretation is true and the other is false in any case. "The law . . . being thus rendered more precise and definite," we are now told, it can be employed to make redundant the hypothesis of the electrotonic state (§ 231): the theory of magnetoelectric induction, namely that it is caused by *cutting* the lines of magnetic force, now applies also to the volta-electric induction, and there is no need to explain this fact by the electrotonic state theory. The explanation is this: when the current is created, lines of force emanate from the conducting wire; they are cut on their way by the adjacent wire in which an induced current is created. When the current is broken, the lines return home, being cut again on their way back by the adjacent wire, causing a new induction.

A few difficulties arise here. First of all, one hypothesis is abolished, but another is introduced; we may now abandon the electrotonic state but we have to assume the *motion* of lines of force in its stead. Second, it would seem that the refuted idea that the induction is due to the change of *intensity* of the field of force would more readily explain volta-electric induction since we know without any additional hypothesis that by creating a current we vary the field's strength.

It is not easy to understand Faraday's idea at this stage. It is usually due to the inductive style that some part of an idea in a paper has to be guessed, and possibly in Faraday's time people were more trained in guessing. We may better take a hint from Faraday's diary.

We remember that he read the first paper on 24 November 1831 and went for a holiday. On 5 December he is back at work. Here is the beginning of his entry of the 9 December (p. 394): "Today went still more generally to work, for *some of former directions only partial*, and obtained I think very satisfactory and *reconciling results*."

This suggests that there has been a conflict in Faraday's theory. And indeed there was. He accepted Ampère's hypothesis, and even if he did not, his experiments with electromagnets[6] suffice to show the conflict. A coiled

6. *Diary*, 1:374, 1 October 1831: "Upon breaking the contact for a minute or two and then renewing it the attraction was reproduced, but when contact was broken for a *shorter period* the attraction was *not so strong*, and when broken for an instant only it scarcely appeared

wire exerts induction (when it conducts and in relative motion) according to the cutting of lines theory, while the same wire exerts induction (when a current is created or broken) according to the electrotonic state theory. The electrotonic state theory assumes that due to this state a wire resists the induction. Now it follows that when we create an electromagnet a wire in its vicinity is in the electrotonic state. Still, according to the cutting of the lines theory, we only have to move the wire or the electromagnet and the wire conducts. According to the electrotonic theory its conductivity should decrease. But if so, Faraday shows, it decreases in such a way as to keep constant the ratio of conductivity between metals. The magnetoelectric induction shows no relation to volta-electric induction in spite of the apparent similarity, and while the electrotonic state stops the former entirely, it does no more than reduce the magnetoelectric induction, and perhaps has no effect on it. And why should electrotonicity resist one induction entirely and the other not?

An attempt is evidently made to give a nonfield interpretation of magneto-electric induction. The problem is how to state the fact of cutting the lines in a nonfield language, or to explain the field theory in more traditional terms. Usually the cutting is involved with a transition from a place where a strong force acts to another where a weaker force acts. Can this be a clue to the explanation?

The answer is not only negative, but surprisingly shows the *"singular independence"* (§ 220) of the force; it is *not* bound to the magnet. The magnet rotates and the force stays still. *The force is freed from its material center.*

The lines of force that first entered in a modest way gain more and more experimental support. It seems hopeless to retain Ampère's program of abolishing magnetism—at least at present.

Now that we have disposed of Ampère's program, the situation is very much simplified. Our assumptions are these: (a) magnetoelectric induction is due to the cutting of lines of force; (b) all induced currents are due to

---

at all. When iron coils first receive magnetic state they attract strongly. When contact broken they lose that peculiar state gradually, and if before it is much diminished it be renewed attraction is only small. *Attraction proportionate to approximation to natural state and to intensity of peculiar state to which it is rising* . . . Still doubt that pure Electromagnets will produce Arago's effect."

This shows that he had more reasons at first to assume the electrotonic state than later. The experiment is evidently inconclusive and was not reported in the paper. And he later did show that Arago's effect is obtainable from pure electromagnets (§ 129). This is the evidence that he was aware of the conflict before he was able to solve it, and therefore before he published anything about it.

magnetoelectric induction; (c) all magnetic lines of force are due to currents. Evidently (c) includes Ampère's hypothesis. It explains the induction of the rotating magnet; it is also testable by obtaining Arago's effect in a rotating plate in the vicinity of a conducting wire; it is likewise testable by obtaining magnetoelectric induction from moving two wires one of which conducts, and so on. (These are all extremely delicate experiments.)

Take as premises the two hypotheses (a) and (b) above plus the fact that, by creating and breaking a current, induction occurs in an adjacent wire, and you may conclude that the adjacent wire cuts lines of force. That lines of force can move in space we know, since we obtain the same result whether the wire moves and the magnet rests (relative to the earth or what you like), or vice versa. The problem is how do lines move in space when a current in a wire is created and broken? The answer is by a new hypothesis: when a current is created, the conducting wire emits lines of force into space, and when the current is broken, they return home (§ 238).

The sending of the lines to the field and the calling them home again, then, results from the attempt to unify the two obviously connected phenomena —induction by variation of the strength of the current and by variation of its (relative) location. This is an astonishing result. The field gains more and more reality, independent existence. It calls for further considerations of many kinds. Faraday, true to his maxim "Work, finish, publish" (Gladstone, *Faraday*, p. 123), publishes the results as they stand and goes on thinking. For the problems that arise are many, since the development of the views and their novelty are tantalizing.

There is little reference in the literature to the crucial point, to the development of Faraday's idea of the lines of force emanating from and returning to the conducting wire. Williams, who quotes (*Michael Faraday*, p. 205) the relevant passage (§ 238), says no more there than that Faraday "now had . . . to assume . . . the propagation of . . . force through space" (i.e., the build-up and collapse of the field). The reason for the general reticence is one difficulty that besets all serious students of Faraday, and one that we shall encounter repeatedly. Later in life Faraday became bolder and clearer in his expression, but he never went back to explain the less-clear expressions of the early parts of his *Researches*: he either corrected himself on a point of error, or made do with a cross-reference. On the case at hand even the greatest student of Faraday's writings, James Clerk Maxwell, was not at all at ease (*Treatise*, § 541, 2:188): "I am not certain with what degree of clearness he then [after writing his § 238 on the build-up and collapse of the field] held the doctrine afterwards so distinctly laid down by him [in 1851], that the moving conductor, as it cuts the lines of force, sums up the action due to an area or section of the lines of force [§ 3082]. This, however, appears no new view of the case after the investigations of the second series have been taken into account." What Maxwell seems to express here is his astonishment at how rich the second series of 1832 seemed to him when he reread it after he had studied the twenty-eighth series of 1851.

## The "Original Views"

Soon after Faraday published his second series, he started to speculate. One of his speculations is the idea of magnetic and electric *waves*. The second is of an *electric* field in analogy to magnetic field. His 1832 speculations are still entirely unknown. In part they were published in his diaries but excited no comment so far; in part they are still unpublished.[7]

The difference between Faraday's 1832 speculations and his previous ideas is that while the previous ideas were invented in order to explain his discoveries, the latter speculations were invented in order to arrive at further discoveries. The first are heretic explanations of refutations of accepted views; the latter are attempts to get rid entirely of the accepted way of looking at things and to create an independent way of looking at things—as a new program for research. Let me outline this development.

Soon after Faraday finishes his second series, he writes in his diary (1:407, 7 January 1832):

> 291. *Is not the evolution of electricity in the wire caused by an electro magnetic pole a presumptive proof that time is required in electric circuit, and perhaps much time*; is not effect due to the wire going in the direction of the current in one part and then against it in the other?

> 292. The electricity in the wire is in the same direction as it is in that side of the circular theoretical current which it is approaching and the reverse of the current in the side it is leaving.

7. The one published comment on the 1832 unpublished speculation of Faraday (*Nature* (1938), p. 141) is entirely unconnected with Faraday's researches; also it is quite inaccurate; I shall refrain from discussing it.

This is hard to follow. Let me first introduce some background material. The induced current is manifest by a deflection of the needle. Query: is the current instantaneous, is it manifest for only a short time, or is it manifest for quite a sensible time? Answer: the induced current that deflects a galvanometer flows for quite a long lapse of time; if a current flows for less than a certain time interval, it will not effect the galvanometer even if it will be sufficiently strong to magnetize a needle in the helix through which is passes (*Experimental Researches in Electricity*, § 69). How long, then, does it take the lines of force to move? Suppose that the lines move into their appropriate position instantaneously when the current is created. Why, then, is the current not instantaneous? Because the instantaneous flow of lines causes an instantaneous electric tension, but an instantaneous electric tension does not cause an instantaneous current; rather, a current starts instantaneously to build up, but the resultant maximum flow occurs after a short time elapses. This conclusion is contrary to the view accepted at the time. Yet Faraday assumes this to be true and asks for an explanation of this time lapse. He gives a false explanation in the above quoted passage, he soon sees its defects, and then refutes it empirically. He then returns to the view that immediately after the cause of the current is created, it flows in its maximal intensity. This amounts to saying, in view of the fact that induction takes time, that when we create a current, the lines of force emanating from the conductor *slowly* spread in space. Here is the relevant entry from his diary (p. 424, 8 March 1832):

> 390. If the soft iron were taken slowly to the poles, there was no convulsion of the frog, but always if taken up rapidly.
> Again at first could not find the convulsion on breaking contact, but on the making the rupture rapidly by knocking off the connecting iron then got the convulsion strongly . . .
>
> 393. Time of travelling of magnetic impulse.
>
> 394. Time of travelling of impulse of electric induction.
>
> 395. Query application of theory of vibration.
>
> 396. When the travelling wire moves only through magnetic curves of equal intensity—can the effect of induced current be due to any thing else than relief on one side of wire relative to its position to the curves and tension on the other, i.e., to time required in propagation?—for the motion requires time

and implies occupation of time in the powers producing
the tension (tangential powers?).

The most exciting part of this passage is also the most enigmatic one:
"395. Query application of theory of vibration." In the *Encyclopaedia Britannica* article that Faraday read in childhood, three theories of electricity are mentioned, not two: the two-fluid, the one-fluid, and the vibrations. The third is not meant to be comprehensible; it is the merest suggestion. After all, heat, which at the turn of the nineteenth century was taken to be a fluid, was claimed by some eccentrics to be vibrations—because heat is produced by rubbing. So is electricity produced. So maybe electricity is vibrations too, perhaps only slightly different vibrations. In every new turn Faraday asked himself, how does this effect the idea of electricity as vibrations? Here, let me show, is the first promising reply.

Faraday discovers here the idea that the act of creating and breaking a current takes time. He tests it by two steps: (1) A swift action causes a strong induction. The magnetic force of an electromagnet is stronger if a soft iron bar is placed in it. Therefore the insertion and the taking out of a bar causes induction in an adjacent wire. If the iron is taken out slowly, no current is sensible, but if it is taken out quickly, a sensitive galvanometer (a frog's leg, in our case) shows a trace of current.

So, the intensity of the action is proportional to the intensity of its result, namely the intensity of the induced current. (2) Now he shows that the creation of the contact takes time. He breaks one current in two different ways, by an ordinary switch and by knocking off with a blow a loose piece of metal that is a part of the circuit. If the current is small enough, then breaking it fast, but not breaking it slowly, will show on the galvanometer. Now the current that still runs after the circuit was broken, runs, of course, for a sensible lapse of time—due to the fact that the lines of force return to the wire. And so, both emanating from, and returning to, the wire (upon creating and breaking the current), *take time*. Faraday assumes both—for reasons of symmetry.

It may be claimed, in criticism, that the delay is due to the fact that creation of a current is a slightly delayed result of the making of the contact that creates the circuit. Evidently, however, this does not work in the case of breaking of a contact in which, clearly, the current stops immediately when the circuit is broken. And so, if we insist on symmetry between making and breaking of currents, the criticism will be invalidated. Hence Faraday had to insist on lines of force not only going to the field but also going back home.

I find this to be an ingenious piece of research. Why was it never published? Faraday himself had no time: wonderful as the results of the experiments are, the train of ideas connected with them immediately suggest a new and a far more interesting experiment, on the delayed action of magnetism, and Faraday wants to carry it out himself. Later historians did not report this because Faraday's assumption of symmetry between making and breaking of currents was soon refuted by the discovery of self-induction, and his whole theory was soon greatly modified.

Later in his life Faraday freely offered suggestions to other experimenters to follow up; he tried to explain to people how fruitful his ideas were. But even then nobody took up his suggestions because of their heretic character. In 1832 he did not yet suspect that he was doomed to solitary research. He was certain that his views would be taken up and although he did not publish the previously described experiments, he was convinced that it was possible that some people would, by serious reading of his second series, consider the same conclusions (which are explicitly mentioned there) and try the same experiments, the attempts to observe the delayed action, which he intended to make. He could not publish the idea that his theory of delayed action should be tested, as at that time ideas did not count, only experiments counted (see above, p. 41). Nonetheless he was anxious to claim priority, even for an idea, and he wrote it in a note that he sealed and wished to be preserved by the Royal Society, in accord with a tradition inaugurated by Boyle and followed by quite a few, including Lavoisier. Here is the covering letter to his sealed note (MS, Royal Society archive), addressed from the Royal Institution, and dated 12 March 1832:

> ... It contains certain views of magnetism & electricity arising from my late investigations which are I believe peculiarly my own. I wish to work them out experimentally but as that will require time I am anxious to place a record of my views in a sure place so that if they prove important, a date may be referred to at which they may be proved to be my own.

Faraday's sealed letter is slightly different from those of Boyle and Lavoisier. There, too, priority of ideas is at stake, but the pretense is that a priority of facts is defended. Ideas have no claim of priority, we know. I do not know if Faraday was the first to place a sealed letter in official hands even though it contained no new fact. But, clearly, Faraday's case was delicate enough; his honor had been questioned too often already, and, induction or no induction, historical truth should be protected at least for the sake of one man's honor if not for its own sake.

Here, then, is the *Original Views* (MS, Royal Society archive):

> Certain of the results of the investigations which are embodied in the two papers entitled *Experimental Researches in Electricity*, lately read to the Royal Society, and the views arising therefrom, in connexion with other views and experiments, lead me to believe that magnetic action is progressive, and requires time; i.e. that when a magnet acts upon a distant magnet or piece of iron, the influencing cause (which I may for the moment call magnetism) proceeds gradually from the magnetic bodies, and requires time for its transmission, which will probably be found to be very sensible.
>
> I think also that I see reason for supposing that electric induction (of tension) is also performed in a similar progressive way.
>
> I am inclined to compare the diffusion of magnetic forces from a magnetic pole, to the vibrations upon the surface of disturbed water, or those of air in the phenomena of sound; i.e. I am inclined to think the vibration theory will apply to these phenomena, as it does to sound, and most probably to light.
>
> By analogy I think it may possibly apply to the phenomena of induction of electricity of tension also.
>
> These views I wish to work out experimentally: but as much of my time is engaged in the duties of my office, and as the experiments will therefore be prolonged, and may in their course be subject to the observation of others: I wish, by deposing this paper in the case of the Royal Society, to take possession as it were of a certain date, and so have right, if they are confirmed by experiments, to claim credit for the views at that date: at which time as far as I know no one is conscious of or can claim these but myself.
>
> M. Faraday

Royal Institution
12 March 1832

Faraday's statement of his view is very brief and not explanatory. He is here interested not to explain but to claim priority. The idea is this. Since it takes time for the lines to move in space, and since moving a magnet in space causes, we know, moving of its lines of force, it is possible that the moving of a magnet causes a *delayed* motion of its distant lines of force. Assume a magnet located in one place. It acts on another small magnet (placing it in the direction of the lines of force). The big magnet is now moved to another place. According to the accepted view, in the same moment that the big magnet is placed in the new location, the small magnet is forced to change its direction in accordance with the new situation. According to Faraday, only a little later will it respond; it will retain its *old* position a little longer. The lines of force do not move *rigidly* with their magnet but elastically. Therefore a curious phenomenon can be traced. If we move a magnet to and fro in the presence of a compass, then according to both the accepted and the new views the needle of the compass will oscillate. There is, however, a contrast: if Faraday is right, the oscillation of the needle will *not* be simultaneous with the oscillations of the magnet. The effect of an oscillating magnet spreads like waves. This is a crucial experiment between Faraday's and the old view. The experiment was first carried out only[8] by Marconi.

Why Faraday could not confirm it is pretty clear in retrospect. He was mistaken as to the velocity of the waves. He assumed it to be very small, while it is, for all we know, very big (the velocity of light). Soon he returned to the view that currents take time to evolve, and his error in this place may be the reason for his ill success. But he did not give up his view of magnetic waves. On the contrary. His refutation of the hypothesis that magnetic waves are very slow led him to the view that they are very quick and thus to the electro-magnetic theory of light. But I shall return to this later.

Another point is not less important. Faraday stated twice in his *Original Views* that he considered electric tension or electrostatic force to be of the same nature. This almost amounts to the assumption of an *electric field*. It is not precisely a theory of electric lines of force since it only says that the electrostatic action is delayed, progressive in time, but not that in a static case the forces are arranged in space as the magnetic forces are. The difference is minute; but not insignificant. And I think that it took time until Faraday realized that the propagation of the change of the electrostatic force in space

8. Hertz experimented with standing waves and, therefore, although it confirms one part of Faraday's view, it is not as straightforward a confirmation of the full idea of Faraday as Marconi's.

in a definite velocity suggests a field theory of electricity. My evidence is from his diary: if he had scruples as to publication of ideas, he had no scruples as to putting them in his diary; yet only a fortnight later he inserts there the idea of electric lines of force (p. 425, 26 March 1832; italics in the original):

> 398. Convinced that . . . if electricity still and needle moved in opposite directions, should become a magnet, for then the electricity and metal are relatively *moving* and that seems the only condition required . . .
>
> [Negative Results]
>
> 402. The lines or directions of force between 2 electrical conductors oppositely electrified may be called *electric curves* in analogy to *magnetic curves*. Do they exist also in the electric current wire?

It is of no significance to try to nail down the date of birth of an idea since ideas may develop like organisms. Nevertheless, my date for the birth of the idea of the field theory is 26 March 1832. In retrospect the 1831 theory was indeed a field theory; but this only happened to be, under the pressure of circumstances. It was a local affair. From now on Faraday is determined voluntarily to interpret facts according to the field view even when there is no urgent need to do so. He is after a new philosophy of nature. He had diverged too far from Newtonianism to attempt a compromise; he feels a need for a new world view, a new framework. He does not yet declare the idea that all natural phenomena are field phenomena, but in 1832 he tries to extend to field interpretation in line with this idea, which he declares only many years later.

### Fields and Matter

That forces travel is only one of many manifestations of the independence of force, although the most remarkable one. It is the most remarkable one for a few reasons. In the traditional theory there exists nothing in the material universe save space and time, matter, and its properties. The accepted view was that of Cotes: forces are properties of matter.[9] Now, if forces travel, they

9. See Alexandre Koyré, *Newtonian Studies* (Chicago, 1965), Appendix C.

are not properties, since we know that (as Democritus had stated) space is either filled with matter or void. The void has no property. Empty space is the same everywhere. Forces, therefore, must be bound to matter during travel. The more striking effect of forces travelling in time is that the force is, at least for a brief time, independent of any matter, whether placed in its starting point or in its end point. This is a philosophical topic—and one that belongs to traditional metaphysics. Not that the dealing with it had no influence on the development of physics. On the contrary, my aim here is to show how this purely philosophic topic affected the history of physics. Scientifically, delayed action was by no means a problem. Any wave phenomenon is certainly a delayed action, and prior to Faraday many phenomena were assumed to bear wave characteristics. But waves without a medium, without matter of which they are properties, were philosophically forbidden, forbidden by a certain metaphysical view of the universe. This is not surprising. It leaves one with alternatives. Faraday and his followers abandoned Newtonianism and dealt with delayed action from a point of view of a new principle; Gauss and his followers did not abandon Newtonianism even though they were perhaps ready to modify it ad hoc in order to incorporate in it the idea of delayed action by traveling forces—ignoring for a while the question of just how this can be done.

Much ink was used to support the myth that the British are more empirically minded and more conservative than the Continentals who are metaphysically minded and radical. This is my counter example. Let me quote Gauss's idea. It was written in a private letter, and for obvious reasons—he had not yet a scientific theory in which to incorporate the idea, and scientists were not to publish even mildly metaphysical views. At that very period Faraday was violating this iron rule and publishing bold metaphysical ideas; Gauss was behind on two counts. Here is the quotation from Gauss (Gauss, letter to Weber, 1845, published in 1867, *Werke*, 5, p. 627; translation by O'Rahilley, *Electromagnetics*, 1938, p. 226):

> I would doubtless have long since published my researches, were it not that at the time I gave them up I had failed to find what I regard as the keystone: namely the derivation of the additional forces—to be added to the mutual action of electrical particles at rest, when they are in mutual motion— *from the action which is propagated not instantaneously but in time as is the case with light.*

Faraday had priority both of having originated and of having published the idea of force propagated in space. How much Gauss was dependent on Faraday I do not intend to discuss; I only wish to point out the evident fact that both were inspired by the same developments. Gauss and his followers tried to modify Coulomb's theory because they tried to retain a fundamental Newtonian idea—that action is possible only between two bodies—while for Faraday the field was starting to take the place of matter. The great difference is between the idea that the action travels in space and the one that it travels in the medium. This will be manifest by contrasting the views of two authors on this issue. First comes Maxwell's view that he propagated before he gave up mechanism (*Treatise*, § 866, 2:492): "*We are unable to conceive of propagation in time* except as either a flight of a material *substance* through space or as a propagation of a condition of motion or stress in a *medium already existing in space* . . ." (This he said against the Gaussians, quoted below.)

Maxwell was a persistent and stubborn but never dogmatic mechanist. He believed in mechanism, he believed in the field theory, and he tried to argue for the consistency of this dual position. In this attempt he could not but conceive his mechanism as more fundamental, and this led him to his inability to conceive of a third possible motion, as quoted here. Of course when Maxwell failed to conceive of these two possibilities that he alleged to be exhaustive, he found another. But before he failed, he was a consistent and persistent mechanist who defended his view in an admirable way before he abandoned it; and his defense and failure left us with one of the most imaginative and important achievements of science.

Maxwell's failure convinced people of the importance of fields, while Faraday's success did not. That of course does not justify those people who ignored Faraday's new ideas altogether. Still, the historical fact is that many people waited for Faraday's ingenious discoveries to be explained mechanically and his wonderful theories to be reconciled with Newton's principles. Kelvin succeeded (see below, p. 272) in reconciling one of Faraday's heretic theories with accepted doctrines, and it soon gained public recognition. So people waited for further success. Here Maxwell rendered a great service. He took upon himself a genuinely philosophic task: he tried to examine the possibilities of reconciling scientific theory and philosophic principles. And he was so well versed both in the theory (of Faraday) and in the (mechanical) principles, and he was so able, that his failure showed mechanists (himself included) how hopeless their case was, how ad hoc and unrational the defense of the principles became. This philosophic approach, the stubborn yet nondogmatic attempt to stick to one's principles, was more fruitful than the attempt to adapt some of Faraday's ideas to the old framework, to alter the principles slightly, according to the good old tradition of surreptitious changes.

There is little doubt that the problem, the philosophic problem, that Maxwell was tackling was well known and widely felt. Even the possibility that there may be a motion not permitted by traditional principles was noted. I wish to illustrate this by quoting another passage, this time by C. Neumann, of the Gaussian school, who spoke of this something which is capable of moving in empty space without itself being matter "as a stimulus to motion or, to use a better expression, as a *command* which is given and emitted by one point and is received and obeyed by the other; we assume that this *command* requires a certain *time in order to travel* from the place of emission to the place of reception."

O'Rahilley, who quotes this passage (*Electromagnetics*, 1938, p. 186), comments that "the transcendental anthropomorphic language of Neumann is as irrelevant to the science of physics as is the elastic language of Maxwell." O'Rahilley points out in the same vein (p. 88) "that Faraday not only performed experiments but indulged in daring and rather metaphysical speculation" that he, O'Rahilley, rejects. In brief, O'Rahilley dislikes speculations, and the more daring they are the less he approves of them. At most he is willing to accept a speculation when it is well integrated in a scientific theory that he has to accept on its scientific merit.

This, I think, is the traditional attitude of most scientists. This, I think, is what prevents them from joining the avant-garde in spite of all their avant-garde outlook. For, the avant-garde develops and takes seriously daring ideas before they become scientific; indeed they render them scientific in order to make the multitude of scientists notice the novel and daring ideas.

At least this is historically true of Faraday and of Maxwell. I do not wish to imply that the majority cannot join the avant-garde, only that as long as the majority hate metaphysics they cannot. Moreover, it is not enough to develop a metaphysics, one has to be ready to be daring. This is exemplified by the case of Neumann, who definitely and consciously broke away from it by conceiving the command traveling in space free of matter. Now we do not agree nor are we supposed to agree that Neumann's command is an idea; but, he tells us, it is *not material* either. It was Faraday who, for the first time in the history of thought, assumes consciously something that was neither material nor spiritual. Neumann's general position was lost somewhere in the middle between the traditional view and this new one.

One can, of course, invert the argument and say that as Faraday's force travels in space it is an independent *thing*, even an *essence*, or whatnot. This, however, is evasive. In Faraday's time there was a definite view of all things as *spiritual or material things*, and there was an accepted theory that *every thing is either material or spiritual, and what is neither is not a thing but merely a property*. And Faraday for the first time entirely broke away from this view that had been unanimously accepted for about two and half millennia, declaring force to be a thing, or a property of empty space, or a cause that is neither matter nor spirit; in short, something that defies sacred traditional categories— one way or another.

The difference can be exemplified by the case of Hertz, who, when giving up an attempt to explain Maxwell's equation mechanically, declared them to be meaningless—in accord with the views of his former teacher Helmholtz; he could not imagine a true description of the world except for mechanics. When he accepted Faraday's *Original View* because, for the first time, he had confirmed the *Original View* and discovered (as he thought) in 1888 the delayed action—when he did so he was fully aware of the change, of the break with tradition. He then fully accepted Faraday's explanation of forces traveling in space, and he then fully contrasted it with traditional views (*Electric Waves,* London, 1893, p. 122):

> The most direct conclusion [of Hertz's experiment] is the
> confirmation of Faraday's view, according to which the electric
> forces are polarizations *existing independently in space*. For
> in the phenomena which we have investigated such forces
> persist in space even after the causes which have given rise
> to them have disappeared. *Hence forces are not simply parts
> or attributes of their causes*, but they correspond to changed
> conditions of space. The mathematical character of these
> conditions justifies us then in denoting them as polarizations,
> whatever the nature of these polarizations may be.

These are beautiful remarks, beautifully worded. Hertz is still noted amongst contemporary writers as an arch-antimetaphysician. But this is only a part of the story. It is easy to side with this thinker or that, and it is still easier to waver. I do not wish to praise Hertz because he finally landed on Faraday's side. Rather, I wish to make it clear that Faraday raised difficulties, both regarding his own views and, more so, regarding more traditional ones. And the difficulties were severe and deeply philosophical. Indeed, the strongest objection Faraday raised against his traditionalist opponents was from his philosophical skepticism and search for depth. This was marvelously expressed by his follower Oliver Heaviside (*Electrical Papers*, 1:337: "Even if were solve all matter into one kind, that kind will need explaining. And so on, for ever and ever deeper down into the pit at whose bottom the truth lies, without ever reaching it. For the pit is bottomless."

To conclude, we have thus far discussed the further breakaway from tradition of the *Original Views*: the field theories of 1821 and 1831 emphasize that forces exist in (empty) space; the 1832 theory and the *Original Views* assume forces traveling in space. Let us now discuss the *mode of action* of the traveling forces, note the novelty of the idea, and take account of the fundamental character of the problems that this gives rise to.

### Action at the Vicinity

Action at a distance was considered to be unsatisfactory by those who assumed it, Newton, Franklin, and others. Counter to their view of action at a distance, they considered the ideal explanation to be an assumption of *action by body impact* or *action by contact*. The rejection of the idea of action at a distance, of course, need not be a return to Descartes' idea of action by contact. Some attempts to return to action by contact, however, are historically important, namely certain attempts to create mechanical models of the aether, as well as statistical mechanics.

There is an ambiguity here—largely due to Maxwell's early belief in Cartesianism that led him to attempt a theory of action by contact; his inductivism and the prevalent atmosphere would have rendered any explicit contrast of his own views with those of Faraday bordering on an expression of disrespect which, of course, he was very anxious to avoid. When he later changed his views, he had little time to explain them since he died young. Meanwhile Faraday had receded into ancient history. Let me, then, clarify the situation briefly.

Faraday had a new theory of action, neither Cartesian, nor Newtonian. Unlike any Newtonian theory, it is not a theory of action at a distance, and like Descartes' theory, it is that of action in the vicinity. (It is also termed "near-action.") Action by contact as postulated by Descartes is one kind of action in the vicinity, it is action carried by a material agent, whether a medium or a moving body. To comprehend Faraday's non-Cartesian idea of action in the vicinity, we may, following Faraday's suggestion (see p. 209), conceive of the usual actions transmittable by the moving body or the elastic medium, and then think of these actions continuing to appear in the same way while the agent is annihilated, say, by God's act of will. Not that the annihilation causes the action to become action in the vicinity. Newtonian gravity would still be an action at a distance if nothing of the appearances changes after God's annihilation of the planets. (The action will be assumed of course to work on the images that are real though not material.) But if the stone that I throw at the glass house will not change its behavior though its matter be annihilated, its action by contact in the vicinity will become an action in the vicinity but not by contact.

But we must notice two points: (1) Although Hertz's experiment refutes a theory of action at a distance (Coulomb's theory) and although it makes it hardly credible (though not inconceivable) that a simple mechanical theory of electricity is possible, it does not establish one theory of action in the vicinity. Nor can it refute an irrefutable theory like "all action is at a distance." (2) Two theories in particular were available in Hertz's time, both of action in the vicinity, which assume the idea of free forces traveling in space. The one theory is indeed that which Hertz tested by his experiment and it is Maxwell's development of Faraday's view of space being full of forces in each instance. The view is that once a change occurs in the field of force it spreads in all directions with the velocity of light. The change is localized at first, and immediately spreads. The second theory, of Gauss, Riemann, Neumann, and others, is also a theory of action in the vicinity, and thus somewhat Faradayan, but it does not assume fields of force, only forces emitted from one body, freely moving to another body, and thus causing the change. Thus this approach is a compromise between Faraday and Newton. It assumes that only bodies can act on bodies, they do not give actions or forces a full status of independence, of substantiality; but they do, by the force of Faraday's experiments, deviate from tradition so far as to enable forces temporary independence, some freedom, though only as messengers. I think it is fair to say that Gauss and his followers were rather forced to accept a Faradayan view while the Maxwellians wanted to accept as much of Faraday's ideas as they could. Both had mechanistic scruples; but only Maxwell and his followers, notably Poynting, Heaviside, Hertz, and Einstein, ultimately became antimechanists. But the only persistent Faradayans of our century are Einstein and Schrödinger. And the main idea of Faraday that they accepted is the entire breakaway from mechanism, the entire freedom from any assumption of matter. This idea is the boldest and most ingenious view of Faraday—his *anti*materialism: *matter has to be explained*.

# 5    Faraday's Methodology

Faraday had to reconcile the doctrine of prejudice with his tendency to speculate. The doctrine of prejudice plainly forbids all speculation. When he speculated, he probably did not think he was seriously violating it. When he violated the inductive style of presentation, he had before him concrete (presentational) problems which he thus wished to solve, rather than methodological principle. But sooner or later the principles of the received methodology had to be considered, and his deviation became too obvious to overlook. It should be remembered that the scientific language in Faraday's time was highly standardized. (So it is to some degree now, but only in the attempt to appear as professional as possible.) To break from a standard language is by no means an easy task, and it may cause misunderstandings of an obvious kind. When Davy said that he found no solution that can be decomposed but that in which the solvent is water, everyone knew that he had announced more than a mere fact; that he made a hypothesis ("water is essential to electrolysis"). When Faraday said that he could not find diamagnetism in gases, people read him in the same manner, namely that he implied a similar hypothesis (see *Experimental Researches in Electricity*, 3:488), even though he had said previously that he thought that all matter has some diamagnetism, and although by then he used to make all his conjectures pretty explicit. This kind of difficulty of communication engaged him constantly and kept him from delving too deeply into more fundamental points of methodology.

Faraday frequently explained patiently the simplest of his fundamental ideas about matter and space in various papers and in private letters. His reader's difficulties were always before his eyes. He tried to introduce his reader to his own mode of thought, his errors, his trains of ideas. He often wrote with a great simplicity, grace, and utmost kindness. The beauty of his character is expressed in his writings no less than the beauty of his ideas in every case in which he succeeded in controlling his immense pedantry. He had a personal style and a thoughtful consideration both for his reader and for other writers; sometimes, regrettably, even to an obsession. But even this is quite understandable: they were so sensitive he could hardly argue with them without offending them. Yet he appeased them all. And hardly anything that he wrote was not original. In fact only in one paper did he confirm someone else's discovery (of self-induction), and despite the tremendous originality of that paper, he attributed everything in it to the original discoverer. That his researches so seldom refer to other people's work is seldom his fault: he worked almost entirely in isolation, and attacking that isolation was his chief object, indeed, obsession.

## A New Trouble

In 1821 Sir Humphry Davy accused Faraday of having plagiarized from Wollaston. In 1834 Dr. John Davy accused Faraday of having plagiarized from his brother Sir Humphry. As the case with Wollaston was highly problematic, so it was with Davy. And both contributed to Faraday's development of a new style of scientific writing.

This example sounds most improbable. And so I should say this: There was another incident of a possible charge of plagiarism (involving the wrong dating of an issue of a journal), and quite an insignificant one.[1] Faraday was much annoyed but cleared it up with much unnecessary fuss. One reason for the importance of the charges for Faraday is that he handled them on the level of moral principle. How much Dalton owed to Higgins was debated in his day and in later days; the debate is still open. He did not take part in the debate, and his honesty was curiously never at stake in his own lifetime or later.

There is not the slightest doubt that (a) Faraday was utterly honest and (b) that he was utterly wrong in stooping so low as to defend his honesty. We

---

1. The plagiarism case here alluded to has led to the tradition, says S. P. Thompson (*Michael Faraday*, p. 267), of viewing verbal communications to learned societies as publication. I do think that this is an exaggeration; anyway, with the development of scientific communication this innovation became inevitable. The problem incidentally was already raised by Boyle; see reference in n. 15, p. 41, above.

are fortunate, I think, that he did defend it. He was, indeed, the opposite of Dalton. He was more fervently honest than that placid old Quaker, and therefore his honesty could be easily challenged. He was ambitious and vulnerable —as Dalton never was—and so he tempted malice. Also, he was so much more concerned and so much more talented. His concern and engagement led to general improvements. Even his fervent conservatism was for him an instrument of social reform. He really asked for involved cases of accusation; involuntarily but conspicuously he posed as raw material for any *cause célèbre.*

The problem that he faced when he was preparing his paper on magneto-electric rotation in 1821 was a problem of acknowledgment of an idea. This is in itself a revolution. True, theoreticians did acknowledge or were supposed to acknowledge ideas. But even there it was problematic, since not the idea was significant but rather its foundation on experiment, its acceptance by analysis, and so on. In experiments proper, the honor of having performed them was given to the one who had performed them and solely and entirely because he had experimented and published. Undoubtedly, one experimenter was praised more than the other; but this is a kind of afterthought; it was less important that one was praised highly or in passing—the main thing was to be mentioned at all, to have made a contribution, however minute, to the stock of human knowledge.

The code of acknowledgment was determined by the Royal Society in its foundation. The regulations of the society had been proposed by its first president, Lord Brouncker, and seconded by Robert Boyle. The defense of the code can be found in Boyle's publications of that period. He says explicitly that acknowledgment and the like are bait to make people experiment and publish: make it easy and rewarding, and more people will experiment and publish. This, of course, discriminates in favor of the rich.

Opponents of the Royal Society complained about it. Thomas Hobbes, the only real giant amongst the opponents of the Royal Society, said in his *Considerations Upon His Own Reputation* (p. 53), everyone who has enough money can buy expensive telescopes and furnaces, but not everyone can write a book like Hobbes on the nature of things. And adversaries of the Royal Society repeated variants of this remark (see Isaac Disraeli's delightful "Calamities and Quarrels in the Royal Society").

Somehow, the criticism was not developed. Of course, a rich man can, in addition to purchasing laboratories, hire hordes of research assistants. So did Tycho Brahe, and so did Robert Boyle himself. One of Boyle's assistants was Robert Hooke, who soon became a leading scientist in his own right. On the Continent doctors were often engaged to ghostwrite doctoral dissertations, some of which included new experiments (however insignificant). Yet the idea of purchasing discoveries and thus gaining immortality has never been attacked.

Not that it has never happened. Davy himself, as a young man, was employed by a phony research institute, designed merely to finance his research in return for the claim of his supporter for coauthorship of his papers. The case terminated abruptly, and Davy was whisked off to London to the newly founded Royal Institution. Such cases still happen, even in our own day and age. Somehow they manage to be overlooked. Quite rightly, I suppose.

Sociologically insignificant as these cases may be, they may become intriguing in some unusual circumstances, such as those forcing us to reflect on the difference between servant and assistant: we may find out that young Michael Faraday was hired as a servant and proved to be a very competent assistant. The master refused, in this case, to set his servant free, violated the rules of the game, and spoiled the game entirely, for himself as well as for a good many people; just like the inventor of professional "sport."

The clash about the liquefaction of chlorine in 1823 led to insinuations and threw doubt on the character of a man whose obsessive aim was to keep his record meticulously clean. When Davy's brother repeated the insinuation in public many years later, in 1834, Faraday felt obliged to publish a reply that is an exact and detailed description of the story. The story needs no further comment; I only wish to present it sketchily from a new angle, namely its influence on Faraday's writing career. Here is first Faraday's description of the background to the incident (*Experimental Researches in Chemistry and Physics*, p. 136):

> Having to give personal attendance on both the morning and the afternoon chemical lectures, my time was very fully occupied. Whenever any circumstance relieved me in part from the duties of my situation, I used to select a subject for research, and try my skill upon it . . . . The absence of Sir Humphry Davy from town having relieved me from a part of my laboratory duty, I took advantage of the leisure and the cold weather . . .

Davy had suggested to Faraday some experimental preparations. As Faraday took pains to prove, Davy never told him what experimental results he anticipated. It is also clear from the above quotation that he had not *instructed* him to experiment, since the poor man could experiment only in his spare time, even though he had very little time to spare, when Davy was out of town. Clearly, also, Faraday had not asked for the suggestion: Davy simply made it to Faraday.

So Faraday took advantage of the leisure and the cold weather and started experimenting. (In the original paper he says, "I took advantage of the late cold weather.")

He employed a new method of compression, and liquefied chlorine. It was then quite late in the evening. Davy happened to return to the Royal Institution, and with him came his friend Dr. Paris, who later wrote his biography. Dr. Paris noticed with his sharp eyes some oil in a glass tube. He scolded the assistant-servant for not having cleaned the tube properly.

Faraday does not explain. He breaks the seal of the tube. The oil disappears, to Dr. Paris's great surprise. Dr. Paris knew the smell of chlorine, no doubt; and one can smell chlorine even if one has a severe cold; he well understood the situation. He ran to Davy and told him the story. "Upon mentioning the circumstances to Sir Humphry Davy after dinner," he tells us, "he appeared much surprised; and after a few moments of apparent abstraction [what a nice expression!] he said, 'I shall inquire about this experiment tomorrow.'"

Well, it was too late to do anything, and the two envious friends went to bed. In the morning Dr. Paris found a note on the table in the room where he slept. The note reads

> Dear Sir,—the *oil* you noticed yesterday turns out to
>           be liquid chlorine.
>                    Yours, faithfully
>                              M. Faraday

It just "turns out" so.

Faraday wrote a paper and the declining, miserable, neurotic Davy added a note. The note states (a) that he had "desired" Mr. Faraday to make the experiment; (b) that he had anticipated three alternative results, one of which came true; (c) it also contains a general description of the new method employed by Faraday to liquefy chlorine.

This was sufficient to spoil the game. Davy desired and anticipated and therefore the experiment was his. As he wrote in a private letter (quoted by Faraday, *Experimental Researches in Chemistry and Physics*, p. 139, note),

"The experiment on the condensation of gases were made under my direction and I had anticipated, theoretically, all the results."

This high-handed tone was new to the scientific community; and so were directions to perform experiments. At that very time professional chemistry began. Firms paid poor chemists for making chemical analyses. Prior to 1831 Faraday himself, when very hard up, used to make experiments under such directions. But these were not scientific investigations, and there was no theoretical anticipation of results. With Davy the story was different. Faraday's comment on Davy's disturbing claim is, as usual, straight as a die—very proud and very humble: "It is evident that he considered the subject his own; but I am glad that . . . he never said he informed me of his expectations." That the subject was Davy's own, Faraday was ready to admit ("I have never . . . denied . . . Davy's right to his share, etc."). But Davy, in his attempt to grasp a straw, claimed that Faraday was his own—assistant or help or servant; and on this Faraday does not even comment.

But the matter is more delicate. Davy anticipated the results. Did he also prescribe the complete circumstances of the experiment so as to have had the right to claim that Faraday only did the menial job? Faraday used a new method of obtaining high pressure that Davy, in his note added to Faraday's paper, describes in general terms. This description is quite redundant, since it is only a repetition of Faraday's own description of his own application of the method, except that Faraday spoke of chlorine and Davy on gases in general. Evidently Davy tried to give the impression—without making an explicit claim—that the method was his; and by that showed that it was not. Indeed, Faraday asserted that Davy gave him no instruction concerning pressure. Davy insisted that the discovery was his. Faraday was reluctant to claim priority, but even less so to give way to his unjust master. He found an ingenious solution (beginning of the "Historical Statement," *Experimental Researches in Chemistry and Physics*): he decided to search in experimental papers for such circumstantial descriptions that would enable him to claim that their authors developed the method of liquefying gases, perhaps liquefied gases even though unwittingly. This would be an elegant compromise. To his surprise he found that chlorine had been liquefied over twenty years previously, consciously and intentionally; the discoverer soon communicated with him, claiming his rights.

But the problem of principle was not thus solved. If experiments can be anticipated, and if anticipation effects claims of priority, then anticipations must be laid bare. If Faraday did not see this for himself, poor Paris, in his embarrassment and catching a straw in the wind, showed this to him. It was in no better context than his embarrassment with Faraday that Paris, the biographer of Davy, had to argue from the importance of anticipations. For he tells the story of the chlorine incident and quotes Faraday's laconic note (quoted above) in order to prove that it was Davy, not Faraday, who made the discovery. For, he argued, the note of Faraday shows that when experimenting Faraday was not aware of what he was doing and only later tested his own two conjectures concerning it as reported in his paper.

It seems hardly conceivable that so pathetic an argument requires comment (as I said, the smell of chlorine is not easy to overlook, and this fact is rather common knowledge). But Faraday was obsessive. To begin with, Faraday put the story slightly differently. "I puzzled out for myself in the manner Dr. Paris described that the oil I had obtained was condensed chlorine," he says (p. 138) in a gush of sarcasm which is so amusing, so straightfaced and humble, so historically accurate and proper, yet so harsh on the miserable Paris. Then he tells us of his "thoughts at that moment" in which Paris entered (p. 138), and the thought was, as it happens, that the oil was chlorine!

So much for Davy's accusation concerning chlorine. While at it he also accused Faraday of disloyalty and disrespect toward Davy, his old benefactor. The story is simple: Davy had said he had discovered no solvent for electrolysis other than water. Literally this is doubtlessly the truth; but Faraday read this as the hypothesis: only water can be an electrolytic solvent. And he attributed this hypothesis to Davy and refuted it. Davy's brother was infuriated, claiming Faraday should have read Davy literally. Faraday answered (*Experimental Researches in Electricity*, 2:215): "*Why, there can be no doubt that if I have proved that water was the only* [*electrolytic medium*], *Dr. Davy would have claimed the discovery for his brother*"; he would have insisted on deviating from the literal meaning. This indeed, was quite a common practice, and though Faraday does not say so, he must have been aware of this fact.

From then on Faraday wrote in order to be read literally. He was not successful at first (see p. 77, above), but sooner or later he was. Indeed, this effort to be read literally is the hallmark of Faraday's style.

## Faraday's Style

Faraday's interest in matters of style was very early. Here is a letter to Abbott of 31 December 1816. It deals with the style of these youths' private communications, and with the problems he was facing (*Life and Letters*, 1:235):

> I must confess that I have always found myself unable to arrange a subject as I go on, as I perceive many others apparently do ... I always find myself obliged, if my argument is of the least importance, to draw up a plan of it on paper, and fill in the parts by recalling them to mind, either by association or otherwise; and this done, I have a series of major and minor heads in order, and from these I work out my matter. Now this method ... introduces a dryness and stiffness into the style of the piece composed by it; for the parts come together like bricks, one flat on the other, and though they may fit, yet they have the appearance of too much regularity; and it is my wish, if possible, to become acquainted with a method by which I may write my exercise in a more natural and easy progression. I would, if possible, imitate a tree in its progression ... where every alteration is made with so much care and yet effect, that though the manner is constantly varied, the effect is precise and determined.
>
> ... I beg that you will communicate to me your method of composing; or, if it is done spontaneously and without an effort on your part, that you will analyse your mental proceedings whilst writing a letter, and give me an account of that part which you conceive conducive to so good an end. ...

The beginning of a new style can be detected in Faraday's "On the Existence of a Limit to Vaporization" of 1826. The first half of the paper is purely theoretical, and the second half is *not* a description of his tests of the theory but rather a discussion of their relevance to his theory, which is so presented as to enable people to repeat them even though the description of the necessary circumstances is made by the way. This is a striking innovation —and a new style, which was later developed independently by others. Faraday himself did not develop this new style. I do not know why. I suppose that he was persuaded not to experiment with style, and forgot all about it until he met with the concrete problems of style mentioned in the previous section —which led him to a completely different direction of stylistic innovation. That Faraday's new style was a great innovation is, in itself, a significant historical fact. Let me quote here two interesting comments on the novelty of Faraday's style, one from a friend of his, Liebig, the other from his greatest follower, Maxwell. They show not only the striking novelty of his style but also his triumph. Here is, first, Liebig's comment (quoted in *The Faraday Lectures*, p. 79):

> I have heard mathematical physicists deplore that Faraday's records of his labours were difficult to read and understand, *that they often resembled rather abstracts from a diary*. But the fault was theirs, not Faraday's; to physicists who have approached physics by the road of chemistry [i.e., to Liebig himself], Faraday's memoirs sound like an admirably beautiful music.

Bacon, Boyle, and Hooke recommended writing in the form of a diary; so did Priestley, whose style was admired by Lavoisier, by Goethe, and many others. We hear from Liebig, however, that scientists were in difficulty to understand Faraday's notes because they were actually written in the form of a diary. This is not serious, but it does refer to a true innovation. In his *Experimental Researches in Electricity*, Faraday did describe his anticipations, his trains of reasoning, his confirmation, and his disappointments; he tells us about surprises, and about his hopes. He tells us about the significance of many experiments that he describes. His observations are used as arguments pro and con. *It is not the diary method that others disliked, it is the dialectic method of the diary*.

It is interesting to see Maxwell's comparison of the style of Ampère, the great inductivist, and that of Faraday. (Maxwell does not tell us, however, that Ampère's method of presentation was once universally accepted.) Faraday's method of trial and error (or action and reaction as he called it) is a more adequate description of the actual procedure than Ampère's inductive description, he admits (*Treatise on Electricity and Magnetism*, 2, § 528); nevertheless, scientific writing should be cast in Ampère's inductive language. Maxwell had recognized that Faraday was isolated because of his revolutionary approach Still, he thinks "it was perhaps for the advantage of science that Faraday . . . was . . . left at leisure to do his proper work, to coordinate his ideas with his facts . . ."

Maxwell's own style, I may mention in passing, was far from being inductive. But, to return to our topic, let us notice this: Maxwell discussed style of presentation as an insignificant marginal item; according to Liebig,

Faraday's style was made a big issue of. No doubt, the big issue was Faraday's heresy, not his style. Even today heresies are confused with other faults; but today a heresy could hardly be confused with a faulty style: today style is not so problematic as in the 1830s.

Faraday developed his style as he developed his views of science. And these became increasingly heretic. Slowly he developed new ideas about science, which are very modern—more modern than those of all his disciples, for example—up to, and excluding, Einstein.

Today we all agree that scientists employ their imagination—that Newton, for example, was highly imaginative. Yet, we know, Newton did not like to speak of his own imagination, nor did his biographers prior to Sir David Brewster (1831). Faraday stressed the fact that he tried to employ his power of imagination, and even systematically. This was noticed by most of his followers. His main pupil, Tyndall, wrote essays on the "Use and Limit of Imagination in Science." Today we take it naturally; then it was a revolution. Van't Hoff devoted his inaugural address to it as late as in 1878. Science was freed, once and for all, from its inductive basis. From then on experiment took a new place, as a check on the imagination, not as a substitute for it. Faraday's major contribution to scientific method is this: it does not matter where you start—if you have an opinion, try to test it, and proceed in this way. A note should be added to gratify priority hunters. The idea itself is not Faraday's; I suppose it was first presented in 1661 by Robert Boyle. Faraday's contribution is double. First, he spread this idea, through writings of his own and of his disciples. Second, and more impressive, he practiced it systematically—which is more than many scientists do even today. Here is a letter that the mature Faraday wrote to a boy in his teens, who had written to him suggesting to him a new theory of matter (*Faraday Lectures*, p. 118):

Royal Institution 16th June, 1834

Sir,

I have no hesitation in advising you to experiment in support of your views, because, whether you confirm them or confute them, good must come from your exertions.

With regard to the views themselves, I can say nothing about them, except that they are useful in exciting the mind to inquiry. A very brief consideration of the progress of experimental philosophy will show you that it is a great disturber of pre-formed theories.

I have thought long and closely about the theories of attraction and of particles and atoms of matter, and the more I think (in association with experiment) the less distinct does my idea of an atom or particle of matter become.

I am, Sir, your etc.

## The Doctrine of Prejudice

The permanent element in Faraday's methodology (as we find it in all his papers and notes of lectures) was Dr. Isaac Watts's doctrine of prejudice that he accepted lock, stock, and barrel. One can find it propounded in his "Inertia of the Mind" (*Life and Letters*, 1:261), which he read in 1818, and in his "Mental Education" (end of *Experimental Researches in Chemistry and Physics*), which he read in 1855 and I shall now briefly discuss.

The peculiar point about the doctrine of prejudice is its naïve and sincere view of enlightenment. Perhaps this was what made Faraday adhere to it so tenaciously. In his "Mental Education" he identifies education with *self*-education, and he promises that *everyone who could train himself to resist prejudice could be as successful as he was* (p. 483).

The paper is largely devoted to attacks on spiritualism. He explains there why spiritualistic table-turning and clairvoyance are not sciences, offering us the feeling that in this explanation hides the secret of the greatness of science. One reason he gives very clearly: the pseudoscientists choose favorable evidence to support their favorite theories (their prejudices) not seeing that only results of tests may be scientifically considered as evidence. The second reason is more important. He does not state it explicitly, but he tries to show very clearly, and by ample use of arguments, emotionally heavily charged. He severely censures the pseudoscientists for not attempting to solve any existing scientific problem; particularly, he urges them to correct some of the scientists' mistakes. This, I suppose, is a new and very important methodological element. It amounts to saying more than what Faraday usually said, namely that we start with hypotheses rather than with experiments. It says that we start with problems, attack them by hypotheses, which we then attack by experiment.

The last observation that I want to make on Faraday's "Mental Education" is this: he makes some historical remarks on the theories of his predecessors Davy and Wollaston, whom he genuinely admired. But he refers not only to their successes but also to their failures, their "errors." I do not know how to impress on my reader the novelty and revolutionary approach of this description, but I can only say again that most books on the history of science that I happen to have read, and even recent ones, have not yet adopted Faraday's approach—at least not fully. (When they do point out an error, they do it scornfully and with an incredible arrogance.)

Faraday's conclusion is rather platitudinous, I am afraid (though very revolutionary for any indictivist). He finds that *all men err, even scientists.* And, he repeatedly and emphatically asks the public, why should they not be permitted to err? (At the time it was actually forbidden for scientists to err!) Beneath this question one can find a great struggle in Faraday's own mind. Let me present it in this way: what, to Faraday's opinion, was more important, fact or theory? I cannot answer this question in general, and I cannot answer it for Faraday. However, I think it is quite clear that according to any theory of prejudice, fact is predominant. Boyle and Newton, Locke and Watts, Faraday and Maxwell would have to admit that theories are only "superstructures" that are stronger the more they are founded on more facts, that they are significant merely to the extent that they are reflections of our knowledge of fact.

But Faraday could not yield to such an opinion, and he therefore vacillated all his life. There are two reasons why he could not accept the idea that fact is predominant. One reason is very obvious and simple. This experimentalist, the crowned king of experimentalists, not only found all his facts by being led by hypotheses, but more than that, his interest was never in mere facts. From 1831 onward he was guided by one problem, a theoretical problem, which he ventured to solve.

The other reason why he could not agree with the emphasis on facts is because he knew very well that *there exist no hard and fast facts.* All believers in induction, from Bacon to Keynes, accept facts "as they are." Faraday's approach was completely different. If he had a theory, he was as stubborn as a mule about it. If Mother Nature said "No," he argued with her: theoretically, it must be so, he said (*Experimental Researches in Electricity*, § 190). Most of his experiments were carried out again and again for years, in spite of failures as clear as any experiment can ever be. But, of course, the last word was Mother Nature's. If he was refuted experimentally, he was only too willing to admit it publicly and he was candidly thankful to his critics. Yet he could always reinterpret failure in order to elicit from it a new sign of hope. It is only a wonder that he more often got the desired "yes" than the persistent "no." There is no explanation for this. Kohlrausch said: "He smells the truth"

(*Discoverer*, p. 55). Bence Jones speaks of his unfailing intuition and Helmholtz of his inconceivable instinct. His technique, however, was to employ the theory of Kant, Whewell, and Duhem, the theory that we *interpret* facts in the light of our theories: he was a master of reinterpretation. *There exist no hard and fast facts* in the sense that it is for us to use our faculty of judgment and decide whether the given fact is or is not a sufficient test for our hypothesis, and if it is, where we should try to locate the error.

But there exists an incoherence here. The doctrine of prejudice, or inductivism in general, is a passive theory. It tells us to accept facts completely, and to accept a theory, to commit ourselves to it, exactly according to the measure of probability afforded to it by facts. Inductivism never raises the problem of making a hypothesis, or of reinterpreting facts. Since Bacon, all inductivists, even Boyle, supposed themselves to be operating with all the possible theories, ignoring the fact that in reality we operate only with all the available theories, not with all the possible ones. And inventing a theory and suggesting it to the public even though it was not confirmed was considered pride; inventing a new interpretation to evade a refutation was prejudice. For what was noticed was not the act of invention, but rather the fact that the inventor propagates his hypotheses, often in the face of facts, that he falls in love with the children of his own imagination, that he is "prejudiced." And Faraday indeed was in love with his own views. And he well knew it.

The only way out that Faraday could see is to assure his readers that he offered his views for further consideration, in order to enable people to use them and to criticize them. He reiterated that he had no intention of making propaganda for his views. In fact, while presenting his speculations to the public he made propaganda against speculation—which quite understandably caused confusion among his readers, including his chief biographer Bence Jones. His propaganda against speculation was, of course, based on his view that only facts are reliable—which implied that he was making propaganda against all theories as such. And this even increased the confusion. However, by reliable facts he meant facts free of interpretation, and he believed in the existence of such facts vehemently but purely in the abstract.

There was schism in his inductivism. He himself was always interested equally in theories and in facts. In 1818, he still believes in the naïve view of unity of all intellectual activity—the unity of discovering and theorizing, of making pure and applied science, and of science and morals (*Life and Letters*, 1:255):

> The wise man, however, will avoid partial views of things.
> He will not, with the miser, look to gold and silver as the
> only blessings of life; nor will he, with the cynic, snarl at
> mankind for preferring them to copper and iron. He will
> contemplate society as the proper state of man, and its artificial
> but necessary institutions and *principles will appear to him
> the correct and advantageous result of natural causes.* That
> which is convenient is that which is useful, and *that which is
> useful is that which is valuable. It is in the relative position
> of things one to the other that they are to be considered and
> estimated*; and whilst a man makes use of them no otherwise
> than wisely to supply his wants and virtuous pleasures, the
> avaricious trader has no reason to call him a fool of nature,
> nor the moral philosopher to name him the victim of society.

Even when he avidly hoped that theory and fact unite, his emphasis was on theory; it is, indeed, on such a note that he chose to conclude his series of chemical lectures in the City Philosophical Society (*Life and Letters*, 1:259). At that time, his views were orthodox inductivist, merely with an emphasis clearly on theory. And by theory he meant, as everybody else, what we should now call highly confirmed hypotheses. Yet, of Newtonian optics, which he had accepted in 1816 as "the conclusion that is now generally received," he says in the same lecture of 1819 from which the quotation below was taken that it is "purely hypothetical," "yet undecided." He does not yet accept the newly announced undulatory theory of light, but, probably seeing it in a serious competitor to the old theory, the latter becomes a "hypothesis" rather than a "conclusion." The change had tremendous results; it finally led him to discover the *transitory character of all theories.* The following is perhaps a most characteristic expression of Faraday's views (p. 310):

> Ever since the world began, opinion has changed with
> the progress of things; *and it is something more than absurd
> to suppose that we have a sure claim to perfection, or that we
> are in possession of the highest stretch of intellect which has
> or can result from human thought. . . . and yet with all this
> practical evidence of the fallibility of our opinions, all, and
> none more than philosophers, are ready to assert the real truth
> of their opinions . . .*

*. . . All I wish to point out is . . . the necessity of cautious and slow decision . . . and the continual guard against prejudices . . .*

The more Faraday was convinced of the transient nature of theories and of his colleagues' resistance to change, the more he became convinced of the doctrine of prejudice and of the supremacy of facts; the more he got involved in his work, the more he became convinced in the impossibility of dividing fact from theory and of the subsequent supremacy of theory. And the conflict deepened all his life.

An instance from his work following his discovery of his field theory of 1832 will be as good as any. We remember that he tried, in 1832, to view all phenomena as instances of fields. Since electrochemistry involves transport of matter along lines of electric force, his attention centered now on electrochemistry. To begin with, he says (*Experimental Researches in Electricity*, § 478) that "the general facts of electro-chemical decomposition are agreed to by nearly all who have written on the subject," while (§ 479) "the views of men of science vary much as to the nature of the action by which these effects are produced." He therefore tested the suggested theories and refuted some of them by most skilful experiments. But this did not induce him to stick to generalizations. And although he was not at all certain as to its truth, he was "bold" and "hasty" enough to present a theory to the scientific world (§ 563) "wishing . . . to submit it to the *test of publication and discussion.*"

So far so good; indeed most impressively bold and avant-garde; and it does not even matter if he hoped that his theory (§ 497) "might be considered, not as an increase of that which is doubtful, but real addition to this branch of knowledge [i.e., electrolysis]." His self-assurance grows, and with it his emphasis clearly returns to theory rather than to fact.

It has to be remembered that his theory of electrolysis (as all his theories) was not accepted for a very long time. (This gives some justification to his doctrine of prejudice.) In spite of his refutation of it, the voltaic contact theory of the pile continued to gain popularity and its followers continuously made ad hoc corrections to it to escape the refutations. "Not feeling . . . that the problem has yet been solved, I venture to give the view which seems to me sufficient, upon *known principles*, to account for the effect" (§ 616).

But people still were not convinced. So he developed his theory (1834) to such an extent as to make the contact theory unable to account for the new "general facts" that he discovered by testing his theory. These most severe tests that he put this theory to really made him believe that his theory is doubtlessly true, or, as he said, actually removed the previous "doubtful knowledge" (§ 876):

> Such knowledge is the early morning light of every advancing science, and is essential to its development; but the man [Faraday] who is engaged in dispelling that which is deceptive in it, and revealing more clearly that which is true, is as useful in his place, and as necessary to the general progress of the science, as he [Volta] who first broke through the intellectual darkness, and opened a path into knowledge before unknown to man.

With the greatest appreciation for the new tone of this passage, which makes Faraday's first indication of the new and less intolerant approach toward refuted theories, I cannot help regretting that he forgot what he said fifteen years earlier about scientists' inability to view with doubt their own ideas.

It would be unfair to suppress the fact that he wrote the following lines (1838; § 1377) that contradict almost all he said about methodology, though it would be nice to think that he wrote them only in the heat of the bitter struggle between his theory and the contact theory.

> The latter is the view which, being adopted by Poisson and Biot, is also, I believe, that generally received; and it associates such two dissimilar things, as the ponderous air and the subtile and even hypothetical fluid or fluids of electricity, by gross mechanical relations; by bonds of mere static pressure. My theory, on the contrary, sets out at once by connecting the electric forces with the particles of matter; *it derives all its proofs, and even its origin in the first instance, from experiment*; and then, without any further assumption, seems to offer at once a full explanation of these and many other singular, peculiar, and, I think, heretofore unconnected effects.

Among the merits of his theory he does not mention its resistance to his most exciting tests, but its origin—the experiments by which he tested it.

I really could not find out how he reverted to Bacon's views. Perhaps his quest for certainty and his inability to be satisfied merely with generalizations pushed him to this view, and perhaps he was influenced by his friend Herschel, whose book on induction was published in 1831, the year in which Faraday started his *Experimental Researches*. In any case, Faraday's critical approach did not allow him to persist in this attitude. In the introduction to the first volume of his *Experimental Researches in Electricity* (1839), which includes the last quotation (1838), where he acknowledges some criticism against him and rejects some, he says,

> There are, no doubt, occasions on which I have not felt
> the force of the remarks, but time and the progress of science will
> best settle such cases; and, although I cannot honestly say that
> I *wish* to be found in error, yet I do fervently hope that the
> progress of science in the hands of its many zealous present
> cultivators will be such, as by giving us new and other
> developments, and laws more and more general in their
> applications, will even make me think that what is written
> and illustrated in these experimental researches belong to the
> by-gone parts of science.

The thoughtfulness as well as the depth of feelings expressed here are remarkable. He was the first man after Boyle who saw that theories, even those that are the best of their age, are apt to become obsolete. And this he saw in the midst of a society that was familiar with ample instances to "prove" the contrary. His great sorrow about his contention that his theories may become obsolete springs from his conviction that in this case he would have been found "in error" and thus "prejudiced."

But the doctrine of prejudice, after all, being self-contradictory, is like the biblical manna in which everyone can find a different taste. And Faraday's taste always was critical; "prejudiced" or not "prejudiced," he allowed the possibility of having been erroneous; and in 1840, in a letter to his friend de la Rive concerning his theory of the pile, he is more careful, even though he still thinks he is right (*Life and Letters*, 2:108):

> The constancy of [those] on the opposite side made me,
> however, think it not unnecessary to accumulate and record
> evidence of the truth, and I have therefore written two papers

> . . . My object in experimenting was, as I am sure yours has
> always been, not so much to support a given theory as to learn
> the natural truth. And *having gone to the question unbiassed*
> *by any prejudices,* I cannot imagine how anyone whose mind
> is not preoccupied by a theory, or a strong bearing to a theory,
> can take part with that of contact against that of chemical action.
> However, I am perhaps wrong saying so much, for, as *no one*
> *is infallible,* and as the experience of past times may teach us
> to doubt a theory which seems to be most unchangeably
> established, so we cannot say what the future may bring forth
> in regard to these views.

But if theories are but opinions and views, does it not mean, to return
to my question, the fact is more important than theory? And indeed, in the
same year, 1840, he presents a view that is strikingly similar to Boyle's
opinion, much more so than in 1819 (*Experimental Researches in Electricity,*
2:266):

> A man who advances what he thinks to be new truths, and
> to develope principles which profess to be more consistent
> with the laws of nature than those already in the field, is
> liable to be charged, first with self-contradiction; then with the
> contradiction of facts; or he may be obscure in his expression,
> and so justly subject to certain queries; or he may be found
> in non-agreement with opinions of others. The first and second
> points are very important, and every one subject to such charges
> must be anxious to be made aware of, and also to set himself
> free from or acknowledge them; the third is also a fault to be
> removed if possible; the fourth is a matter of but small
> consequence in comparison with the other three; for *every*
> *man who has the courage, not to say rashness, of forming an*
> *opinion of his own, thinks it better than any from which he*
> *differs, so it is only deeper investigation, and most generally*
> *future investigators, who can decide which is in the right.*

Is forming an opinion the result of "rashness" or of "courage"? Is it right or is it wrong to form an opinion? Faraday is ambiguous. We try to understand him by examining his own example (2:272),

> there is the theory of one electric fluid and also that of two. One explains [electric tension] by the difference in degree or quantity of one fluid, what the other attributes to the variation in the quantity and relation of two fluids. Both cannot be true. That they have nearly equal hold of our assent, *is only proof of our ignorance*; and it is certain, whichever is the false theory, is at present holding the minds of its supporters in bondage, and is greatly retarding the progress of science.

The example is more puzzling than enlightening. It is entirely neutral as to the question, should the holders of the one-fluid theory and of the two-fluid theory have propounded their views in public or not? Surely, Faraday could not apply the doctrine of prejudice in order to dismiss other people's speculations only in order to allow himself to speculate. True, this practice was common; but Faraday could never employ it. Did he hold the view that all speculation is evil, as the doctrine of prejudice asserts, or did he deny it to be so?

It is hard to say; the most coherent answer one may get from his work is that speculation, though not necessarily harmful, is very probably harmful, namely very dangerous. If so, then why did he speculate? The answer that most clearly emerges is that he simply could not resist it, although for years he tried. He was not only assisted by his imagination. He was swept along by it. But this answer, true as I believe it is, is insufficient. For if one of his characteristics was his tremendous power of imagination, the other was his no less forceful self-restraint. Let me illustrate the conflict with heartbreaking quotations:

> I must keep my researches really *experimental*, and not let them deserve anywhere the character of *hypothetical* imaginations. (1833)

> Must always work practically; never give final opinion except on that. (1834)

> Speculations, dangerous temptations; generally avoid them; but a time to speculate as well as to refrain, all dependent

upon the temper of the mind . . . *may be right*—but may
*be all wrong*. Thus see how little . . . is known as fact, and
how *much* is assumption . . .

As I begin by a warning against *speculation*, so end by
a warning against too much *assurance*. What is the experience
of past ages—all *sure* in their days except the most wise—yet
how little remains, and are we wiser in our generation? . . .
We may be *sure* of facts, but our interpretations of fact
we should doubt . . . (1844)

I cannot doubt that a glorious discovery in natural
knowledge, and of the wisdom and power of God in creation
is awaiting our age, and that we may not only hope to see it,
but even be honoured to help in obtaining the victory over
present ignorance and future knowledge. (1849)

ALL THIS IS A DREAM (1850)

It is not the duty or the place of a philosopher to dictate
belief, and all hypothesis is more or less matter of belief;
he has but to give facts and his conclusions, and so much of
the logic which connects the former with the latter as he may
think necessary, and then commit the whole to the scientific
world . . . for future judgement. (1856)

In my early life I was a very lively "imaginative" person,
who could believe in the "Arabian Nights" as easily as in
the "Encyclopaedia," but facts were important to me, and saved
me. I could trust facts. (1858)

To complete this set of quotations, there should be a corresponding list
of Faraday's admissions of failure to obtain certain experimental results, from
the polarization of light by electrolytes in 1834 to the effects of electricity
on gravity in 1851. But these quotations are more involved, and so I postpone
them to their proper places in my narrative. Let me merely conclude this
list of quotations with a brief note, found in his "research drawer" after his
death (S. P. Thompson's *Michael Faraday*, p. 241):

THE FOUR DEGREES
The discovery of a fact.
The reconciling of it to known principles.
Discovery of a fact not reconcilable.
He who refers all still to more general principles.

M.F.

It is very clear that here there is neither any room for the doctrine of prejudice, nor any of Faraday's problems concerning refutations. But I do not know if the fact that this note was found in Faraday's research drawer is sufficient ground to assume that in this note there is the record of a resolution of his conflict.

I do **not** think that we can get an entire picture of Faraday's research without realizing the existence of that conflict. Faraday was both an inductivist and a critical thinker. Only by development did his critical spirit gain ground over his inductivism. My question was, why did he speculate? I answered this, saying that he was swept along by his own imagination. But this is an insufficient answer, because he had a marvelous power of self-restraint and at least he could resist publishing his speculations. Although he held an ambivalent view of the function of speculations, he knew that experimentally he was aided by them. This is his critique of inductivism. He also had a growing conviction that whether his own speculations were true or false, others held to an orthodox speculation that evidently was false. This is his application of the inductivist doctrine of prejudice. When he shyly presented his views as a possible alternative to the old views, he had hoped that the old views would vanish. They did not. Later he used his own views as a tool to overthrow evidently false views. As he put it in a letter of 1855 (*Life and Letters*, 2:362):

> . . . I think that men are beginning to look more closely
> to [my theory] than they have done heretofore, and find it
> a more serious affair than they expected. My own convictions
> and expectations increase continually . . . [even though] I
> always tried to be very critical on myself before I gave anybody
> else the opportunity, and even now I think I could say much
> stronger things against my notions than anybody else has.
> Still the old views are so untenable *as a whole*, that I am clear
> they must be wrong, whatever is right.

**Faraday's Methodology**

Though Faraday went back and forth to the last, the above quotation represents, in my view, the correct and basic resolution of his conflict; while acting in accord with it, he pushed forward best; but he wavered all his life, though he had the correct solution slowly emerge while he wavered. Perhaps the clue may lie not so much in Faraday's faith in facts, but in the function of these in his activities.

## Theory and Fact

We had on several occasions met Faraday's protestation of his faith in facts, in all facts, even in minute facts. There is evidence that Faraday could dance about and hug people who showed him new facts. There is the story that someone was disappointed to witness Faraday's demonstration in a public lecture of a minute and well-known experiment but later relented upon hearing a member of the audience express his admiration of that experiment as the highlight of the lecture. There is a story about an elderly gentleman who tried to impress Faraday with an experiment demonstrating that a piece of cork floating in a vessel will be close to the wall of the vessel if it is half-filled but move to the center of the water's surface if the vessel is filled. He was disappointed to learn that Faraday knew this fact, and Faraday had to comfort him and reassure him. Faraday's own preference was to observe the sky and lightning, and there are a few testimonies about his excitement during thunderstorms and his discussions with painters, especially Turner, on the variety of sights in the sky. But this preference of his was personal and extrascientific, we are led to believe: scientifically, it was repeatedly alleged, even the smallest fact was important—to Faraday as to anyone else; his success was, we are told, rooted in his realizing just this.

Today the discussion about minute facts looks quaint and antiquated. What its significance in history was is hard to assess; certainly it had more than one role. First, stressing minute facts was an admonition against dogmatism: the dogmatist will not relinquish a beautiful grand theory because of a nasty minute fact; but he ought to, and no fact is nasty, indeed no fact is minute. This is Bacon's teaching. Second, it follows that every new fact, however seemingly minute, is publishable. This was Bacon's and Boyle's proposal.

Though the ideas are now antiquated, the style they have generated is still alive. In most biological journals, for example, experiments must be reported in a fixed style: brief optional introduction, description of instrument, of experiment, of results, and concluding optional brief discussion. In a few journals of the social sciences this style has been instituted, with proper variants, when social scientists try to imitate the style of the natural scientists. In physics this style is almost extinct, thanks to Faraday more than to any other individual. But Faraday had no intention of altering any style; he was working on problems and altered the accepted style by the way.

In 1833 we find Faraday working on electrolytes. He says he was interested in electrolysis because he wanted to see the transition, he thought he could see it better if he froze the battery, and was surprised to discover that ice is a nonconductor. He took a trough, so-and-so many inches long, so-and-so many inches wide, so-and-so many inches deep, with such-and-such a solution, and with so many electrodes of given size and specifications. This is as unreadable as any paper in the inductive style before or after. The introduction is cryptic, and followed by an unexplained detailed description of apparatus, including much that is obviously immaterial.

We can assume that colleagues and contemporaries of a writer can comprehend his work because they can, and usually do, easily repeat his experiment, and because they are familiar with his background and hence with his problem —at least to the extent that his introduction is a sufficient hint. In the example at hand, whatever Faraday's specific problem was, and specific surely it was, since it related to currents, and since everyone at the time was concerned with currents, the introduction was quite sufficient. But his specific concern and the preoccupations of his colleagues soon diverge. He goes on furiously more or less in the same manner, putting accent on facts that agree with his theory and refute accepted theories. When he comes up with specific inductive capacity he states his case more boldly: he was looking for facts, he says, that would decide between his views and the current ones. Still, no response. No one even takes up the topic of specific inductive capacity. Faraday becomes increasingly isolated.

In 1839 he interrupts his research due to depression and illness for a period of about four years. In 1843 he prepares a new mode of attack—he writes a note to himself, putting much stress on points of style of presentation (*Life and Letters*, 2:166). The topic itself is theoretical, concerning the field view of magnetic poles with regard to polar forces and the law of conservation of force; the facts referred to are not particularly novel or even interesting. Yet he tells himself emphatically, "Avoid any particular language. Should not pledge myself to answer any particular observations, or to anyone, against open consideration of the subject. Want to direct the thoughts of all upon the subject, and tie them there . . ." In brief, he was determined to give the inductive style its last chance, aiming only "to direct thoughts of all upon the subject and tie them there . . ." He could employ the rigorous traditional style.

He did not publish that paper. Instead, he published a very similar paper on static electricity. I do not know why he finally decided to write the one rather than the other; the idea applies to the two so similarly that his biographer H. Bence Jones was confused and had the impression that he published both.[2]

The paper on static electricity has earned Faraday a minor reputation amongst dogmatic historians of science. Whether thanks to Whittaker, or to other writers, it is customary to read into Faraday's paper of 1843 not the idea of polarity (as clearly intended though never fully stated) but the idea of conservation of charge! But we must press on, merely noting that in 1843 Faraday had his last—and highly orthodox—fling at the inductive style.

When he at last published his view on magnetism, in 1844, he made it explicit and did *not* avoid any particular language but presented his field theory in its first explicit statement. What he actually achieved, Helmholtz tells us (see quotation p. 196, below), was only to confuse his readers. In any case, they went on ignoring him as a thinker. In spite of illness he worked very hard, experimenting and explaining his views, still trying desperately to "direct the thoughts of all upon the subject and tie them there . . ." His experiments caused great confusion in his opponents' camp, for they still showed an incredible pig-headedness in ignoring his explanation. He was almost desperate. He stressed that his views are most helpful for discovery, he explained that anyone who would follow him, experimenter or mathematician, would be guided by these views to new facts and new theories—it is all to no avail.

The strangest thing about Faraday's attitude to facts is that he refused to accept their verdict when the verdict went against him; he stubbornly tried again and again to squeeze the right result out of nature. He never disregarded the facts; he only tried to reinterpret them, to go round them. What he found so horrid is that his peers simply ignored his facts.

Clearly, then, when Faraday only presented facts and no theory, it was his hope that the facts would speak for him. He wanted not merely to report

2. Bence Jones says "He sent to the *Philosophical Magazine* a paper on static electrical inductive action." He then quotes the note on the style of the intended paper on static magnetism. He then says "He also sent a paper to the *Philosophical Magazine* on static electrical inductive action, and [a quite different paper] on the chemical contact theory . . ."

facts but also, and mainly, to draw attention to his own ideas, plain and simple. He did not apply measure and measure, and he was ready to welcome disagreement—but not reticence. I will not discuss the classical passion to draw attention by making a contribution. The topic has been covered in Carl Becker's classic *The Heavenly City of the Eighteenth Century Philosophers*. Moreover, most writers of histories of science and biographies of scientists share this sentiment. What is not noticed by such writers is the possibility that contributions are made yet not recognized, that one may be robbed of one's right for posterity.

It may be well, therefore, to offer positive evidence of the isolation that Faraday suffered, at least in order to show its enormity. It is hard to assess his isolation before 1839, how much his breakdown reflected external conditions, how much internal ones. But after that the isolation had set in, and he had to learn to live with it. Let us consider, as a sort of measure of his isolation, the attitude of the *Encyclopaedia Britannica* toward him. In the ninth edition, after his death, it published Maxwell's essay on him, which is justly considered a classic. In the seventh edition, of 1842, none of Faraday's anti-Newtonian views are mentioned. Even his 1831 discovery is only mentioned. Incidentally, the *Encyclopedia Metropolitana* of 1845 should also be noted for its taboo on Faraday; yet, I think, the *Britannica* stood out for its dogmatism even then. The 1842 edition of the *Britannica* includes a list of theories about the cause of lightning. Since the situation was problematic and the list was an obvious indication that the truth of the matter was not known, the article could easily include Faraday's theory—lightning is a discharge due to ionization—without any commitment. But Faraday's views are not even hinted at in that article.

When an author is ignored, he may be ignored for good; alternatively, his existence may be grudgingly acknowledged by implication: he graduates from nonexistence to the status of an anonymous opponent; later he may even acquire the status of an opponent, and even the status of a predecessor. Faraday skipped much of all this, but he was, once, the anonymous opponent of the *Britannica*: the eighth edition of the *Britannica* of 1853–60 (where Faraday's discovery of 1831 is described but by carefully chosen quotations and in a most noncommittal manner) contains a fierce attack on those who do not adhere to the widespread views. The attack, I believe, is very representative. It is therefore well worth quoting (1:740):

> It must indeed be confessed, that after all the progress which
> Electricity and its younger branch Galvanism have made,

the hypotheses commonly received are exceedingly vague and unphilosophical. In cultivating these attractive sciences, experimenters would seem to satisfy themselves with the exercise of a *looser and humbler species of reasoning*. It is rather *amusing* to observe the complacency with which *some ingenious persons* describe the play and vagaries of the Electrical Current, whose existence was never proved. *We are acquainted only with electric attraction and repulsion, and with the transmission of electric influence:* All beyond these elementary principles, rests on *hasty conjectures*. Instead of adopting one or two fluids it were safer to suspend the assumption of any . . .

The Theories proposed by Aepinus and Cavendish are entitled, however, to the praise of great ingenuity . . . The latter most accurate philosopher likewise stated . . . though he did not explain the grounds of his conclusions. Coulomb agreed with him . . . and the Balance of Torsion showed . . . These were real discoveries, deduced from nice and cautious observations . . .

Experimenters, it seems, are kindly permitted "to satisfy themselves with the exercise of a *looser and humbler species of reasoning*," of an inferior mode of thinking. But, inductively speaking, we know of nothing but attractions, repulsions, and conduction! Let me explain the above claim for a special status for attraction and repulsion. Thomson (Lord Kelvin) and Tait were the first authors of a textbook of mechanics who employed the sharp distinction between motions, kinematics, and forces, dynamics. They were the first who presented kinematics independently of dynamics in a systematic fashion. Previously, people could hardly observe motion toward a center or motion from a center; they usually saw in these cases attractions and repulsions. (It was the same error, we may remember, that Faraday made in 1821. But he soon refuted his own error. Most people were considerably less able.) This is why the above-quoted passage from the *Britannica* defends Coulomb and others in spite of the fact that their views had been refuted.

The treatment Faraday received from the *Britannica* was quite general. His friend Schoenbein, who shared some of his views (see *Correspondence*, p. 46), but definitely not all of them (see p. 71), was struck by the conspiracy of silence. In a letter dated 26 April 1843, he says (p. 105), concerning electro-static induction,

I only wonder that our Continental philosophers have as yet not paid that degree of attention to the subject . . . It is perhaps a certain laziness, inherent to human nature, that makes even men of science unwilling to shift out of old-beaten tracks and enter into paths newly opened, though these should happen to be ever so well laid out.

The conspiracy remained. We can say exactly when, for the first time, the topic of electrostatic induction was aired in a manner satisfactory to Faraday —not accepting but merely respecting his views—and we have his expression of how this effected his mental health. It seems clear that recognition, small as it was, came in the nick of time, when his powers were slowly fading to the point that his illness made it quite impossible for him to continue his campaign. Almost before a total defeat the new ray of hope appeared. Here is a letter to Tyndall about it written by a sick old man of sixty-two, whose chief illness is loss of memory, to a young good friend, and it is pathetic just because the ray of hope puts him off guard for a moment and shows the depth of his anxiety and despair:

> Here we jog on, and I have just undertaken the Juvenile Lectures at Christmas, thinking them the easiest thing for me to do. Reading . . . is my weighty work, and because of the call it makes on memory I have now and then to lay them down and cease till the morrow. I think they encourage me to write another paper on lines of force and polarity, etc., *for I was hardly prepared to find such strong support in the papers of Van Rees and Thomson* [Lord Kelvin][3] *for the lines as correct representants of the power and its direction*; and many old arguments are renewed in my mind by these papers. But we shall see how the maggot bites presently; and as I fancy I have gained so much by waiting, I may perhaps wait a little longer.

Indeed, his memory and vigor were revived, and he published in December 1854 a paper commenting on the two papers here mentioned; another paper

3. In 1845 Kelvin encouraged Faraday—but in private and at Faraday's own instigation (see Williams, *Michael Faraday*, p. 383).

follows in January 1855 and still another in February. This practically ends his *Experimental Researches in Electricity*. If anybody seriously doubts the mental source of Faraday's fits of giddiness and forgetfulness (mercury poisoning is currently blamed for it), then he should explain the enormous emotional susceptibility of Faraday's illness to encouragement and discouragement.

He continued to experiment, and to lecture, and to correspond with anybody who was interested. He was very gratified by Maxwell's nondogmatic attitude toward gravity; he saw the beginning of a new approach. Then, his experimental paper on gravity was rejected by the Royal Society. His active powers soon declined; he even gave up his lectures in the Royal Institution with the explanation that is sketched in a note (*Life and Letters*, 2:450) that refers to his loss of memory, his hesitation and uncertainty, and even "dimness and forgetfulness of . . . *standard* in respect of right, dignity, and *self-respect*" (incidentally, the psychoanalytically minded reader may find it relevant that Faraday had difficulties in the spelling of the words "withhold," "wearies," "successful").

Being in this state of mind, and doing work that demanded tremendous concentration, it is not at all surprising that he invested ever decreasing amounts of work; what is surprising is that the significance of his work increased up to the very end. His last preparation of an experiment was to deflect electromagnetic waves. The last experiment was an attempt to discover the very important effect of magnetism on the color of the source of light (Zeeman effect). These were his last and sporadic efforts, preceded by two series of research experiments. His last series of experiments was on the connection between gravity and electricity; here he had no shred of success; Einstein had some, in Eddington's observations of 1917; but electrogravity constitutes, even now, the greatest and most difficult problem in physics.

In brief, Faraday's last research, though in retrospect very exciting, at the time could not but be a severe discouragement. His research on electrogravity ended with no result and the rejection of a paper (probably the first), and each of the loose ends he picked was very ambitious and beyond his reach: he could not know how fruitful they could be; his powers declined to the point of no return. He became a senile old man. Toward the end he was hardly able to talk and could only express his great pleasure when watching the sunset.

We see, then, that facts can be encouraging or discouraging; it much depends on contexts, social, intellectual, even emotional.

## The Development of Faraday's Critical Style

Here is a simple contrast between the inductive style of presentation and the debate or the argumentative or critical or dialectical style. The traditional high inductive style, as advocated and practiced by Boyle, Hooke, in part even Newton, Priestley, Davy, and many others, is characterized by (superfluous) circumstantial descriptions of facts (in abundance), by putting facts on the table, by arguing only by implications, by surreptitious improvement of the views of past thinkers, and by presenting one's views by hints—or, at most, sketchily in the end of one's essay. The argumentative or dialectical style is not necessarily characterized by an explicit mentioning of the name of an opponent or by an attack on some view or another; the role of polemics, if any, is incidental to the argumentative dialectical style. The argumentative style is first of all characterized by the presentation of the *problem situation*, by the presentation of the problem that one wishes to attack and the setting that lends it significance, by an attempt to present some views as a suggested solution, and by an attempt to criticize the proposed views—perhaps also to summarize the results of this criticism. For this purpose it is traditionally considered advisable, I think, to try to make the best presentation of the best solutions previously suggested to solve the problem, perhaps with some improvement, and to contrast these with the new solution. This is not essential, though of a great help.

Now, of course, there are degrees and shades of different mixtures of styles. One might, indeed, expect in history the occurrence of some graded or smooth transitions from one style to another. Now, the high tide of the inductive style, especially in Britain, was in the mid-eighteenth century; it was interrupted by the dispute concerning phlogiston; and it deteriorated into polemics and quarrels. Indeed, the main difficulty in a gradual or smooth transition from the inductive style to the argumentative style is to get rid of the inductivist doctrine of prejudice that identifies all argument with polemics. And now to Faraday.

Faraday, we saw, was concerned with stylistic problems from his early age. In 1832, while engaging in his most fruitful thoughts, he bound a volume of offprints of his early papers, including as a preface some comments on them, and expressing (*Life and Letters*, 2:55) his self-critical attitude both concerning the content of his work and concerning its style.

The style of his first two series of the *Experimental Researches in Electricity* is inductive; I do not think they are different in manner of presentation or style from many other papers of that time, even though they are somewhat exceptional in one way, in the presentation and the explicit criticism of his own theory of the electrotonic state. It is perhaps obstinacy (and perhaps affection and respect for Ampère) more than anything else that made him refrain from criticizing others explicitly. Soon Lenz's theory was accepted as the explanation of Faraday's 1831 discoveries. Since that theory is refuted by experiments described in Faraday's first series, he never bothered to argue against it. Later Weber's theory was fairly widely accepted. He found no need to criticize it since it was unsatisfactory from the start.

Faraday felt very hurt that he was ignored; what he wanted was not acceptance but attention—the older he became, the more he felt the wish to attract critical attention. In accord with the critical canons, he criticized his best opponents. But even then, he lost patience with them, he regretted the need for controversy—he never decided between inductivism and criticism. Much as I sympathize with his inner conflict and with his loss of patience with his opponents, I think we must admit that he was in error. One item of evidence is so weighty, I think it will suffice. It is this. William Whewell was both a very respected and important thinker, and friendlily disposed to Faraday, even a bit of an admirer; he was not a dogmatist: he was one of the few who have ever stated clearly that Faraday had refuted Coulomb's law. Yet he stated, as late as in 1857, that Lenz's theory explains Faraday's theory, and that it is based on Newton's third law (*History of the Inductive Sciences* [1857], 3:531). True, Faraday had shown in 1832 that induction occurs even in motion in a homogeneous field (i.e., in a field of forces of equal magnitudes), and this does refute both Lenz's law and Newton's third law (as understood then). But at least in part the muddle was due to Faraday's early inductive style and his refusal to take up the cudgel.

In 1833 Faraday changes his mode of attack. He still conceals his views, but now he is carefully preparing the ground. After his two great papers comes a paper that aims at an offensive but is still fairly conventional: he unites all the different electricities, so that at the most one or two electric fluids exist, and he prepares the overthrow of the one-fluid theory (as it allows nonpolar forces). The paper is rather inductive both in matter and manner and is one of Faraday's less exciting. The problem at hand is fully stated, and the attempt is made to show that all the known electric effects are common to electricity of different sources. He thus "proved to his own satisfaction, at least" the identity of all electricity. At the end of his paper he gives a general and vague hint as to his field explanation of currents. Both Tyndall and Helmholtz give this as an example of a puzzling passage. Since previously everybody spoke in the same cryptic language, and since Faraday was the first to speak explicitly, I find this a bit harsh.

The only noninductive element in this third series is in the introduction, where Faraday mentions the existence of different views of the subject. And, for the first time he explicitly and publicly deviates from his beloved master's view. Years before, a parliamentary committee had some difficulty, we are told (see Thompson's *Michael Faraday*, p. 43), in learning from Faraday that Davy's safety lamp is not quite safe.[4] Now he deviates publicly. Later, in his researches on the electric pile he explicitly refuted Davy's theory that water is also necessary to the pile. He also claims that Davy's theory is too general. Dr. Davy, we remember, opened a fierce counter attack and Faraday answered carefully and quietly (1835), but not without irony. From then on, when he republished papers, he did so without changes and he added footnotes wherever he thought he had made erroneous statements. In later researches (1842) he argues more explicitly against the current theory of the pile and he presents facts as "experimental arguments"! In 1840, he writes an open reply to an open letter of criticism by Dr. Hare (*Experimental Researches in Electricity*, 2:262), saying that he greatly appreciated his critic's judgment, yet had no need to make any revision save mere rewording and clarification. In a second published letter to Hare in 1841 he draws a sharp line between criticism (that

---

4. There was a violent priority dispute between Davy and Stephenson (the inventor of the railway). Davy's major point was that Stephenson's lamp, though earlier, was not safe. His own was neither. Stephenson is undoubtedly justified in claiming that the invention of Davy should not be described as Davy's invention of the safety lamp, whatever else the case may have been. Historians still speak of Davy's safety lamp as if it were really safe. Faraday himself, understandably, was very angry whenever the topic was raised. All he would say was, it was a "disgraceful subject" (Thompson, *Michael Faraday*, p. 269).

No doubt Faraday was unwilling to admit that here he had been compromising. Though to the parliamentary committee he said the truth, and though he added in pencil to the inscription on Davy's safety lamp in the Royal Institution the deadly comment "The opinion of the inventor" (*op. cit.*, p. 43), he did offer high praise of it in public lectures in 1817 and in 1829. Literally the eulogies may have been quite correct; yet the spirit of the eulogies is questionable.

For my part I think Faraday thought safety lay elsewhere: in ventilation. And he did all he could, but on the quiet, to raise standards of ventilation. This also led him to the study of ventilation as a technological problem, which he solved successfully for light houses where, however, the problem lay less in safety and more in the prevention of darkening of glass by soot. See Jeffreys' bibliography, items 290, 321, particularly important 329, 332, and 335, also 339. Obviously Faraday felt that both Davy and Stephenson were not sufficiently sensitive to the fact that coal mine accidents had not been eliminated, and that their petty priority dispute was diverting public interest from a real issue involving many lives.

should be offered and accepted in a friendly spirit) and controversy (involving personal conflict) (2:275); "criticism," he says, "is of much value." This idea, implicit in many writers' works, especially Kepler's and Galileo's, and a cornerstone of Whewell's philosophy, can hardly be found so explicitly stated in a brief fashion even in our own less sensitive age. It took Faraday years to come to the expression of the idea of criticism as something that may call for some chagrin but never for annoyance. (This, indeed, is in the preface to the first volume of his *Experimental Researches in Electricity*, quoted above.) It was Einstein who did away even with chagrin. Without some measure of historical perspective, we cannot possibly appreciate the immensity of Faraday's (and Einstein's) contribution.

Faraday made criticism something reasonable by stressing the difference between the personal and the intellectual (*Experimental Researches in Electricity*, 2:262); and between stimulating criticism that should be acknowledged with gratitude and apologetic defense and attacks that should be ignored (p. 276). Faraday, in brief, was setting new standards of publication. The standards were not introduced in one day, but they did become common. Maxwell could criticize his friend Kelvin in scientific and semiscientific publications without causing much surprise; this is simply an incredible novelty, the realization of one of Faraday's dreams. The standard that he tried to implement he presented in many papers, private letters, published letters, and private conversations. Here is an instance (3:506; *Life and Letters*, 2:299): ". . . they are felt to be imperfect, and may perhaps even be overturned; but . . . as such a result is not greatly anticipated, it was thought well to present them to the members of the Royal Institution and the scientific world, if peradventure they might excite criticism and experimental examination, and so aid in advancing the cause of physical science."

## Faraday on Civil Arguments

In line with this principle, and with enormous emotional effort, Faraday practiced his principles in the hope that they would be noticed, reporting on all this only in letters to friends. In one such letter he confesses, "I write and write and write . . . I have to criticize [my papers] again and again before I let them loose . . ." (*Life and Letters*, 2:256). In another he tells how he purges all his public expressions of all marks of annoyance at petty opponents (*Discoverer*, p. 49). When he finds worthy opponents, he even embroiders his replies with comments on criticism, replies, and the like. Yet, before 1850 he encountered no serious rival. Weber, for example, was considered for a while to have explained Faraday's discoveries; he scolded Ampère for having been too hasty in his theorizing; but he mentions no theory by Faraday. Nor did de la Rive, Faraday's friend, and others. Although Faraday refused to argue with Dr. Hare because he had already stated his experimental arguments against Hare's electrostatic theory in his first paper on electrostatics (in reply to Hare he only wished to clarify some misunderstandings), he did continue to argue from experiments against the contact theory of electrolysis (as action at a distance). His excuse for this was that he found new experimental arguments, new discoveries. On the whole, Faraday really declined to argue, though he regularly said he was against controversy but for argument. Evidently, his aim was to objectivize science, to exclude personal elements from scientific method, and to exclude matters of belief. But he only made it hard for himself when he expressed this by saying that "all hypothesis is more or less a matter of belief" (*Life and Letters*, 2:352). Here the vestiges of his inductivism confused issues. He thought that objectively speaking we can only present facts, mention hypotheses, and show the logical relations between them. This is not the whole story. We can objectively discuss the logical relations of statements of facts to sets of competing hypotheses, whether they are equivalent, independent, or contradictory, and what, in the latter case, could be done in order to decide between them in the manner of a crucial experiment. All this is objective though it may involve a personal element. People may take such a process personally. In fact Faraday himself did so; and then he tried hard to exclude the personal element. Obviously, the right approach is to rather ignore the personal element and stick to the objective element in any dispute. This, however, is hard to notice in the absence of worthy opposition.

In 1850 two worthy theories were presented that assume action at a distance. They are both praised in Faraday's introduction to the third volume of his *Experimental Researches in Electricity* as theories that are compatible with all the facts he knew. The first, of electrostatic induction, was that of Faraday and Kelvin; the second, of magnetocrystallic action, was that of Knoblauch and Tyndall. This was Faraday's great opportunity, and he took it eagerly. Tyndall was invited to the Royal Institution and soon became a professor there. In November 1850 Faraday writes to Tyndall (*Life and Letters*, 2:276), ". . . it is wonderful how much good results from different persons working at the same matter. Each one gives views and ideas new to the rest. When science is a republic, then it gains; and though I am no republican

in other matters, I am in that . . . I am, Sir, your very obedient servant."
In April 1851 he comments on a paper by Tyndall. He starts his letter (*Life and Letters*, 2:294) with a lament on his loss of memory and inability to read mathematics. Nevertheless, he adds, "I am able fully to appreciate the value of the results you arrived at . . . exceedingly well established and of very great consequence. . . . Nature is our kindest friend and best critic in experimental science, if we only allow her intimations to fall unbiassed on our minds. . . ."
In 1854 he writes to Tyndall about the return of his memory caused by public recognition of his work. In 1855 Tyndall and Faraday exchange open letters, published in the *Philosophical Magazine* and both addressed from the Royal Institution; both contained severe and open attacks on each other's views—in the friendliest terms. In 1858 Faraday writes Tyndall on his mountaineering adventure (*Life and Letters*, 2:407), "I won't give you any scolding. I dare say my wife will when you see her." Such a degree of intimacy Faraday never achieved with anyone else outside his narrowest family circle.

With Tyndall's aid Faraday set the tone for public scientific discussions. It soon became quite normal for discussions to be regularly seasoned with brotherly remarks. This has also another source: the post-Faraday period was that of popular lectures after Faraday's own fashion, and especially in imitation of his juvenile lectures (the admission to which had no age limit). They were of this sentimental character both because Faraday had no children and loved all children with whom he came into contact and because he tried to lure people, and especially the younger ones, to try and think on his lines.

There clearly is also some lack of confidence expressed in this brotherly mode of disputation. There is the fear that the opponent would take it amiss and the feeling of a need to reassure him that all is done with the best of intention. For my part, I find this method of brotherly argument unnecessary and even slightly dangerous. It may lead to dogmatism. It may lead to the distinction between brotherly disputes with those with whom we essentially agree and hostile dismissal of the views of those with whom we differ in fundamentals. But on the whole Faraday's mode of brotherly argument was successful. Most of his followers soon learned to argue objectively and maturely, and to ignore altogether the personal element in a dispute.

Science has a logic of its own. Once two people start to criticize each other seriously, they find themselves working in friendly-hostile cooperation, to use Popper's apt phrase. But the process of making this friendly-hostile cooperation the institution of science is not a matter of the inner logic of science, but also of trial and error—especially error. Clearly, Faraday could not effect such a major change in the scientific climate single-handed. Such changes come about neither as the result of single individuals' endeavors nor as the result of masses of people blindly pushed along the paths of progress by sheer historical forces. Significant changes are conceived by a few individuals, critically debated by more, and implemented by still more. It is impossible to ascertain the exact degree of Faraday's contribution here. That he was a significant contributor is all I have sought to illustrate.

## Realism and Fictionalism

Faraday was convinced in the thirties that his lines of force would become respectable; the more lines of force one cuts with a wire, the stronger proportionally is the current they create in the wire. The sincere respect for facts, he felt, was sufficient to guarantee him full success. He was soon deeply disappointed. All his life he remained of the opinion that he should not have been so cruelly disappointed. In the year 1857, when he was sixty-five and close to the conclusion of his career, he wrote to a friend who agreed with him about a heretic view. The view is that of the conservation of gravitational force, which we shall discuss later. Here is what Faraday wrote to his heretic friend (*Life and Letters*, 2:389):

> If you would cause your view . . . to be acknowledged by scientific men; you would do a great service to science. *If you would* EVEN GET THEM TO SAY YES OR NO *to your conclusions* it would help to *clear the future progress.* I believe some *hesitate because they do not like their thoughts disturbed.* When Davy discovered potassium it annoyed persons who had just made their view of chemical science perfect; and when I discovered the magneto-electric spark, distaste of a like kind was felt towards it, even in high places. Still science must proceed . . .

It is not that Faraday ever urged people to make up their minds or to comment on his papers. Throughout his life he was aloof and insistent on not imposing on people. A few months after he had written the above, he wrote to Maxwell, saying (*Life and Letters*, 2:390) that if he had asked Maxwell to comment on his, Faraday's, recent papers, then he, Faraday, had clearly been in the wrong. And this is much more in line with his general attitude. Nevertheless, he could not help but think that those who were exercising their right to ignore him were doing so from sheer dogmatism and to the detriment of science.

When Faraday realized that recognition was not forthcoming, he entered a frantic phase of hard work. He tried to drown his opponents with experiments that they could not cope with and with snippets of his ideas that accommodate these experiments very comfortably. This brings his story roughly from 1833 to 1839, to the publication of the first volume of his *Experimental Researches in Electricity* (of 1831 to 1839), and to his first nervous breakdown, the chief symptoms of which were giddiness, forgetfulness, and disgust both with thinking and with meeting people.

When he recovered from his breakdown, he came out, after a brief period of hesitation, with a whole new philosophy of nature, which he contrasted with the received philosophy of nature. Clearly, the dogmatism of his opponents was fundamentally philosophical. His facts had been acknowledged, and if theories accepted at the time were not in full accord with his facts, men of science were trying hard to remedy the situation even though they were not frank enough to say so in public. What they silently rejected were his fundamental ideas.

Faraday was destroyed by his supreme efforts to suppress his tremendous fury at all this. This is understandable but not very commendable—indeed, not very philosophic. Even in our enlightened twentieth century, it is not easy, sometimes impossible, to make men of science discuss the philosophy of nature. And it is extremely hard to make men of science admit that received scientific theories are defective. Even men of science who these days work hard to remove certain imperfections from received scientific theories often publicly deny the existence of these imperfections. It is very regrettable but true that science as a social phenomenon is sharply divided between the workshop and the shop window, that the lay onlookers are invited to look at the shop window, that the laymen (the very word comes from religion) are authoritatively informed that things are under control. Faraday took it all so hard because science was for him a childhood ideal of the loftiest kind, somewhat of a dogma, indeed.

Now, the view of science as always under control, this superficial and intellectually least significant theory of science, is nowadays called positivism. Positivism can be characterized in different ways; different strands of it may be distinguished. It says, roughly, though science is not complete in the sense that some of its achievements lie in the future, it is complete in the sense that each of its achievements is complete and final and unquestionable and can never be overthrown—at least almost entirely so. Positivism can be characterized as the claim that science does not include any philosophy of nature, is not bound by any philosophy of nature; the positivist claim is that science recognizes only two kinds of assertions: assertions of facts of experience and of nature, and assertions of pure logic and mathematics; both kinds of assertions are (practically) final and unalterable, and science is nothing else but these two kinds of assertions and their ramifications, and their occasional slight rectifications.

There are two strands of positivism, inductivism and fictionalism as I shall call them.

Inductivism is the belief that scientific theories are truths about nature inasmuch as they contain parts of the true philosophy of nature; it is the belief that when science is complete it will include a demonstrated philosophy of nature. Indeed, philosophy of nature concerns itself, for example, with the question, is matter continuous or atomic; and science by now can assure us that matter is atomic. In due course science will answer positively—demonstrably—all questions of the philosophy of nature. But men of science should not aim at attaining any philosophy of nature since this will prejudice their research.

Inductivism is one version of realism. It is characterized by the claim that scientific theories are proven by facts. Those who claim that scientific theories are proven but not by facts are called apriorists. Realists who deny that science can ever prove its doctrines are called skeptics. Following Boyle, Faraday was a skeptic regarding scientific theory but not regarding facts.

The remaining possibility is that scientific theories are often false. For example, the ancient astronomer Ptolemy was a follower of Aristotle and hence a believer in perfect circles, one who considered his own epicycles and eccentrics false. He presented them as mere pieces of fiction, as machinery to describe phenomena, not as realities proper. Philosophers who oppose skepticism in science and who nevertheless deny that proof is possible in science tend to view science as a whole as nothing but a piece of fiction. This extreme fictionalism is called instrumentalism by John Dewey and by Sir Karl Popper. Whereas fictionalism was the most current view about science—especially astronomy—throughout the Middle Ages, it became extremely unpopular in the seventeenth century when Kepler and Galileo refused to accept Copernicanism as mere fiction, the way Jesuit astronomers had done, and insisted on its realism. In the nineteenth century, fictionalism was revived by Faraday and his friend Grove, and independently also by Helmholtz. It soon spread, became instrumentalism, and has now won popular assent as the most sophisticated version of positivism.

Faraday was no positivist; he was not even a fictionalist. But he did suggest a fictionalist compromise between his own views and those of his opponents. Of his three modes of attack, his early inductivism, his middle expression of his own philosophy of nature, and his late fictional compromise, the last was all too successful.

His idea of compromise was very simple. Fictional lines of force may but need not turn out later to be real as well: *what is unreal must be purely fictional; but what is endorsed as fictional without prejudice to its reality may turn out to be real after all.*

It was not easy to convince people to try his ideas even as fiction. Moreover, many who agreed stated sharply (with Helmholtz and young Hertz) that unless lines of force agree with the more traditional philosophy of nature which they endorsed it will forever remain fictional. Others still said (with Mach and Kirchhoff) all scientific theory is fictional; reject both the old and the new philosophy of nature. Today this view is still dominant amongst physicists. There is no more to it than to moral cynicism, the natural step following morally naïve views. After inductivism comes fictionalism; after that we may settle for skepticism—for a more tentative, realistic view of science.

Faraday had two fundamental contentions. First, that his principles were rejected not because of their own illegitimacy but because they competed with older principles (Newtonian, he believed, though not to Newton's own liking) that were themselves illegitimate. If people insisted on older principles, he suggested they revive Euler's mechanistic or Cartesian principles: Euler's space was full of matter—the aether—that could be viewed as the carrier of lines of force. Once people introduced the aether to legitimize lines of force, he felt success was guaranteed: the lines of force would take root and the aether would only be a nuisance that people would sooner or later have to dismiss.

Faraday's defense of his view was not by proof—though he never gave up hope of proof, all his skepticism notwithstanding—but by two new, indeed most avant-garde, kinds of argument: it stands to criticism better than the old view, and it is more useful for experimenting. Both kinds of argument are exciting, even today.

### Faraday on His Program

And so we come to Faraday's speculation and program—or rather to his methodological justification of his views. The main justification is his view of imagination: an imaginative approach to discovery is fruitful, the more so when it is more universal and poetical. In a letter he put it thus (*Correspondence*, p. 149): "You can hardly imagine how I am struggling to exert my poetical ideas just now for the discovery of analogies and remote figures respecting the earth, sun, and all sorts of things—for I think that is the true way to work out a discovery."

How seriously can one claim truth, even mere likelihood, to the products of one's imagination? Was one committed to one's imagination? Did this lead to fictionalism?

As to the problem of commitment, Faraday always considered it significant. We do not know if lines of force exist and therefore we should not commit ourselves to believe that they exist, that they are physical. Meanwhile we shall use them as possibly fictititious but useful instruments, as tools with which to express statements of fact as well as hypotheses. But when our aim has been achieved and our hope fulfilled, we shall be able to unite all the hypotheses concerning lines of force into one hypothesis; then its testability will be so high that nature will have to tell us the secret, to show us the truth or falsity of the idea of lines of force. And nature may answer affirmatively. Then the happy and glorious moment will come, and we shall be permitted to commit ourselves to our belief in lines of force and rejoice in it.

Let this be so. Shall we then be able to explain the lines of force mechanically? Perhaps; but we should no more commit ourselves to mechanism than to its opponent, the theory of physical lines of force. Faraday never ruled out the possibility of a mechanical or any other kind of explanation of the theory of lines of force. But, of course, if they can be explained satisfactorily, mechanically or not, they are in a definite sense real and yet in another definite—and deeper—sense they are not. The explanation of lines of force will make them as real as, say, colors or gravity. But if another theory can be found to explain them satisfactorily, a crucial experiment may prove them limited in explanatory power and not real in the sense of not being final. From this we may draw an interesting lesson: even if the lines are not real, we are permitted and even advised to use them, because insofar as they are truly representative, they should be explicable by the real and final theory, be it mechanical or not.

Personally, Faraday was enthusiastic about the finality of the lines. Methodologically, he ruled the problem out.

If the program of using lines of force is fruitful, Faraday argued, we may forget about the view of the world as a system of lines of force and just use the lines themselves. As much as the hypotheses that this procedure will suggest may be true, they will be sooner or later deducible from the competing theory, *if* that theory is true. So we need not oppose the practice of believing one world view and employing another, especially if we are really as sure that we are right as some pretend to be.

Still, with all this deep insight, Faraday did not convince people. If one reads carefully works of his contemporaries (e.g., Grove's *Correlation*, particularly the conclusion), one may find here and there some slips of the pen—some field concepts used unnoticingly. But even Tyndall, the mechanist consciously ready to employ field concepts, tried to use them sparingly. And so Faraday tried harder to compromise.

According to the mechanistic program the different kinds of matter should be reduced to one. The most widely accepted kind of matter was the luminiferous aether, which transmits light. Faraday explicitly denied its existence. But he never ruled out the possibility of its existence all the same. Now, if his theories be true, the first suggestion that mechanism makes as to the mode of the actions that he discovered is that some other aetherial media transmit the electric and the magnetic action. The next step would be to unite these aethers. And this mechanistic program has much in common with his own program of uniting the actions of light, electricity and magnetism, though not the mode of transmission of these actions.

This is the point that Faraday stressed. This is also the program of Kelvin and Maxwell. And when Maxwell united the actions in order to unite the media that transmit them, the unification succeeded but the attempt to create the theory of the medium that transmits the unified action failed.

This is how ultimately Maxwell and his followers quit mechanism—by first taking up Faraday's compromise suggestion. Only Kelvin still waited for an aether that will solve all problems—as late as in 1904. Again and again, Faraday suggested thinking in terms of lines of force, leaving open the further problems concerning one aether. Not that he had hoped that the idea might be taken up uncritically. He only wanted people to give his view a fair chance. And we cannot do justice to our opponents unless we sincerely attempt to adopt their point of view and think in their terms. And this is all Faraday tried to accomplish—in a religious conviction that after this everything will follow suit in a proper manner.

But there is more to Faraday's suggestion. He genuinely thought that the fruitfulness of his speculations will be the last judge. He could not bridge the gap between his specific theories and his grand speculations. For this he needed a mathematician. He wanted a mathematician to think in terms of lines of force and produce a theory to unite, at first, electromagnets and optics. He was convinced that once such a theory has been produced success would be assured. Meanwhile he only stressed the first step of his argument. And it was very characteristic of Faraday's mode of arguing to dwell as long as necessary on one step in the argument before he produced and developed the next step.

But this belongs less to methodology than to tactics. As to tactics, I will not argue against Faraday. The circumstances are not sufficiently known, and tactical decisions are less clearly arguable than theoretical problems unless there can be a free exchange of information. As to the purely methodological aspect of the discussion, I for one am generally (though not absolutely) against compromise. Contrast is usually the more interesting and the more inspiring. And, without any qualification or justification, we should try to train ourselves to think like Faraday in more than one framework and according to more than one program.

Let me now quote Faraday on this issue. First, his public letter to Tyndall. In the preface of that letter Faraday says that he is ready to consider any concrete criticism of his view, but that Tyndall's criticism is too abstract. He explains why he does not think it is serious criticism: "I may say, however, that the idea you suggested presents no difficulty to me . . . What happens in the medium may, according to my knowledge of facts, happen in space . . ."

This is slightly ironical. What Faraday meant is, of course, that Tyndall should try to refute him by finding some facts rather than by repeating his own old principles in contrast to Faraday's new principles. Faraday keeps his metaphysical convictions to himself and so, he implies, should Tyndall too:

> You are aware (and I hope others will remember) that
> I give the lines of force only as *representations* of the magnetic
> power, and do not profess to say what physical idea they may
> hereafter point, or into what they will resolve themselves.
> *Advancing no principle*, I say, . . . The following points . . . are
> always shown truly by [experiment] . . . and they, with
> considerations arising from the principle of the conservation
> of force, seem to me to be left unexplained by and in opposition
> to, the usual [Newtonian] hypotheses. No difference arises
> about the laws of magnetic action and their mathematical

> development; and that, simply because they are as yet applied
> only partially, and thus far are in accordance with *all* the
> views taken, including mine. . . . On my part I endeavour not
> to assume anything, but only to draw such conclusions from
> the assumptions already made, and the phenomena now
> discovered, as seem subject to experiment and tangible by facts.

To sum up this argument we may put it thus: excluding all problems of metaphysical principles, we compare hypotheses and facts. The accepted hypotheses are well applicable in a given domain of facts, but when we try to apply them to new facts they are refuted. Faraday's own theory explains them with a high degree of simplicity, and it also explains why the accepted theories are applicable in a given domain of facts.

This contention contradicts the methodological view common to many thinkers from Newton to Whewell. According to the accepted view, the more general theory is needed because the previous theory, the "lower level" one, is in need of explanation and unification with other "lower level" theories. Faraday said the "lower level" theory is limited in its application, as failure to extend its application to new phenomena illustrates. This point is nowadays attributed to Poincaré and Duhem. Faraday's view also contradicts the methodological view, now in fashion, of Heisenberg, which he labeled as "closed theories." A closed theory, Faraday argues (for the view was already then advocated), is closed by its refutations. Heisenberg argues that the field of applicability of a theory is not necessarily well-defined. Faraday, on the contrary, argues that we want to define it, and that we do define it both by the refuting facts and by a better hypothesis that tells us what is the domain of applicability of the older hypothesis and why. Later the better hypothesis may be closed by new refutation; but on this Faraday only touches. Instead of following up this point, he tries to show the methodological superiority of his program:

> Some persons may feel surprised that I dwell upon points
> which are perfectly and mathematically explained by the
> hypothesis of two magnetic fluids, as, for instance, places
> of little or no action (3341, etc.). My reason is, that being
> satisfied by the phenomena of diamagnetism etc. that *that
> hypothesis cannot be true*, all these and such like phenomena
> acquire a new character and high importance which they had

not before, and amongst other philosophical uses, point most emphatically to the essential relation of the dualities and their equivalency in power. They do not contradict the old hypothesis when that is partially applied, but they are not the less strong and striking as evidence in favour of the view of lines of force.

Faraday's definitive discussion on these matters is to be found in his *Experimental Researches in Chemistry and Physics*, the paper on "The Conservation of Force," his last speculative paper of 1857–58. I shall here present my own summary of its lines of argument with a running commentary. The paper begins with a comparison of two programs. One tries to establish merely a hypothesis that all forces are conserved and the other, the stronger form of the same program, tries to show that they are even of identical nature and that therefore every force can change its appearance and assume any form of known force. Faraday advocates the second version.

The first objection to such an idea is that it is metaphysical. To this Faraday has a methodological reply. He does not argue about the status of the idea but of its effects on research. The idea, he says, leads to some interesting and testable consequences; "to inquire, therefore, whether power, acting either at a sensible or insensible distance, always acts in time, is *not to be metaphisical*" (ibid., p. 444).

The next objection is more difficult: the idea contradicts a well-confirmed hypothesis. According to Newton's theory, gravity cannot be directly converted to electricity (it can first turn into inertial force or kinetic energy and then to electricity). The problem is how to accept Faraday's program and still accept Newton's theory. The answer is simple: we must reinterpret Newton's hypothesis (ibid., p. 445):

> Allowing the principle its force, we ought, in every hypothesis, either to account for its consequences by saying what the changes are when force of a given kind apparently disappears, as when ice thaws, or else should leave space for the idea of conversion. *If any hypothesis, more or less trustworthy on other accounts, is insufficient in expressing it or incompatible with it, the place of deficiency or opposition should be marked as the most important for examination; for there lies the hope of a discovery of new laws or a new condition of force. The*

*deficiency should never be accepted as satisfactory, but be
remembered and used as a stimulant to further inquiry; for
conversion of force may here be hoped for. Suppositions may
be accepted for the time, provided they are not in contradiction
with the principle.* Even an increased or diminished capacity
is better than nothing at all; because such a supposition, if
made, must be consistent with the nature of the original
hypothesis, and may therefore, by the application of experiment,
into further tests of probable truth. The case of a force simply
removed or suspended, without a transferred exertion in some
other direction, appears to me to be absolutely impossible.

Here a program is laid down frankly and boldly. We accept a principle.
If a well-confirmed hypothesis in in conflict with the principle, then, in spite
of facts and confirmations and in spite of the fact that our principle is accepted
without empirical support, unconfirmed and metaphysical, we prefer the
principle to the most confirmed hypothesis. But we do not ignore the hypothesis,
nor the fact that it does not comply with the principle. We try to bend the
hypothesis to conform with the principle—so bold we are. And the new "supposition" or the interpretation of the hypothesis in the light of the principle,
or the hypothesis as it now looks after we have bent it, should now be rendered
testable and tested, and thus a discovery may be made. And if we fail, we shall
try a new supposition—we shall try the process all over again. The negation
of the principle, says Faraday, "appears to me to be absolutely impossible."

If the principle be accepted as true, we have a right
to pursue it to its consequences, no matter what they may
be. It is, indeed, a duty to do so. A theory may be a perfection
as far as it goes, but a consideration going beyond it is not
for that reason to be shut out. *We might as well accept our
limited horizon as the limits of the world.* No magnitude, either
of the phenomena or of the results to be dealt with, should
stop our exertion to ascertain, by the use of the principle,
*that something remaining to be discovered, and to trace in what
direction that discovery may lie.*

This is the justification for preferring a principle to a well-confirmed
hypothesis. A confirmed hypothesis, Newton's theory of gravity, is a horizon,

a limitation. We want to transcend it. The principle helps us, guides us to a possible discovery.

This, I think, is a sufficient argument against the well-confirmed hypothesis. But what about the principle? It "appears to me to be absolutely impossible" that the principle is false. Nevertheless, what if it is? Faraday is not a man to forget such a question. Here is his reply (ibid., p. 459):

> But, after all, the principle of conservation of force may by some be denied. *Well, then, if it be unfounded even in its application to the smallest part of the science of force, the proof must be within our reach, for all physical science is so. In that case, discoveries as large or larger than any yet made may be anticipated. I do not resist the search for them, for no one can do harm, but only good, with an earnest and truthful spirit in such a direction. But let us not admit the destruction or creation of force without clear and constant proof.* Just as the chemist owes all the perfection of his science to his dependence on the certainty of gravitation applied by the balance, so may the physical philosopher expect to find *the greatest security and the utmost aid* in the principle of conservation of force. All that we have that is good and safe, the steam-engine, the electric telegraph, &c., witness to that principle,—it would require a *perpetual motion*, a fire without heat, heat without a source, action without reaction, cause without effect, or effect without a cause, to displace it from its rank of a law of nature.

This argument, strong as it is, seems to me unacceptable. The hypothesis that no perpetual motion is possible is not incompatible with Newton's theory of gravity. It is a poor show to argue that Newton's hypothesis, though well-confirmed, must give way to a principle, and then defend the principle because it is a well-confirmed hypothesis. I do not think it easy to find a crude logical flaw in Faraday's arguments. But I failed to criticize my present criticism of Faraday. And I think that on this point, the theory of interpretation that will be developed in the present volume offers better arguments. Not that it matters much from the point of view that interested Faraday; but it might if we wish to have a forceful theory of interpretation—forceful enough to be applicable to the present problem-situation in physics.

Faraday was anxious to establish his principle. He hoped that it would be refutable to so high a degree that when it was tested and resisted refutation it would be well-confirmed as a consequence. Were it so, we would merely have to follow his own advice and reject his principle as one that had turned into a well-confirmed hypothesis, as the new horizon to our world. We would then invent a new principle that would guide us toward a refutation of that confirmed hypothesis.

Faraday was absorbed in employing his principle to widen existing horizons; he could not be bothered with the question of what should be done when that principle becomes the new horizon. He was too anxious there and then to apply the principle to concrete cases, to raise concrete problems (ibid., p. 461):

> It is perfectly true that we cannot always trace a force by its actions, though we admit its conservation. Oxygen and hydrogen may remain mixed for years without showing any signs of chemical activity; they may be made at any given instant to exhibit active results, and then assume a new state, in which they again appear as passive bodies. Now, though we cannot clearly explain what the chemical force is doing, that is to say, what are its effects during the three periods before, at, and after the active combination, *and only by very vague assumption can approach to a feeble conception of its respective states, yet we do not suppose the creation of a new portion of force for the active moment of time* . . . A part may at the active moment be thrown off as mechanical force, a part as radiant force, a part disposed of we know not how; but believing, by the principle of conservation, that it is not increased or destroyed, *our thoughts are directed to search out what at all and every period it is doing, and how it is to be recognized and measured.* A PROBLEM, founded on a physical truth of nature, IS STATED and, BEING STATED, IS ON THE WAY TO ITS SOLUTION.

And, he shows in detail, those who believe in one of two versions of the principle will state the problem differently than those who believe in the other; and they will search for the solution in different directions.

This is now the full answer: If we have a principle, it creates problems; and the statement of a problem is a step toward its solution. I find this still a bit positivistic to my taste. I do not see why Faraday should endorse a view for pragmatic reasons alone, even if the word "pragmatic" means not cash value but scientific value. And I do not believe that all problems that are interesting need be soluble. Nevertheless, I have no doubt, Faraday's philosophy is one of the most enlightened ever.

Let me conclude by stating that it is my impression that Faraday's point was fully and explicitly endorsed by his disciples. Allow me to quote J. J. Thomson's *The Corpuscular Theory of Matter* (London, 1907, p. 1): ". . . a theory of matter is a policy rather than a creed; its object is to . . . suggest, stimulate and direct experiment . . . [and] lead the observer . . ." The language is unmistakenly Faradayan. This passage has been quoted by I. B. Cohen in his *Franklin and Newton* (p. 285) as a point applicable to Newton's program. And so it is; but the eighteenth-century Newtonians were not as clear about this as the late-nineteenth-century Faradayans. By now, of course, physicists have abandoned the matter, and apart from a stray philosopher of science, such as Sylvain Bromberger,[5] only a few historians of science (Koyré and his followers, mainly) notice this point.

5. See Sylvain Bromberger, "A theory about the Theory of Theory and about the Theory of Theories," in B. Baumrin, ed., *Philosophy of Science, The Delaware Seminar*, 2 (New York and London, 1963), 79–105, especially 104–5. In the penultimate paragraph Bromberger says a metaphysical theory "often generates a field of investigation whose" explanatory theory "must be created." He also speaks there of two kinds of acceptance, one of believing an explanatory theory to be true and one of accepting as sound the questions that a metaphysical theory gives rise to. Imre Lakatos has recently elaborated these different senses of acceptance, and his work has gained considerable attention. See Imre Lakatos, "Changes in the Problem of Inductive Logic," in I. Lakatos (ed.), *The Problem of Inductive Logic*, Amsterdam, 1968, pp. 315–417.

# 6    Faraday as a Discoverer

### The Miracle of Faraday

> If Newton, not quite without reason, has been compared
> to a man who ascends to the top of a building by the help
> of a ladder, and cuts away most of the steps after he has done
> with them, it must be said that you have left to the follower,
> with scrupulous fidelity, the ladder in the same state as you
> have made use of it . . .

So wrote a famous adversary to Faraday toward the end of Faraday's philosophical career (*Life and Letters.* 2:350). Indeed Faraday developed from a
discoverer to a methodologist, to a public figure who influenced views on science
and the scientific tradition no less than the scientific views themselves. He
did it in part directly, but mainly indirectly, by being a personal example,
by "leaving the ladder which he made use of."

Let me make my thesis clear. The fragmented pictures we have of Faraday
—the discoverer, the speculative thinker, the methodologist, the person, the
Early Victorian, the grand old scientist—all these can be brought together in a
somewhat rounded picture that is not divorced from history. And the way to
bring these together is by noticing the fact that Faraday did not remove the
ladder or the scaffolding: he described the way he had developed his discoveries.

In our own day, revelations (like James Watson's *The Double Helix*)
about the seamy side of research are frowned on by almost no one (really only
by the President of Harvard University and his like). And even those who do
frown are concerned with gossipy revelations, not with their methodological

and philosophical implications. We are less scandalized by such matters today than Faraday's contemporaries were. The reason is obvious. Until Faraday's time, the model had been Newton; since then, Faraday is a model too.

Newton concealed his method and largely presented his results inductively. So did Ampère. In between there was little variation. The little variation there was may be first noticed in the works of Joseph Priestley. Many writers, he says, try nowadays to present their discoveries as if they were confirmations of their theories. But, he continues, had they stuck to chronology, it would be clear that their discoveries were accidental and not predicted on the basis of their theories. Since that time, quite a few thinkers have risen to the challenge and make their discoveries after publicly announcing them on theoretical grounds. Ampère himself did so, thus having it both ways: he predicted his discoveries during a public lecture and reported them in the succeeding lecture. Oersted made his discovery in public. We have a letter from Davy to a friend promising to decompose nitrogen before their subsequent meeting. He failed, of course; but the idea is devilishly clever: write a letter to a friend; if your prediction is correct, he will publicize it; if not he will not betray you. The practice went on, I suppose, as long as people felt that publishing prematurely entailed risk. Lord Kelvin, who died in our own century, still followed it. "As someone had said, he made discoveries in his public lectures: it is certain that he threw out new ideas which were often lost through the want of a verbatim report," comments a reviewer of some of his collected works in the *Glasgow Weekly Herald* of 8 June 1911 (p. 4). The very description of Kelvin's practice that we have here marks that the era was over: the reviewer could not imagine that a man like Kelvin needed to test his ideas in public before publishing them. In biology, we know, the practice is still extant; in physics Faraday has managed to oust it at long last.

Physicists, indeed, are now more liberal and may view a paper, even a significant paper (such as that of Bohr, Kramers, and Slater, or that of Goudsmit and Uhlenbeck) as merely flying a kite; yet historians of science still follow the classical vein of considering a contribution to science as something positive and and definite—a discovery, a verified theory. Attitudes toward Faraday are still in this vein: all his discoveries are presented as either accidental or confirming his predictions. Of all his speculations, usually only those are cited by historians and biographers that have been confirmed. Let me mention but one example. In his comments on Faraday's very important paper, "Thoughts on Ray Vibrations," S. P. Thompson says (*Michael Faraday*, p. 193): "At the dates when the earlier biographies of Faraday appeared, neither that doctrine [of the electromagnetic origin of light] nor this paper had received the recognition due to its importance. Tyndall dismisses it as 'one of the most singular speculations that ever emanated from a scientific man.' Bence Jones just mentioned it in half a line. Dr. Gladstone does not allude to it . . .''

And why does Thompson consider it important? Because it was confirmed, or rather because this is what he thought. Thompson emphasizes that Faraday had looked for Kerr's effect, for the photoelectric effect, and for Zeeman's effect; had Thompson lived later, he would mention with the same enthusiasm and with equal justice that Faraday was looking for Compton's effect when he tried to detect any change of color of a ray due to transition through matter. Since he thought Faraday was mistaken in his search for this change of color, he did not even allude to this part of Faraday's research. No doubt there is something very important in the use of later developments of our knowledge for a reevaluation of past developments. But I cannot help thinking that there is something degrading in the simple criterion of evaluation that I have else-where termed standard-up-to-date-science-textbook-worshipping. It is funny that Thompson should censure his predecessors while employing the same criterion they held.

Undoubtedly our major objective is the truth, and therefore, the more Faraday helps us to come nearer the truth, the more we should remember him with gratitude and respect. But this is not the point most emphasized by his biographers. Rather, with each new confirmation of a conjecture by Faraday, and the latest occurred about a century after his death, we are apt to hear more about his penetrating intuition, his mystical power, his knowledge of nature akin to that of a magician and a clairvoyant. Now, doubtless, there was something uncanny, something of a miracle in Faraday's ingenious search for gravitational effects on electromagnetic waves, for the photoelectric effect, for Zeeman's effect, for Compton's effect, and even for later discoveries; it is most amazing. For my part, however, I find, say, Faraday's search for *transversal* electric forces no less impressive—even though nothing whatsoever resembling them in any way have been found as yet. And if I consider Faraday's theory of gravity as the peak of his research, it is not, I wish to stress, because Einstein entertained a view very similar to it. Thompson, who was the first biographer to pay tribute to Faraday's "Thoughts on Ray Vibrations," did not mention at all his thoughts and experiments concerning gravity. Nowadays they are more popular, since Bragg declared (in his 1931 centenary lecture at the Royal Institution) that Eddington's eclipse observation (which was made as a crucial experiment between Newton's and Einstein's theories of gravity) confirms

Faraday's hunch. I really do not think it is Einstein's theory that gives Faraday's theory its significance. It only illustrates this significance.

There are two uncritical elements in measuring Faraday's research by the yardstick of the standard-up-to-date-science-textbook-worshipper. One is the ignoring of his failure and the emphasis on his success in hitting upon views accepted today. If we sincerely accept today's theories as our measure, at least we have to contrast success with failure. But, of course, we cannot accept this yardstick seriously because of its second weakness—we cannot think highly of Newton when we accept a corpuscularian theory of light and lowly when we accept an undulatory theory of light. Our yardstick becomes too unstable! Most important, we cannot possibly understand what was Faraday's "ladder" while looking only at his successes. And so I must fully reject the standard of evaluation so commonly accepted—the method of exalting Faraday's success in stating views now incorporated in the body of accepted theories. Faraday's "ladder" was to try and apply his grand speculations repeatedly, and in the face of failure, in order to make new discoveries. Moreover, his grand speculation itself is not accepted today by any scientist (even heretics like Schrödinger or Einstein did not fully accept his views).

In brief, the standard implicitly (but clearly) employed by all of Faraday's biographers and the majority of historians of science omits that element of Faraday's views that seems to me to be the most significant for an understanding of his method.

Faraday's success up to 1831, even including his greatest discovery, that of magnetoelectricity, is a very great success, no doubt, and yet no more surprising than the success of quite a few scientists before and after him. But his lifetime work, taken as a whole, is really unique. It is true that some scientific theories, like those of Newton, Maxwell, Einstein, and Schrödinger, are in one way or another comparable to Faraday's electromagnetic theory and each in its own way superior to it. But the researches of none of these giants exhibit such a richness of discovery, such an ever-increasing force of development of theory, such a magnificent poetic beauty as the three volumes of Faraday's *Experimental Researches in Electricity*.

These *Researches* are in a distinct manner unique, incomparable. By saying this I give the clue to my characterization of the miracle: Faraday worked like a group of people. Not only did he both theorize and test, he also theorized on different lines, as if he were ready to defend with all his heart now this theory, now the other, and now the old one again. But I shall come to that later. The miracle, to view it from the inductivist angle, is that Faraday was the first to realize the inductivist ideal. As if in possession of a science-making machine, he produced his discoveries at regular intervals, disturbed only by his illness, from 1831 until the end of his career; and he produced one great discovery after the other with the apparent ease of a conjurer.

For inductivists, Faraday the discoverer was an animal of a most peculiar species. They were just as surprised at the fertility of his research as a spiritualist would be at his first encounter with a ghost. Again and again they claimed that a stream of discoveries is possible, nay, inevitable, provided that we really suspend judgment. And then one who suspends judgment does produce discoveries in streams and leaves them confused and open-mouthed. But the surprise was only temporary. Faraday's success, they were told, is indeed due to his suspension of judgment and hatred of speculative thinking. But why is suspension of judgment unique in the history of discovery? This is bound to remain wrapped in mystery.

### De la Rive on Faraday

> After all, though your science is much to me, we are
> not friends for science sake only, but for something better in a
> man, something more important in his nature, affection,
> kindness, good feelings, moral worth . . .
>
> Faraday to Schoenbein[1]

Auguste de la Rive was a close friend of Faraday. As we have noticed, Faraday had no wide circle of friends or colleagues and practically no acquaintants. Even his family circle was small and close. He corresponded very extensively, but of his correspondents only Schoenbein and de la Rive stand out, perhaps also Matteucci. His relations with Schoenbein were those of close colleagues; their friendly correspondence fills a volume. There is little to say about it, however, that is not about day-to-day affairs, whether of research, a bit of scientific gossip of the best kind, or personal encouragement and appreciation. The most important aspect of this correspondence, I think, is the mutual encouragement of two rebels; this may indeed relate to the fact that Schoenbein had been a student and a disciple of the notorious Schelling. This leaves us with de la Rive, whose correspondence with Faraday is second only to Schoenbein's—both in volume and in content.

1. *Life and Letters*, 2:439.

Faraday met young Auguste de la Rive during his European tour, when Davy was the guest of honor of Auguste's father, Gaspard, a Swiss professor of chemistry. Faraday was welcome there in a natural manner, and the elderly professor treated him as an equal in all respects. (As gossip has it, this led to a clash between host and guest of honor.) It seems to have been a unique experience in the whole of Faraday's life: he seems to have treated Auguste de la Rive as a brother, and he seems to have relaxed only in his company. Faraday could not relax even on holiday. He kept extensive journals while not working, and in one such journal, on a holiday prescribed by doctors, he describes a day of walking in mountain country, covering forty or fifty miles in heavy rain, and a night deprived of sleep because of noise in a Swiss hotel. But in de la Rive's home he could rest. When he became old and tired, he remembered a sunny afternoon on de la Rive's lawn, lazying with the children and being offered a glass of water by the lady of the house. Having nothing else to write de la Rive but feeling obligated to write something, the old man mused with gratitude upon the memory of that restful afternoon. This is not to say that all his letters to de la Rive were reminiscences; many of them are very substantive, both experimental and theoretical. Old de la Rive had encouraged Faraday to write to him about his work, and this was Faraday's first serious scientific correspondence (it was also published by the old man). It flowed from the father to the son quite naturally and smoothly. Thus, few could claim closer acquaintanceship with Faraday than de la Rive. It is therefore quite understandable that his obituary notice on Faraday had great impact, even if we entirely ignore its tremendous intellectual and artistic force.

Here are a few passages from de la Rive's once famous *Notice sur Michael Faraday* (1867, translation both in the Annual Report of the Smithsonian Institute, 1867, and in the *Philosophical Magazine*, 34 [1867], 410):

> Without children, a complete stranger to politics or to
> any kind of administration, except that of the Royal Institution,
> which he directed as if he would have directed his own house,
> having no interest but that of science, and no ambition but
> that of advancing it, Faraday was of all *savants* the one most
> completely and exclusively devoted to [science] . . .
> One may easily understand what must be produced
> under such circumstances by a life thus wholly consecrated
> to science, when to a strong and rigorous intellect is joined
> a most brilliant imagination. *Every morning Faraday went*

*into his laboratory as the man of business goes to his office,*
*and then tried by experiment the truth of the ideas which he*
*had conceived overnight, as ready to give them up if experiment*
*said* no, *as to follow out the consequences with rigorous logic*
*if experiment answered* yes . . .

This is an impressive passage, echoed in other impressive passages, including one quoted at the beginning of a classic work by Hermann Weyl on quantum theory, repeated in the closing pages of a classic work by Karl Popper on the logic of scientific discovery.[2] As for the context of this passage, the yes-or-no view of experiment, which is presumably de la Rive's, whether it fits Faraday's attitudes is questionable, as I have ventured to show: when Faraday expressed distaste for "doubtful knowledge," he fits this characterization fairly well; when he expressed his deep-seated skepticism, he does not.

As for the rest of the above quotation, I can hardly comment on it since it is more personal than scientific and the present study is not much of a personal biography. The idea, however, that the more devoted a man is to science, the more results he can expect is inductive rubbish; nor does the rest of it fit the facts unless we can show that the agony of childlessness and the readiness to spend any amount of time with every child encountered is less taxing than having children and neglecting them to the care of wife and nurse in the style current in that period.

I might say in passing that, all appearances to the contrary, de la Rive's description of Faraday's blissful childlessness is sincere and honest: it is expressed in a friendly and appreciative letter to Faraday himself, written as early as 1852 (*Life and Letters*, 2:316; Gladstone's *Michael Faraday*, p. 170): ". . . thanks to the goodness of God," he said, "you have not suffered any of those family misfortunes which crush one's life." I may even say, perhaps, that de la Rive was uncomfortably conscious of Faraday's envy of his domestic bliss and oblivious of his "family misfortunes." To quiet his own discomfort, he imagined Faraday's blissful working conditions in an idealized fashion—in utter symmetry, I suppose. "You possess that which best contributes to peace of mind and serenity of spirit," he said, explaining that he was referring to Faraday's religion.

De la Rive's image of Faraday as a stranger both to family life and to politics and administration is rather erroneous. Yet there is no doubt that

2. Hermann Weyl, *The Theory of Groups and Quantum Mechanics*, 1931, p. xx, quoted in Karl Popper, *The Logic of Scientific Discovery*, 1959, p. 280.

Faraday himself somewhat misled de la Rive: Williams quotes (*Michael Faraday*, p. 357) a letter from Faraday, written in 1849, saying that he never meddled in politics because he thought little of politics "as one of the games of life" and because he felt scientific men should concentrate on the progress of philosophy and not be disturbed by the passions of men. As Faraday explained elsewhere (*Life and Letters*, 2:204), he considered politics in his day not yet open to the critical spirit. He had, I suppose, the choice between playing no part in politics or revolutionizing the field; but he was too conservative for the latter. No one would say of Ampère that he was a stranger to politics, since he declared that the storming of the Bastille was one of the three significant events of his life. (Another was the loss of his father to the subsequent Terror.) Faraday, his younger contemporary, was educated by a French refugee and soon was faced with the Napoleonic disillusionment ("The disgrace of France," he called the Louvre). Consequently he became a conservative. And as a conservative he could more easily be characterized as a complete stranger to politics. Yet of the two he gave more time—much more—to public service, and quite free of charge, too.[3] He spent much time in engineering and in invention and in governmental and public inspectional and administrative work of all sorts. The records of his labors are astounding. When he thought other people could do a given job, he declined to accept it, but all too often he was the only volunteer. And it was his principle never to apply for a patent and to decline remuneration for serving the government—which he did with the same sense of duty that made him a devoted scientist. His work in lighthouse inspection and administration alone was enough to occupy one man's full energy and concentration. To repeat, he was a work-maniac.

So much for the opening phrases of de la Rive. The idea that all his intellectual activities went to science is nearer to the truth, even though less by intention than by expediency. In principle he was all for a broad cultural education.[4] He entertained an ideal of a widely informed public with a taste

3. See Jeffreys' bibliography, pp. vii, xix, xx. See also Roy M. MacLeod, "Science and Government in Victorian England: Lighthouse Illumination and the Board of Trade, 1866–1886," *Isis*, 60 (Spring 1969), 16, text to n. 45 and nn. 45–46. See also Williams, *Michael Faraday*, pp. 488 ff.

4. The following quotation from another obituary notice is exaggerated (Chemical Society of London, *Faraday Lectures*, London, 1928, p. xi): "Faraday had naturally a great love of literature, especially of fiction and drama. In early life he acquired some knowledge of Latin and of several modern languages; and he was well read in the great English classics . . ." In fact, he knew no Latin, and the several modern languages he knew were English, some French, and less Italian. Even his French was not very serviceable: Plücker stopped writing to him in French and switched to English after they met in person.

for the arts and the sciences *alike*. Let me mention one of many examples—
the concluding section of an early lecture on magnetism of 1827—in which
he speaks of the lecture evenings in general (*Life and Letters*, 1:398), expressing his hope "that literary subjects shall be intermingled with those of science
and art." He spoke in this vein all his life. Personally he drifted from this
ideal. In his youth he sang (bass) and played the flute. In later life he had a
free ticket to the opera, yet he seldom had the time to go. Similarly, he was a
member of the Royal Academy but soon neglected his interest in painting.
Socially, however, he was an educational reformer, not without influence,
who was consulted by various authorities. He stressed the need for experimental
science in all schools and fought the tendency to offer only a narrow cultural
education in vocational schools.

Back to de la Rive. Faraday was successful, we note, because he was
devoted to and in possession of the gifts of imagination and rigor. And now
comes de la Rive's account of Faraday's development of this idea of imagination
and rigor (p. 412):

Is it true that the man of science who wished to interrogate
nature must set himself face to face with his apparatus, make
them act to derive facts from them, and wait until these
facts have appeared, in order to deduce their consequences,
and all without preconceived ideas? Most certainly the
philosopher who could advance such an opinion [Bacon] has
never experimented, and in any case *this method has never
been that of discoverers; it was assuredly not the one adopted
by Faraday*.

There is a second method also which is not his, although it
is truly worthy of attention *and often* fertile of results. This
consists in *taking up known phenomena and studying them in
great precision, carefully determining all the elements and
numerical data so as to deduce therefrom them laws which
govern them, and often also to show the inexactitude of the laws
to which they were supposed to be subjected*. This method requires
great previous study, great practical talent in the construction
of apparatus, remarkable sagacity in the interpretation of
the results furnished by experiment, and lastly much
perseverance and patience. . . .

A third method, very different from the last mentioned,

is that which, *quitting the beaten track*, leads, as if by INSPIRATION, to those great discoveries which open new horizons to science. This method, in order to be fertile, requires one condition—a condition, it is true, which is but rarely met with,—namely genius. Now this condition existed in Faraday. Endowed, as he himself perceived, with much imagination, he *dared* to advance where *many others would have recoiled* . . . Still always wishing for facts, and accepting theories with difficulty, he was nevertheless *more or less directed by preconceived ideas*, which *whether true or false, led him into new roads*, where most frequently he found what he sought, sometimes indeed what he did not seek, but where he constantly met with some important discovery.

I have quoted de la Rive on method in full because I do not know how to abbreviate it without giving a false impression. It is not unusual that when men of science talk about method inaccuracy, confusion, and ambiguity abound. In this case, perhaps more than usually, the apologetic purpose of the ambiguity is what I find intriguing. It is possible to read de la Rive thus: there is *first* the official purist inductive method that has never been tried (this point had been made by a few commentators on Bacon's work around the mid-century); there is *second* the quantitative inductive method, with minor corrections all along, which most scientists use; there is the *third* imaginative method open *only* to men of genius.

There is no doubt that de la Rive's aim was to offer praise, but to prevent the praise from causing attempts to emulate its object. In this, I must add in all fairness, de la Rive was merely echoing an opinion which had been stated in the press before[5] and which seemed to have been quite popular amongst his contemporaries.[6]

5. Not only was this said of Faraday, it was said before by Laplace concerning Kepler (though perhaps less crisply) in his *System of the World*, Book V. This, indeed, seems to be the origin of de la Rive's idea: geniuses have a special dispensation to speculate at their own risk.

6. For example, J. B. A. Dumas, Faraday's friend since the European tour, said in his Faraday Lecture (*Faraday Lectures*, London, 1928, p. 2), both "In the study of Nature conjecture must be ENTIRELY PUT ASIDE, and vague hypothesis carefully guarded against. The study of Nature begins with facts . . ." and "A long familiarity with the exact detail of phenomena can alone give to a man, as it did to Faraday, THE RIGHT TO BE BOLD; but he is also, like Faraday, restrained, when he has a thorough appreciation of the limits of man's knowledge."

This attitude, it is true, is implicit in Herschel's *Preliminary Discourse* (see my "Sir John Herschel, Philosophy of Success" in Russell McCormmach (ed.), *Historical Studies in the Physical Sciences* [Philadelphia, 1969], pp. 24 ff.).

Faraday's method was to "quit the beaten track" and imagine new ideas, says de la Rive. But, he adds immediately, this is the privilege of the man of genius alone (p. 413): it is "barren and even dangerous with mediocre minds"! A few pages later (p. 419) this is followed by a mystifying discussion of the function and place of Faraday's speculations; this makes it clear that de la Rive considered not the speculating as the act of "quitting the beaten track": speculating was merely a part of "more or less indirect consequences" of "quitting the beaten track." What exactly was that act of imagination, how it differed from the act of speculating, and how did it lead Faraday to new roads —all this is left obscure.

In de la Rive's *Treatize on Electricity*, which consists of three thick volumes, Faraday is often mentioned as a clever and profound scientist etc. etc., and Faraday's discoveries are often mentioned and discussed at length. But in this work references to Faraday's theories are cursory and often unfair;[7] in the first volume there is a defense of Ampère's theory and an implicit attack on Faraday; Faraday's lines of force are mentioned in that volume once (p. 365), and as a mnemotechnical device, as a means to memorize the right-hand rule, relating directions of currents to directions of magnetism. The obituary notice is more generous. De la Rive briefly mentions there the content of Faraday's atomic speculation; he admits that the difficulty it comes to solve is real and even disturbing (to adherents of the accepted doctrine). That he still hoped the difficulty may be resolved within the old system is not in itself unreasonable, of course, especially since he noted the significance of the issue involved (which I shall later discuss)—materialism versus immaterialism. I quote only a brief passage of his discussion (p. 420): "We are convinced that it is not by *denying the existence of matter, properly so called, and admitting only the forces*, that we shall succeed in solving the difficulties . . . but rather . . . by modifying the ideas hitherto accepted . . .

Here, at least de la Rive clearly states Faraday's natural philosophy. De la Rive also adds that the expected solution should come on lines proposed by Clausius, and he points out that Clausius had a fair measure of but not complete success. And he censures, therefore, those who claim that the received atomic doctrine had achieved the status of certitude. It is, as yet, not as certain as Laplace's *Mechanique Celeste*.

---

7. See Williams, *Michael Faraday*, pp. 372 and 404. See also my forthcoming "Field Theory in de la Rive's Treatise on Electricity."

It is often said of great men that they are difficult. They may be difficult in the psychological sense—demanding much from themselves and constantly struggling and uneasy, they may convey the sense of constant struggle and irritation that goes with them. Though this is not true of all great men, it is true of many of them in the last few centuries. To be merely psychologically difficult, however, is neither here nor there. Many people are difficult to this or that degree, and without the excuse of their genius, as Shaw has pointed out in his *Doctor's Dilemma*. Strangely, difficult men of genius annoy us more than others because we cannot ignore them as we can ignore the others. They appeal to the better in us, whether by animating our nobler sentiments or by impressing our nobler friends. And this is a kind of difficulty in that quite often we do not know how to cope with our better selves and we feel at a loss—and in a search for a way out we work up our anger.

Faraday was a very difficult man. He was, however, as kind and sweet to de la Rive as David to Jonathan. And the latter, of course, was at least equally courteous and friendly, perhaps much more so. Yet, I have the feeling sometimes he must have found him barely tolerable.

Of course, there can be no explicit evidence for my view, and so it sounds both light and nasty. Yet I wish to present it as my general impression from his letters to Faraday and from his obituary; as my explanation for his inability to communicate with Faraday and his unreadiness to tell Faraday some of the harsh things he said of him in his obituary; and, mostly, in deep sympathy with him, especially since he got rather a raw deal (Faraday's biographers do not even mention his obituary). It seems to me that both Faraday and de la Rive had to make enormous concessions to each other, not in order to compromise ideology for friendship but in order to reconcile ideology with plain liberalism. They symbolized for each other the intellectual stalemate of their outlooks. It would be natural if de la Rive would have taken all this with equanimity and Faraday with irritation. But history does not always yield to rational reconstruction. It seems clear to me that in all respects of their interactions de la Rive paid more heavily than Faraday. Except that he could enjoy the company of one of the greatest spirits of the age, without the ability to return in kind.

## Tyndall on Faraday

If Bence Jones's biography of Faraday is the most faithful and detailed biography, and if Gladstone's biography is a portrait of an admirable old professor ("the professor" he is called in that book), then Tyndall's work is the monument to Faraday's genius erected by a man of science who could well appreciate Faraday's discoveries. The title of the book, *Faraday as a Discoverer*, is very becoming: for Tyndall the aim of science is discovery of new facts. Whether, like Tyndall, one appreciates Faraday more as a discoverer, as a faithful observer of detailed facts, or, like Einstein, more as a natural philosopher, as an originator of a bold idea, such a preference is at least partly a matter of taste, perhaps even of peculiar personal interest. But there can be no clear-cut distinction here. The view advocated in the present study is that Faraday the discoverer was mainly aided by Faraday the thinker; Tyndall's view is only slightly different. Yet I wish to strain the difference to its breaking point.

To whatever extent we may say that the stress on Faraday's facts or ideas is a matter of taste, at least partly such a taste must be considered philosophical. We know as well as we know anything in history that Tyndall's philosophical taste was inductivist, that his temperament and his judgment both came down on the side of fact, and that similarly for Einstein it was theory that played this dual role. We also know that Faraday showed great ambivalence facing this choice. And we can show by means of logic that this ambivalence can be resolved on the (Popperian) theory that the interplay between theory and fact is dialectical, that theory and fact enhance each other not by mutual support but by mutual nudging and criticism. We know from history how important Faraday considered criticism. Putting all these factors together we can easily present a more coherent picture of Faraday than historical truth warrants. Arthur Koestler has presented in his *The Sleepwalkers* a fairly convincing picture of Kepler as a Popperian. It is much easier to do so with Faraday. We can take warning from Tyndall's effort to make a coherent but unhistorical picture of Faraday—an inductive picture, but not in the traditional Baconian style.

Tyndall's view of Faraday is greatly influenced by the view of the importance of imagination in science; as was the avant-garde view of scientific method, originally propounded[8] by Whewell and Faraday. With this stress on the role of the imagination, in a book on Faraday, which, its author claimed, was a compression of Faraday's life-long work while retaining its spirit intact (preface to 2d edition), surely one would expect Tyndall to present Faraday's

8. Perhaps Sir David Brewster has priority for this view as expressed in his life of Newton of 1831 in the chapter on Newton's method. But I have not sufficiently checked this point. There is Colleridge and there are his Continental predecessors to check on this point, including Boscovich and Kant (e.g., the preface to the second edition of the first *Critique*).

philosophy of nature, his speculations, as the axis of Faraday's researches. After all, in his open letter to Tyndall, Faraday had said that much rather clearly.

But Tyndall's presentation of the role of imagination in Faraday's work is different, and utterly divorced from Faraday's speculations—which in fact he considers the results of poor imagination.

Tyndall introduces Faraday's power of imagination, "a power which Faraday possessed in an extraordinary degree," in order to explain the fact that in 1831 Faraday succeeded where others (Ampère and Arago among them) failed: "he united vast strength with perfect flexibility" (p. 24). This means, I take it, that convinced that he was right he went on searching, but never twice in the same place. But Tyndall does not explain, except to refer (p. 26) to "Faraday's power of lateral vision, separating, as it were, from the line of expectation." This means, I take it, that Faraday could look forward but keep glancing sideways, that he could keep more or less on course while taking cues for correction along the line, that he could stubbornly retain his vision in essence but regularly modify it in detail. To this, incidentally, I am quite ready to agree. The question, however, is, what was the essence of Faraday's vision? The answer is, Faraday's vision of the whole system of laws of nature as laws of fields of force; in brief Faraday's speculations. These, however, are not even alluded to early in Tyndall's book.

Rather, as if in an attempt to show that he has less disregard for Faraday's vision than others, he attacks those who viewed Faraday from a purely Baconian position. Referring (p. 28) to the view of him as "a purely inductive philosopher," Tyndall says bluntly, "a great deal of nonsense is, I fear, uttered in this land of England about induction and deduction." Faraday, he stresses, "was at this time [1831] full of the theory of Ampère, and it cannot be doubted that numbers of his experiments were executed merely to test his deductions from that theory." And so, first of all, the Baconian theory is false.

Nevertheless, Tyndall does ascribe to Faraday a clear adherence to Bacon's doctrine of prejudice: "Faraday always recommended the suspension of judgment in cases of doubt," he says (p. 32). "Now, however," he continues, "the time for theory had come." The theory, of 1831, is that currents are produced by cutting lines of force (p. 33).

Clearly for Tyndall, then, "induction" means discovery without a theory in one's head, while "deduction" means deduction from a hypothesis so as to *test* it in order to refute it or else to verify it by new discoveries.

This is in fact Tyndall's thesis: Faraday made hypotheses and tested them, thus coming to more and more discoveries. He emphasizes throughout the whole book the conflict, the dialectic interplay, between two elements—Faraday's imagination and his hatred of things doubtful. The outcome of this conflict was Faraday's constant urge to test the offsprings of his imagination (p. 51):

> I have already once used the word "discomfort" in reference to the occasional state of Faraday's mind when experimenting. It was to him a discomfort to reason upon data which admitted of doubt. He hated what he called "doubtful knowledge" and ever tended either to transfer it into the region of undoubtful knowledge, or of certain and definite ignorance. Pretence of all kinds, whether in life or in philosophy, was hateful to him. He wished to know the reality of our nescience as well of our science. "Be one thing or the other," he seems to say to an unproven hypothesis; "come out as a solid truth, or disappear as a convicted lie."

Here Tyndall presents a popular version—a vulgar one—of Whewell's philosophy of science. It is an idea which in the mid-1930s was very widely and enthusiastically hailed as the greatest and last discovery in the philosophy of science—the so-called verification principle of meaning. The truth value of a hypothesis (i.e., the answer to the question, is it true or false?), says the principle, must be decidable (i.e., the hypothesis should be proven or its negation should be proven). And while explaining this deep idea, Tyndall confuses nescience or lack of knowledge or ignorance, with the knowledge that some view is an error; he similarly confuses error with lie. Descartes did so over two centuries earlier, by an ingenious though faulty argument; Tyndall was merely swept away by his rhetoric, I think: when he applied it to Faraday he gave it an ingenious twist: Faraday hated doubt but generated new and hence doubtful ideas; and so he had to verify or refute a new idea every day. What kept him running was his conflicting tendencies—imagination plus the quest for certainty. Never a moment of rest; never a dull moment.

Next comes a condensed report on various researchs, mainly concerning the experiments on the electric pile, the theory of the pile and the tests of the theory. It repeatedly illustrates the view that Faraday made his discoveries by testing his own hypotheses. The report is rather factual, according to the inductive style. It ends with Faraday's theory of conversion of forces of nature into one another, and with a quotation from Faraday on the indestructibility of power. On this his comment is very strange: rather than acknowledge Faraday's priority over Joule and Mayer, he says (p. 78), "These words ... illustrate the fact that before any great scientific principle receives distinct enunciation by individuals, it dwells more or less clearly in the general scientific mind. The intellectual plateau is already high, and our discoverers are those who, like peaks above the plateau, rise a little above the general level of thought at the time."

My immediate response to this passage is very different from my considered response. The first is to consider it a mystification and irrationalism, as well as a gross unfairness to Faraday, who was more "a little above the general level" than Mayer or Joule. My considered response is different. The idea expressed in this passage is clearer and more rational than the one that Robert Merton and T. S. Kuhn, among others, have recently popularized under the title of "multiple discovery." Tyndall shows in two respects a higher degree of rationality than these two later scholars. First, Tyndall confines himself strictly to major ideas—since smaller ones, such as Faraday's theory of magneto-electric induction, are clearly not often made in a multiple manner. Second, he explains by what mechanism we arrive both at the multiple discovery and at the attribution of it to one individual, whereas they neither give a mechanism nor do they comment on the fact that we do make acknowledgments and offer rewards to single individuals. Superior as Tyndall's idea is by comparison to some famous ideas, it is nonetheless not really very impressive. Indeed, it is pretentious. What Tyndall should at least have noted as missing is some measure of excellence, of that "little above the general level."[9] Was it Mayer, or Joule, or Faraday, or Seebeck, or Oersted? Tyndall pretends to see no problem here. But we must proceed.

Faraday's research on static electricity of 1837: "the idea of action at a distance," we hear, "perplexed and bewildered him" (p. 82). "He loved to quote Newton" about it. His theory is that electrostatic force is transmitted

---

9. Tyndall's defective argument is rectified only by Williams, I think. He says (*Michael Faraday*, p. 403) that what was missing in Faraday's theory (for it to count as the discovery of the principle of conservation of energy) was the determination of a universal constant that would have made the theory quantitative. Williams thinks this is essential, whereas others might feel differently about it, especially since Faraday did test his theory quantitatively: What Joule added to Faraday's experiments was indeed the determination of universal constants, the universal factors of conversion. For my part I think it is not important to decide whose study amounts to "*the*" discovery, as long as we understand what each person did, and also, perhaps, notice the degree to which one person helped another.

through the particles of matter, from one particle to its neighbor, to the contiguous one. This theory, Tyndall finds, does not solve the problem, since the atoms are distant from each other, and the problem is thus only shifted (p. 83):

> Faraday does not see the same difficulty in his contiguous particles. And yet, by transferring the conception from masses to particles, we simply lessen size and distance, but we do not alter the quality of the conception. Whatever difficulty the mind experiences in conceiving of action at sensible distances, besets it also when it attempts to conceive of action at insensible distances. Still the investigation of the point whether electric and magnetic effects were wrought out through the intervention of contiguous particles or not, had a physical interest altogether apart from the metaphysical difficulty. Faraday grapples with the subject experimentally.

This is the thin edge of the wedge, and so I have quoted it in full. Here is an example, says Tyndall, of Faraday's display of metaphysical incompetence that matters not since it is accompanied by high scientific competence. The argument, indeed, is valid—perfectly convincing, even—but its premise is palpably false. Tyndall attributes to Faraday a view that Faraday had not held. In his first presentation of his views Faraday spoke of contiguous—meaning adjacent—particles. This was in the 1830s; in the 1840s Faraday presented his view of particles openly: every particle extends, being a field of force, all over the universe; and it has a center that is what we usually call the (localized) particle. This is today quite a well-known idea; in the 1860s it was so novel that Tyndall could not seriously consider it. Ignoring Faraday's ideas, and Faraday's difficulties in handling it, Tyndall could say he had "grappled with the subject experimentally." How sad!

On the next encounter with Faraday's speculations, Tyndall's presentation deteriorates further. Faraday's research on static electricity—where Faraday tried to show that there is no electric fluid but only electric condition of matter—culminates with his effort to explain discharge or current not as the flow of an electric fluid but as the collapse of the electric field of force (and the generation, in its place, of some other, usually magnetic, field of force—since force is indestructible). With this Faraday terminated his first series of *Experimental Researches in Electricity* in 1839 and headed toward his first emotional collapse. Tyndall's discussion of Faraday's theory of the current is condescending. And in his condescension, he defends Faraday against still more vulgar deprecators of his theory of the current. Here is Tyndall's mock-defense (p. 88):

> It would . . . be easy to criticise these researches, easy to show
> the looseness, and sometimes the inaccuracy, of the phraseology
> employed; but this critical spirit will get little good out of
> Faraday. Rather let those who ponder his works seek to realise
> the object he set before him, not permitting his occasional
> vagueness to interfere with their appreciation of his speculations.
> We may see the ripples, and eddies, and vortices of a flowing
> stream, without being able to resolve all these motions into
> their constituent elements; and so it sometimes strikes me
> that Faraday *clearly saw the play of fluids and ethers and
> atoms*, though *his previous training did not enable him to
> resolve what he saw into its constituents*, or describe it in a
> manner *satisfactory to a mind versed in mechanics*. And then
> again occur, I confess, *dark sayings, difficult to be understood*,
> which disturb my confidence in this conclusion. It must, however,
> always be remembered that he works at the very boundaries
> of our knowledge . . .

So the criticism of Faraday on the current is valid, but obviously valid and so cheap, says Tyndall. Faraday, we must in fairness remember, had no training in mathematics and in mechanics, and so he was handicapped. Criticizing him for his handicap is cheap. Moreover, Faraday "clearly saw the play of fluids and ethers and atoms"! Tyndall himself feels uneasy and admits there exist passages in Faraday "which disturb my confidence in this conclusion"—what an understatement!—and that he labels "dark sayings, difficult to be understood." Much that is supposedly the domain of theology is merely the domain of dogmatics, religious *or* scientific: "dark sayings, difficult to be understood . . . the boundaries of our knowledge . . ." Bah!

Oddly enough, in an irony of logic, the last quoted criticism of Faraday's theory of the current clashes violently with the previously quoted criticism of Faraday's theory of electrolysis by contiguous particles. Clearly, on the quaint hypothesis of Tyndall that Faraday had imagined atoms and the aether and the ripples and the eddies, then clearly Faraday was presenting a theory with no action at a distance, only with action by contact. Even if Tyndall is right in criticizing Faraday's theory of 1836 by saying it did not eliminate action at a distance but only reduced the distance through which action was traveling to subatomic magnitudes, even then Tyndall should add that in 1839 all this changed and Faraday "clearly saw the play of fluids and ethers on atoms," thus fully eliminating all action at a distance. But this would be taking a eulogistic apology seriously.

It is strange to find in a eulogistic apology a remark on Faraday's lack of "previous training" in mathematics and in mechanics. It is even most unfair to Faraday: Tyndall's defense was written, after all, in 1868, after Kelvin had failed, and even Maxwell had publicly admitted to having failed, to do what Faraday could not allegedly do merely due to lack of previous training. And in Britain these two individuals were among the two or three most qualified mathematical physicists.[10]

But it is hard to criticize Tyndall harshly. He was the only one who so far criticized Faraday fully, openly, and boldly. And if his criticism is slightly too narrow-minded for my taste, he surely had no ill intention and he did try to do his best. He really was convinced that with a proper training one could solve all problems since the truth is, in essence, already known to us. Even though he could not understand Faraday's theory of the current, it was not merely his dogmatism and narrowness—his inability to break away from mechanism even hypothetically. It is also Faraday's inductive style that made it difficult. I know of no comment on Faraday's theory of the current save that of Tyndall, and I confess that I too found it pretty difficult to comprehend, though by no means "obscure" or naïve.

I shall later return to this theory. Tyndall's point, we remember, is that Faraday's method, indeed the method of science in general, is that of induction and deduction. From his theory of current, we learn, Faraday made one deduction that was verified. The deduction is that electric tension, like currents, moves in *time*, that counter to the common belief the current does not flow through the whole conducting wire in the very moment of the creation of the contact with the two oppositely charged bodies. In this very context, we remember, Faraday also made predictions that were refuted; but, apparently, refuted predictions do not count, and Tyndall omits mentioning them.

We leave, then, Faraday's research on static electricity, being reminded

10. The third was probably Stokes. E. T. Whittaker understands Stokes to have endorsed Faraday's view of the current as a vibration.

again that it is "by no means always clear" (pp. 90–91), and even with the admission that "the difficulty will be most felt by those who are best trained in *ordinary* theoretic conceptions." And the explanation is that Faraday "does not know the reader's needs, and he therefore does not meet them." This explanation I fully accept, though in a different sense. What are "the reader's needs" is, in my opinion, some argument against dogmatism in general and against mechanistic dogmatism in particular. This is not supplied during Faraday's earlier period of research. Later, Faraday comes closer to doing so, and in reporting this Tyndall's task becomes now more and more delicate.

After the story of his rest, namely his breakdown, and a few more remarks on his character, we "quit the man and go on to the discoverer" (p. 96). Now we come to Faraday's discovery of the relations between light and magnetism. This, we are told, is due to Faraday's idea that electrostatic induction is transmitted through contiguous particles and to his knowledge (?) "that polarized light was a most subtle and delicate investigator of molecular condition." Faraday himself says that his discovery of interaction between magnetism and light is rooted in his theory "that the various forms under which the forces of matter are made manifest have one common origin. . . . they are convertible, as it were, to one another . . ." Tyndall quotes this on page 99. On page 97 he offers a different presentation, illustrating the view that we have encountered earlier: Faraday stuck to his views in essence but altered them in detail under the pressure of experience. These two explanations, Faraday's and Tyndall's, of the same fact will not conflict if we assume the essence of Faraday's view to be the speculation on the conservation of force. This compromising view should be unacceptable to Tyndall, since Faraday's theory of conservation of force is doubtful and metaphysical, whereas Faraday's scientific researches were intended to dispel doubt, and whereas the scientific law of conservation of force belongs not to Faraday but to others. Tyndall nevertheless accepts this compromising view.

Here, then, is Tyndall's description of how Faraday developed his experiment on the interaction between magnetism and light (p. 97):

> After his return from Switzerland he was beset by these thoughts; *they were more inspired than logical:* but he . .
> proved his inspiration true. His dislike of "doubtful knowledge" and his effort to liberate his mind from the thraldom of hypotheses have been already referred to. Still this rebel against theory was incessantly theorizing himself. *His principal*

> *researches are all connected by an undercurrent of speculation.*
> *Theoretical ideas were the very sap of his intellect—the source*
> *from which all his strength as an experimenter was derived.*

This is very nice. Here, we have the main thesis that I wish to advance in the present volume about Faraday's mode of work—stated by Tyndall, in contrast to almost everything else Tyndall says on the same subject. I do not like the imagery, but I endorse the statement.

The relation between light and magnetism that Faraday had discovered was first observed in heavy glass. Other bodies were tried too, but with no success. Here Tyndall provides a mechanistic explanation to this failure—regrettably without a clear statement that it is his own, not Faraday's. Tyndall uses this explanation as the link between Faraday's discovery of the relation of magnetism and light and the following discoveries of Faraday—namely the magnetism of all matter and the magnetic forces of crystals. Tyndall then declares (p. 121) that Faraday "proves that the action of the magnetic forces in crystals, though . . . molecular, is an *action at a distance*."

Tyndall had presented Faraday trying, in his theory of contiguous particles in electrolysis, to eliminate action at a distance and not noticing that he only reduced its magnitude. He had then presented Faraday clearly imagining, in his theory of the current, the aether whirling and moving atoms so that all action at a distance is eliminated. Now he presents Faraday solving a problem, in his magnetocrystallic theory, by simply and frankly postulating action at a distance. Tyndall's attempt at a coherent picture of Faraday results in a picture of a thoroughly muddled thinker; and, I think, not quite unintentionally.

The truth of the matter, let me add in passing, is that the theory in question (of magnetic action of crystals at a distance) is not Faraday's but Tyndall's. True, Faraday had briefly sketched it and rejected it before Tyndall developed and presented it in detail. Hence, Tyndall, in all truth and modesty, could—and did—attribute Tyndall's theory to Faraday. What we must remember is that for any inductivist the scientific truth is more important than its history. And so, we need not be surprised that Tyndall now relates his own researches on magnetocrystallic forces (p. 124). He describes his lecture in the Royal Institution in Faraday's presence, the fact that his view which he then propounded was in disagreement with Faraday's view, and Faraday's exemplary behavior in that situation. Regrettably he does not explain the disagreement. He only mentions (pp. 128–29) that the theory that he, Tyndall, then defended was later proved, and that it was at first originated by no one else but Faraday himself. He then praises eloquently Faraday's "admirable instinct which always guided him" (p. 130), mentions a few of the correct results of his own work, and then comes to the point: Faraday was right in declaring that magnetocrystallic force is neither attraction nor repulsion, we are told, yet he was still wrong, since Tyndall himself succeeded in explaining the phenomena by assuming *both* attractive and repulsive forces (p. 131). As a result of his work, "the most perplexing of those facts were shown to result from the action of mechanical couples." It all sounds very nice and clear. Fortunately it is all just a piece of Victorian fiction. But we shall come to this topic later on. Here I should only say, the only theory of Faraday which de la Rive mentions in his *Treatize* is that of the magnetic condition of all matter (diagmanetism); Tyndall was overidiosyncratic in suggesting that he could beat Faraday just here.

Skipping the ultimate part of Tyndall's report on Faraday's discoveries of facts, I pass now to his final report—on Faraday's speculations.

The discussion, one may think, is perhaps not necessary, since Tyndall's volume is devoted to Faraday the discoverer, not Faraday the natural philosopher. Yet, for the sake of completeness and in view of the connection between the two, Tyndall presents Faraday's speculations (p. 146).

First comes Faraday's view of atomism. Faraday's chief point is, I understand Tyndall to say, that habitual usage of words should not cause dogmatism. Or, in Faraday's language, only the factual part of any atomistic description can be fully confirmed by subsequent tests but not the theoretical part, which is always doubtful. Here Tyndall objects (p. 147): "Facts cannot satisfy the mind," he declares. This, I think, makes it quite safe that Tyndall would not do justice to Faraday's speculations. To clinch matters, Tyndall drives his point home: "*The objection of Faraday to Dalton, might be urged with the same substantial force against Newton,*" he adds triumphantly in a mode of a *reductio ad absurdum*. When did Faraday assert that Newton's theory is certain? Did he not often imply in his writings that it is not certain? But Tyndall, in spite of his very close relations with Faraday, could not even hint[11] at the fact that

---

11. In his famous lecture on "Science and Imagination," Tyndall argues against ascribing uncertainty to atomism. That shows that he did see the problem. However, he does not mention the name of those against whom he argues. As he states that he admires their caution though he thinks it is misplaced, and as the same argument is employed there as the one quoted above, it is clear whom he had in mind. Yet I do not know why in one work he could mention explicitly whom he attacks and in another not, unless even hinting was considered unpleasant.

he was a heretic. Rather, he simply admits that if one must be strict, then one should say of every theory that the world is built *as if* that theory were true. He makes it clear, however, that this is logic-chopping; at least in the case of Newton, but Dalton's case is not weaker than Newton's.

So much for Faraday's demand to doubt Dalton's theory. We shall soon see that Faraday had some criticism of Dalton's views, and that Tyndall himself quotes it; but somehow he views Faraday's criticism of Dalton's more relevant to Faraday's ideas than to Dalton's! Before coming to Faraday's own atomic speculation, Tyndall adds one more aside (p. 148) on Faraday's use of his own speculations: "He incessantly employed them to gain experimental ends, but he incessantly took them down, as an architect removes the scaffolding when the edifice is complete." And he quotes approvingly Faraday's caution against viewing hypotheses as if they were proven facts.

This is, of course, very correct by Tyndall's standard: Faraday's doubt concerning Dalton's hypothesis is culpable and concerning his own is commendable. After all, we all know that Dalton is right and his critics and denigrators are in error. We should doubt falsehood, but believe the truth. Unfortunately, however, it is not fair to Faraday.

Faraday intended, in 1844, to present to the world his idea that each atom is spread, as a field of force, over the whole universe, though it has a localized center. He started by criticizing the identification of the atom with its localized center or its immediate environment—a view he ascribed to Dalton. He claimed that, empirically, the number of atoms that a given piece of matter contains is no clue to the size of that piece of matter. In fact, if any atom of matter is localized, then most of the part of space occupied by any piece of matter seems to be empty.

This, so far, is not really criticism of any fundamental idea. True, it was a shocking novelty at the time, but in due course it became an obvious part of the theory. In the twentieth century the idea is generally accepted that localizing atoms merely leads to viewing atoms as very small in comparison with intermolecular space.

Now, says Faraday, if most of space occupied by matter is empty, then the conductivity of matter as well as the nonconductivity of matter, given the accepted doctrines of conductivity, must both be ascribed to empty space. That, says Faraday, is absurd.

To value the force of this criticism we must take account of the then-accepted theory of conductivity. This is rather easy: conductivity was viewed then as the existence of free passage. Hence, clearly, Faraday's criticism of the then-current theory is devastating. Yet, it is really too much to expect, as he clearly did expect, the whole world to understand his argument and subsequently consider seriously the rejection of the (Daltonian) view of atoms as localized. It was all so much ahead of the times—in the sense of employing so much that had not yet been absorbed or digested by most scientists. We must remember that de la Rive sincerely thought that Faraday's depriving of atoms of their locality is the destruction of matter altogether, and thus the capitulation to the idealistic enemies of science who view the world as nothing but a dream!

Tyndall presents Faraday's ideas sketchily, adding that they had a "profound, strange, and subtle character," and that "we have to take [them] into account in dealing with Faraday's later researches." He says nothing more about Faraday's "Thoughts on Ray Vibrations" except that they are of a similar type—much, we remember, to S. P. Thompson's annoyance. He stresses again that Faraday himself constantly deprecated his own speculations, that he only used them as means of experimental discovery but otherwise thought them worthless to the point of being always ready to change them (p. 152): "His theoretical notions were *fluent*," he says, emphasizing the word "fluent," and explaining that Faraday correctly had considered any *fluent* idea not serious. It is not fair to ridicule Tyndall here, as he was expressing the most widespread prejudice of his age; now that we have deviated even from Newton's theory of gravity, it is easy to consider Tyndall as a naïve dogmatist. Perhaps he was.

Tyndall did not learn from Faraday's nondogmatism. All Faraday's antidogmatic assertions he interpreted as attempts to weaken Faraday's own anti-Newtonianism and subsequently as permission for Tyndall to sustain his dogmatism. Yet Tyndall fully emphasizes the fact—and he is the only biographer of Faraday who was ultimately ready to admit, even though quite marginally—that Faraday was guided by an anti-Newtonian idea (p. 154):

> Let it be remembered that Faraday entertained notions
> regarding matter and force altogether distinct from the views
> generally held by scientific men. Force seemed to him an
> entity dwelling along the line in which it is exerted. The
> lines along which gravity acts [similarly contained forces] . . .
> Such views, fruitful in the case of magnetism, barren, as yet,
> in the case of gravity, explain his effort to transform [gravity
> into magnetism] . . .

Had this beautiful passage been an expression of common knowledge—even of knowledge common to Faraday's biographers alone—I would not have found it necessary to write the present volume. Had L. Pearce Williams written his work as an exegesis . on this passage, I would not be publishing mine. Here we have an open and clear view of what Faraday's heresy was, and how it guided his researches. Contrary to the view of forces acting at a distance between particles of matter, believed by almost all men of science, Faraday saw forces stationed in space; even concerning gravity he held this unusual view. I do not know of any study of Faraday that stresses this view—not even Tyndall's, need I say, and not even that of Bence Jones (who followed Tyndall's footsteps closely).

Tyndall acknowledges, to return to our topic, the methodological value, the heuristic significance, of Faraday's speculations. He never for a moment stops to consider that perhaps they are true. He even quotes Faraday to say "I have been so accustomed to employ them . . . that I may have unwittingly become prejudiced in their favour . . ." The impression clearly is, to the extent that Faraday took his speculations literally he was prejudiced even by his own verdict! We know that this is a false reading that only a Victorian may consider charitable. The truth is that Faraday, in compromise with his environment, devised later in life two distinct readings of his theory of force—a literal reading for himself and an "as if" reading for the hesitant. Tyndall knows this. Indeed, he now comes to say so himself. And so I cannot any longer escape commenting on his presentational technique, and I must describe it in its generality and criticize it in full.

Tyndall's interpretation accords with a very widespread philosophy, largely shared by Faraday himself—in theory, and more so in practice. Subsequently, there are arguments from historical facts supporting both Tyndall's reading and mine. Of course, what supports my reading opposes his; and vice versa; much evidence is in agreement with both readings, of course, and as such it is no argument hither or thither. Nowadays we expect an author to present evidence contrary to his reading and to explain what makes him retain his view contrary to the evidence; he should not be content to argue how things should have happened since it is too easy to bend history to fit any interpretation. Now Tyndall does not conceal all the evidence against his reading—he even quotes casually a significant part of it; at times he even unnoticingly changes his reading; at times he simply speaks of the evidence as obscure, as dark sayings; once he even explicitly states that possibly certain evidence goes against his reading. All these means of self-criticism are presented—tossed, really—quite uncritically. Particularly since his Faraday fits Tyndall's image of the scientist and since Tyndall's Faraday so often supports Tyndall's scientific ideas, I think Tyndall's story is, ultimately, too apologetic by criteria acceptable to us today. We can scarcely ignore the fact that Faraday's heresy caused him severe conflicts with the scientific community. Tyndall merely hints in this direction, stating "that Faraday entertained notions regarding matter and force altogether distinct from the views generally held by scientific men." He shows, too, a readiness to quote Faraday to say perhaps there is an aether, but not to quote him to say "I dismiss the aether" (p. 158); to quote him against dogmatism in conjunction with field ideas, but not in conjunction with action at a distance; to alter chronology (p. 159, top); and to harmonize Faraday's views with those of his opponents (pp. 163–76). Tyndall ends his report with a disarming "I do not know whether Faraday would have subscribed to what is here written," with a repeat of Faraday's caution against prejudice, with a repeat that Faraday's ideas are partly obscure, that he knew no mathematics (pp. 175–77). By and large, however, all these ploys are less significant than the fact that Tyndall's work contains an extensive report on Faraday's speculations.

Tyndall's report of Faraday's speculations is far more than what most other biographers of Faraday include in their studies. Even L. Pearce Williams, whose study is the most recent, the most comprehensive and extensive, and the most theoretically oriented, is not superior to Tyndall as a reporter of Faraday's speculations—and thus of the problems and conflicts and struggles that Faraday encountered. The modern reader, in particular, can easily overlook many of Tyndall's small efforts at beautification, and benefit from the story as he has presented it.

### Bence Jones on Faraday

"To write a life of Faraday seemed to me at first a hopeless work," writes Bence Jones in the beginning of his biography. Ultimately, when no one else volunteered, he "made the attempt to join together" Faraday's "own words, and to form them into a picture of his life which may almost be looked upon as an autobiography." True to this program, he "arranged the material for memorial of Faraday in the simplest order, with the least connecting matter," the exception being "some admirable summeries published by Dr. Tyndall."

The connecting material by Bence Jones is too scanty for comment. One might well expect this benign elderly Victorian to have suppressed or glossed over some of the less pleasant material, but again, one cannot complain of his criteria for selection: most of what he selected is of great interest to some kind of reader or another, and what he omitted was what many would have considered scandalous to publish—such as matters relating to Faraday's expulsion from the Sandemanian Church, though he was an elder (he returned a few years later and became an elder again). Perhaps one should notice the amusing fact that the material "arranged . . . in the simplest order" is arranged seemingly chronologically and consecutively—but not always so. For example, Bence Jones sometimes (e.g., 2:178–79) changed the order of paragraphs in a lecture by Faraday, placing the warning against dogmatism at the end of a lecture rather than in the beginning—in line with Tyndall's reading. But I really do not see that much harm could be done this way.

Bence Jones's own concluding remarks of about two or three pages are all that remains, then. They are remarkable.

In his conclusion Bence Jones gives the character of Faraday—his science, his personality, his religion. As a scientist Faraday seems to Bence Jones to be primarily a man who trusted facts and who had a vivid imagination, who "throughout his life" held views "different from those held by others," which led him "to form plans for the broadest and newest, as well as the exactest, experiments"; he even believed in the transmutation of metals (a fact overlooked by other biographers, though here he was in complete agreement with Davy and with William Prout).

Bence Jones concludes his impressive scientific portrait with what is perhaps the best nineteenth-century summary of Faraday's daring speculations. I shall quote only one sentence: "He immaterialized matter into 'centres of force,' and he materialized the directions in which matter tends to move into 'physical lines of force.'"

This is very exciting—exact, crisp, and beautiful: Faraday is not an idealist, as de la Rive suggests: he deprives matter, or atoms, of materiality, in order to grant materiality to something as abstract as directions, and directions not even of motions but of tendencies to move!

Second comes Faraday's personality—love of truth, kindness, and energy; perhaps also "his strong religious feeling" that led him to "his marvellous humility." Third comes Faraday's religion, which I shall skip.

This is all Bence Jones has to say—facts, imagination, and a new natural philosophy leading to new experiments; and an unusual personality. Perhaps the present study is merely an elaboration of Bence Jones's summary. I do not accept all his detailed assessments; I particularly dissent from his identification (2:385) of force with energy (and the conservation of the one with that of the other) which he accepted from Tyndall and Maxwell. These, I feel, are minor corrections; what matters is that Bence Jones did not conceal the documents that reflect Faraday as the heretic natural philosopher. Doubtless, Faraday's later biographers all too often ignored these documents; it is not inconceivable, however, that the post-Maxwellian English Faradayans, particularly Poynting and Heaviside, were much influenced by Bence Jones in their holding an immaterialist theory of matter. Anyway, it is not by its influence alone that a writer's labor may be valued.

## Helmholtz on Faraday

Helmholtz spoke of Faraday and his work in his introduction to the German edition of Tyndall's book, and in his Faraday lecture in the Royal Institution about ten years later. Helmholtz's remarks on Faraday are brief but weighty; in addition, they have exercised a tremendous influence.

In his introduction to the German edition of *Faraday as a Discoverer*, Helmholtz says of Faraday's discoveries (*Nature*, 2 [1870], 51),

> Most of them burst upon the world as surprises, the products apparently of an inconceivable instinct; and Faraday himself, even subsequently, was hardly able to describe in clear terms the intellectual combinations which led to them. These discoveries, moreover, were all of a kind calculated to influence in the profoundest manner our notions of the nature of force. In the presence of Faraday's magneto-electric and diamagnetic discoveries more particularly, it was impossible for the old notions of forces acting at a distance to maintain themselves, without submitting to essential expansions and alterations. The clearer expression of these changes is at the present hour the object of physical science.
>
> In what way such extraordinary results were achieved is naturally a question of the first interest to the investigator who strives after similar though more modest ends . . .
>
> The principal advantage [of Faraday] rose undoubtedly [!] from the fact that his intellect was not too soon subjected to theoretic fetters, but enjoyed its freedom in the presence of natural phenomena; and that instead of book-learning he

permitted the fulness of Nature herself to operate upon his open mind. The disadvantages are, perhaps, of a subordinate kind; but they reveal themselves in quite an unmistakeable manner [!] when he strives to give expression to his ideas; and to supply, by all kinds of sensuous imagery, the want of mathematical culture. This is manifestly the way in which he alighted upon his Lines of Force, his Ray Vibrations, and other notions, which bewildered the investigators of his time, and the truer and clearer meaning of which has been in part made out by mathematical theory since Faraday himself ceased from his labours.

Faraday's discoveries, says Helmholtz, were "the products, apparently, of an inconceivable instinct," since even Faraday himself "was hardly able to describe in clear terms" the theories "which led to them." (Why does Helmholtz call Faraday's theories "intellectual combinations"?) And, yet, Helmholtz admits, "moreover, [they] were all of a kind calculated to influence . . . our notions . . ."! (He uses "moreover" where "yet" should be more appropriate.)

Helmholtz's description is not meant to be either antiintellectual or irrationalistic. His claim that Faraday excelled in discovery because he was "not too soon subject to theoretic fetters," because "instead of book-learning" he observed—this is but an echo of Bacon's doctrine of prejudice, an echo as in Rousseau's *Emile* who is taught to read not books but the Book of Nature, an echo as in Dr. Thomas Thomson's explanation of Priestley's discovery of oxygen as rooted in his nonscientific background, an echo as in Paul de Kruif's more recent and still best-selling *Microbe Hunters*, where we are told that Leeuwenhoek fortunately could not read Latin and so he could discover the microbe world. Faraday used Bacon's doctrine of prejudice to advantage. But other usages, less serious, are possible. Voltaire had a fairly dim view of savages, yet he described a noble savage, Huron by name, who was able to study all existing knowledge during his few months of imprisonment, as his mind was free of prejudice. In Fenimore Cooper's novels the Canadian Indians are savage and the American Indians are Noble Savages, empty-minded and thus free of our decadent prejudices and ready to absorb facts of Nature. Helmholtz's Faraday is both empty-minded, ready to absorb facts of Nature—and yet theoretically oriented by some "intellectual combinations." The great Helmholtz, how much trouble Faraday must have caused him!

Indeed, Helmholtz admitted that Faraday caused a need for "essential expansion and alterations," but he could not free himself from the old notions altogether. "The clearer," i.e., the Newtonian mechanistic, "expression of these changes is at the present hour the object of physical science," he claimed. Faraday's theory and Maxwell's equations were not false, they were unclear— he knew of no mechanical explanation of them, and he thought that to search for such an explanation was "at the present hour the object of physical science." There is no reason to object to such a program; but only as one possible program; to imply that physics is either mechanical or nonscientific, or at least not put in a clearly scientific expression, is a slight exaggeration, I think.

The result envisaged by Helmholtz is most enjoyable. Once there was some metaphysical element in physics, electric and magnetic fluids, and all that; Faraday has expelled them. Admittedly he has expelled them at the expense of introducing other metaphysical ghosts—lines of force, ray vibrations, and similar confusions. But these are now exorcised and replaced by mathematical formulas and a delightful freedom from metaphysics can now prevail. Helmholtz dismisses Faraday's lines of force and such bewildering things: Faraday wanted them from his ignorance of mathematics, and we, Helmholtz et al., that is, aided by modern mathematics, can do without them. True, Helmholtz still needs a "clear expression" of electromagnetic theory; the formulas are not yet quite available. Clearly, however, in his opinion we shall be soon in possession of them, and then we shall live happily ever after with no metaphysical nuisance to bother us.

> It was these ideas that Faraday sought in his riper labours to purify from everything theoretical, which was not the true and immediate expression of the facts. More especially he opposed the action of forces at a distance, the assumption of two electric fluids and of two magnetic fluids, and, in like manner, all hypotheses which contradicted the law of the conservation of force, of which he had an early presage, though he singularly misapprehended its mathematical expression.

What should we make of such a piece of muddle when it comes from the pen of such a great thinker who excelled both in science and in philosophy? Why is action at a distance metaphysics but the law of conservation of force scientific? And why does Helmholtz say Faraday "had an early presage" rather than "early announced" the law of conservation of force? How did Faraday "mis-understand" the law? Clearly Helmholtz here claims priority on the strength of the unexplained assertion that his own announcement of the law, though later than Faraday's, is clearer. Neither the assertion, nor the basing of a priority claim on it, is any near being clear enough for consideration.

But priorities are silly. The question of metaphysics is more important. How did Faraday "purify" physics "from everything that is theoretical"? We are not told. About a decade later, the same message is repeated more clearly, where Faraday is more simply and clearly praised for having expelled metaphysics. (This praise was repeated almost literally by Mach in his *History of Mechanics*, 5:i.) But let us take one step at a time. In 1881 Helmholtz is more confident, since he is assured that the strongly felt need for a "clear expression"—for a mathematical formulation—of Faraday's ideas is by now fully satisfied (*Faraday Lectures*, p. 135).

> *Nobody can deny* that this new theory of electricity and
> magnetism, originated by Faraday and developed by Maxwell,
> is in itself well consistent, in perfect and exact harmony
> with all the known facts of experience, and *does not contradict
> any one of the general axioms of dynamics*, which have been
> hitherto considered as the fundamental truths of all natural
> science, because they have been found valid, without any
> exception, in all known processes of nature.

This is a bit cocksure. "Nobody can deny," we are told, that Maxwell's theory is consistent with Newton's. We need not jump from the year 1882, when Helmholtz said this, to the year 1905, when the young Einstein replaced Newton's mechanics with a theory consistent with Maxwell's. We need not even insist that the consistency at the very least requires the aether-drift which in the year 1881 Michelson had failed to detect. We need no detailed history here: when Helmholtz says that no one can deny that the theories of Newton and of Maxwell are consistent with each other (and with a given class of factual statements), we may inquire whether there was any consistency proof available. There was none. And so the claim that "no one can deny" the consistency is a mere boast at most. Such boasts of great success are possible symptoms of anxiety. The present case is no exception.

In the opening of his lecture we encounter an admission: there was something to worry about: "Nevertheless, the fundamental conceptions *by which Faraday was led to these much admired discoveries* have not received an equal amount of consideration. They were very divergent from the trodden path of scientific theory and appeared *rather startling to his contemporaries.*"

How much Helmholtz has changed in one decade! Now lines of force are no more "sensuous imagery" due to Faraday's "disadvantage" (his ignorance of mathematics); they are really "startling" scientific "conceptions." Again we face metaphysics in science, since Faraday only excluded the electric and magnetic fluids in order to introduce lines of force and all that. But, no; now that the lines of force are *"really"* scientific, they are factual. Having his speculations verified, again Faraday appears in his true light, as an antimetaphysician (p. 132):

> His principal aim was to express in his new conceptions only facts, with the least possible use of *hypothetical* substances and *forces*. This was really an advance in general scientific method, destined to PURIFY SCIENCE FROM THE LAST REMNANTS OF METAPHYSICS. Faraday was not the first, and not the only man, who had worked in this direction, but perhaps nobody else at this time did it so radically.

This is a repeated claim. It has been made in the eighteenth century of Newton,[12] in the nineteenth century of Faraday, in the twentieth century (by Carnap) of Einstein. The reason is simple: scientific progress is, allegedly, averse to metaphysics; and so wherever you see scientific precision, you see a deathblow to metaphysics. Or, once you notice that salvation is not achieved in one stroke, you can say, the more science we have, the less metaphysics we need. This was stated clearly in the conclusion of Bohr's Faraday lecture (*J. Chem. Soc.*, February 1932, p. 384) with reference to Helmholtz's just-quoted passage. I think Bohr's conclusion is worth quoting:

> . . . As Helmholtz so forcefully emphasized, Faraday's general scientific method allowed him more than anybody else to contribute to the great aim "to purify science from the last remnants of metaphysics." In concluding this lecture, I may

12. The usual formulation, due to Alexander Pope I think, was that Newton had cleared the heavenly spheres of their cobwebs. The imagery relates to Bacon's best-known parable—of the spider, the ant, and the bee (*Novum Organum*, 1, Aph. 56), with the spider symbolizing the Reasoner who spins metaphysical speculations out of his own head.

be allowed to express the hope that modern endeavours in
atomic theory have not in this respect betrayed the great
example which Faraday has set us and that the new aspects
of natural philosophy . . . far from involving any mysticism
foreign to the spirit of science will be found to have contributed
to the great common aim.

This idea, too, is already adumbrated by Helmholtz, who thought Maxwell
did even better than Faraday in cleaning up the mystery. To use Helmholtz's
words, let me quote the following passage (p. 132):

Now that the mathematical interpretation of Faraday's
conceptions . . . has been given by Clerk Maxwell, we see
how great a degree of exactness and precision was really hidden
behind the words, which to Faraday's contempories appeared
either vague or obscure; . . . for I confess that many times I
have myself sat hopelessly looking upon some paragraph of
Faraday's description of lines of force, or of the galvanic current
being an axis of power, etc.

I am afraid this is not an exact report; but it is a candid report of a serious
attempt to understand Faraday. It illustrates, again, how mistaken Faraday
had been in his assessment of his contemporaries' abilities to understand him
and to alter their views as a result. Not only Faraday's contemporaries, but
even Helmholtz, a younger contemporary who shared much of his thoughts
on the conservation of force, found it hard to follow him. Admittedly, the
difficulty was partly rooted in dogmatism, both scientific (the adherence to
Newton) and methodological (the *idée fixe* concerning mathematical language
and precision); this, however, does not make the difficulty less genuine.

Faraday's strongest argument was commonsense: follow my example and
make as many discoveries as I did, he said again and again. Helmholtz has a
comment on this too (p. 133):

A single remarkable discovery may, of course, be the
result of a happy accident, and may not indicate the possession
of any special gift on the part of the discoverer; but it is
against all rules of probability, that the train of thought which

has led to such a series of surprising and unexpected discoveries, as were those of Faraday, should be without a firm, although perhaps hidden, foundation of truth.

This is queer logic. When Helmholtz says that one discovery can be accidental but it is improbable that . . . one would expect him to continue: that so many discoveries as Faraday made were accidental. But this Helmholtz could not say. Instead he says: it is improbable that Faraday's theory is not true, even though its (mechanistic) true foundation is perhaps hidden. Thus instead of concluding the improbability of many accidental *discoveries*, he switches to the alleged improbability of the falsehood of such a well-confirmed *theory*, the improbability that by accident all the discoveries fit into the preconceived scheme. Now, although it is indeed improbable that theory and fact fit accidentally, there may be other and more probable reasons for the fit than the alleged truth of the theory. Evidently, this is how some of Faraday's contemporaries looked at matters. If Faraday's discoveries confirm his theory well, why did his contemporaries reject it? And in a direct continuation to the above-quoted passage Helmholtz gives a futuristic answer to this question: "We must also in his case acquiesce in the fact that the greatest benefactors of mankind usually do not obtain a full reward during their lifetime, and that new ideas need the more time for gaining general assent the more really original they are, and the more power they have to change the broad path of human knowledge."

Original thinkers are fated to be rewarded, Helmholtz tells us, but only posthumously. But inductivism and futurism do not match so well. We cannot have it both ways: either one wants a high degree of originality and let History decide upon it, or one wants us to conform to "the general axioms of dynamics" and look for high probabilities. Yet Helmholtz expects both from Faraday; hence he himself cannot honor him until it is too late. In 1870 Helmholtz presents Faraday as a confusing and confused rebel. In 1881 Faraday is tamed; what Helmholtz mentioned of his work is what Helmholtz, by now, kindly accepts as very highly probable. Helmholtz's acceptance of Faraday's ideas in their mathematical formulation on the basis of ample confirmation is crucial both in the history of science and in the history of philosophy. Helmholtz could declare Faraday to be the liberator of science from metaphysics while holding tenaciously to Newtonian dynamics. This was done by requiring either a proper Newtonian interpretation of the theory—as the Faraday-Maxwell theory—or the acceptance of it only on the "as if" level—as Maxwell's equations. The next step, taken by Mach, Poincaré, and Duhem, was to view all physics as merely mathematical equations, as one big "as if" amply confirmed by experience. It is in this context that we must view Helmholtz's scant remarks on Faraday as highly influential—indeed expressions in them are traceable to many later writers. Influential as it was, however, one can hardly take seriously such shoddy treatment.

## Gladstone on Faraday

John H. Gladstone's biography is the most popular of the works I here discuss, written by a personal friend. Still, the miracle of Faraday's success is discussed in it (p. 60) and some suggestions as to a solution are made, and rather extensively. "The first element of success that we meet with in his biography," we are told (p. 61), "is the faithfulness with which he did his work"—any work that he undertook. "His love of study" and "his enthusiasm" are recorded (p. 62) as further sources of success. "His perseverance in a noble strife was another of the grand elements in his success" (p. 62). Next come his perseverance and playfulness (p. 62), which serves as a jumping board for a long—and just, of course—discussion of Faraday's poetic love of nature—especially of thunderstorms—and his great disappointment in the fact that scientists are by and large as petty as tradesmen (pp. 87–89). After the discussion of his character Gladstone comes to the method of research. Here he quotes Faraday's statements on suspension of judgment. Next comes the discussion on the method of Faraday's working (p. 124): "The habit of Faraday was to think out carefully beforehand the subject on which he was working, and to plan his mode of attack. . . . He would describe fully to the instrument maker . . . He would give Anderson [his only assistant] a written list of things . . . at least a day before . . . etc., etc."

This is an interesting account of an eye-witness. The significance of Faraday's mode of work is not only technical. There was a personal component, to be sure: Faraday worked very intensely and for long hours; and so he needed much preparation, physical and mental, before every plunge. His assistant was a compulsively slow worker, but precise like the retired sergeant that he was. The more ceremonial was the preparation for a long intense day at the lab, the clearer was the degree of theorizing that had gone into it. Preparing an experiment always demands prethinking, yet from the early days of the Royal

Society this was overlooked. But when one saw Faraday coming to the laboratory prepared to perform a great number of a wide variety of experiments, always having in mind what to do if the result of the experiment is this or that or the other, then prethinking could no longer be ignored.

Again, we see, inductivism was the faith of the leisurely gentleman; and whatever Faraday was or tried to be, he never pretended to be a man of leisure. He was a gentleman of the working class, whatever exactly this may be. Here is a reminiscence of an assistant at University College, London, where Faraday came to perform some experiments (p. 132): ". . . Mr. Faraday working with great activity; his motions were wonderfully rapid; if he had to cross the laboratory . . . he . . . ran . . . and when he wanted anything he spoke quickly . . ." though he spoke seldom—as he describes in his letter to Hansteen of 16 December 1857 (italics in the original):[13]

> We have but one assistant and he is an ordinary workman . . . I have never had any student or pupil under me to aid me with assistance; but have always proposed and made my experiments with my own hands, working & thinking at the same time. I do not think I could work in company, or think aloud, or explain my thought at the time. Sometimes I and my assistant have been in the Laboratory for hours & days together, he preparing one section apparatus or cleaning up & scarcely a word has passed between us:—all this being the consequence of the *solitary & isolated* system of investigation; in contra distinction to that pursued by a Professor with his aids of pupils as in your Universities.

This is strongly reminiscent of Maxwell's remark that we are fortunate that Faraday was left to work in isolation; it must reflect something that was observed and uttered more than once. Again, when we speak of the isolation that Faraday suffered—and he doubtlessly did suffer from it—there must have been a large element of choice involved. In the mid-nineteenth century there

13. I am grateful to Professor Svein Rosseland of the *Institutt for Teoretisk Astrofysikk*, of Oslo University, and Miss S. Tunold of the manuscript department there for the photostat of this letter. On 20 July 1955, Professor Rosseland kindly informed me that the original letter had "remained in custody of this institute until . . . the occasion of the Faraday Jubilee" of 1931 when it was handed over—probably to the Royal Institution.

was little notice or understanding of the psychology of conflict. Nowadays the matter is too trivial to mention.[14]

Perhaps the greatest weakness of Gladstone's biography is its Victorian smoothness. Faraday had tried hard to reflect it and only it, and Gladstone was glad to observe it and only it. He does mention one cloud over his serene Faraday: his great regret was that he had no children and no disciple. But he does not connect this with Faraday's mode of work—though he quotes de la Rive on Faraday's method of working. Nor does he speak of the role of Faraday's speculations in his experiments. As ever, his descriptions are technical, plastic, and superficial. "He loved to speculate, too, on Matter and Force . . ." he says (p. 149), adding a quotation from Helmholtz—on Faraday's attempt to "purify" science "from everything that is theoretical" and on his dim foresight of the conservation laws!

To conclude, Gladstone's work is rather popular; a kindly work, only somewhat spoiled by quoting rather uncritically de la Rive, Helmholtz, and others. The picture it conveys, impressionistic as it is, is charming and seems quite correct. Faraday's industry, love of study, perseverance, love and respect for nature, well-organized work, well-thought-out experiments, and his aim to unify science, all these contributed in this or the other way. As for Faraday's love for speculation, his suspension of judgment, and his lack of deductive power, these are less important points of the picture and Gladstone does not enlarge on them. The merit of Gladstone's work is in its own proportions: in narrating minor anecdotes, in detailed discussion of Faraday's mannerisms, of his sincerity, hard work, tenderness, and all those characteristics that are very much to be esteemed; I do not intend to discuss them. Gladstone had first-hand information; anyone interested in these points should refer to his chatty and enjoyable book.

## Conclusion

Faraday the discoverer was aided by many things: his personal characteristics like perseverance, his critical approach, a great deal of luck, and also by an idea. Of course, he was lucky in having such an idea; but the point is that

14. For detail see, for example, Faraday's letters to Matteucci, especially of 18 February 1843 and of 20 March 1857: "My health and spirits are good but my memory is gone and it, like deafness, makes a man retreat into himself. . . . when I try to remember it, all is slow to to me, and you are so active and *spirituel* that it seems to me as if you were out of my sight." For a case of deafness and its similar psychology, see Matthew Josephson's life of Thomas Alva Edison.

somehow he did have an idea, and a *new* idea, a revolutionary idea, off the track, or call it as you like. In simple language, the idea contradicted the accepted views.

I shall not discuss here the more recent literature on Faraday. I shall only mention that the central point of Faraday's career, his clash with accepted opinion, is less clearly reported in our century than in the last one. On the whole, one can say, it is more absent than present and, in some cases, by intent. Perhaps the last biography of Faraday to give some feel of the situation is one that is, in a sense, the last first-hand report. It is the biography by Silvanus P. Thompson, the founder of the Institute of Electrical Engineers in London and also the biographer of Kelvin. His life of Faraday contains a few original anecdotes and other material not to be found elsewhere. Later works on Faraday are increasingly views of him as integrated in his historical background—especially since views on the continuity of the history of science have since gained popularity.

On the whole, the story of the historiography of Faraday's discoveries is sad. First they were orthodoxly described without a word of explanation. Later, the question of Faraday's miracle was raised: how could he be so successful, and so systematically successful. A reviewer of the three volumes of Faraday's *Experimental Researches in Electricity* in the *Philosophical Magazine* (1855, pp. 297–98) gave a sketchy reply that was very promising as a start; but then Tyndall apologetically showed the way of reconciliation between facts and inductivism, and others followed suit. Let me quote here a part of the anonymous review in the *Philosophical Magazine*. The editors tell me that they have no record of the reviewer's identity. I can hardly avoid, however, noticing the similarity between the view on methodology here expressed by the reviewer and the philosophy of William Whewell that, together with the expression "inductive philosophy," make him a likely candidate, especially since the review compares the novelty of the conceptual framework of Faraday's *Experimental Researches* to that of Kant's *Critique of Pure Reason*.

> We may not make Faraday's mode of symbolizing the operations
> of nature our own, but when we reflect upon the success which
> has attended his efforts, on the fact that his peculiar symbols
> enabled him to foresee results of which no other electrician
> dreamed, and which after a lapse of twenty years accident
> has brought to light, *we are warned against being dogmatic*
> *on theoretic matters, and learn the salutary lesson, that the*
> *competent and earnest searcher after truth has other avenues*
> *than our licenses scientific turnpikes into nature.*

. . . None of our hypotheses would have prompted us to seek these results [magnetoptics], they would rather have dissuaded us from the attempt . . . The method of true scientific investigation is probably incommunicable; it belongs to the individual rather than to the system, and our contemporaries, we think, miss their mark when they point at Faraday's researches as simply illustrative of the power of inductive philosophy. Faraday's researches are illustrative of the power of strong and independent soul, *expressing itself after its own methods, and acknowledging no mediator between it and Nature* . . . The value of Faraday's discoveries consists in a *great degree in the amount of intellectual power which they call into action.*

Here the admission that Faraday had been guided by a heretic view leads to a call to shake our dogmatism. Tyndall said the heretic thoughts were only "as if," only means of generating new empirical hypotheses. Tyndall hinted, and Helmholtz asserted, that only the mathematization of Faraday's ideas would gain them respectability—either on the understanding that in a mathematical formulation their realistic claim would vanish, their "as if" nature would become conspicuous, or on the understanding that we must reconcile them with more old-fashioned views. This led to the development of the "as if" view of science in general, which is very popular amongst physicists today. Faraday himself became known as one who believed in an aether—which would render his ideas rather conventional. A few scientists, even historically minded ones, were surprised to hear from me that Faraday denied the existence of the aether: they thought this idea belongs to Einstein.

# 7  Faraday's World View

Faraday's world view developed in three stages. First, he assumed the existence of lines of force, magnetic and electric; and he developed the idea of their motion in space. Second, he developed the Oerstedian idea of conservation of force. Finally, he saw matter as mere configuration of the field of force. I have described the first stage in chap. 4 above; I now come to the two further stages. The most amazing fact about Faraday, biographically speaking, is that he developed all three stages between 1832 and 1834.

## The Laws of Conservation of Force and of Energy

Tradition identifies the law of conservation of force with the law of conservation of energy. There is even some traditional justification for this, since the vis viva of Leibnitz can be identified both with force and with kinetic energy—and both Laplace and Lagrange had proved the law of conservation of kinetic energy in the Newtonian system of gravitational force. Of course, the law as presented today says that the sum of kinetic and potential energy is constant; this, however, is not to say that energy conserves, but that kinetic energy conserves in that when it seemingly disappears it merely hides as potential energy. The idea that potential energy is real and resides, therefore, in space, is Faradayan; it belongs to Maxwell and Poynting.

But let us ignore this point, as well as all other differences between the various historical cases of conservation laws. Assume, then, with all the text-books on the subject, that in any system of forces energy is conserved because all forces have to abide by the laws imposed on them by Newton. What is the significance of this law if, after all, it is a mere theorem of dynamics?

Here is the answer, as given in 1885 in *The Philosophical Transactions of the Royal Society* (p. 307) (in the same volume in which Poynting argued for free floating energy!), and by J. J. Thomson, the disciple of Faraday and Maxwell and later the discoverer of the electron:

> . . . the view (which we owe to the *principle of Conservation of Energy*) that every physical phenomenon admits of a dynamical explanation is one that will hardly be questioned at the present time. We may look on the matter (including, if necessary the ether) which plays a part in any physical phenomena as forming a material system and study the dynamics of this system by means of any of the methods which we apply to the ordinary system in the *Dynamics of Rigid Bodies*. As we do not know much about the structure of the systems we can only hope to obtain useful results by using methods which *do not require exact knowledge of the mechanism of the system*. The *method of Conservation of Energy* is such a *method*, but there are others which *hardly require a greater knowledge of the structure of the system* and yet are capable of giving us more definite information . . . [as] Lagrange's equations and Hamilton's method of Varying Action . . .

J. J. Thomson says that the use of the law of conservation of energy is a short-cut: if you know what forces operate in a system, you may deduce the law from that knowledge, or you may use that knowledge and not use the law at all. However, when you do not know the forces that operate in a system, at least you know that they obey the law of conservation of energy, and this may be useful information in itself.

This is hardly new, and even if it were, it would not be very important—techniques are useful but not usually very interesting. Moreover, in the very first of the above-quoted sentences, J. J. Thomson managed to ask whether Newton's dynamics is applicable to all systems, answers in the affirmative, and justifies it as a consequence of the law of conservation of energy. This last point sounds extremely puzzling: the law follows from Newtonian mechanics; it is not quite equivalent to it. Perhaps, however, J. J. Thomson thinks otherwise. His last-quoted sentence may be the claim that Lagrange and Hamilton had proved mathematically the equivalence of the law of conservation of energy with Newtonian dynamics (Newton's law of force and of action and reaction).

Let us suppose this to be the case. This would not deprive Newton's theory of its significance, nor would it diminish the significance of the mathematical discoveries of Lagrange and of Hamilton; but it would deprive the law of conservation of energy of all importance: it would reduce it from the status of a new idea to the status of a merely new formulation of an old idea.

The answer to this objection must be this: though mathematically Newton's general laws of force are equivalent to the law of conservation of energy, philosophically the conservation law is more fundamental. Let us, then, discuss the philosophical aspect of the law as argued by some early nineteenth-century physicists.

The theory behind the laws of conservation, whether of matter or of motion or of anything else, is that *nothing comes out of nothing*. On this theory Leonardo based his view that a *perpetual motion* machine is impossible. On the basis of this theory Locke proved the law of causality. This theory—since nothing comes out of nothing, *perpetual motion* is impossible—was applied by Stevin, Descartes, Leibnitz, Rumford, Davy, Lazare Carnot, Roget, Faraday, Mohr, Mayer, and Joule. This is the end of the story, and there is little else to add to it, I am afraid.

One may puzzle about this: no *thing* can be created; granted. But why not force, motion, momentum, or energy? These are *not* things! After all, we do see creation and annihilation constantly take place before our eyes; when we say that *things* are not created, we do not mean houses, for instance, which rise and fall, but the bricks from which they are made, or more precisely the *matter* from which they are made. *Matter* cannot be created or destroyed; houses can; and perhaps also motion, force, or energy! The answer to this is the following most important traditional (invalid) argument.

Traditionally, two things exist on the deepest level of existence: matter and its properties. Properties are essential or accidental, and the accidental properties, too, can change (e.g., the accident that a certain piece of matter is shaped like a house). Essential properties of a thing are, by definition, those that make it what it is: take away from a thing its essential property and it lost its being what it is: take away from a house its ability to function as a dwelling and it ceases to be a house—a ruin or a structure or anything else it may be, but as essentially a house is a dwelling, destroy a dwelling and you have destroyed a house. Now if the essential property of matter is its motion, then motion conserves with matter: take away its motion and it is matter no longer.

So now the deduction is valid: matter conserves, x is essential to matter; hence, x conserves. But this will not do. What we wish to explain is the conservation not of motion but of the *quantity* of motion, not of energy but of the quantity of energy. And the argument thus far is at best qualitative (even this is disputable). The transition from qualitative considerations to quantitative ones in the above argument is sheer fallacy. Yet on this fallacy such great ideas rest as Mayer's paper on heat as energy. We see now why the literature on *the* principle of conservation of energy is so vague. So let us now ask a much more specific question. What is the status of the statement "the energy of a closed system is constant" within Newtonian mechanics? The answer is very simple. It is a theorem, *not* a principle; it is a theorem that may be used by a *method*, a method of applying mechanics to systems the inner structure of which is unknown to us. For *if* mechanics is universally true, then the principle—that is, the theorem—is true too.

The controversy about the question, to whom shall we ascribe the honor of having discovered *the* principle of conservation of energy, is unsettled as yet, in spite of the great quantities of ink poured on this issue. What is *the* principle? There are at least two forms of the principle sharply distinguished by Faraday (though he spoke of force rather than of energy), and systematically confused in all the elementary textbooks and popular presentations which I chanced to check: one of *conservation* and one of *convertibility*.

The law of conservation of energy is that we cannot destroy energy; that whenever energy seemingly disappears, it only changes its own form. When electricity is discharged, for example, it is *transformed* into heat, magnetism, light, or any other form of energy. In this form the principle has roots in antiquity. In another, stronger form, the law is that of *convertibility*. It says more than that energy conserves. It says that energy *can transform* from *any* given form to *any other form*. This is a slightly different form of an idea that no one but Oersted and Faraday ever forwarded. We know that gravity can vary into motion, and motion into heat, electricity, and other forms of energy. Oersted argued that electricity can be directly altered into magnetism. Newton's theory *forbids* the conversion of gravity to any other form of energy except motion: Faraday argued that it is still possible to *convert* gravity *directly* into electricity or heat.

Then there is the difference between force and energy. Faraday had *no* principle of conservation or conversion of energy. He had only announced the *principle of conservation and conversion of force.* And this principle was rejected by Faraday's followers, even though they paid to it lip service, and identified it with the law of conservation of energy. Mayer and Helmholtz spoke of the conservation of FORCE, not of energy. Energy is a property of a system, and systems do not exist in nature; *we* make them. Forces, on the other hand, are *causes*, more "real," they have effects. A cause *equals* its effects, says Mayer. Therefore, he argued, forces are indestructible. Helmholtz's memoir of 1847 is *also on the conservation of force (kraft)*.

The basic ideas of Helmholtz, at least for the present discussion, are two. The first is that the law of conservation of force agrees with Newton's theory. The second idea is that the principle is well worth pursuing. Helmholtz, far from claiming priority, collected all the available material in order to show how fruitful is the application of the law. He claimed for the law the status of *tentativity*. He claims in the memoir of 1847, where he advocates the new principle, that the only *ultimate* explanation is that which follows Newton's program in all its purity: only atoms and central forces are the ultimate constituents of physical reality. His own program was to have the *law of conservation of force* as *tentative*, as some crutch to be finally eliminated—a means to the end of fulfilling Newton's program.

Helmholtz's memoir of 1847 is not as revolutionary as Faraday's paper; but it is revolutionary in its own way. This is, presumably, why it was rejected by the editors of *Annalen der Physik*. It contained a program, and one that was well argued for. In a way, Grove, in his *Correlation of Physical Forces* of 1842, argued for the same program, though on the basis of fictionalism in general. Anyway, the law of conservation of energy certainly cannot go to Helmholtz; if not to Leibniz, it must go to Lagrange and Laplace. When in 1800 Volta claimed that his pile was a perpetual motion machine, his claim was refuted at once. Faraday, for example, never defended the law of conservation of energy but rather took it for granted that Roget's argument from this law against the contact theory of the pile is very strong, as anyone must admit! What Faraday found hard to explain to his contemporaries, rather than take for granted that they knew it, was the law of conservation of force.

## Faraday on the Conservation of Force

There are two reasons for the attempt to identify the conservation of force with the conservation of energy. First, the conservation of energy is a corollary of Newton's theory. Second, energy was not supposed to be a real thing, only a property of a material system: energy can be transferred from one thing to another, but a system that is closed to energy-transfer, a system that does not lose or gain energy to or from another system, does not lose or gain energy at all. Energy cannot be created or annihilated, but nevertheless fixed energy is not a thing but a property, not of a thing but of a closed system of things.

Faraday insisted that forces reside in empty space, and that energy resides in empty space too; Maxwell tried to speak of the conservation of energy alone; he admitted that force and energy reside in space, and therefore filled space with aether—free-floating energy did not make good sense to him at first. When he tried to imagine the aether in all detail and failed, he was ready to assume the existence of energy freely floating in empty space; at least so Poynting understood him, and so did Einstein too. A similar development occurred to Hertz. Einstein, who started with energy in empty space and developed special relativity, kindly noted that both Maxwell and Hertz missed the opportunity to do so chiefly due to early death.

Einstein always loved to find other people responsible for his success: it was partly his deep sense of history, partly his excessive but simple humility. His own success, he said in his preface to Max Jammer's *Concepts of Space*,

> became possible only because the concept of the material object was gradually replaced as the fundamental concept of physics by that of the field. Under the influence of the ideas of Faraday and Maxwell the notion developed that the whole of physical reality could perhaps be represented as a field whose components depend on four space-time parameters. . . . There is no "empty" space, that is, there is no space without a field . . .

There is no doubt, however, that Maxwell found it difficult to give a mathematical formulation to Faraday's theory of conservation of force. For long it has been taken for granted that Maxwell had formulated mathematically all there is in Faraday's intuitive idea. In recent years, especially since the development of plasma physics, this has been shown to be incorrect. Maxwell has much improved certain ideas of Faraday—but at the cost of neglecting others. Sometimes by intention. Only in the post-Einstein period can we appreciate Faraday's idea that inertia should not be introduced axiomatically but deduced from the principles of the field theory. It sounds prophetic, but it actually is a part of Faraday's immaterialism: after all, before Faraday, matter was identified with gross matter, namely with mass, namely with inertial and gravitational mass or with mass possessing inertia and gravity. And Faraday wished to assume only the existence of fields of a variety of forces—including gravity—and their laws of conservation and convertibility. And so in his system there was no room for inertia. Indeed, as Leibnitz had already observed, for inertia one needs inertial systems, and for these one needs empty space partly occupied by matter.

Let us, then, follow Faraday's intuitive idea of conservation of force. As forces conserve, he argued, gravitational forces *cannot vary*—inversely as the square of the distance, or in any other way. They must be *fixed*. If the earth is *created*, there cannot be a creation of force to act on it. If it moves, there cannot be a force created to act on it in its new position, nor can the force that acted on it a minute ago act on it now, since it has for this purpose to *vary*. Hence all the forces of the sun that may ever act on any body *already exist now*. And they can be said to reside in the sun or in space, but they cannot be radiated from the sun. But, Faraday continued, if we must assume the *pre-existence* of all the forces of the sun that may act on the earth or any other body at any time, then we should better assume their *distribution in space*, to refrain from assuming *action at a distance* (*Experimental Researches in Electricity*, 3:579).

Thus far the field of force is merely an extension of Newtonian forces, Newtonian forces, so to speak, are embedded in Faradayan field. Some modifications, however, are necessary, when precision is increased or a drastic change occurs. If the sun is annihilated, for example, then the earth will notice this at once according to Newton, but only some time later, according to Faraday. He could not specify the speed, merely suspecting it to be the same as the speed of light, but he insisted it was a finite speed, not the infinite speed of Newtonian action at a distance.

Next comes a serious deviation from Newton's theory of matter. If gravitational forces can convert to electric forces, as Faraday insisted, then gross matter may convert to electric matter—which is a contradiction in terms in the old system since matter is by definition permanent! It is no surprise that Faraday's contemporaries refused to understand him!

Let me conclude this section by quoting a flyleaf advertising Faraday's lecture on the force of chemical affinity—doubtless written by Faraday himself.

ROYAL INSTITUTION OF GREAT BRITAIN

30 March 1840

Syllabus of a course of seven lectures on the force usually called chemical affinity, by Professor Faraday F.R.S.

The object of the course will be to illustrate the nature of the force; *the change produced by it*; the circumstances *facilitating or retarding its action*; *variations in its strength*; *its definite nature*; its consequences in relation to organic and inorganic matter; its conditions as *local force* in ordinary cases, and its exertion as current or *dynamic force* in the voltaic pile.

Local force is a force acting on a body; dynamical forces act on other things, like lines of other forces. A force can be intensified or *exalted* by concentrating the field, as in the case of bringing two charged bodies nearer to each other. This may indicate how much wider is Faraday's concept of force than the usually accepted one.

## Conversion of Forces

Faraday's fundamental idea that led him to the majority of his great discoveries, if not to all of them from 1832 onward, was his idea that all forces can vary not in quantity or in size but in appearance. A gravitational force can change directly into electricity, magnetism, heat, crystallinic force, chemical affinity, and so on. Each force can directly vary into *any other force*. (Also, forces can be concentrated or spread.) If he knew that electricity can be generated by heat, he wanted to convert heat into electricity. He could use heat to rotate a piece of cloth on glass and thus convert heat into electricity via motion; but he wanted to convert heat directly into electricity. He wanted to convert radiant heat (or rays of light) into electricity, he wanted to extract from a crystal its crystallinic force and transmit it in a wire; he imagined in 1834 hundreds of possible laws of conversion of force upon which he experimented, as indicated in notes to his lecture of June 1834 on this theory (R.I., MS., partly quoted in *Life and Letters*, 2:47–48):

Lectures on Electrical and Chemical Problems; Last Lecture, 21 June 1834.

The extraordinary power of matter which we have thus traced exhibiting itself as the cause of chemical electrical and calorific effects exhibits another set of phenomena unlike any of these but equal to any of them in the irregularity and generality of its action. . . . *We cannot say that any one is the cause of the others,* but only that all are connected and *due to a common cause* . . . And even gravitation may perhaps be included . . . Consider in connection with this the supposed magnetic relations of the earth sun and planets to each other. . . . Electricity will be the connecting link of body and mind and the agent by which the use of the corporal faculties are subjected both to the judgement and the will. But better to refrain from presuming too much upon our present day better knowledge.

This idea[1] was compared by Faraday (*Life and Letters*, 2:47) to the myth of Proteus, who changed his appearance many times before he was captured. Faraday was so haunted by the idea that he could hardly speak of any natural phenomenon unless in relation to this "grand generalization" (as Bence Jones called it). He interpreted every fact in the light of this theory and saw everywhere the problems involved. Out of his lecture notes I selected the following example both because it is of an early date, 1836, and is on a subject about which he published almost nothing after 1831—heat. I quote the beginning and end of the notes (R.I., MS.):

1. For the origins of the modern Proteus myth see A. J. Paris's life of Davy, 1:308; and note that it may well have Boscovichian or Kantian background. Faraday's version here, however, is a field theory proper. Faraday added in the margin of this passage, "Correlation of Physical Force MF 1853." The title is that of Grove's lectures, delivered in 1845 and published in 1846. Hence, according to Faraday's own judgment, this is the earliest public expression of his fully fledged ideas.

The crucial passage here is "we cannot say that any one [force] is the cause of the other." Mayer said that forces conserve since every cause equals its effect. Grove, by contrast, said that if electricity causes magnetism and vice versa, each is the essence of the other, which is absurd. Hence the theory of laws of nature, or of essences, or realism, is false. Grove advocated, instead, a version of fictionalism, which later Mach claimed priority for and called functionalism. Faraday seems to be the first to advocate a realism which clearly defies the classical (Aristotelian) doctrine of essences. This is a remarkable achievement. Even its independent rediscovery as a conclusion that Whitehead rightly drew out of Einstein's theory and called process philosophy deserves more attention and appreciation than it has thus far received. That Whitehead opposed general relativity was advertised by all his detractors; that he was one of the few consistent students of Einstein's world-view is less well-known. Even nowadays the title "process philosophy" arouses tremendous ambivalence—partly because Whitehead was not evenly clear and rationalistic throughout his philosophical career.

Some general considerations of the nature of the particles of matter—and their associated powers—these are for us [gravitational] *attraction—heat—electrical forces*.
The great object now is to identify these forces or refer them to *one common cause*.

Very varied forms which the power of heat assumes
Repulsion—⎫
Sensible—⎪
Latent—⎬ These conditions and distinctions are very striking but we search for a law to which all these can be reduced.
Radiant—⎭

In taking the effects into consideration I shall pursue that order which will best enable us at last to review the general characters of this power—Must limit myself in some way and shall therefore rather try to anticipate or lead to further results.

*Nature of Heat*
Old notions amusing. One Two favoured theories. Have power of moving it by conductors and radiation from body to body and place to place—difference in this respect and the power of attraction—though approximation made in late times—hence idea of its independent nature and motion of *caloric*—but there is never any change in the weight and it is state only induced as a property of matter.

In sun's rays a close association with luminous and chemical agencies of peculiar kind—Newton's query whether radiant heat and common matter are not convertible with each other.

Curious that with respect to expansion where there is the least matter [gases] there is most increase in bulk—leads to speculations on the condition of heat and its attachment or relation to the particles of matter—and this is closely related to the probability that the *specific heat* is the same for all. bodies when taken in their equivalent proportions . . .

Fresnel says that there is a material repulsion at sensible distance between two hot bodies . . .

Some bodies on solidifying expand instead of contract *water, iron, bismuth*—most important bearing and shows that solidity is not mere approximation or affinity . . .

Nothing nearly as bold was published by Faraday for many years. The idea that heat and light are conditions of matter, that Newton's speculation on light and common matter being interconvertible—which makes common matter a condition of matter, of course—all these are very daring ideas. The conclusion of the lecture shows again his mode of thought. He discards caloric when it was in the peak of its popularity for the same reasons that he discards electric fluids. He ends with a problem that interested him most—the constitution of matter.

## Matter and Force

Faraday often spoke of "the forces of matter"; the phrase is indeed peculiar to him. Of course the official view also ascribed to matter certain forces—primarily of gravity. Also, under certain pressure, it was admitted that matter possessed Volta's contact forces, chemical affinity, and elastic forces. Faraday viewed the situation very differently. In 1833 he had a first estimate of the magnitude of the forces of chemical affinity. And although these forces are negligibly small in comparison to nuclear forces, his discovery was not less surprising in his day than Rutherford's in his day. It set his imagination free; he visualized matter, any small piece of matter, a small pebble, a piece of paper, as a store of titanic forces, as a prison of a mighty Proteus. The forces were by comparison so enormous that they put matter in which they resided completely in the shade. Their function became more and more significant. "Instead of looking at a fulminating silver as a torpid mass," he expressed his view in cursory notes to a later lecture (1845) (*Life and Letters*, 2:204), "rather represents half-a-dozen Afriks chained together and struggling for liberty—a link between chemical and mechanical forces."

It is impossible to understand his development of his electrostatic theory without noticing that he was trying to develop his idea of the electric conditions of matter; and it is impossible to understand his immense concern with the electric condition of matter without seeing in this his attempt to come closer to the realization of a dream—to liberate the enormous molecular forces that he had first measured and that Davy had declared to be electrical in nature or origin. "Common matter" is electrified, and electrified matter is just the terminals of the electric lines of force. If two electrified bodies attract each other, it is because lines of force tend to contract like muscles. They also exert lateral pressure on each other, so that they look more like a muscle, and when a bundle of lines contracts, it becomes thicker like a muscle. If we put some dielectric, glass, sulphur, or other nonconductor in the electric field, it attracts to itself the lines of force. Moreover, when one line of force becomes a line of discharge, a current so-called, it attracts to itself other lines of force. A discharge looked to Faraday like a huge storm. If a condenser is discharged, lines of force are swallowed by the line of discharge, the current; if the condenser is constantly charged afresh, there is a whirl of lines arriving to the walls of the condenser and being then attracted to the current, always leaving after them their traces —magnetic lines of force. When two electrified bodies are moved toward each other, it is the concentration of the field that *is* their approximation to each other; when we electrify a body or two, we only transfer the lines of electric force from one place to another, or more adequately, we change the field's *structure*. When we generate or destroy a field, we again only change the field's structure: we make Proteus change his cloak.

Space, motion of matter in space, action, structures—all these were translated into laws of structures of fields and the laws of their transformation—or rather into dreams about such laws. In Newton's theory, introducing a new body into space, or even changing position of a single body, causes a change in the whole situation—as Boscovich had argued. With Faraday all this is more so. A small test body moves along the lines of force; but this is only a first approximation. In fact the field has now changed entirely: the test body has attracted to itself lines of force and broken the equilibrium. Newton's law of parallelogram of forces is *not* assumed; it follows as a first, or rather should follow, as a very rough, approximation to what really happens. This may suffice to transmit the sensation that "common matter" is fading away when fields are discussed—that more and more it becomes a mere characteristic of the field. Instead of saying that the dielectric, the piece of glass or sulphur, attracts to itself lines of force, we can say that the place of concentration of the field *is* the glass or the sulphur. This raises myriads of problems. Why, sulphur is yellow and glass is transparent, sulphur is soft while glass is hard. They can both be transferred from one place to another, electrified, broken, and what not! How will the field view account for all these differences and changes?

This is exactly the point: one may now try seriously to imagine how we can explain all those things by sticking to our idea that the piece of glass or of sulphur is just the concentration of the electric field, and a configuration of the field in general. We have to translate each of the glass's properties, its weight, transparency, form, and so on, to field properties, and search for *laws connecting* the field of gravity and the field of transparency, and the field of hardness and the field of transparency, etc., etc., etc., in order to accept ultimately this piece of glass or this sheet of paper as a *configuration* of the *universal field* of forces.

What happened now to matter? Two answers are possible, Faraday says. Matter, in the ordinary materialistic sense of the word, is either pushed to a metaphysical realm, or denied its existence, annihilated altogether. Of course, Faraday admitted the existence of common matter, say this table. If you asked him why my elbow cannot penetrate it, he would tell you that the lines of force are so strong and tense that my elbow can neither penetrate nor bend them. But my elbow is a field of force, too. And so, some fields are penetrable by others to a great degree, some not. And so it goes.

## Against Dalton

Spend a few thoughts sometimes on the puzzling enquiries concerning *vacuum and atoms*, the doctrine of infinites . . . Do this on purpose to give you a more sensible impression of *the poverty of our understanding*, and *the imperfection of your knowledge*. This will teach you what a vain thing it is to fancy that you know all things.

Dr. Watts[2]

There is a letter from Faraday of 1834 in which he stated that he was much puzzled by the atoms. He spoke in favor of atomism as such, including the view of atomicity of electricity, yet he expressed his reluctance to commit himself to Dalton's atomism because it introduced the idea of essential differences between atoms of different chemical elements. In his time this was considered an antiatomistic view, rather than a wish to replace Dalton's atomism by another version of atomism. After Niels Bohr has caried through this idea and explained the various chemical atoms by assuming two more fundamental physical atoms, or elementary particles, the heavy proton and the light electron, there is no need to argue about this problem, the feasibility of the idea. New problems are now at stake. The number of elementary particles

2. Isaac Watts, *Improvement*, 1:i.

again increased, although not to 92 or more, to quite an enormous figure, and they call for a *new* explanation.

Faraday wished to explain the chemical properties of matter, all properties of matter in fact, by field assumptions, in order to have all atoms of matter under the same heading. His own suggestion was that each atom is a *center of force*. The volume of each atom has thus to be eliminated: it has to shrink to a point, or expand to cover the whole of space, as one wishes to look at it. Here is Faraday's characterization of his speculation on atoms (*Life and Letters*, 2:177):

> . . . a speculation respecting that view of the nature of matter which *considers its ultimate atoms as centres of force*, and *not* as so many little bodies surrounded by forces, the bodies being considered in the abstract as independent of the forces, and capable of existing without them. In the latter view these little particles have a definite form and a certain limited size. In the former view such is not the case, for that which represents size may be considered as extending to any distance to which the lines of force of the particle extend. The particle, indeed, is supposed to exist only by these forces, and where they are it is.

Here is an extract from Faraday's lecture notes (R.I., MS.; see also *Life and Letters*, 2:177–79):

> Atomic constitution—physically—it breaks—hence divisible to particles; to atoms. First notion is that particles fill the space of the lump *entirely*: this consistent with the idea that matter is *continuous*: but then effect [compressibility] suggesting *intervening space*.
>
> This assumption accord with notions of liquifaction and vaporization. Hence elasticity of air, but now perceive that particles are assumed to feel each others influence when not in contact.
>
> Yet warning facts here and there—also in gases THE SPACE IS AS MATTER IN PHYSICAL PROPERTIES CANNOT TELL DIFFERENCE—leads on to view that centres of power or atoms

are excessively small and the space and powers around them
large.

*Crystallization* . . .—remarkable that best investigator of
crystalline phenomena is light and that light is considered
as depending on aether supposed to fill the whole space or bulk
of the crystal so THAT WHICH IS CALLED SPACE IS TO THE LIGHT
ASSUMED TO BE MATTER. . . .

. . . The view that physical chemistry necessarily takes of atoms
is now very large and complicated; first many elementary
atoms—next compound and complicated atoms. System within
system, like the starry heavens, *may be right*—but *may be all
wrong.* . . .

Now Electric considerations . . . How does a body conduct
by the particles or space? here BEGIN ELECTRICAL DOUBTS.
Next as to SPACE BETWEEN particles;—is not the heaviest nor
the lightest metals that conduct best—for *Platinum Iron &
Tin* nearly alike yet very different in weight—*lead* much
heavier than tin, much lighter than *platinum*, is only half
as good a conductor as either. *Copper* . . . *Iron* according to
atomic theory has most particles in given space yet very bad
conductor.
Again Potassium a metal and conducts:—with oxygen makes
a non-conductor but now far denser . . .

Again influence of heat on conduction. Fluoride of lead
solid not conduct: fluid conducts like a metal. All this refers
to the properties of matter much more to the space than the
particles but then SPACE MUST BE TAKEN TO BE THE MATTER.

So space may be proved to be an insulator in non-conducting
bodies—or—a conductor in conducting bodies. If an insulator
it is proved not to exist by conducting bodies.

These illogical and contradictory conclusions follow upon
the assumed admitted corpuscular theory of matter . . .

If any of the properties of matter be referred to the
atmosphere of power around the atoms, that is MAKING SPACE
MATTER, for it is not a difference in degree that I am discussing
but a difference in kind: for *may* then say that the atom is

*a mere mathematical centre* and power is adjusted around it—then
all the bulk must be considered as matter and matter will
be continuous . . . this allows many things that the old theory
does—as that matter may be mutually penetrable or that
two substances or three or four may exist in the same amount of
space . . .

Even in old notion of matter another matter is in theory
of light (undulatory) supposed to pervade all space both without
and within bodies. . . .

. . . for instance, water is not two particles of oxygen side by
side, but two spheres of power mutually penetrated, and the
centres even coinciding . . ."

In brief, the field of forces already makes space material in a certain sense,
and Dalton's atom becomes anyhow a small part of its sphere of influence, of
the whole atom. And how can a crystal effect light, if its atoms were merely
confined to these Daltonian small spheres?

I have perhaps to explain here the phenomena mentioned. Light waves
are, according to the accepted theory, similar to waves on the surface of the
water, only that the surface can be in any direction and not only horizontal.
If we imagine many surfaces of water in vertical, horizontal and any other
direction, all of them vibrating, we have a better picture of the phenomenon.
Now in the crystal the atoms are ordered in space in rows and columns (not
necessarily perpendicular to each other). The row of atoms in a tourmaline
crystal, or icelandic spar, will permit the transition of this light wave, which
moves on an imaginary surface parallel to it but not on that perpendicular to
it. Now Faraday asks how is this possible if the atom is confined to a small
space and if the amplitude of the wave (the height to which it rises above the
surface on which it moves) is smaller than the calculable distance between
two columns of atoms that prevent it from passing? Furthermore, the light
wave is supposed to be not a vibration of water but of aether. In other words,
his opponents assume space to be empty when discussing atoms and they assume
it to be full when discussing light. "That which is called space," says Faraday,
"is to light assumed to be matter." It is not really aether that transmits
light.

The same holds for conductivity. How does matter conduct? If we permit electricity to be transmitted by the billiard balls of iron or copper, then we have to admit that if we concentrate them, conductivity increases. To this Faraday offers some counter examples. If we allow space between the billiard balls to transmit electricity, then rarification of matter must increase its conductivity. To this again he offers counter examples. I am afraid Faraday's counter examples are not convincing; they only show how little the accepted theory explains: Dalton's atomic theory has no application to electric conductivity and so, at least, it must be further developed.

Next comes a still heavier attack. We attacked Dalton optically and electrically; now we attack him chemically, on his own grounds. For reasons of physical chemistry, Dalton's atom is too complex; it has to be SPLIT somehow into simpler elements. "*System within system*, like the starry heavens, *may be right* . . ." This is an anticipation of Niels Bohr's theory of 1913. It is not the one he subscribes to; his imagination, however, works for his *opponents* as well. If you wish to retain the particle, he tells them, you must split the atom and view it perhaps as a solar system; you must simplify your assumptions.

The final point includes a curious slip—water is mentioned instead of oxygen (molecular oxygen). It seems clear to me that the possibility he plays with is very doubtful: in his theory two atoms, it seems, cannot coincide any more than in Boscovich's. But as his ideas are not sufficiently worked out to clearly exclude this possibility, he mentions it. But I feel one cannot attach so much importance to mere lecture notes. All I wished to illustrate is the incredible scope of his imagination and probing of diverse possibilities—even wild anticipations; and for some reason his lecture notes illustrate this better than his papers or even diaries and letters. I do not know why. I have no idea how much of the notes he did use, and we know that he always prepared more experiments, observations, comments, or theories than he possibly could present in one lecture. Perhaps he needed leeway to improvise yet be well prepared. Or did he hope that a wild youngster would be taking notes?

### The Place of Faraday's Atomism

Apart from the lecture notes and one printed allusion, as well as a few remarks in his *Diary*, Faraday had kept his views on atomism fairly much to himself—so that after he gave the lecture and published a short paper, there was a radical change in his public image. What made him decide to change?

Initially, Faraday was inhibited particularly because he had such outlandish speculations; concealing them led him to a nervous breakdown; he then came fully out into the open. This is not to say that others had not speculated before, whether theoreticians or experimenters. It was rather the great novelty of Faraday's speculations, as well as extreme orthodoxy in avoiding wild speculation until 1844, which made their appearance on the scene in 1844 ever so much more noticeable. They were soon wrapped in silence; but they seem to have left quite an impact.

Silvanus P. Thompson, in his life of Faraday, seems to suggest (p. 226) that Faraday made his speculations public in response to a rumor that he was belittling Dalton. This is rather silly. It was Davy, not Faraday, who was vexed by Dalton's popularity, as Dr. Thomas Thomson testifies in his *History of Chemistry*. Funnily, Davy's jealousy did drive him to some criticism of Dalton, and Faraday was doubtlessly familiar with all this, since at places he even deliberately echoed Davy. Yet Davy had nothing to offer of the intellectual caliber of Faraday's speculations. It is a bit surprising that Thompson, who was an unusually appreciative and agreeable person, should have reported such pointless rumors (which, of course, most probably did take place sometime, somewhere); he even adds (*loc. cit.*) that Faraday once made a mistake concerning the priority of some discovery.[3] Evidently he was wondering why Faraday came out with his speculations when he did, and had no better theory than a mere psychological accident. It is clearly a very unsatisfactory mode of explanation. As Bence Jones has noticed (*Life and Letters*, 2:176), Faraday was then of the opinion that it was, in Faraday's own words, "time to speculate."

The corroboration to the theory that Faraday's lecture on atomism was based on mere psychological accident is that the lecture was a stand-in for a shy friend—Sir Charles Wheatstone (of Wheatstone's bridge and of early telegraphy)—whom Faraday tried for years to bring to talk to the public and who ran away in stage-fright minutes before the lecture was to start. This story is doubtless true, yet to think that this event is what made Faraday decide to speculate in public suggests a psychological insensitivity. I need not go into all the very interesting questions that this silly theory pushes aside. Rather, let me note here that Wheatstone's shyness and stage fright were no secret, least of all to Faraday, who not only knew him well, but also stood in for him quite regularly before, and yet not with any astounding speculations of his

3. He was alluding, I suppose, to *Experimental Researches in Electricity*, § 57; in which case he misread his text.

own but rather with facts and details prepared by Wheatstone himself.[4] I shall later show that the empirical topic of Wheatstone's undelivered lecture had a crucial place in the speculative topic of Faraday's lecture that replaced it.

Faraday's first speculative lecture was given in January 1844; it was soon published. He repeated it at Easter 1844—I have quoted his lecture notes—in a more extended form. What the January lecture has that the Easter lectures omit is, first, Faraday's expression of hesitation and, second, his ideas of where he differs from his predecessors—both in his explanation of the shape of the atom and in his subsequent theory of the possibility of atoms interfering with each other, thus retaining their individuality yet being able to combine and reshape. It is obvious that these are not ideas thrown off the cuff, but a fairly well-prepared lecture. Here are the three points I have mentioned. First, his hesitance (*Experimental Researches in Electricity*, 2:289).

> . . . I feel myself constrained . . . to admit them, and cannot
> do without them, but I feel great difficulty in the conception of
> atoms of matter which . . . are supposed to be more or less
> apart from each other, with intervening space not occupied
> by atoms, and perceive great contradictions in the conclusions
> which flow from such a view. . . . the atoms of Boscovich appear
> to me to have a greater advantage over the more usual atom . . .

And so, the story developed, there and then, and is still extant, that Faraday was a follower of Boscovich in matters atomic. But this is highly inaccurate. In the same lecture he makes it clear—Boscovich's atom is a mere approximation. In the same lecture he also says that Dalton's atoms are approximations. Clearly, his theory synthesizes both—not to mention Kant's extended particles that though not atoms, extend to cover the whole of space just like Faraday's atoms. Faraday sounded bold enough even without mentioning Kant—supposing he knew enough about his particles. Moreover, even regarding his attitudes toward Dalton and Boscovich he could easily be misunderstood. Faraday had to defend Boscovich more than attack him and attack Dalton more than defend him if he wished to give the impression that he accepted a bit from each. Here

---

4. See Jeffreys' bibliography for lectures that Faraday "delivered from materials supplied by Charles Wheatstone," items 156, 160; and for "lectures delivered for Charles Wheatstone" by Faraday, items 167, 173, 176, 177.

is a passage, regrettably overlooked by those who consider him Boscovichian plain and simple (p. 292):

> With regard also to the *shape* of the atoms, and according to the ordinary assumption, its definite and unalterable character, another view must now be taken of it. *An atom by itself might be conceived of as spherical, or spheroidal, or . . . as a dodecahedron,* . . . But . . . that which is ordinarily referred to under the term *shape* would now be referred to the disposition and relative intensity of the forces. The power arranged in and around a centre might be uniform in arrangement and intensity in every direction outwards from that centre, and then a section of equal intensity of force through the radii would be a sphere; or the law of decrease of force from the centre outwards might vary in different directions, and then the section of equal intensity might be an oblate or oblong spheroid, or have other forms; or the forces might be disposed so as to make the atom polar; or they might circulate around it equatorially or otherwise, after the manner of imagined magnetic atoms. In fact nothing can be supposed of the disposition of forces in or about a solid nucleus of matter, which cannot be equally conceived with respect to a centre. . . .

Faraday conceives his atom, then, as a center of force *surrounded by a field whose intense part is shaped like a Daltonian atom.* The advantage of this is that now space is nowhere empty and atoms are everywhere continuous. But how do atoms combine and separate? (How do they retain their individuality?) Faraday replies (p. 293):

> the manner in which two or many centres of force may . . . combine, and afterwards . . . separate again, may in some degree be illustrated by the beautiful case of the conjunction of two sea waves of different velocities into one, their perfect union for a time, and final separation into the constituent waves, considered, I think, at the meeting of the British Association at Liverpool . . .

. . . in 1837, on the application of Fourier's mathematical theory of the conduction of heat to the phenomenon of waves (of tides, in this case). The application of Fourier's theory to atomic phenomena is now commonplace. It was the
nonmathematician Faraday who first suggested it. The suggestion comes
astonishingly near to Schrödinger's theory of the material waves, as some
writers have recently noticed.

What happened now to matter? Faraday argues that one may if one likes
ascribe to his mathematical points materiality. But this, he contends, is gratui-
tous; he prefers to identify matter with fields.

Following his report on Faraday's atomic speculation, Bence Jones quotes
(*Life and Letters*, 2:179 ff.) "two remarkable letters" from two medical men,
in response to reprints of the speculation that Faraday had sent them. One is
by a traditionally minded writer who reads Faraday to be a Boscovichian and
fails thus to notice that Faraday's forces are not all central. The other, no less
critical, is more perceptive. It is by one Dr. Mayo, and I wish now to quote its
highlights.

> Your atmosphere of force, grouped round a mathematical
> point, is . . . rather superseding the material phenomena which
> it pretends to explain. It resolves . . . all matter into a
> metaphysical abstraction . . .
> . . . But what is the mathematical point?
> The question . . . is whether [any hypothesis] best interprets
> phenomena or is at least at variance with them; the objection
> you take to [Daltonian] atoms on the ground of their uncertain
> magnitude . . . presumes that we pretend to more knowledge
> of them than [we do] . . . Indeed, your mathematical point
> is either a simple negation, as having neither magnitude or
> parts; or is itself, after all, a material atom . . .

Mayo's first point is that an explanation of the kind presented by Faraday
goes beyond what is to be explained, that in a definite sense it denies the truth of
what it comes to establish. This is true. If we wish to explain matter, we must
not assume it; we thus deny its existence as substance. This disturbed Mayo,
especially as he justly noted that Faraday's theory of matter was not satisfactory, untestable, metaphysical. It was merely a part of a *program* for establishing such a view, a program that still exists and is still feasible. (Faraday's

general program being deterministic, is not defensible; but his program to explain particles is.) This already answers Mayo's second criticism, which is this: What does Faraday's mathematical point explain? Nothing. Faraday's theory explains hardly anything. Mayo expected too much from it all at once, yet he blamed Faraday for expecting too much from Daltonian atoms. Mayo's third criticism is that the mathematical point must be material. That this point interacts with its field does not show that it is matter, or else the whole of space is matter, which is to say the same thing in a different language. To put it still differently, once we assume a field, we have no obligation to materialize any part of it, center or no center. That the center will have a special function is not at all a bad idea, but its main function is not to reintroduce Dalton's atom as such—it is to reintroduce it as an approximation.

Nonetheless, I may perhaps interpret Faraday's mathematical point in two ways and discuss each of them; but I stress that this is inessential. Let us take the following atomic hypothesis. In an otherwise empty universe, the center of the atom is a center of spherical symmetry. This sounds entirely untestable; but in a framework within which forces and their mode of action are well described, it is very testable. In fact it is very similar to Lorentz's electron theory. In order to make Faraday's atom and Lorentz's electron identical we have first to endow both with mass. This would fall outside Faraday's program since he demanded to consider mass (heavy as well as inert) as a property of the field, not of the mathematical point. This may be overlooked when gravity and mechanics are not at stake. Let us further shrink Lorentz's electron into a mathematical point. This will make its self-energy infinite: it is held together by an infinitely large force. Yet we may view the center of Lorentz's atom as a mere center of symmetry, endowed with peculiar properties (like "electromagnetic mass" or other properties) that are spread in space. This is one interpretation of the mathematical point. Being a center it has, because of peculiar properties of our theory, some special properties, such as symmetry.

But this is an evasive argument. Consider again a theory in which the center of symmetry has no other peculiar property. Is it still a center? Has it still some sort of peculiar interaction with the rest of the field? The answer, I think, is in the affirmative. The whole significance of Faraday is the—unintentional, I suppose—breaking of the barrier between geometry and physics. Being a geometrical center is for him by no means a *purely* geometrical property. We cannot say that the resultant properties of the center, its motion, acceleration, and so on, are purely geometrical. This is the second, more general and satisfactory interpretation of the "mathematical point." For, the atom should not be identifiable with certain properties that distinguish one point from any other; it should be an explanation of the Daltonian atom; it should be a field with physicogeometrical properties. But all this is, of course, hindsight. It illustrates how explosive the ideas of Faraday were, not that he was the herald of Einstein.

I do not know what, if any, was Faraday's reaction to Mayo's letter. Mayo was critical and not approving; but he was understanding and even appreciative; most important, he got the main points of Faraday's argument. It is regrettable that his letter was published only in Faraday's biography and was never discussed; by now, of course, its argument is obsolete.

## Faraday's Interpretation of Light

After matter was abolished, there was no point in retaining the aether. The aether was introduced to "save the phenomena" or rather to save the principle that mere space cannot interact with matter, cannot house pure energy: waves are regular motions, and motion is the property of matter: the nothing has no properties. This principle and the wave theory of light together imply that space is not empty. Only to Faraday this is not so: since space *can* have properties, there is no need for the aether. Or, as Einstein put it (*The Times*, 4 February 1929; reproduced by permission of the Einstein Estate):

> The great range of phenomena which could be calculated and predicted to the finest detail by the use of this [wave] theory [of light] delighted physicists and filled many fat and learned books. No wonder, then, that the learned men failed to notice the crack which this theory made in the status of their eternal goddess. For in fact *this theory upset the view that everything real can be conceived as the motion of particles in space.* Light waves were, after all, nothing more than *undulatory states of empty space,* and the space thus gave up its passive *role* as a *mere stage for physical* events. The aether hypothesis patched up the crack and made it invisible. The aether was invented, penetrating everything, filling the whole space, and was admitted as a new kind of matter. Thus it was overlooked that by this procedure *space itself had been brought to life.* It is clear that this had really happened,

since the aether was considered to be a sort of matter which could nowhere be removed. It was thus to some degree identical with space   itself, i.e., something necessarily given with space. Light was thus viewed as a dynamical process undergone, as it were, *by space itself*. In this way the field theory was born as an illegitimate child of Newton's Physics, though it was cleverly passed off at first as legitimate.

To become fully conscious of this change of outlook was a task for a highly original mind, whose insight could go straight to essentials, a mind which never got stuck in formulas. Faraday was this favoured spirit. His instinct revolted at the idea of forces acting directly at a distance, which seemed contrary to every elementary observation. If one electrified body attracts or repels a second body, this was for him brought about, not by a direct action from the first body to the second but through an intermediary action. The first body throws the space immediately around it into a certain condition which spreads itself into more distant parts of space according to a definite spatio-temporal law of propagation. The condition of space was called *"the electric field"*. The second body experiences a force because it lies in the field of the first, and *vice versa*. The "field" thus provides a conceptual apparatus which rendered unnecessary the idea of action at a distance. Faraday also had the bold idea that in appropriate circumstances *fields might detach themselves from the bodies producing them and speed away through space as free fields; this was his interpretation of light.*

This is in fact all that should be said about Faraday's comment on the theory of light. (1) Aether is superfluous; it is indistinguishable from empty space. Therefore it is simpler to view light as a field phenomenon. (2) The field in question may be an electromagnetic field.

The locus classicus of Faraday's dismissal of the aether was a lecture he read in the Royal Institution in 1846 and published in that year under the title "Thoughts on Ray Vibrations." S. P. Thompson, we remember, was indignant, at the turn of the century, at the fact that Faraday's earlier biographers had ignored this paper. Thompson admired this paper because it heralded the electromagnetic theory of light that turned out—he was assured —to be true. Later writers have recently noticed Faraday's abolition of the aether because this, too, had turned out—to their satisfaction—to be true. I feel most reluctant to enter such company. It is obvious to me that practically all of Faraday's theories are false, that the very existence of genuine electric currents and of asymmetry between negative and positive charges make most of his ideas plainly outmoded, that even the most Faradayan theory still extant, namely general relativity, would have greatly surprised Faraday in quite a few respects. My own admiration of Faraday is rooted in his boldness, not in his success. In many cases people are all too gladly ready to acknowledge boldness in retrospect as amply justified by subsequent success. This is illogical: boldness involves risk.

The purpose of Faraday's "Thoughts on Ray Vibrations" is to identify the waves of the wave theory of light with the "lines of force which connect particles, and consequently masses of matter together; a notion which as far as it is admitted, will dispense with the aether . . ." (*Experimental Researches in Electricity*, 3:447). He goes on to explain that this idea developed out of his view of matter not as "little bodies . . . independent of . . . forces and capable of existing without them" but, on the contrary, "as centres of force." In his own view, atoms do not have "a definite form and a certain limited size:" in his view, "the particle indeed is supposed to exist only by these forces, and where they are it is." (Again we see, unlike Boscovich's atom and like Kant's, Faraday's is of infinite size.) Clearly, if things are not matter but forces, waves are not of matter but of forces; the simplicity of the conclusion defies explanation.

As an argument he says this: electric currents move with the speed of light, and are constituted of vibrations. So, possibly currents differ from light chiefly in that the former move through so-called insulators and the latter through so-called conductors. In the 1830s, and throughout the rest of his career, Faraday declared the difference between conductors and insulators to be not of kind but of degree. The upshot is now clear: current and light waves are the same; a conducting wire and interstellar space are essentially the same—differing only in degree.

Here Faraday at his boldest and most admirable is in error, and even in gross error. So I am the first to express admiration of this argument in print. Incidentally, the factual error on the basis of which the argument rests is Wheatstone's. The "Thoughts on Ray Vibrations" were, originally, a lecture on "Wheatstone's Electromagnetic Chromoscope" (R.I., MS, April 1846), and the lecture notes read, in part,

|               | Vibrating of Light                                      | Of Electric Current                        |
| ------------- | ------------------------------------------------------- | ------------------------------------------ |
| The Medium    | Ether<br>is in the masses<br>between particles          | Metals<br>by properties<br>of particles    |

but why this difference in our views.

So inclined to dismiss the Ether—though not vibrations —perhaps the undulations are in the lines of force . . . Gravitating force—so lines of inductive electric force now can shake lines of Magnetic and Electric force . . . So why may not the vibrations of light and other rays [!] exist (in a high species of vibrations) in the lines of force . . .

When one takes seriously Wheatstone's alleged fact—the speed of currents in metals equals the speed of light—and Faraday's argument from it and the lack of a basic distinction between conductors and insulators, then one sees why Faraday was so intent on having Wheatstone speak, and how it was that when Wheatstone was going to lecture in 1844 and at the last moment disappeared, Faraday was there and then ready with his atomic speculation. But back to "Thoughts on Ray Vibrations" of 1846 where he declares he "can shake lines of force."

The paper is six pages long, and contrapuntal in theme: it raises difficulties with the aether and extols lines of force. He considers the sizes of the aether's atoms and its elastic properties, and finds it uncomfortable any way he looks at it. This part we need not discuss now. And he shows that the little he knows about lines of force, such as their elasticity, makes them all very congenial carriers of ray vibrations. That field's vibrations are identical with light rays he does not say as yet.

Faraday repeated his electromagnetic theory of light in later publications and on a number of occasions. I shall only quote one passage (§ 3075), which is most often quoted—for obvious reasons:

. . . for my own part, considering the relations of a vacuum to the magnetic force and the general character of magnetic phenomena external to the magnet, I am more inclined to the notion that in the transmission of the force there is such an action, external to the magnet, than that the effects are merely attractions and repulsions at a distance. Such an action *may be a function of the aether*; for it is not unlikely that, *if there be an aether*, it should have other uses than simply the conveyance of radiations . . .

We see here again that Faraday thought for his opponents. Additionally, this is a compromise suggestion.[5] But the concluding part of this passage is often used as a representative of Faraday's views. Tyndal quoted it in evidence for Faraday's support of the aether, and so did Maxwell (*Treatise*, § 782, 2:432 note), and so did many others, including the influential historian of science E. T. Whittaker, in his *History of Theories of the Aether and Electricity*. Clearly, some authors still consider Faraday as really an aetherist rather than as one who intended seriously to "dismiss the aether but not the vibrations." Others, who like to see Faraday as the precursor to Einstein, prefer to quote the opening part of the passage. As the passage itself represents both views, we may well admit, he thought on two lines simultaneously.

It is not difficult at all to say how Faraday's attack and his defense of matter and aether intertwine—he did these alternately in the act of self-criticism. It is more difficult to say what he invented first, his attack on matter or his attack on the aether. The first was published in 1844, the second in 1846; in the second he says the second followed the first, and in a sense this is doubtlessly true: when matter is abolished, it is hard to see why we need the aether. Yet his abolition of matter came from his field theory, which in itself is a theory without any aether, without any need for any aether. Clearly, once he endowed lines of force with reality, he ascribed to them different roles in succession, thus rendering various previously postulated entities jobless and thus being able to dismiss them. And each such development demanded special elaboration. Here, then, the order of his thoughts is less a case of internal development and more of an accidental matter.

5. The reference in the above-quoted passage makes this clear. Faraday's cross-references are, incidentally, always pedantic and sometimes full of irony and wit.

### Conclusion: Faraday's Program

In retrospect we can see Faraday's program as a very simple one: explain every theory as an approximation to some theory about lines of force and design crucial experiments between the two.

In retrospect we can also say that Faraday carried out a small part of this program. In fact, he more often developed a very peculiar procedure, which, in my opinion, is the unique characteristic of Faraday, most idiosyncratic to his metaphysical and experimental bent, and to his lack of readiness to develop mathematical theories in detail. He used his metaphysical theories to interpret given theories, and while hardly crystallizing the interpretations into clear scientific theories from which empirical corollaries could be deduced for the purpose of crucial experiment, he tried various possible empirical corollaries that might follow from some, as yet unarticulated, scientific theories. This is why he experimented so much and tried so many versions of an experiment, until one version came his way.

No doubt, this is not the most efficient way to go around; Faraday was working under a severe handicap that could more easily be overcome by collaboration. Maxwell was not right in saying that Faraday was fortunate in his isolation. We can illustrate this by showing that where Faraday's conception of a scientific theory was clearer, his experimentation was more fruitful. His conception of gravitational field theory, in particular, was not clear enough to guide his experiments, and Stokes even found his experiments on electro-gravity somewhat pathetic. And his conception of a field explanation of inertia was even poorer, and so he had no experiment at all on this topic.

In a lecture in 1847 (see p. 88) he says:

> . . . now INERTIA is considered by some to be the great distinction of matter and that which alone indicates a nucleus to it, in certain views which I shall not go into here. For my own part I only see in it that law of nature by which force cannot be annihilated, but must produce its equivalent effect. It IS A CASE OF THE CONSERVATION OF FORCE . . . The effect of retention or transfer of any other force in nature than mechanical force seems to me to be just as good a case of the *great law* under which inertia comes . . . though it have not the same name.

Inertia is a case of conservation of force, declares Faraday. I doubt that this sounds convincing in any interpretation. The only printed reference to inertia is of 1848, when he mentioned it in a manner showing that he was quite aware of its significance. It was one of his suggestions to solve his problem (§ 2576) whether the peculiar interaction of magnets and crystals, magnecrystallic force, originates in the magnet or in the crystal. One of his suggestions (§ 2591) is that magnetism may be polarizable by crystals and therefore act on crystals in a manner that reduces the obstruction due to polarization. He continues thus:

> In making this supposition, I do not forget the points of inertia
> and momentum; but such an idea as I can form of inertia
> does not exclude the above view as altogether irrational. I
> remember too, that, when a magnetic pole and a wire carrying
> an electric current are fastened together, so that one cannot
> turn without the other, if the one be made axis the other
> will revolve round and carry the first with it; and also, that if
> a magnet be floated in mercury and a current sent down it,
> the magnet will revolve by the powers which are *within* its
> mass. With my imperfect mathematical knowledge,[6] there

6. Although Faraday made no secret of his "imperfect mathematical knowledge," his mention of it in a philosophic publication sounds peculiar. The inductive code included two important rules. First, one had to speak to the point (though, as if unknowingly, add redundant circumstantial details). Second, one had to avoid personal talk (though one had to talk in first person and report one's observations as well as, occasionally, one's curiosity). There were minor deviations that one could master, such as talk about the weather, at least in England. There are cases when Faraday did talk about the weather, regarding both the liquefaction of chlorine and the use of heavy glass to analyze sunlight—both very famous cases. There are other cases too (such as *Experimental Researches in Chemistry and Physics*, p. 51). In addition, one could express personal feelings of diffidence on the point at issue—but only when the point was a bold one, thereby expressing the desire not to be quoted if one's bold point was not favorably received. Indeed, here Faraday boldly declares an experiment contrary to Newton's laws, despite the weakness of his mathematics; that reported weakness, however, makes his expression diffident. We remember (see p. 62, above) that the experiment is recorded in the *Diary* entry for 21 January 1823 as opposed to Newton's laws. Significantly, Faraday manages to add so much personal color to the paragraph here quoted. He says "I remember." When he is mathematically daring he has no need to blame his poor memory for his poor mathematics. Also he refers to the magnet rotating on its own axis with the same expression, instead of giving a pedantic reference as he usually does. The experiment (see p. 101, above) was crucial in the development of the field concept in 1832. In retrospect, Faraday seems to ascribe its ability to encourage his speculative bent to its conflict with Newton's laws. In a relaxed mood Faraday could see all his crucial moments as liberations from Newton's laws (see, for example, his 1831 letter, p. 69, above, relating his 1831 discoveries to his old rotations of 1821 and contrasting them with the views of "the mathematicians"). In a relaxed mood, then, Faraday was a rebel, with no fear of the mathematicians and readiness to put forth a contradictory judgment, as well as a man of good memory and not a pedant. But, generally, the very position of a rebel that he occupied was his symptom neurosis (in the sense of Allen Wheelis's *The Quest For Identity*.)

seems as much difficulty in these motions as in the one I am
supposing, and therefore I venture to put forth the idea. The
hope of a polarized bundle of magnetic forces is enough of
itself to make one work earnestly with such an object, though
only in imagination, before us; and I may well say that no
man, if he take industry, impartiality and caution with him
in his investigations of science, ever works experimentally in
vain.

What Faraday says is this. No one as yet knows how to square the laws
of inertia and of conservation of momentum and of momentum of momentum
or angular momentum (rotation) with certain experimental finds. Therefore,
he ventures to suggest a new hypothesis which is equally problematic vis-à-vis
these laws. And this new hypothesis is very stimulating and suggests series
of new experiments. All this hardly indicates a view concerning inertia and
momentum, and it is no accident that Faraday goes back to magnetism rather
than dwells on inertia.

Of course, what he says about the difficulty vis-à-vis inertia and momentum
is true. Of course, the solution accepted today has to do with currents as the
flows of negatively charged massive particles—a view utterly objectionable to
Faraday. Of course, his suggestion that he did not have to bother with inertia,
particularly not with his own—seeming or true—violations of it, is true too.
Yet, to complete his world view he did need a clearer view of inertia.

There is little doubt that Faraday was conscious of his unification of
geometry and physics, of space and of matter. Yet, his geometry was not in
any sense a substitute for Euclidean geometry—chiefly because he did not
know what to do with inertia, because he did not see how to deduce the laws
of conservation of momentum, the classical Newtonian conservation laws, from
his theory of conservation of force. Even Einstein could not fully do so: his
general relativity geometrizes only gravity and assumes inertia of sorts as a
postulate, not as a corollary. His generalized relativity might have done that
if it were successful. But meanwhile the whole program had to be scrapped
because of the indeterministic character of quantum theory.

With this I conclude my general discussion of Faraday's program; I shall
now add some details about the process by which Faraday filled space with
lines of force and thus moved toward the development of his program.

# 8 The Electrification of Matter

The first period of Faraday's major work is easy to characterize as his study of the material medium—as the crystallization of a partial program within his general program. The period started, we remember, in 1832, with the combined single explanation of the two discoveries of 1831. It ended in 1839 or so, and it concerned electricity in all its forms. Electric currents are induced, first in the vicinity of moving magnets, and second in the vicinity of currents when their intensities vary. The first fact is explained by the hypothesis: cutting of magnetic lines of force induces currents. The second fact is declared the first fact in disguise: varying the strength of a current is moving around magnetic lines of force. This idea Faraday tried to apply to all phenomena, especially to currents: electric currents *are* aspects of the magnetic field. The gain from this is that it replaces electric action at a distance with action through space: even though when we switch a current on we see the action of it at once anywhere else, the action still moves through space, and this is detectable by the phenomenon of induction.

And so, Faraday tried to find various experiments where *intervening space* comes into action, where *the medium* affects the situation most noticeably. As a first step he began to consider the intervening space or the medium when filled with matter, to try and correlate the electric action and *the intervening material medium*.

This is the program of Faraday's first period. It was surprisingly successful, but not surprisingly it was misunderstood: his readers saw him concentrate on the *material* medium rather than the material *medium*. That *the medium could be empty space* was for them too bewildering. This misunderstanding did not relieve all the bewilderment: even when the medium is material, the results of Faraday's ideas are very unorthodox. Their application to electro-chemistry showed that *matter has electrical properties.* This was already sensed by Davy, but never clearly stated by him. Faraday now compels his opponents to admit this heretic theory that one and the same material particle has *both* gravity and electricity. He assumed this particle to be roughly a Daltonian atom. He applies the view of the connection between lines of force and particles of matter to electrostatics. He refutes Coulomb's theory of electric action at a distance by showing how decisive is the function of the material medium of electrostatic interaction. He tries to explain certain electric processes on the same lines as his explanation of electrochemistry. The results are important yet less satisfactory. He tries again and again to encourage people to take up his program. It was only partly taken up. Only after Maxwell's success did many Faradayans continue the research. The most successful of them was J. J. Thomson. Faraday's idea was partly confirmed—particles have both mass and charge—partly refuted—they are *not* only Dalton's atoms but also some much smaller, and these *do* flow in electric currents proper, and they are charged with only one kind of electricity. This is a clear deviation from Faraday's views, which puts a clear wedge between electrolytic (and dielectric) conduction and metallic conduction. Nonetheless, the next step, of Rutherford and Bohr, was a (probably independent) utilization of the idea that was fundamental with Faraday: if electricity has material properties, then we can *identify* electric matter and ordinary matter. In this roundabout way it was ultimately assumed that ordinary matter has mainly electromagnetic properties. When Rutherford invented nuclear physics, this assumption became outdated as well.

Faraday's speculations and experimental researches are linked thus. He wished to show that the universe is one field. For this he tried to show in his first period of research the "electric conditions of all matter," and in the second period "the magnetic conditions of all matter." Throughout the two periods he tried to convert every force directly to every other force and measure the constancy of the intensity of each force in transition—centering on electricity in the first period, and on magnetism in the second. From time to time he probed into empty space itself, but usually with meager results.

Though Faraday's success was incredible, it may be noted that most of his experiments were failures and that much as he was successful he was very far from his goal. Only the great success of his electrochemical researches, for example, mask his deeply disappointing failure to decompose all elements into hydrogen. As he suspected, he could not match the intensity of what we call today nuclear forces. In the same way, we can say, he spectacularly succeeded in showing the electric conditions of insulators, of *non*conductors (allegedly nonelectric), like glass, sulphur, resin, and so on; but he failed to explain the electric conditions of metals. This was the background to J. J. Thomson's discovery of the electron and to the later discovery of the role of (so-called free) electrons in metals. Now that the ideas of constitution of matter, though still very vague and unsatisfactory, have so progressed, the greatness and boldness of Faraday's ideas can easily be overlooked. According to the views accepted in his day, matter and electricity were two entirely different substances. The only electric conditions of matter known at that time were two. The first is Gray's discovery (of the early eighteenth century) that some matter conducts electricity and some does not. The second was that of electrochemistry (of 1800). These, then, were the natural spearheads, and the starting point of his research into the electric conditions of all matter, as described in the first volume of his *Experimental Researches in Electricity* of 1839.

## Electricity as Power

Faraday's first two series are dated November 1831 and January 1832. The Third Series is dated January 1833. The majority of its space is devoted to a research usually labeled as "the identity of electricity." It is a report on an attempt to obtain the various characteristics of electricity (tension, decomposition, deflection of needle, and so on) from the different sources of electricity (voltaic, common or frictional, magneto-, thermo-, and animal). Faraday argues that he tried to establish the identity because some individuals doubted it; he did not state what his own interest was in the problem. Moreover, we know that there are some observed differences between the various electricities, and one can always insist that they are very significant, and even Faraday admitted that, for instance, he failed to obtain a spark from electricity evolved by heat, though he easily obtained it from common (frictional) electricity. In spite of the obvious differences between the various electricities, Faraday claimed (§ 450) that he established in the third series, at least to his own satisfaction, the identity of the various electricities. What his arguments were in favor of this view of the identity of the electricities were never publicly discussed. The theory of the Third Series was not mechanistic, while the identity of all electric fluids was a part of the mechanistic program. In the forties both the *Encyclopaedia Britannica* and the *Encyclopedia Metropolitana* ignored practically all of Faraday's theories save that all electricities are identical, and presented this theory as one based on finding similarities and inferring identity.

But what should one do about the *dis*similarities?

Half a year later, in the beginning of his Fourth Series, Faraday claimed (§ 450) that he had explained the apparent differences between the various electricities, and especially those between common (frictional) and voltaic electricity (§ 451):

> The great distinction of the electricities obtained from
> these two sources is the very high tension to which the small
> quantity obtained by aid of the machine may be raised, and
> the enormous quantity (371.376.) in which that of comparatively
> low tension, supplied by the voltaic battery, may be procured;
> but as their actions, whether magnetical, chemical, or of any
> other nature, are essentially the same (360.), it appeared
> evident that we might reason from the former as to the manner
> of action of the latter; and it was, to me, a probable consequence,
> that the use of electricity of such intensity as that afforded
> by the machine, would, when applied to effect and elucidate
> electro-chemical decomposition, show some new conditions
> of that action, *evolve new views of the internal arrangements
> and changes of the substances under decomposition*, and perhaps
> give efficient powers over matter as yet undecomposed.

In brief, the theory is that all apparent differences are due either to difference of *degrees of tension* or to the difference of *quantities of electricity*. This is obviously a highly testable and interesting theory, and of consequences that Faraday mentions only in the next series.

The reason is obvious: facts that can be stated without reference to theory, such as the similarities that Faraday discusses, were traditionally viewed as independent of all theory, and traditionally had to be presented so. This is the traditional inductive style. Faraday tried to conform to it for as long as he could. But his real intent was to establish further tests, to compare both tensions and qualities of electricities acquired from the different sources. And here Faraday's presentation becomes less inductive, since here the inductive mode of presentation is not available, since here he was testing a theory. Faraday had to explain *what* we measure by the galvanometer. His idea was that we measure the *work* that acted on the needle when deflecting it. And he showed that the *work* invested in the friction machine is proportional to the *work* that the total current, when passing through the galvanometer, worked on the needle. No doubt, the total work invested in the friction machine is much bigger than the work invested in the galvanometer; but this is only because the greater part of it is diverted through other channels—mainly heat. Indeed, the ratio of the quantity of electricity passing through a wire and the heat evolved in it is also constant.

*If* we assume all electricity to be power or work or energy, then we can compare the quantities of electricity evolved from different sources, by their action on the galvanometer's needle. In this manner Faraday could find that the electricity evolved in a minute voltaic pile that acts for two or three seconds evolves the same quantity of electricity as his big friction machine evolves in about thirty revolutions. Thus, his concept of universal force enables him to have a glimpse of the enormous forces hidden in the chemical properties of matter. We may still remember how overwhelming was the discovery of the immense quantities of nuclear energy. Faraday was as surprised when he found the magnitude of chemical energy.

In brief, Faraday tested the idea that a given absolute quantity of electricity can turn into a definite amount of heat, mechanical work, chemical decomposition, or magnetic work. Put the other way round, the thing makes no sense any longer. The deflection of the needle can be shown to depend on the amount of work invested in the friction machine or on the size of the voltaic battery and other conditions of it. But of comparison there is no way to speak unless we first make the hypothesis. And the hypothesis cannot be made on the basis of similarities since it has to explain dissimilarities.

Thus, inductivism, or the inductive style, is one possible reason why Faraday's third series failed to have any effect on the public; its heretic character is another. Indeed, it is doubtful if its heretic character has ever been observed: neither contemporary commentators nor writers on Faraday from Tyndall to Williams seem to have suspected it.

Faraday's idea was that of the conservation of force. *By the same amount of force invested to create electricity the same amount of action may be obtained by utilizing this electricity.* The "*absolute quantity of electricity*" is for Faraday a *quantity of force.* By discharging equal quantities of electricity, measured by the work invested in creating them, a magnetic needle is *deflected* to equal arcs (Faraday made a mistake here), equal wires are equally *heated*, and the same *chemical action* is evolved from them: equal quantities of matter are decomposed by them. Faraday claimed that although the *tension* of the pile is much lower than the tension of the friction machine, the *absolute quantity* of electricity evolved in the pile is enormous, after a few seconds of immersion of two minute pieces of metal into the acid the quantity of electricity, *measured* now by the *deflection* of the needle, is equal to the quantity evolved by thirty turns of the wheels of a large friction machine.

Faraday's subsequent theory of the voltaic pile is very famous; its source was traditionally overlooked. Here we see it clearly: the researches on the pile were made in order to *compare forces* and illustrate the *indestructibility* of force. By decomposition we spend electric force, therefore we gain chemical force. And the first testable theory of chemical force was proposed by Faraday in January 1833. By his theory we should be able to correlate the various measurements of the *absolute quantities of electricity*, the measurement by mechanical work, by electromagnetic work (to effect the needle), by chemical work (of decomposing chemicals), and by heating.

All this is implicit in the Third Series. A part of it was made explicit half a year later in the Fifth Series where Faraday claimed that he had already stated the same view in the Third Series. He had done it, but not explicitly.

A few final remarks on the Third Series. Faraday gives a description of current (§ 283):

> By *current*, I mean anything progressive, whether it be a fluid of electricity or two fluids moving in opposite directions, or merely vibrations, or, speaking still more generally, progressive forces. By *arrangement*, I understand a local adjustment of particles, or fluids, or forces, not progressive. Many other reasons might be urged in support of the view of a *current* rather than an *arrangement*, but I am anxious to avoid stating unnecessarily what will occur to others at the moment.

Currents may be conductions of one or two fluids, but the main property of a current is that it is a change. What change it is Faraday explicitly refused to state as yet. In the end of the third series he implicitly states that it is "progressive *forces*"; it is, I understand, either the conversion of electric forces or the change of position of the forces. It is not merely a flow of particles of the electric fluids or a new arrangement of their positions, not merely "local adjustment of particles"—particles may not exist at all. This tempts one to compare Faraday's theory of the current with that of Georg Simon Ohm, first published in 1827 but left unnoticed for quite some time. Unfortunately, it is quite unclear even today what Ohm's theory was and why it aroused so much resistance.[1] What is clear, however, is that Ohm's law views the quantity of electricity that flows in a current in a unit of time as proportional to the electric tension that produces the current, and the factor of proportionality is the conductivity that is peculiar to the conductor.

Flow = tension × conductivity, or, when we consider resistance to be the inverse of conductivity, tension = resistance × flow.

As to the comparison of Ohm's theory of 1827 (which was unknown to Faraday) and Faraday's views, what is common to both views is first the identification of the electricities and subsequently the identification of all the electric *tensions*. The difference is this. While for Ohm *tension* was the central factor of the electric situation, Faraday considered the *absolute quantity of electricity* to be the central factor. Ohm believed that electricity is an indestructible fluid. By the electric machine, he thought, we do not create electricity, but electric *tension*. Faraday believed that electric forces are created —though not from nothing; he believed that mechanical forces become electric forces, the increase of the concentration of which, their exaltation, *is* the *increase of the tension*. We may say, on one hand, that nowadays we rather accept Ohm's view than Faraday's view, although we no longer believe his view that the electric fluid is void of the properties of ordinary matter (inertia, gravity). On the other hand, we may say that nowadays we accept Faraday's view that we can create absolute quantities of electricity, and that even the material properties of the electron (of which Faraday did not know) are convertible into force. However, clearly in all those experiments that Faraday describes *save* those of electric decomposition, Ohm's theory is more accurately applicable than Faraday's (even though with modifications): the *current's intensity*, the *electric tension* times the conducting power of the conductor causes the maximum deflection of the needle and heats the wire, and causes mechanical work. Only in the case of electrochemistry and in cases where the discharge is very rapid is Faraday's theory of the absolute quantity of electricity approximately correct. But Faraday predicted (note to § 853), and confirmed his prediction, that the conducting power of a wire is independent of its length. *Ohm's theory makes it clear that here Faraday was in error.* Still, Faraday

---

1. See Morton Schagrin, "The Resistance to Ohm's Law," *American Journal of Physics*, 31 (1963), 536–47.

surely found many quite accurate methods to measure it and thus he was able to find both Ohm's result as a first approximation and the absolute quantity of electricity involved in the chemical action of the atom. To make this point more accurate we may say this: Faraday considered the absolute quantity of electricity to be something like electric energy. He thought that we can increase (or exalt) its intensity by compression. Now we think that the *tension* is the energy and that the compression of the energy is also *investment of more energy* in the system. Here lay Faraday's error: he did not yet notice that compression of electricity demands *work*. With this correction Faraday's theory would give the same results as Ohm's, even though the theories would still be different, and Faraday's theory would, with this correction, be richer and more to our taste. This explains why he got fairly correct results. His experiments are such that the missing factor in them plays a negligible role. The main point is, however, not that he was right, but that he had a highly testable theory, which now he tried to test by investigating the chemical action of the voltaic pile.

The clearest point where Faraday's view is correct, quantitatively, and approximately, is in the most crucial junction: Faraday first showed that equal quantities of electricity deflect the needle to equal distances, and this became his prime measure of quantities of electricity. Now, whether this is true or not, much depends on what Faraday meant by quantities of electricity, which may be problematic. But we do not have to discuss this difficult point: we know independently of all this that he used a ballistic galvanometer, so-called, a galvanometer that, for all practical purposes, may be viewed as one in which the discharge is instantaneous. Even in later theories, where the quantity of electricity is roughly the total charge, Faraday's theory holds well enough for ballistic galvanometers. But not for galvanometers in general. How lucky Faraday was and how much his success was rooted in the general vagueness of even his knowledge of electricity at the time are hard to assess; but, obviously, all galvanometers at the time were in fact ballistic: the error was in fact a second order or marginal error at the time.[2]

The experiments of converting energies and of measuring the rates of conversion are usually attributed to Joule.[3] Justification may be sought in the fact that Faraday was measuring forces, not energies; but Joule too was measuring forces. I shall not enter this point here. Let me, however, quote Tyndall

2. See my *Towards an Historiography of Science* (1963), nn. 57, 59, 60.
3. See note 9, p. 179, above.

(*Discoverer*, pp. 52 ff.), to show that he was quite aware of the point I am raising.

> . . . he inferred the possibility of comparing, as regards quantity, electricities which differ greatly from each other in intensity. His object now is to compare frictional with voltaic electricity. . . . and found that the needle of his galvanometer swung through the same arc, and coloured his moistened paper to the same extent, as thirty turns of his large electrical machine. . . . In his subsequent researches "On the absolute Quantity of Electricity associated with the Particles or Atoms of matter" [seventh series] he endeavours to give an idea of the same amount of electrical force involved in the decomposition of a single grain [one-fifteenth of a gram] of water. He is almost afraid to mention it, for he estimates it at 800,000 discharges of his large Leyden battery. This, if concentrated in a single discharge, would be equal to a very great flash of lightning; while the chemical action of a single grain of water on four grains of zinc would yield electricity equal in quantity to a powerful thunderstorm.

The status of Ohm's law in nineteenth-century physics still confuses readers of Faraday's texts. In Maxwell's equations we have the electromagnetic potentials and the current and changes of system as given. From this we can conclude the intensity of the electromotive force, and we can define resistance or conductivity as the ratio between the intensities of the electromotive force and the current or vice versa; this can be defined for any current or portion thereof. Ohm's law says that given a means of a current, a channel, whether a given wire or a given jet of water from an open faucet, its resistance is independent of tension, current, or the surroundings. This law is utterly unrelated to Maxwell's equations. This is a fact that is as obvious as it is often overlooked.

Faraday tried to explain why a wire conducts (see p. 228): in it electric waves transmit forces. Maxwell denied this: electric waves, he says, accompany the magnetic waves that Faraday had viewed as light waves. And so a lacuna was left in Maxwell's theory.

Is Ohm's law true? Most people answer in the affirmative as a matter of course. But take a wire and make it into a coil, and self-induction will greatly impede its conductivity. Even when not coiled, if a wire is long enough its self-induction will severely impede its conductivity, as Kelvin's study of telegraphy illustrates. But all this may be written off as mere electromagnetic induction, which is quite irrelevant. Well, then; the classical equation of impedance tells us that the conduction by a wire in a given system does not depend solely on the wire's resistance (as defined in the discussion of Ohm's law), and not solely on resistance of the wire plus the electromagnetic induction of the system, but also on the electrostatic condition of the system. We shall discuss Faraday's views on electrostatics soon; here suffice it to note that he viewed electrostatic properties not as of charges of charged bodies, but of whole systems. And in 1838 he had explained at length that currents, too, were dependent not only on tensions and wires but on systems as wholes. In 1854 he carried this idea even further by showing empirically that the mere coating of a telegraphic wire with this insulator or that, which changes the electrostatic condition of the system while leaving the system otherwise unaltered, may make quite a difference. He said then (*Experimental Researches in Electricity*, 3:516), "A striking proof of a variation of the conduction of a wire by variation of its lateral static induction, is given in the experiment proposed sixteen years ago (1333)." He describes his experiment and adds triumphantly, "Why is this? the quantity of electricity is the same, the wire is the same, its resistance is the same . . ." Here, incidentally, the word "resistance" is used as in Ohm's law. . . . But the law is refuted.

There is no doubt that Ohm's law is false. It is replaced by the impedance equation, and only when impedance due to electrostatic and electromagnetic induction is negligible is Ohm's law serviceable. Why? Faraday tried to explain, but he was in error; his ideas about induction were quite good, but about currents in conducting wires he went awry.

Of all commentators and biographers of Faraday, only Williams discusses Faraday and Ohm (*Michael Faraday*, p. 210). He quotes the second series of 1832, where Faraday varies the conductors in electromagnetic induction and gets currents that vary in proportion to the conductivity of the conductors. Williams comments: "This is one of the times when Faraday's lack of mathematical training and his distaste for mathematical formulation prevented a general law from being recognized. What Faraday had stated is clearly Ohm's law. . . . Had Faraday taken one final step of putting his view into the equation . . . , he would have provided an enormous stimulus to the progress of electrical science. . . . Although its exactitude is evident . . . the passage could be, and probably was, read as a qualitative restatement of the relative conducting powers of the various metals." Williams is right about Faraday's early work: it looked qualitative—at first even to Maxwell (see above, p. 103)—though it was quantitive. But Williams is in error about the agreement between Ohm and Faraday. We can use Ohm's law to correct Faraday's view that the length of a given wire does not influence its resistance, and we can use Faraday's view and experiments to develop the impedance equation that by far supersedes Ohm's law.

This discussion of the relations between Faraday's and Ohm's views covers the period between 1833 and 1854. Faraday said in 1833, we recall, that since what matters is the absolute quantity of electricity, we may ignore the differences between high-tension, low-flow spark and a low-tension, high-flow galvanic current. He sustained this idea of the third series of 1833 throughout his career and merely elaborated on it. I think this is as astonishing as Maxwell's similar discovery concerning Faraday's second series of 1832. This is, indeed, Faraday's methodology—to speak in extreme generalities and add the details as he went along—a methodology already outlined in his lectures to the City Philosophical Society at the very beginning of his career (see p. 31.) Let us, then, follow some of the details.

## Electricity and Matter

Faraday's third series—on the identity of all electricities—is of January 1833. The fourth series—on electric conductivity—is of April of the same year. In 1600 William Gilbert thought that all matter divides into electric (i.e., that which can be electrified, like amber) and nonelectric (metals). In the early eighteenth century Stephen Gray refuted this theory by showing that when metals are *insulated* they can be electrified. He divided matter into conductors and nonconductors. Faraday's theory was, on the contrary, that *all* bodies are conductors, though to different degrees: some conduct more readily than others. Or, in Ohm's language, some bodies have low resistance and others have high resistance. (Low conductivity is high resistance, of course.) From now on the term "nonconductor" or "insulator" designates any body that conducts very badly. A perfect nonconductor, Faraday claims, does not exist. In addition, Faraday shows, it is not merely the chemical character of a body that decides its conducting power (or resistance) but also its physical state, its being a solid, a fluid, or a gas. Here is Faraday's description of this discovery.

381. I was working with ice, and the solids resulting from the freezing of solutions, arranged either as barriers across a substance to be decomposed, or as the actual poles of a voltaic battery, *that I might trace and catch certain elements in their transit*, when I was suddenly stopped in my progress by finding that ice was in such circumstances a non-conductor of electricity . . .

382. At first the experiments were made with common ice, during the cold freezing weather of the latter end of January 1833; but the results were fallacious, from the imperfection of the arrangements, and the following more unexceptionable form of experiment was adopted.

383. Tin vessels were formed, five inches deep, one inch and a quarter wide in one direction, of different widths from three eights to five eights of an inch in the other, and open at one extremity . . .

Faraday hints here at his purpose—to "catch certain elements in their transit"—and reports this as a part of a naïve diary-style report, referring to the cold weather in January, and to a poor experiment, and moving briskly to his report in the high inductive style with all details and his instrumentation, relevant or irrelevant. The initial purpose of the experiment, "to catch certain elements in transit," namely electrochemical currents, is shelved for a while and conductivity is proved to be quite universal and dependent on various conditions, solidity, heat, and, of course, electric tension.

There are a number of new discoveries. First, insulators conduct, contrary to Gray's theory. Similarly, Faraday finds a refutation of Davy's theory that resistance is proportional to heat. Faraday discovered "extraordinary" materials for which there is another refutation to Gray's theory. Ben Franklin first discovered that although water conducts, ice does not.[4] But the fact was forgot-

4. Benjamin Franklin, *Experiments and Observations on Electricity*, edited by I. B. Cohen (Cambridge, Mass.: Harvard University Press, 1941), Letter IV, Benjamin Franklin to Peter Collins, 29 April 1748, p. 198: "A dry cake of ice . . . prevents the shock, which one would not expect, as water conducts it perfectly well."

ten. Faraday pursued the hint and overturned the view that was universally accepted at that time: the fluidity of a decomposable material and the ability of electric current to decompose it need not go together. His § 449 is an indication of his intention. His aim is to find a *voltaic criterion* for distinguishing the chemical elements, a method to test a hypothesis that a given chemical is an element. Decomposition only refutes hypotheses that *some* materials (as potash) are elements, but not more. (In fact there is no electric criterion of this kind, and so, all spectacular success notwithstanding, and although Faraday's subsequent theory goes a long way in this direction, his search is doomed to failure. The problem here posed by Faraday was ultimately solved by Henry Moseley in the beginning of the present century by X-ray photographic method.)[5]

Even superficially the fourth series is impressive; and we have not yet come to the main point. Up till now I have discussed only what is explicit in the fourth series. Four years later, in 1837, Faraday himself found it necessary to render the implicit part of that series quite explicit (italics in the original):

> 1164. When I discovered the general fact that electrolytes refused to yield their elements to a current when in the solid state, though they gave them forth freely if in the liquid condition (380. 394. 402.), I thought I saw an opening to the elucidation of inductive action, and the possible subjugation of many dissimilar phenomena to one law. For let the electrolyte be water, a plate of ice being coated with platina foil on its two surfaces, and these coatings connected with any continued source of the two electrical powers, the ice will charge like a Leyden arrangement, presenting a case of common induction, but no current will pass. If the ice be liquefied, the induction will fall to a certain degree, because a current can now pass; but its passing is *dependent upon a peculiar molecular arrangement* of the particles consistent with the transfer of the elements of the electrolyte in opposite directions, the degree of discharge and the quantity of elements evolved being exactly proportioned to each other (377. 783.). . . . As, therefore, in the electrolytic action, *induction* appeared to be the *first* step, and *decomposition* the *second* (the power of separating these

5. See Whittaker's *History*, 2:24, or the obituary notice in *Proc. R. S.* (*A*) 93 (1917).

steps from each other by giving the solid or fluid condition
to the electrolyte being in our hands); as the induction was the
same in its nature as that through air, glass, wax, &c. produced
by any of the ordinary means; and as the whole effect in
the electrolyte appeared to be an action of the particles thrown
into a peculiar or polarized state, I was led to suspect that
common induction itself was in all cases an *action of contiguous
particles*, and that electrical action at a distance (i.e., ordinary
inductive action) never occurred except through the influence
of the intervening matter.

1165. The respect which I entertain towards the names
of Epinus, Cavendish, Poisson, and other most eminent men,
all of whose theories I believe consider induction as an action
at a distance and in straight lines, long indisposed me to the
view I have just stated . . . on the point . . . it is only of late,
and by degrees, that the extreme generality of the subject
has urged me still further to extend my experiments and publish
my view.

Faraday says, first the nonconductivity of ice led him to the view that
electric tension or polarization sets in the battery before decomposition starts;
this is doubtful since his desire to "catch certain elements in their transit"
already includes this view. Indeed, the same view that he first says he concluded
after discovering that ice is an insulator, namely in 1834, he then immediately
says he concluded "only of late," i.e., in 1837. Of course, there is no contradiction here, since he is speaking about different degrees of ambivalence, ambiguity, and generality: it was very hard for him to admit that his old electric
heroes had been mistaken. But enough of that. Let us merely record that
the fourth series opens the way to both Faraday's electrochemical researches
and his electrostatic ones.

The fifth series follows in two months' time. Faraday's theory of force
applied to the pile destroys by experiment *all* extant theories of the pile, and
there were at least six major such theories under discussion at the time. The
main point under discussion was whether the main factor was the *attraction*
between the metals in the pile and the fluid (the contact theory), or the chemical
actions between the various chemicals (the chemical theory). No one denied

that the metals interact with the fluid, and therefore the metals were called "poles" (like magnetic poles). No one denied either that chemical processes are here involved. The problem was that of *cause*[6] and effect—what is the cause of the electric current. Faraday not only came down heavily on the chemical side and against the contact side; he showed that the poles were entirely superfluous and denied that contact played any role at all.

Revolutionary as Faraday's work was all the way, this fact could easily be ignored until one comes to his all-out attack on the electrodes as poles. This can be seen from Tyndall's report, which starts to falter just at this point. Though Faraday develops in his fifth series his single-mindedness and its expression, Tyndall's report of the fifth series starts on a muffled note. He opens his discussion saying, "Faraday has now got fairly entangled amid the chemical phenomena of the pile." This is merely a mystification. He wished to refute the accepted views and test his own theory of force. The experiments that Tyndall so well describes are all of this character. Faraday varied all the circumstances relevant to the action according to the accepted views, while retaining the constancy of the circumstances he thought relevant (amount of electric work invested), and he showed that the results are unaffected by the variations. These experiments, I find (it is mainly a matter of taste), are some of the most beautiful and delicate ones that Faraday every performed. And, as Tyndall says, they are some of his most accurate. I copy here a few of Faraday's drawings (Pl. IV). When $p$ and $n$ in Figure 50 are highly charged, a current flows from them to the pieces of paper $a$ and $b$ that are soaked with chemicals. The current, not any action of $n$ and $p$ on $a$ and $b$, causes the decomposition.

In Faraday's figure 51 a train of such elements is described. Faraday now imagines every molecule of matter to be of such character—each molecule is composed of two parts. By electric charge the molecules order themselves along the lines of the electric forces (figs. 53, 54); when electric force is invested, it moves the particles that compose the molecule, the *ions*. Each ion moves in

6. A characteristic example of the mode of approach is a report on Berzelius's work. Berzelius was undecided for a long time between the contact and the chemical theories. Here is a report on his work, from a review of his Yearly Statement of 1829, published in the *Edinburgh Journal of Science* (3 [1830], 3): "Though in his treatise upon the *Theory of the Electric Pile*, published in 1807, he advocated the chemical theory, yet later experiments have convinced him, that, however intimate may be the connection of chemical action with the phenomena of Galvanism, yet that they have not their origin in this action, or at least cannot in all cases be accounted for without the cooperation of the conducting power supposed in electric theory."

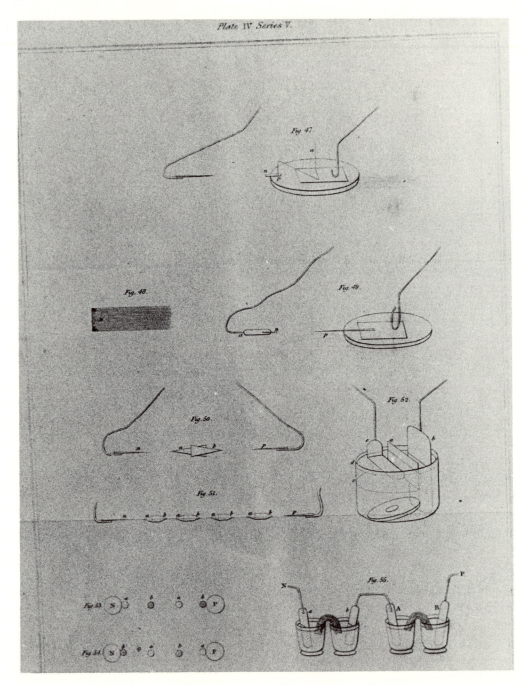

Plate IV Series V.

Fig. 47.

Fig. 48.

Fig. 49.

Fig. 50.

Fig. 52.

Fig. 51.

Fig. 53.

Fig. 54.

Fig. 55.

a definite direction. The first ions in each such train are released as the decomposed chemicals. If we have a position $\overset{a}{\bigcirc}\overset{b}{\bigcirc}\overset{a}{\bigcirc}\overset{b}{\bigcirc}\overset{a}{\bigcirc}\overset{b}{\bigcirc}$ and we invest enough *force* to move each ion two steps, we then get the position $\overset{a}{\bigcirc}\overset{a}{\bigcirc}\overset{b}{\bigcirc}\overset{a}{\bigcirc}\overset{b}{\bigcirc}\overset{b}{\bigcirc}$ and two ions of *a* and two ions of *b* freed. This explains the fact (discovered by Oersted) that the discharge of the two parts on the opposite sides is their definite chemical proportion. There is now a definite relation between chemical proportions and electric quantities since, Faraday argues, the amount of decomposed chemicals is directly proportional to the absolute quantity of electricity invested. That a current flows in the decomposed material as well as in the pile had been discovered by Ampère. Faraday here shows the mechanism of the current, but the model is not a mechanical model. He therefore gains confidence, and now he feels he has to present more fully his theory of the current (italics in the original):

> 517. *Judging from facts only*, there is not as yet the slightest reason for considering the influence which is present in what we call the electric current, . . . as a compound or complicated influence. It has never been resolved into simpler or elementary influences, and may perhaps best be conceived of as *an axis of power having contrary forces, exactly equal in amount, in contrary directions.*

> 518. Passing to the consideration of electro-chemical decomposition, it appears to me that the effect is produced by an *internal corpuscular action*, exerted according to the direction of the electric current, and that it is due to a force either *super-added to*, or *giving direction to the ordinary chemical affinity* of the bodies present. . . .

Faraday expresses here a theory—the current is an axis of force—that was too hard for his contemporaries to comprehend on two quite different accounts. It was a new kind of abstract explanation, and it was too sketchy—indeed, too sketchy to be viewed an explanation, as yet, by any standard. These two difficulties, however, reinforced each other: being unsympathetic, his readers were impatient with him. But their lack of sympathy was dogmatic. They refused to admit, though they knew it to be the case, that he showed that the fluid theories are only very clumsily, if at all, applicable to electrochemistry. He replaced this with a very sketchy theory of the current—merely seeing it as a bipolarity. One can hardly see, it is true, how currents like this can take place in the vacuum between two plates. Of course, Faraday himself could not explain this as yet; he even suppressed his idea that there was no important difference between the material medium and the nonmaterial medium. All he said was that the chemical force and the electric force are one, and that polarizing these along certain lines was a current, and a current was the change of electric forces into chemical forces. Even the flow of ions was for him a secondary effect: the chief point was that under a certain polarization electric forces turned into chemical forces. All this was still much too abstract to make sense to his contemporaries.

In retrospect we may see here, perhaps, a hint at unifying electrostatics with electrodynamics and ordinary curresnt with voltaic currents. Electrostatic situations are those in which space is polarized (as well as the matter in it). A current occurs when those forces act, namely transform. This is a *dynamic* theory of the current. (Ampère's theory is not; it assumes that the dynamic phenomena, the action of the current, is the consequence of the current that takes place because of other causes; it does not identify the current with its action.) To say, with Faraday, that this theory is judgment from fact, however, is simply false. It is a field theory, and thus a highly abstract hypothesis. Perhaps this remark by Faraday gave rise to Tyndall's criticism.

"An 'axis,'" says Tyndall (p. 62) in a critical comment on the above statement, "here can only mean a direction; and what we want to be able to conceive of is, not the axis along which the power acts, but the nature and mode of action of the power itself. He objects to the vagueness of De la Rive; but the fact is that both he and De la Rive labour under the same difficulty. Neither wishes to commit himself to the notion of a current compounded of two electricities flowing in opposite directions; but the time had not come, nor is it yet come, for the displacement of this provisional fiction by the true mechanical conception." Faraday's theory, being abstract, does not fit into Tyndall's mechanical framework; therefore it is not physical, but purely geometrical. In 1868 Tyndall could conceive no line but a purely geometrical line. No wonder that even the specific theory of the voltaic current is, to Tyndall, "hardly presentable in any tangible form to the intellect." Tyndall was right in presenting Faraday as one who refused to commit himself to the bifluid theory. But Faraday did not labor under the same difficulties as de la Rive. He had a testable theory of the current, vague as it was, and he intended now to test it.

## Short-range Forces

We are already in the problem that leads to the sixth series, where chemical combinations and its intimated conditions and results are investigated. The sixth series is of November 1833, about five months later than the fifth series. The problem discussed here is that of *catalysis*, a phenomenon discovered over a decade previously and soon neglected until Faraday took it up. It is the fact that the presence of certain metals in a vessel accelerates or even triggers the chemical combination of the gases in it. Somehow catalysis does not seem to be in the main line of Faraday's thought, and so the sixth series is usually ignored. Tyndall, who commented on each series, explained the motive for the series thus (*Discoverer*, p. 64): "Faraday would never be satisfied with a deduction if he could reduce it to a fact." The point was this: when using platinum poles in a battery, we observe small, fast-rising bubbles and large, slow-rising ones; knowing that oxygen is heavier than hydrogen, we tend to assume the slow bubbles to be of oxygen and the fast ones of hydrogen—but Faraday showed the contrary to be the case.

So much for Tyndall's rather unexciting summary. Let us, instead, follow the series in a little detail. We begin with the extant theories of the subject.

Döbereiner's theory of his discovery was that catalysis occurs because— and only if—the metal that acts as a catalyst is charged. This was refuted by Dulong and Thenard, who found that even an uncharged metal is catalytic provided that it is *clean* (§ 609). Faraday further refutes another theory, or two, or three—and then produces his own theory; and this time theory frankly precedes experiments. First, he assumes (§ 618) *all solids are catalysts*; they are all capable of urging chemical combination. Second, Faraday claims that catalysis is a result of attraction (§ 619) between the metal and the gases that it helps to combine with each other. These forces are similar to cohesion (§ 620), the power to absorb vapor or hypometric action (§ 621), adhesion (§ 622), and the power to cause crystallization (§ 623). These actions depend not on the chemical affinity between the particles of the different materials but on their *proximity* (§ 624), and particles of gases can come very close to the surface of the solid placed in their vicinity (§ 628). Like many of Faraday's theories, this one was forgotten and revived independently by the physical chemist Michael Polanyi (better known as a philosopher) in a much more elaborate theory, published in 1914 and 1928—to be ignored as too revolutionary, but to be generally accepted around 1960.[7] I now quote Faraday's § 626 in full because it is important evidence that as early as 1833 Faraday deviated from Dalton's atomic theory, which here he thinks may be erroneous:

626. . . . the condition of elasticity under which the gases are placed against the acting surface. We have but very imperfect notions of the real and intimate conditions of the particles of a body existing in the solid, the liquid, and the gaseous state; but when we speak of the gaseous state as being due to the mutual repulsions of the particles or of their atmospheres, although we may err in imagining each particle to be a little nucleus to an atmosphere of heat, or electricity, or any other agent, we are still not likely to be in error in considering the elasticity as dependent on *mutuality* of action. Now this mutual relation fails altogether on the side of the gaseous particles next to the platina, and we might be led to expect *à priori* a deficiency of elastic force there to at least one half; for if, as Dalton has shown, the elastic force of the particles of one gas cannot act against the elastic force of the particles of another, the two being as vacua to each other, so is it far less likely that the particles of the platina can exert any influence on those of the gas against it, such as would be exerted by gaseous particles of its own kind.

627. But the diminution of power to one half on the side of the gaseous body towards the metal is only a slight result of what seems to me to flow as a necessary consequence of the known constitution of gases. An atmosphere of one gas or vapour, however dense or compressed, is in effect as a vacuum to another . . . the particles of watery vapour appear to have no difficulty in *approaching within any distance* of the particles of air, being influenced solely by relation to particles of their own kind; and if it be so with respect to a body having the same elastic powers as itself, how much more surely

7. See Michael Polanyi, *Knowing and Being* (Chicago, 1969), 95, nn. 1–3.

must it be so with particles, like those of the platina, or other limiting body, which at the same time that they have not these elastic powers, are also unlike it in nature. Hence it would seem to result that the particles of hydrogen or any other gas or vapour which are next to the platina, &c., must be in such contact with it as if they were in the liquid state, and therefore almost infinitely closer to it than they are to each other, even though the metal be supposed to exert no attractive influence over them.

Faraday here rejects the theory of the atom as "a little nucleus to an atmosphere of heat" whose elasticity is due to the elasticity of the heat (caloric) atmosphere; he accepts Dalton's theory that atoms of different gases do not interact even when in the same vessel. In the inductive style of the day he does not name the author of the view he rejects, but names the author of a view he accepts as a hint. Of course, Dalton is the author of the rejected view (a variant of the view of Lavoisier). He rejects the view because he wants any two particles to come as close to each other as dynamic calculations require, and this may mean much closer than the Daltonian model of the atom allows. Now, if we accept only Dalton's theory that particles of different gases do not repel each other, but not of their sizes, we may infer that a metal, being less elastic (i.e., composed of particles endowed with less repulsive forces than of a gas), can repel another gas even less; therefore the particles come very close to the metal's surface. Clean platinum, for example, attracts air and after a short time, about one day, becomes covered with the gas particles and therefore no longer attracts water, as experiment shows (§ 364), since water cannot come near it; likewise, it loses its power to cause catalysis.

In brief, catalysis and all the effects mentioned depend on *proximity*, on the two attracting bodies being very near to each other. This is a theory of forces that act only at a *short range*. Nowadays the idea is commonplace. Before Faraday, it was never used; and only Boscovich had suggested it. Here Faraday opens a new horizon, arguing experimentally for his *hypothesis* that catalysis, cohesion, adhesions, hygrometry, and other actions are due to short-range forces. Tyndall ignored the significance of this theory and did not mention it; Faraday anticipated much from further research in this direction. Faraday suggests a general program (§ 656 and note) and a more detailed concrete program for immediate pursuit (§ 660). (He adds that he will not consider as a

competitor anyone who would take up the program that he considered sufficiently promising to pursue. This is not the witty remark that it sounds today,
but a sincere promise of one who had recognized claim stakes for fields of research only one decade earlier.)

## Definite Electrochemical Action

The problem that led to the sixth series was not solved by it. Faraday now
leaves the problem and hurries back to complete his research on electrochemical
decomposition. His seventh series is of January 1834. It opens with a termino-
logical note. The concept "electrolysis" is introduced to designate the process
of electrochemical decomposition, "electrodes" to designate the two sources
of electricity; one, connected with negative charge, is called "cathode"; the positive source he called "anode"; the particles of which the molecule consists
he called "ions"—"cation" and "anion." The names are introduced to prevent
theoretical import, "for I am fully aware that names are one thing and science
another" (§ 666). He is also tempted to introduce a new word to designate
currents, but he refrains from it, repeating that by using the word "current"
he does not commit himself to accepted theory that a current is a stream of
one or two electric fluids (§ 667). As to the research itself, it is traditionally
considered the least problematic of all of Faraday's researches. It is the experimental corroboration of his law of definite electrical action in chemical decomposition: equal quantities of electricity decompose equal quantities of water,
or equivalent quantities of other matter where equivalence is determined by
the laws of chemical proportions. Of course, the study is not considered problematic chiefly because we now view it from the standpoint of the Rutherford-
Bohr theory: we see each atom with one, two, three, or four "chemical"
electrons that may be transferred to atoms with four, five, six, or seven chemical
electrons; we can see the similarity between a hydrogen atom entering a
chemical combination by giving its electron to a chlorine atom or to an iodine
atom, and see that in each case somehow the current is half of that in which
two hydrogen atoms combine with one oxygen atom while each contributes
its electron to that oxygen atom; it is clear that under the same circumstances
the oxygen current will be twice the chlorine or the iodine current. Ignoring
the cases where this description of chemical combination raises problems of a
chemical nature—some still unsolved—we can repeat the last sentence more
accurately thus: if the tension and resistance are the same, then the current

intensity in the oxygen case is twice that of the chlorine case. That is, we use Ohm's law to explain Faraday's law. Without it things were not as easy.

But we may ignore all this and take Faraday's laws as unproblematic. Let us center, then, on the topic relating to Faraday's electrochemistry that is still problematic: his view of atomism. Faraday is usually presented as an anti-atomist, his own protests notwithstanding. In later years it was Schrödinger's objections to being considered antiatomist that did not seem to impress the orthodox: for them there is one and only one atomic doctrine, theirs; and so, anyone who rejects it must be an antiatomist. And so they go on presenting the deviant as a sworn antiatomist. In the seventh series, it is true, Faraday's own peculiar atomism is very strongly manifest. He even expresses his hope that his work will render atomism more real than hypothetical (§§ 845, 867, etc.), and he believes it more directly and closely touches facts than any other research by which people tried to argue for the view that chemical action is merely the electrical action of the particles of matter (§ 850). But he still finds need to express his atomism more boldly (italics in the original):

§ 13. *On the absolute quantity of Electricity associated with the particles or atoms of Matter.*

852. The theory of definite electrolytical or electro-chemical action appears to me to touch immediately upon the *absolute quantity* of electricity or electric power belonging to different bodies. It is impossible, perhaps, to speak on this point without committing oneself beyond what present facts will sustain; and yet it is equally impossible, and perhaps would be impolitic, not to reason upon the subject. Although we know nothing of what an atom is, yet we cannot resist forming some idea of a small particle, which represents it to the mind; and though we are in equal, if not greater, ignorance of electricity, so as to be unable to say whether it is a particular matter or matters, or mere motion of ordinary matter, or some third kind of power or agent, yet there is an immensity of facts which justify us in believing that the atoms of matter are in some way endowed or associated with electrical powers, to which they owe their most striking qualities, and amongst them their mutual chemical affinity. As soon as we perceive, through the teaching of Dalton, that chemical powers are, however, varied the circumstances in which they are exerted, definite for each

body, we learn to estimate the relative degree of force which resides in such bodies: and when upon that knowledge comes the fact, that the electricity, which we appear to be capable of loosening from its habitation for a while, and conveying from place to place, *whilst it retains its chemical force,* can be measured out, and being so measured is found to be *as definite in its action* as any of *those portions* which, remaining associated with the particles of matter, give them their *chemical relation*; we seem to have found the link which connects the proportion of that we have evolved to the proportion of that belonging to the particles in their natural state.

Faraday reluctantly commits himself to atomism here. Again he indicates that he dislikes Dalton's theory of chemical action that is not sufficiently universal and that he was glad to have found at least one law of chemical force that is entirely universal.

Now the electric current is not only the cause of the chemical action, but in the case of the voltaic pile also the consequence of a chemical action (§ 859). This means, however, that not only the action of electricity is atomic, but also, in this case, its source. Is not electricity always of atomic character? This question has somehow gained significance in the current literature on the history of electricity. Anyone who first answered it in the affirmative is a candidate for priority in the discovery of the electron, it is supposed.

This seems rather silly. In a speculative mood everyone since the mid-seventeenth century has viewed electricity as atomic. In the experimental mood, there is no doubt, the electron "belongs" to J. J. Thomson, who measured its properties in 1897. If the question makes, at least at first blush, more sense, then it is because it seems that we can illustrate the atomic or discrete nature of electricity without being able to exhibit a fully fledged electron. For example, the laws of electrolysis, which ascribe definite electric proportions, proportional to the definite chemical proportions, may offer a clue. These laws do not prove that electricity is atomic; but—as Helmholtz put it in his Faraday Lecture of 1881—given the assumption that matter is atomic, they certainly give strong support to the idea that electricity is atomic, at least in matter. Since these laws had been discovered in 1834, long before J. J. Thomson discovered the electron, it is possible that he was preceded by someone to some extent—for example, Faraday.

The ideas presented here, strangely, echo ideas of Faraday himself. And so, it seems, if we want to be subtle and sophisticated, we can say that Faraday was a precursor to J. J. Thomson. This seems to be to be much sophisticated input leading to little trivial output—but I have no objection. The objection, however, comes from the very originators of the idea. Faraday, I have said, is reputed to be an antiatomist. If so, he could not have asserted the atomicity of electricity in matter except, perhaps, as conditional on the atomicity of matter, which he allegedly rejected. So all is in vain.

The evidence in question is toward the end of Faraday's seventh series, in his famous § 869:

> Or, if we adopt the atomic theory or phraseology, then the
> atoms of bodies which are equivalent to each other . . . have
> equal quantities of electricity . . . But I must confess I am jealous
> of the term *atom*; for though it is very easy to talk of atoms,
> it is very difficult to form a clear idea of their nature, especially
> when compound bodies are under consideration.

The paragraph just quoted looks like one carefully worded in the extreme. It contains some high modernisms—no use of the word "matter," for example, but rather "bodies," and some archaisms, in particular the word "jealous," which I think has been misunderstood recently by a few writers. It is used in allusion to Faraday's favorite writer, Dr. Isaac Watts, who used it, in the early eighteenth century, also as an archaism. I hope the reader will bear a small quotation from his *Logic* (bk. 2, chap. 3, sect. 4): on emotional prejudices: "The cure of these prejudices is attained by a constant *jealousy of ourselves, and watchfulness over our passions*, that they may never interpose when we are called to pass judgment of anything: *And when our affections are warmly engaged, let us abstain from judging*."

It really is rather silly to ask seriously if Faraday was a precursor to J. J. Thomson, and to say yes only if his heart was favorably disposed toward atomism. Playing this silly game, however, to say that his heart was against atomism and thus to deny him the dubious honor is, perhaps, a bit too much of a presumption, and with too little knowledge. Of course it does not matter that some historians misread Faraday or anyone else this way or that. My purpose here is to illustrate the innumerable pitfalls of failures of communication. The seventh series, of January 1834, was on the conservative side in expression, and was misunderstood. The eighth series, three months later, was on the bolder side, and was misunderstood too. The boldest, the speculations of 1844 and later, were dismissed as sheer extravagance. A word on the eighth series, then. Its main object is to pick a quarrel: his discoveries and refutations ought to be acknowledged at last. If his empirical refutations of the contact theory do not suffice, he is ready to come forth with a theoretical criticism: the contact theory of the voltaic pile conflicts with the law of conservation of force, the general principle that the nothing cannot generate any power. Faraday was happy to acknowledge P. M. Roget's priority for this argument. Tyndall, we may remember, considered both Faraday and others to be on a high plateau, but Mayer and Joule to be the peaks—the zealous discoverers of the principle of conservation of energy.[8]

The central thesis of the eighth series of 1834 is, again, the theory that voltaic action in the pile and in electrolysis are opposite to each other and that the processes go in one direction of composition (in the pile) or of decomposition (in electrolyte), relative to the intensity of the acting forces; if the electric

8. P. M. Roget, *Galvanism*, § 113, quoted by Faraday in a note appended to the reprint of his seventeenth series, *Experimental Researches in Electricity*, 2:103, and in Whittaker's *History*, p. 181. For Tyndall see *Discoverer*, p. 79, and above, p. 82.

Whittaker also quotes Roget's distinction between tension and the quantity of electricity that it generates. He calls this Roget's principle (shouldn't it be Ohm's?), and adds, "Roget's principle was afterwards verified by Faraday and by DeLaRive," giving their dates as 1832, 1834, and 1836, respectively. This is one of Whittaker's usual pranks (see my *Towards an Historiography of Science*, sect. 5). First, Faraday dates Roget's work as January 1829, not 1832. Second, Faraday expresses regrets in March 1840 concerning his ignorance of Roget's work prior to January 1840. Even in March 1840 he only refers to the argument from conservation, not to what Whittaker calls Roget's principle. As to that principle, Faraday says (§ 1958) it is "a necessary consequence of the chemical theory, and in 1834 I adopted that opinion (891. 908. 916. 988). DelaRive in 1836 gave a still more precise enunciation of that principle." Whittaker's reference to Faraday reads: "§ 908, 909, 916, 988, 1958," though § 1958 is the one at hand, dated January 1840, before Roget is mentioned, and where Faraday carefully avoids identifying himself with de la Rive though he refuses to express disagreement openly (except in private, see note above, p. 77). What sounds very well-documented in a few lines of Whittaker's book takes hours to check, even by a student of Faraday's work, and turns out to be Whittaker's patchwork, not any history. Of course, to say "Roget's principle was later verified by Faraday" is not to say that Faraday was aware of Roget's work; nor that their views on it were identical; it is intended to sound that way without being explicit. Whittaker would have made a great diplomat.

As Williams notes (*Michael Faraday*, p. 404, n. 10), Faraday became aware of Roget's argument of 1829 only through Roget's letter to Faraday of 27 March 1840, which Faraday bound with his copy of the seventeenth series of January 1840. The note to this series regarding Roget was added on 29 March 1840. This typical promptness was overlooked by Williams, who dates the note as some time in 1844 (*ibid.*, p. 403).

force of the affinity is more intense than the external electric force, composition occurs; otherwise decomposition occurs. Forces *cannot* vary; they are constant. All we can do is to concentrate them in order to increase their intensity. His comparison of this with a balance (§ 917) shows his view on forces in general. We cannot increase gravity, we can only put together in a small place more and more gravitational forces; we cannot create them. And as in the balance, the two forces, of chemical and electrical action, "are merely two exhibitions of one single agent or power" (§ 1031).

Now the theory gains more clarity. Chemical forces between ions belonging to different molecules act against the chemical forces between ions of the same molecules—forces that bind them to their molecules. In a voltaic pile the ions depart from their original molecules and combine with other ions or with the metals. Chemical forces are thus released and can be conducted to another place and act there against other chemical forces that will thus be released again. The forces accumulated by the composition in the pile are of smaller intensity; but we can "extoll" them, or concentrate them, in order to enable them to redecompose the materials that, by their own composition, released them. This is the "circularity" of the force, the reversibility of its processes. All the processes involved are causally explained—by assuming the indestructibility of causes. To test this theory Faraday tries to show that one cannot achieve effects stronger than causes; we do not gain anything by going around in the causal circle. Nor do we lose anything. If, however, a force or a tension fails to act as expected, all we have to do is to *intensify* it (§ 994). Thus Faraday found that there exists a *threshold* tension, a minimum necessary tension, of decomposition. The problem, why thermoelectricity does not decompose, is thus solved; we are now able to *compare* the forces of electrochemical bonds, the *chemical affinities* (§ 988).

## The Electrification of Ordinary Matter: Preliminary Remarks

Leaving his theory of the pile in 1835, Faraday, according to his declared program, had come to deal with electrostatics. But then there were two interruptions. One was a return to the problem of voltaelectric induction occasioned by a discovery made by a young man who was not permitted by his father to philosophize and who therefore communicated his discovery to Faraday. Faraday guessed that the effect was due to self-induction: creating and breaking a current in a wire causes induction in an adjacent wire; but the adjacent wire can be connected to the primary wire: hence the change should also create induction in the primary wire itself. In 1831 Faraday had searched for this phenomenon (§ 74), first as a test for his electrotonic state theory. Now that he found self-induction, he returned to the electrotonic state (*Experimental Researches in Electricity*, 2:210). In the next month he declares that he refuted some of his experimental anticipations and withdrew his remarks on the electrotonic state (p. 211). He adds that he intends to write another series—the ninth—on the whole matter. Remarkably, he begins his ninth series by stating that he had been in error. It is very unconventional, original way of writing; even nowadays it is still not conventional. The rest of the paper includes a presentation of the discovery[9]—and of extremely simple crucial tests between the electrotonic state hypothesis and the lines of force hypothesis, without, however, discussing their function at all (§ 1101, etc.); he did not wish to dwell too much on his field theory. "Notwithstanding [the empirical evidence] I cannot resist the impression," he says (§ 1114), that some sort of electrotonic state exists in the wire. Strange!

Half a year later, in June 1835, Faraday presents his tenth series, on a purely technical point, the improvement of the voltaic battery. Here he applied all his new knowledge to technical problems that I shall skip. We have here ten series in less than four years. The next series is of the end of 1837, over two years later. This long lapse was explained by Wilhelm Ostwald (*Grosse Männer*) as a result of excessive fatigue; we know, he says, that Faraday visited Switzerland during that time. But, as Williams assures me, there is evidence that he worked regularly in London all this time. Moreover, his diary shows a clear anomaly here: this is the only research that Faraday published a very considerable time after he started to work on it. At the end of 1835 Faraday was working on experiments that he reported only in 1838. He even refrained from publishing his great discovery of the electric conditions of matter for an entire year. This is very unlike Faraday. Indeed, in the introduction to his eleventh series he explains:

> 1165. The respect which I entertain towards the names
> of Epinus, Cavendish, Poisson, and other most eminent men,

---

9. By the way, the discovery of self-induction is due to Joseph Henry, who made it, according to his own evidence, even before Faraday discovered induction, and who published it after he learned that Faraday had discovered induction and before Faraday discovered self-induction. (This has caused quite an amount of muddle and cross-purposes among various historians of science.)

all of whose theories I believe consider induction as an action at a distance and in straight lines, long indisposed me to the view I have just stated; and though I always watched for opportunities to prove the opposite opinion, and made such experiments occasionally as seemed to bear directly on the point, . . . it is only of late, and by degrees, that the extreme generality of the subject has urged me still further to extend my experiments and publish my view. . . .

This explains much. Faraday was a conservative in taste, and a rebel in fact. He was pushed to rebellion, never suspecting that his idea that scientific research as the quest for truth is hard to reconcile with his idea that existing science is absolutely true. He even thought that if Aepinus, Cavendish, and Poisson can be contradicted, then even the highest achievements of science may be considered as prejudices.

In his notes to a lecture in 1834 he implied that even Newton's theory of gravity may need modification. But clearly the conflict, when coming to actual specific problems, was much more strongly felt. And if Faraday stated so clearly that the respect towards Aepinus and others hampered his research, we may have a glimpse at the immense complication of the situation. But sooner or later he has to come out, as he does, and say what modifications electrostatics must undergo. But let us review the situation first.

Faraday's theory of electrolysis was not accepted for a long time. People, even if they were ready to reject the theory of contact, would not accept a theory of arrangement, law of structure, without having a dynamical explanation of it. We know that magnetism is polarization of the smaller parts of a magnet (since a piece of a broken magnet is a magnet), but this is explained by assuming that magnets, as well as magnetizable bodies, contain small magnetic dipoles. This is Poisson's theory. Later Mossotti and Kelvin assumed Faraday's molecules of matter to be small electric dipoles; consequently Faraday's theory at once appeared to be more acceptable. But to claim that molecules are polarized without claiming that their parts (the ions) are oppositely charged was unacceptable. And, here as elsewhere, Faraday explicitly states that this unacceptable view is exactly what he had in mind. And he now intended to unify electrostatics and electrolysis along these unacceptable lines. He knew that electrostatic forces can electrolyze; what was wanted was to identify these two forces. This heresy is the reason he felt uneasy, out of respect for Aepinus,

Cavendish, and Poisson. But let us take a closer look at the eleventh series.

Faraday still tries to conceal his field theory of the universe, but in presenting a mature and forceful theory of electrostatics, he is unable to conceal his theory entirely, much less his train of thought. He still argues specifically. He discusses fields in nonempty space—refusing as yet to discuss fields *in vacuo*. He sketches his field theory of nonempty space and how he arrived to it; and he expresses his embarrassment at the fact that he succeeds at last in coming into direct and open conflict with the accepted theory of electrostatics:

> 1166. I searched for an unexceptionable test of my view, not merely in the accordance of known facts with it, but in the consequences which would flow from it if true; especially in *those which would not be consistent with the theory of action at a distance*. Such a consequence seemed to me to present itself in the direction in which inductive action could be exerted. If in straight lines only, though not perhaps decisive, it would be against my view; but if in *curved lines* also, that would be a natural result of the *action of contiguous particles*, but, as I think, *utterly incompatible with action at a distance*, as assumed by the received theories, which, according to every fact and analogy we are acquainted with, is always in straight lines.

> 1167. Again, if induction be an action of contiguous particles, and also the first step in the process of electrolyzation (1164. 949.), there seemed reason to expect some particular relation of it to the different kinds of matter through which it would be exerted, or something equivalent to a *specific electric induction* for different bodies, which, if it existed, would *unequivocally prove the dependence of induction on the particles*; and *though this, in the theory of Poisson and others, has never been supposed to be the case*, I was soon led to doubt the received opinion, and have taken great pains in subjecting this point to close experimental examination.

I do not know how to impress my reader with the novelty and significance of this change of style, the entire breakaway from the inductive style and the employment of the frankly argumentative mode of presentation. Perhaps it would help to show that the leading twentieth-century historian, E. T. Whittaker, in his presentation of Faraday's research on electrostatics, still finds it too embarrassing to endorse the novelty; he presents it entirely inductively. "The researches of Faraday on the decomposition of chemical compounds," we are told (p. 184), "led him in 1837 to reflect on the behaviour of such substances as turpentine or sulphur, when placed . . ." and so on. He discovered the "specific inductive capacity," the fact that a condenser will be charged by the same absolute quantity of electricity into two different tensions or intensities if two different electrolytes are placed between its plates. "The discovery raised the question as to whether it could be harmonized with the old idea of electrostatic action" (p. 185). Incidentally, it could, as Kelvin showed over a decade later. Faraday, when reporting on Kelvin's work, mentioned this, in fairness, as Kelvin's view. Whittaker is not so courteous: "The problem [presumably of Faraday] could be satisfactorily solved by forming a physical conception of the action of dielectrics; and such conception Faraday now put forward." That "Faraday now put forward such conception" is very misleading. In 1837 he put forward his conception, which is different from Kelvin's; he suggested the outline of Kelvin's conception—but as a concession to his opponents only, and in 1838. Finally, Whittaker views (p. 185) specific inductive capacity as the discovery—even though not a published one—of Cavendish, and the idea of polarity of electrolytes in the pile as primarily of Davy; Faraday, he says, only developed Davy's idea. Even the electric lines of force Whittaker finds rather a natural development of some idea or another. This is not history but schematic history imposed on the facts: in Whittaker's view no scientific development can ever be revolutionary.

To return to Faraday, here is his line of reasoning. He searched for *curved* lines of electric force (§ 1166), he thought that electrostatic action, electric induction, is different for each chemically different material (§ 1167); in addition, he hoped thus to unite electricity with ordinary (ponderable) matter (§§ 1162, 1168). Here is the end of the long introduction to his eleventh series (§ 1168; italics in the original):

> It was in attempts to prove the existence of electricity separate
> from matter, by giving an independent charge of either positive
> or negative power only, to some one substance, and the utter
> failure of all such attempts, whatever substance was used or
> whatever means of exciting or *evolving* electricity were employed,
> that first drove me to look upon induction as an action of the

particles of matter, each having *both* forces developed in it in exactly equal amount. . . .

Again Faraday tells us, the *attempt to establish the opposite view* drove him toward his own; he now believes that electricity is not a fluid (or the power of a fluid) but a power of ordinary matter, action through contiguous particles. This is how he came to the idea of arranging the material medium in order to curve the lines of force.

## The Electrification of Ordinary Matter: Details

The initial problem, we remember, was raised in an effort to refute the electric field theory (§ 1169): ". . . can matter . . . be charged with one electric force?" If it can, then at least one fluid may exist. Faraday wished to establish bipolarity, and no electric fluids.

Faraday was troubled by a few closely linked problems concerning electricity. What he wanted to show was, first, that there is no electric fluid or electric matter; second, that the electric field is associated with matter; and third, that currents are changes in the field's configuration. The currents that intrigued him were varied: the closed wire with a stationary current; the rapid discharge of a condenser by a wire or, still better, by a spark; the transport of a charged body. What did all these have in common? He further tried to associate this, quite early in the day, with his theory of matter. A particle of matter, he thought, had electric properties; it was, indeed, a bundle of field properties, electric and otherwise. As far as electricity was concerned, particles were terminals of lines of electric forces: whereas magnetic lines of force were closed, electric ones linked negative and positive particles. Hence Faraday wished to have bipolarity everywhere and a complete symmetry between negative and positive charge.

Being as self-critical as he was, he noted with great excitement the lack of symmetry in a discharge tube between the negative and the positive poles, and in sparks in general—including lightning, of course. This led to a line of research that ended up with J. J. Thomson's discovery of the electron. The electron has both mass and charge—as Faraday insisted; but it is always negative, contrary to Faraday's hope. Even the discovery of positrons does not change the fact that usually electrons are negative, not positive; it is perhaps our close dependence on Faraday that has prevented us from finding any explanation for the asymmetry.

Faraday's idea that the transport of a charged body is a current tallies very well with the traditional idea of electric currents as flows of electric fluids; yet it was he, and Maxwell, who noted the significance of this point (see Whittaker, p. 305). I suppose Faraday would be rather surprised to find that all currents in the material medium are transporters, whether, as usual, of negatively charged bodies (electrons), or, occasionally, of positively charged bodies (canal rays and other ions). I suppose it is sheer luck that he did not know this, that he developed a more sophisticated idea of currents as collapsing fields, which gave Poynting his idea of the flow of electromagnetic energy in empty space. By any standard this flow is not of any charge and thus, strictly, not a current. But it is a flow in a field of force and so, to Faraday, a current.

When he was very old and nearly senile, things looked different. One of his last experiments was on the discharge tube, the instrument where currents consist chiefly of electrons flowing freely in near-vacuum and can thus be deflected by magnets. It is nice to notice that a few of Faraday's latest experiments, including his ultimate one, led to spectacular success; it is also nice, perhaps, to notice that his penultimate experiment could be viewed as a disaster to his whole philosophy—or as an impetus and a challenge to push it farther ahead. Sentiment aside, we cannot appreciate or even understand Faraday's electrostatic theory without noticing that it makes it impossible to have a positively charged particle without also having a negatively charged one. This *is* Faraday's idea of electric force as *bi*polar, of electricity as being a field between so-called positively and negatively charged particles.

One of the experiments discussed under this heading is the famous *Faraday's cage*. In an electrified copper cage he tried to find whether the air was electrified. It was not. He then tried to electrify one body without having another body electrified to the opposite at the same time. But once a body is electrified, it will, by *induction*, electrify other bodies in the vicinity. This, he claims, is traditionally inexplicable (§ 1175). Is his claim true? This is a delicate historical question. If we assume both the conservation of the total quantity of the electric fluids and the inequality of the total amount of the two kinds of electricity in every body in its natural or unexcited state, then Faraday's attack is answerable. But the topic is too intricate, as the following will indicate.

According to Coulomb's theory, the absolute quantity of electricity in a body acts according to the inverse square law. Now by absolute quantity of electricity of a body we mean the amount of electricity of one kind that it possesses minus that of the other kind it possesses at the same time. According to Coulomb, equal quantities of electricity of opposite kind neutralize or cancel (though do not annihilate) each other. From this it follows that if we introduce equal quantities of electricity of the same kind to two already oppositely charged bodies, their interaction will change as a consequence. Coulomb's theory, in other words, assumes the zero level of electrification (the so-called zero potential) to be the electric charge of the earth; it assumes that the earth is on the whole charged with equal quantities of the two opposite electricities.[10] Now the experiments in Faraday's cage show that the zero is a matter of convention, that only differences of electrification cause action, not absolute amount of electrification (see § 1178). Therefore, Faraday concluded, it is not the charging that causes the electric action; but the cause of difference in electrification is. In brief, *all electrification is induction.*

The accepted view, Faraday insists, is the opposite of Faraday's; it explains induction by charge: it starts with a charged body; when the charged body approximates a neutral body, it breaks the equilibrium of the neutral body: it attracts one fluid, and repels the other; when, further, we connect the distant side with the earth, the electric fluid will run from it to the earth; the induced body will thus be charged.

Faraday inverted the picture. All electrification is for him induction. We rub two bodies and cause induction; on separating them we only do the same thing as we would do if we *break* the induced body. In both cases power is converted into electricity: in the first it is friction; in the second it is the work of introducing the induced body into the field. Indeed, work is spent then, both according to the accepted view and according to Faraday. But while according to the accepted view, work is the result of acting against force, according to Faraday the work is the cause—the act of conversion of mechanical force into electric force. But Faraday only alludes to all this; he refrains from developing the theory as yet. He drops the subject and looks first for the decisive test, for curved lines of force. As usual, when a theory is sufficiently definite to be tested, he stops developing it and devises a test. I shall not discuss the experiments in detail. The main point, as Tyndall stated, is that the insulator in the

10. In his Second Series, when Faraday discovered currents in a rotating magnet, he concluded that currents flow in the earth. He tried to detect them, failed, and still retained his view. (He thought it explained the aurora.) Thus Faraday's already rotating magnet has a bearing on Coulomb's theory; but this is not a sufficiently clear clash.

*Accepted View*

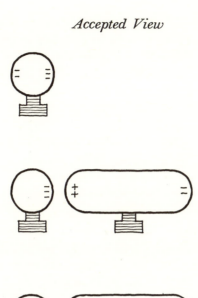

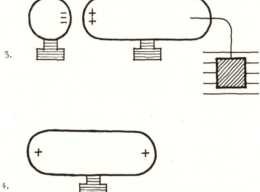

electric field attracts lines of force and thus bends them. He refutes Coulomb (§ 1253) by showing that different bodies have different specific inductive capacity, the action of the same inductive force is different when different

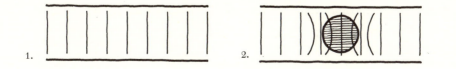

insulators are present between the two interacting bodies; by inducing the insulator the tension between the electrified bodies decreased. These are two refutations, both of which follow from his own theory.

The field presentation of these phenomena is very important. The lines of force *repel* each other (§ 1224), and the repulsion acts against their elasticity. This is why the interior of a condenser does not look thus ||||||||| but thus ((((()))) . The reason why they concentrate in the condenser is that they are elastic and tied to the plates. (Their elasticity explains the difficulty in separating the plates from each other.) Now, presenting a sulphur ball into this space will make it *attract* the lines (§ 1297).

Faraday concludes by saying that the lines of force are imaginary, representative (§ 1304). He does not wish people to attach "a more particular meaning" to them; he wants them to remain no more definite than the present state of science demands. "Further inquiry" will render the explanation more definite. Next (§ 1305) he expresses his view that Poisson's theory, though assuming a very different mode of action, is not in conflict with his own, and may perhaps be applicable to cases of curved lines of force. This is again a challenge. It was taken up by Kelvin, and with the results that Faraday here anticipates. By that time Faraday had progressed so far that he wanted no more expression of reconciliation. Kelvin's theory is important not as the reconciling bridge it was meant to be but as a milestone in the history of the mathematical development of Faraday's ideas.


## The Electrification of Ordinary Matter: Retrospect

It may be useful to make more explicit the views that Faraday feared to stress too much, and those that he made more explicit in the following series with reference to his present study.

Magnetism was reduced to molecular actions by Ampère. Faraday tried to reduce electricity to molecular actions, too. He denied that electricity is a fluid. He claimed that each molecule is a minute *condenser*. A condenser is not two plates charged with fluids but two material bodies connected with lines of force. Now if we move all the positive particles of a body to one side and the negative to another, we have a condenser as large as we want. In this case we do not create forces but merely *vary the field* of force; the electric force acting between two particles of one molecule will diminish in intensity due to the distance, but their sum is the same. When they diminish below a given threshold, the molecule is decomposed.

We see that to Faraday chemical bonds are matters of degree. This is unsatisfactory and therefore significant; it raised the problem specific to short-range forces—namely the nature of the threshold—and thus opened the way first to classical theories of valency and then to the quantum theories of affinity. It is a fact that Faraday did not apply his theory of short-range forces to chemistry; he had no explanation of the threshold. He saw electricity applied so beautifully to the pile, and he did not think of any need to think that electrical force attacks a different, short-range, chemical force. He identified chemical and electrical forces. It is difficult for me to say whether today we consider chemical bonds to be different from electrical forces, or a special case of them. In view of the small magnitude of the molecule, Faraday thought that ordinary chemical force diminishes sufficiently quickly with the distance, so that he could declare not only all chemistry to be electrical but also all electricity to be chemical. This leads straight to a severe difficulty that he clearly recorded in 1836 in his diary (as quoted in *Life and Letters*, 2:76; italics in the original):

> February 1, he writes: "Is evident in voltaic battery with its *tension* and its *spark* that *chemical action is electricity*. Hence also *electricity is chemical action.* Hence electricity of rubbed glass should be chemical action. Hence chemical tension of *acid* and *amalgamated zinc*, before the current passes, must be the same as rubbing glass and amalgam, or rubbing wax and flannel, *in its origin.* Induction of battery poles or electrodes in an experimental decomposing cell, or in the air with a spark, must be the same force. Hence glass electricity and its induction up to the spark must be the same force" . . .

> On August 3 he writes: "After much consideration . . . If electricity exist independently of matter, then I think that the hypothesis of one fluid will not stand against that of two fluids. There are, I think, evidently, what I may call two elements of power of equal force and acting towards each other. . . . But these powers may be distinguished only *by direction*, and may be no more separate than the north and south forces in the elements of a magnetic needle. . . . Law of electric tension might do, and though I shall use the terms positive and negative, by them I merely mean the termini of such lines."

Faraday was too scrupulous in his doubts, here as elsewhere. Had he been able to present the theory in a free atmosphere he would have openly raised the *problem* of why glass is not decomposed by friction. Then, perhaps, science could have progressed more rapidly. In reality, perhaps he would have been dismissed more strongly and ignored altogether. Clearly, he thought that caution was required; evidence much supports his view—his contemporaries were rather dogmatic.

Faraday's papers on electrostatics were written in the form of a discussion —of questions, answers, examination of their validity, and presentation of more questions. And I need not say how they were opposed by his contemporaries— not by an open argument, for which he waited in vain, but by evasion. The first admission that he refuted Coulomb was made by an admirer, the philosopher and historian of science William Whewell, although it took him two decades to gain the courage to make the following statement (*History of the Inductive Sciences*, 1857, 3:523):

> With reference to this, I may remark that, as I have said, the distribution of electricity on a conductor in the presence of an electrized body is so complex a mathematical problem that I do not conceive any merely popular way of regarding the result can entitle us to say, that the distribution which we find CANNOT BE EXPLAINED BY THE COULOMBIAN THEORY, AND MUST FORCE UPON US THE ASSUMPTION OF AN ACTION IN CURVED LINES:—which is indeed, itself A THEORY, and SO VAGUE A ONE that *it requires to be made much more precise before we can say what consequences it does or does not lead to.* Professor W. Thomson [Kelvin] has arrived at a *mathematical proof* that the effect of induction *on the view of Coulomb and of Faraday must*, UNDER CERTAIN CONDITIONS, be necessarily and *universally* the same.

This is a half-hearted admission, even though it is made by an ardent admirer, and only after the two theories—Coulomb's and Faraday's—were considered as partially reconciled. I see no difficulty in putting Faraday's refutation of Coulomb's theory in a popular way, and Whewell was a great popularizer of science. What he could not put in a popular way was not the facts but the *apologetic defense*. Coulomb's theory enables us, though with great mathematical difficulties, to calculate the distribution of the electric charge on a conductor. Faraday refuted the simplest case in it, which demands no calculation: when the charged conductor is a sphere surrounded by another conductor in order to protect it from outside electric influences, then—and this follows immediately from Coulomb's theory—the electric charge will be evenly distributed on the sphere. Hence the sphere will act with the same intensity on a small test body whether it is placed on one side of it or on the other. Now Faraday showed that this will no longer be so if one part of the space between the two spheres is filled with a gas different from air or, still better, with sulphur. This is counter to Coulomb's explicit assertions to which Faraday explicitly refers (§ 1253), and there is no mystery about it nor any mathematical difficulty involved. Whewell's reference to mystery, and to mathematics, and to Kelvin, is spurious.

Moreover, the theory of curved lines affords extremely simple modes of calculating what is so difficult to solve when employing Coulomb's theory. But Whewell did not see that. It was beyond his understanding how Faraday could solve problems that he, an excellent mathematician, found so difficult. He called Faraday "a natural mathematician," yet he did not suspect that Faraday could use a theory that is "so vague" to achieve such accurate results. By "vagueness" and "precision" he did not mean lower or higher testability; mechanical explanations and mathematical symbols were what he wanted.

But let us come now to Kelvin's theory, to which Whewell triumphantly refers as a "mathematical proof." Here is an interesting quotation from a letter that Kelvin wrote (to his father) on 30 March 1845, from Paris (S. P. Thompson, *Life of Kelvin*, 1:28). As the letter indicates, by then he had the theory, but he published it only a few months later.

> . . . On Thursday I made use of that time by going to see
> Liouville (at 12 a.m.) . . . He did not let me go away until
> 4½ . . . He asked me to write a short paper . . . explaining
> the phenomena of ordinary electricity observed by Faraday,
> *and supposed to be objections fatal to the mathematical theory.*
> I told Liouville what I had always thought on the subject of
> those objections (i.e. that they are simple *verifications*), and as
> he takes a great interest in the subject, he asked me to write
> a paper on it . . .
>
> Arago, it seems, has recently heard of Faraday's objections,
> and the uncertainty thus thrown on the theory prevented,
> as Liouville told me, its being made the subject for the

> mathematical prize of the Institute [of France] this year . . .
> However, as Poisson before he died wished Liouville to do
> anything he could for it, I think it will very likely be proposed
> again. . . .

This is a rather pathetic document, all the more so because these scientists had nothing to conceal except their ignorance, yet in concealing it they became dogmatists. And so, the point was never fully discussed and opinions were never contrasted. Faraday had raised by then more important and interesting problems, and the immense significance of his electrostatic research and the real storm that he caused were soon hidden and ignored. Tyndall's praise of the discovery of dielectricity hardly explains its significance. Kelvin at least had the guts to speak (*Mathematical and Physical Papers*, 4:336) of "*Faraday's discovery . . . of specific inductive capacity*, and his now celebrated THOUGH THEN IGNORED, determination of it, for flint glass, shell-lac and sulphur . . .'' Even if we accept the view that indeed Kelvin reconciled Coulomb's theory and the facts that were once considered so fatal to it that they were ignored, we may ask ourselves what *sacrifice* Faraday's opponents had to make in order to afford the reconciliation.

The sacrifice, as Kelvin made clear in his early paper (of November 1845; the above-quoted letter is of March of the same year), is not a small one: it is an admission that matter is electrically polarizable. Something of Faraday's views had to be swallowed if his facts were not to be ignored, and this little was no less than the admission that the constitution of matter involves electrical forces. Here is a quotation from Kelvin (*Reprints of Paper on Electrostatics and Magnetism* [London, 1872], pp. 30 and 37):

> The hypothesis adopted by Faraday, of the *propagation*
> of inductive action, *naturally led him* to the idea that its effects
> may be in some degree dependent upon the nature of the
> insulating medium or dielectric, by which, according to this
> view is transmitted . . . a series of researches instituted to *put
> this into the test* of experiment . . .
> The commonly received idea of attraction and repulsion
> exercised at a distance, independently of any intervening
> medium, are quite consistent with all the phenomena of electrical
> action which have been here adduced. Thus we may consider

the particles of air in the neighbourhood of electrified bodies to be entirely uninfluenced, and therefore to produce no effect in the resultant action on any point: but the particles of a solid non-conductor must be considered as *assuming a polarized state* when under the influence of *free electricity*, so as to exercize attractions or repulsions on points at a distance, which, with the action due to the charged surfaces, produce the resultant force at any point. *It is, no doubt, possible that such forces at a distance, may be discovered to be produced entirely by the action of contiguous particles of some intervening medium* . . . It might also be found that magnetic forces are propagated by means of a second medium, and the force of gravitation by means of a third. *We know nothing*, however, of the molecular action by which such effects could be produced, and in the present state of physical science it is necessary to admit the known facts in each theory as the foundation of the ultimate laws of actions at a distance.

Kelvin, who was to a large extent the defender of the old views, was not entirely on their side; he already thought in Faraday's way, at least in part. Soon Faraday found the magnetic action of the medium to which Kelvin was referring at the end of the above-quoted passage. Sooner or later the mechanical matter had to fade away, leaving room for electromagnetic matter and opening the way to the discovery of the subatomic world.

All this apropos Faraday's problem of what happens when a piece of glass is electrified by friction. For the answer is that some change does occur when glass is electrified—but the change is not chemical or atomic; it is subatomic.

Without any wish to belittle Kelvin's ingenious work—which first hints at the subatomic level—we may, in justice to Faraday, mention that even though he was no mathematician he said (§ 1305) he felt that Poisson's mathematical theory can be applied to his case, and he even provided precisely the idea that Kelvin employed. "The particles of an insulating dielectric," he says in 1838 (§ 1679), ". . . may be compared to a series of small magnetic needles, or more correctly still to a series of small insulated conductors." That seven years passed from the time of this comment to a mathematical presentation of Faraday's view is to me a real wonder; after all it is hardly more than a *new interpretation* of an already existing mathematical theory of Poisson, as

Whittaker has remarked (p. 188). Faraday explained everything, made the great concession by stating explicitly (§ 1679) that the particles may be distant from each other, not really contiguous. He explained patiently that this is the only hope for those who wished to restore action at a distance. "I think it is evident," he said (§ 1680), "that in the case stated," in action on the dielectric thus conceived, "action at a distance can only result through an action of the contiguous conducting particles. There is no reason why the inductive body should polarize or affect distant conductors and leave those near it, namely the particle of the dielectric, unaffected . . ." Coulomb's action at a distance, together with the assumption of a quasi-Poissonian polarity, would explain the phenomena.[11] Still, Arago and Liouville were more apt to give up the view than to add the assumption that material particles are electrically polar. The reason being, I now venture to suggest, that thus atomism as a whole was in a great danger. Indeed, in 1844 Faraday himself argued from his theory of conduction (an extension of the theory of polarization; see next section) against Dalton's atomism.

Faraday's concern with atomism was always great and varied. We saw him looking in electrochemistry for a universal test to the table of chemical elements; we saw him revolting against Dalton's idea that ordinary matter can be fundamentally or essentially different from other matter. His theory of electrochemistry was a successful attempt to find a property common to all matter. We know that in his youth he believed in transmutation of matter and that he repeatedly returned to consider this view. (His friend Schoenbein was the only one of his contemporaries to share with him this secret heresy.) But again and again he thought that the ultimate test to the table of elements would decide this question. I quote here a lecture given in June 1836 because it shows that his electrostatic views were already far developed in 1836, over a year before he published his first paper on the subject, with a special reference

11. Faraday's attitude here is implicitly corroborated in full by Maxwell. See his *Treatise*, § 62, 1:70 and § 430, 2:58: "Mossotti has deduced the mathematical theory of dielectrics from the ordinary theory of attraction merely by giving an electric instead of a magnetic interpretation to the symbols in the investigation by which Poisson has deduced the theory of magnetic induction from the theory of magnetic fluids. He assumes the existence within the dielectric of small conducting elements . . . If [Mossotti's theory] is true, the specific inductive capacity of a dielectric may be greater, but cannot be less, than that of the vacuum . . . if such should be discovered, Mossotti's physical theory must be abandoned although his formulae would all remain exact, and would only require us to alter the sign of a coefficient.

"Of course the value of Poisson's mathematical investigations remains unimpaired [by the rejection of his physical hypothesis regarding magnetic fluids], as they do not rest on his hypothesis, but on the experimental fact of induced magnetism."

to the problems of constitution of matter. He had no idea as yet how to transcend Dalton's theory. He only searched for a better test of it. Here are the notes to his lecture (R.I., MS.; the last paragraph is quoted in *Life and Letters*, 2:85).

### Considerations respecting chemical elements

Elements important—ancient views. Earth Air fire & Salt Sulphur—*How obtained*—from substances around—Bodies from others *not always elements*—sometimes *new compounds* from elements of body—or from action of external matter—or results even more complicated than the original bodies—Cannot decide from chemical nature of bodies for inactive elements produce active compounds and active elements inactive compounds—an important test is recombination and reformation—Final test by weight and proportions—*definite proportions*—then a *limit in this direction*.

Perhaps consideration of *powers of matter* may extend our perceptions of elementary nature—or else give 2 or 3 limited conditions important to know—This in part the principle of Prout & Mainicus hypothetical views . . .[12]

In the forms definite and distinct in ordinary chemical action and then when excited by it acting in its *characteristic* way only on present elements—Is impossible to conceive of bodies having the same electric relations to *these known elements* which they have to known *compound matter* without assuming some *new law of state electricity itself*.

Thus, either present elements are true elements, or else there is the probability before us of obtaining some *more high and general power* . . . an entirely *new* grade of the elements of matter . . .

Once Faraday discovered high short-range forces, he could envisage higher and shorter range as dissolving Dalton's many elements into fewer. This is, of course, nuclear chemistry, described by Faraday most sketchily but, as far as I know, without error. His error was his hope that field theory can explain thresholds, or the division between weak and strong forces. It does not.

12. See *Prout's Hypothesis*, Alembic Club Reprints, No. 20, Edinburgh, 1932, Historical Introduction, p. 7, about Meinecke and the paucity of references to him in the literature.

The amazing aspect is not the correctness of Faraday's foresight or his inability to see its slight incompatibility with his view. The amazing thing is that his concern with the multitude of Daltonian elements and his worry about the lack of chemical changes in electrified glass—that these two meager clues should have taken his imagination so far!

Here is another passage from the beginning of a series of lectures on a very odd subject, *On the Ancient Elements*, of April 1837 (MS. Royal Institution, p. 1):

> Ancients not so wrong—they seem to have had a different meaning for the word element rather than we have and to have meant modes of existence—Now Earth Air Fire & Water are our primeval types at this day of the forms of matter.
> We have probably given a new sense to that word as we have done to *atom and salt* etc.
> . . . The ancient notion of four elements not bad—not so loose as the way in which we use the word atom; or acid; or salt in modern times— . . ."

Speaking of heat a year before, Faraday says, "old notions amusing." Here he says, "Ancients not so wrong"; which is incredibly revolutionary. He starts to see even the point of a false theory, he sees the theory as a framework, a world view. He cannot try to attack Dalton's theory without seeing that even false views may have merit, no matter what the doctrine of prejudice says on the matter. I cannot help thinking that Faraday tried for a long time to transcend Dalton's theory; but he did not know how to do so.

It was never stated, but Faraday's theory of contiguous particles is in itself almost a breakaway from Dalton's theory in that it allows it possible to polarize an element. (This, indeed, soon led Faraday to his breakaway.) Let me explain.

The contiguous particles that are polarized before their decomposition in the electrochemical process are *molecules*. The negative ions or atoms move in one direction and the positive ones in the opposite direction. If the electrolyte becomes solid, it is still polarizable but not decomposable; its ions are bound, but they are free to change position without leaving their domain. The current through the electrolyte is that of decomposition. It goes on until the whole electrolyte is decomposed. The current by polarization is that of the motion of the electrically charged molecule into the direction of the lines of force; it is a current of a maximum absolute quantity that is much smaller than the electrolytic current. Now Faraday's view was that polarization current always accompanies any other current. In addition, he thought as early as 1837 that many discharges, like sparks and the aurora, are *molecular* actions of a somewhat similar kind (§ 1216). No wonder, then, that when he first tried to detect the polarization of a solid he chose a *compound*—turpentine (§ 1227). Next comes sulphur, which is an *element*. And if an element can be *polarized*, then when its ions *are polarized*, each atom has a positive and a negative ion; it is thus definitely not Dalton's symmetric billiard ball.

I do not know how it happened that Faraday avoided referring to this problem; probably he did it consciously, for he avoided discussing it even when he discussed his theory of discharge. He said that discharge is through the medium, that it is a result of the fact that the elements in the polarized dipole easily depart from each other, and that the best conductors are elements. Remembering that he had always in view the application of his discoveries to test the views on chemical elements makes one wonder how much Faraday was aware of the possibility that a chemical atom can break up like a molecule into two parts oppositely charged. In print, anyway, he never expressed such a heresy. When the problem pressed, he diffused Dalton's billiard ball all over space (in the year 1844); but I do not know that he split it, though he clearly wished he could. The ambiguity beyond which the problem is hidden is the ambiguity with which he employed the word "particle." If we identify Faraday's "particle" with Dalton's chemical atom and remember that in Faraday's view, which he developed in the year 1839, each particle is polarizable (§ 1337), and moreover, a current is the result of the fact that in a conductor "the contiguous particles, upon acquiring the polarized state, have the power to communicate their forces" of polarization (§ 1338), then the consequence is that the atom can tear, especially since Faraday adds that "conductors are those whose particles cannot be permanently polarized" (§ 1338). But we do not know what exactly we mean by "particle" or how the particle loses its force of polarization. Still, Faraday makes some stronger indications. He argues that his theory dispenses with electric fluids but adds (§ 1667) that his theory can thus be reconciled with the monofluid and bifluid theories: induction by contiguous particles "may depend upon the association of one electric fluid with the particles of matter as in the theory of Franklin, Epinus, Cavendish, and Mossotti, or they may depend upon the association of two electric fluids, as in the theory of Dufay and Poisson; or they may not depend upon anything which can properly be called electric fluid, but on *vibrations* or other affectations of the *matter* in which they appear."

This is an implicit admission that Dalton's atom can split. The theory he favors is that electricity is the vibration of matter, which is less fantastic than it sounds, and is both the idea he had read in the *Britannica* as well as the fundamental idea of Schrödinger. Nonetheless, if each particle of matter is polarizable and if it can be represented by a model of a mechanical particle plus two electric particles, then at least his contemporaries would conclude, as they did, that he was against the atomicity, i.e., the indivisibility, of the assumed particles of matter, i.e., of Dalton's atoms. That there can be atoms, indivisible particles, which are both electric and massive, of which the particles of chemical elements are composed, did not occur to his contemporaries. They were sufficiently surprised by Dalton's assertion that some particles are molecules composed of smaller atoms. That these smaller ones, the chemical atoms, can again be split was a thing they would not accept. I do not know how much Faraday considered this idea; if he did, then we know that he thought it possible. For one of the great guiding rules of this philosopher is that everything conceivable is possible, that nothing is too wonderful for Nature, that we should work out each such possibility until we reduce it to an experiment. Yet, we know he did not think of the electron in sufficient detail or he would have considered a monofluid current also possible. This far he did not go.

I cannot conclude with a definite statement. We know that Faraday's bold statements shocked people then, and even in our own time. We know that he tried hard to bring his views to a compromise with the views of his opponents. How far his own views went, I, for one, do not know. I shall mention a few examples. Faraday speaks here (in 1837) of *contiguous* particles. Under a heavy attack he interprets (in 1838) "contiguous" to mean "that which is next" and withdraws the meaning "that which touches" (§ 1164, note). Yet in his diary (6 September 1836, 3:88) he speaks of "CONTINUOUS particles." Can it be an error? Before that (3 August 1836, 3:71), he says: "*Lines of electric tension might do*; and although I shall use the terms Pos. and Neg., by them I merely mean the *termini* of such lines." This is an admission of an attempt to hide new thoughts behind old concepts. Even in his diary he only hints at his revolutionary thoughts. "Even metals," he says later (December 1837, 3:226) laconically, "are to me *di-electric*"; he put the emphasis clearly on the "*di*." And that this is revolutionary he knew. How revolutionary, I do not know. And it does not matter very much. In order to understand him, it is enough to notice his intentions to leave as much room in his theory as possible for all sorts of revolutions. As to the problem of the cause of frictional electricity, Faraday solved it first by assuming it to be thermo-electricity (*Diary*, 3:216) and then by assuming that the two rubbed bodies come close enough to be considered one polarized body! And he now has two different theories of discharge. Electrolytic discharge is this in which the particles travel and then carry the electric force with them and are thus decomposed. In other discharges the particles do not travel but transmit their own electric force each to his neighbor along the lines of force. In the framework of his later speculations this idea has to lead, I think, to serious considerations of the possibility that the *dielectric atom* can split. But on the whole I tend to think that this has escaped Faraday's notice.

## Faraday on Currents

We have come to the last and most elaborate item of the first period of Faraday's research—the application of his electrostatic theory to currents in general.

"The ratio of speculation and reasoning to experiment," Tyndall tells us, "is far higher" here than in previous works. For this Faraday himself offers an apology in the opening paragraph (§ 1318):

> I shall necessarily have occasion to speak theoretically,
> and even hypothetically, and even though these papers profess
> to be experimental researches, I hope that, considering the
> facts and investigations contained in the last series in support
> of the particular views advanced, I shall not be considered
> as taking too much liberty on the present occasion, or departing
> too far from the character which they ought to have, especially as
> I shall use every opportunity which presents itself of returning
> to that strong test of truth, experiment.

The ambivalence is obviously on the increase. Be that as it may, I intend to present Faraday's discussion of discharge by following his own line of presentation. These few pages of mine correspond to one hundred pages of his, which are stuffed with descriptions of hundreds and hundreds of beautiful and interesting experiments and very intriguing cross-references.

It would be worth mentioning that Tyndall exempts himself from discussing this series altogether (save for a vague general remark and a mention of one true predication), by admitting that he failed to understand it. It is "obscure," he said. Faraday indeed refused to make any theory of his more definite than necessary for the satisfactory (i.e., testable) explanation of given phenomena. But Tyndall's suggestion that the reader needs some more definite picture of the theory need not apply to the modern reader. It is odd that when discussing Faraday's lines of force Tyndall, like many other mechanists of his day, explained this by the claim that Faraday, not his mechanistic readers, had to visualize his ideas; but when commenting on details of Faraday's ideas, he found them too abstract.

According to Faraday's theory of induction, all charges are dual. The problem is how to generate and destroy the dual charges. As discharge is more varied and better known than charging, Faraday discusses it first. He distinguishes between discharge through a conducting wire, discharge through a dielectric (or nonconducting) medium, and the disruptive discharge. Of the first, he says, he has hardly anything new to say; he repeats the view that there is no sharp boundary between conductors and nonconductors, supporting it by more experiments and a new argument. But this only universalizes the problem of conduction. The discharge by electrolytes happens when charge is *carried* by the contiguous particles. The difference, however, between electrolytic and conductor discharge must be secondary since in principle conduction and insulation are merely matters of degree.

Consider induction to be a primary effect. Assume induction to be polarization. Assume that bodies are capable of tolerating polarization to different degrees, some poorly, and cause the collapse of the induction, some highly, and keep themselves polarized—the conductors and the insulators. If the polarizing agent is present, it polarizes a conductor, which then collapses, is polarized again, and collapses again; the poor polarizer, the conductor, vibrates. The vibrations drain power from the source of polarization, and the drained power turns up in a different form—magnetic power or heat. Subsequently the source of polarization is entirely consumed. This was a condenser with a conducting wire connecting its two plates, vibrating, and neutralizing the condenser. If the medium between the plates of the condenser takes the polarization well, then the situation stays put: the condenser polarizes the insulator between its plates and remains charged.

This was incomprehensible to Tyndall because he could not imagine any polarization without asking where the polarized particles and such were. Today there are extant a few theories about polarized empty space; and any polarization can vibrate and, under certain conditions, emit energy. Faraday's ideas were too abstract in the 1870s, but are not abstract enough in the 1970s.

We should notice, however, how much more definite are modern theories of polarization than Faraday's theory. In his theory the modes in which polarization and transmission occur are not even mentioned; we are only told that the bodies when in the (maximal) polarized state have the power to communicate their forces. Faraday asserted that a conduction is a chain action; as in the case of electrolysis, it resembles the case of bricks transmitted by a row of builders from hand to hand. What is transmitted is fundamentally force, and when it is transmitted we know that the transmitting body is in its maximal state of polarization. And of course, the current, as usual, is dual—the transmission is of forces in two opposite directions. More we do not know. There is no description of how the particles transmit force, and why *all* of them have to be polarized. Still, the theory is already testable.

Take, first, the contention that polarization is prior to discharge. This is tested in the following way: when pure water is put between the electrodes, it is polarized and even conducts a spark. When a solution is in the water, the tension has to rise above a minimum characteristic to the solution before electrolytic discharge occurs. In the electrolysis the current is not a communication of force by chain action, but rather the ions themselves move carrying their forces with them, first being polarized and then able to move. Therefore this current is carried only by compounds; "and by those who have considered the subject and are acquainted with the philosophical view of transfer which was first put forth by Grotthuss, its particles may easily be compared to a series of metallic conductors under inductive action, which, whilst in that state, are *divisible into these elementary moveable halves*" (§ 1347). This analogue is also applicable to the case of ordinary (metallic) conduction, and was meant seriously; he was here mistaken in thinking that ordinary metallic conduction also may lead to chemical decomposition, that the "elementary moveable half" cannot be smaller than the chemical atom. It is clear why the electrolyte has to be a nonconductor; the ion of an insulator has to be unable to transmit its electric power, i.e., to depart from it; the ion must move its current by carrying it (§ 1348). But why this must also sometimes hold for metals is not clear except for the claim that metals and insulators are not fundamentally different. The fact that metals are elements speaks against this, of course. But Faraday is reticent here—he evidently thinks that somehow this must be a minor objection.

Back to the case of current by contiguous particles. The lines of electric force can here be illustrated by suspending small silk particles in oil of turpentine (§ 1350). This is at last the analogue to iron filings as detectors of magnetic lines. The lines of force become lines of discharge when the particles start to move along them; gas bubbles appear in the terminals of the lines (§ 1351). The fact that the minimum intensity necessary for electrolysis is characteristic for each matter is a very promising clue to the properties of matter (§ 1354), as well as the fact that it can be reduced by adding another material into the solution (§ 1355), which acts in a way that a catalyst acts (§ 1356). The fact that electrolytic conduction as well as ordinary conduction (§ 1357) vary by mixing other materials, as well as the fact that electrolytes do not conduct when solid, is also promising (§ 1358). It would take a chapter to sketch the follow-up of all this in later decades.

Next comes the disruptive discharge, spark, brush, and glow. Sparks occur between oppositely charged bodies through the medium (usually air or other gases) when the tension between them is above a given minimum. This minimum, Faraday contends (§ 1360), is the maximum tension that the polarized particle can sustain without breaking asunder. (This is a theory of *ionization*[13] of the medium.) Faraday reports on many very different and very interesting tests of this view. They are more or less inaccurate; he needs higher tensions for the tests than he can generate. He only discovers that the minimum tension does depend on the insulator to quite a high sensitivity. Even the change of the gaseous atmosphere causes a change. The problem then discussed concerns the path of the spark: why does the lightning jump to the lightning rod? Faraday's theory answers it. The line of force that polarizes the particles that are more easily polarizable is the *line of discharge*. The line of discharge is the line of least resistance or least insulation or least ability to sustain the tension of polarization.

Here comes a striking experiment (§ 1412): Faraday finds that two adjacent sparks attract each other (according to Ampère's theory of electro-dynamics); but he could not unite two sparks on their way (§ 1417).

The main problem is, what is the spark, and why the action is transmitted in conductors without a spark while in nonconductors the spark takes place. This he does not answer. The fact that the color of the spark depends upon the gaseous medium impressed him, he says (§ 1423); they are due to the relation of the electric power to the particles, not due to ignition. This, we now know, is false. The effect, for all we know, is indeed ignition, though ignition itself is electric.

13. Whittaker ascribes this idea to J. J. Thomson (see note, p. 294, and compare with Faraday's § 1375). Whittaker connects this research of Thomson with his discovery of the electron. So, historically, the refutation of Faraday came by a *test* of his view.

He continues to discuss the brush, which is a group of sparks in a form of a brush, usually between the pointed end of a conductor and a wide basis of a nonconductor or even the atmosphere in the room or its walls. The *lines of discharge* here are *curved*. The experiments are fascinating but the whole range of problems is too inaccessible as yet. There are many problems hidden here. The sparks need not necessarily appear along the whole portion of the line of force that passes through the air discharge train to the other; why the spark appears in the part of the discharge he does not know (§ 1434). (Evidently the discharge cannot end in the middle of the gaseous dielectric, § 1444.) He suggests that it depends on the intensity. The air particles near the highly charged conductor are polarized to the maximum and transmit its electricity of one kind. This is an explicit theory of the *ionization of air*.

The sound of the brush is explained by the frequency of the single sparks of which it consists, and the pitch of the sound is a measure of the frequency (§ 1431). Now the discontinuity of the brush is explained by the discrete character of the charge transmitted by the ionized gas particle and the *time* necessary for the source of the brush to return to its high tension (§ 1435). Faraday offered this line of thought to be taken up and developed; after Maxwell's success, it was taken up and developed; even some of our most delicate instruments, like the famous Geiger counter, are direct improvements on this research and hundreds of similar ones that I shall skip. They have to be discussed in any prelude to the history of physics of the last century; here we can overlook them.

I skip a large portion of the research to mention the problem of the difference between negative and positive discharge. Since a spark may take place between conductor and nonconductor, we may here search for the *asymmetry* in discharge that would refute Faraday's theory by showing the differences between the case in which the conductor is the one charged positively and that in which the insulator is the positive. Faraday sees this and eagerly plunges into the problem; he finds some asymmetries, but none of any conclusive character. The difference is that a negative discharge (the conductor is negatively charged) can be achieved at lower intensity and transmit a stronger current than the positive discharge (§ 1501). This fact, now known as surface-potential, is, we now know, a refutation of Faraday's theory of the current. But it is not a clear-cut refutation; he thought that the function of the particles of the charged bodies may somehow cause the difference (§ 1504). He now proceeds to show the dependence of the minimum tension of the discharge on the gaseous medium, which is inexplicable according to accepted views.

It may sound odd that when he discovered an asymmetry in the glow discharge, he failed to pursue the hint and refute his own theory. The ordinary neon and argon lights that are nowadays so often used for advertisement, the fluorescent light, and the mercury and sodium arcs used to illuminate highways with their strong bluish and yellowish light, all these are electric glows. (An ordinary bulb is not; there the electricity causes incandescence or heat glow.) Two oppositely charged plates immersed in a tube, the gas within which is rarefied, will soon glow if the electric tension of the plates are sustained by some source of electricity. (This is the usual arrangement of the neon light.) Here Faraday discovers that the glow is disturbed by a small dark space, a space in which there is no glow, near the positive plate (§ 1509). (This is still known as "Faraday's dark space.") He even sees, when increasing the distance between the plates, a glow appearing between the dark space and the positive plate. He now thinks that the glow and spark are only consequences of the discharge, not the discharge itself (§ 1553). This saves the theory but is no explanation of the phenomena. He was carrying these experiments in order to test his theory of discharge through media and the theory that all matter is conducting to some degree. Had he thought here more of his theory of the entire symmetry between negative and positive electricity, and the *duality* of each discharge, as he did when working on the negative and positive spark, he might have refuted the theory, it seems. For, applying a magnet to a glow and examining the deflection of the current would show him that it is (almost) only negative electricity that flows in the glow; only the small portion between dark space and the positive plate employs a small positive current, one that is not easily deflected by magnets.

The great distance between our present outlook and the one that Faraday was trying so hard to develop may easily mislead us: it was only in the late 1850s that (with higher and steadier vacuum and tension) experiment could easily show all these facts—now so well known. When the apparatus was first available in England, in 1858, Faraday, then old and feeble, did carry out the experiments that seem to be fairly clearly in opposition to his theory of discharge. He dug in his heels. He was too feeble to do more than that. History may perhaps look kindly at his stubbornness. The refutation did turn out to be not so crucial. It did show that all currents, contrary to Faraday's views, are convection currents; this would have seemed, in the early days, to accord better with his opponents' views. But meanwhile his followers effected some modification of his views and took account of the facts. They then presented convection currents within Faraday's theory of the current as the collapse of electric fields, and did so so successfully that his opponents were ready to give way fast enough. It is not that the victory of his disciples should vindicate him; the victory simply shows that the earlier defeat was not as clear and final as it might have seemed at first glance.

He now turns to convection currents, to currents that are the motion of charged bodies, big or small (like dust particles) (§ 1442). To test his theory that an insulated body near a charged one is charged due to the motion of particles, he carries out delicate experiments with suspension, smoke, and so on. In this case his theory would allow one-way currents. But he succeeds in showing even a two-way current here (§ 1602).

The theory that the motion of a charged body is a current seems to be a consequence of the old theory as well. It was Faraday, however, who brought it and its importance to light. In later years motion of charged bodies became more important for reasons he did not know. (I have already discussed this point above, p. 238.)

We now come to the vacuum. We cannot create a vacuum—of course: each particle covers the whole universe—and even in "high" vacuum the walls of the vacuous vessels conduct and may mislead the experimenter. Students of the history of electronics may see in this how amazingly accurate Faraday's experiments were.

He gives a general statement, however: his theory does not decide on the vacuum. Perhaps in it the action is at a distance; the theory does not negate this possibility.

Now we come to a discussion of currents in general. The main point is to look at a current as a cause. The discharges take the course of the lines of inductive force, or the lines of the electric field. The current is of dual forces; that is the most important thing for him, and he gives vent to his strong feelings:

> 1628. . . . If, as a first principle, we can establish, that
> the centres of the two forces, or elements of force, never can
> be separated to any sensible distance, or at all events not
> further than the space between two contiguous particles (1615.),
> or if we can establish the contrary conclusion, how much
> more clear is our view of what lies before us, and how much
> less embarrassed the ground over which we have to pass in
> attaining to it, than if we remain halting between two opinions!
> And if, with that feeling, we rigidly test every experiment
> which bears upon the point, *as far as our prejudices will let*

*us* (1161.), instead of permitting them with a theoretical
expression to pass too easily away, are we not much more
likely to attain the real truth, and from that proceed with
safety to what is at present unknown?

1629. I say these things, not, I hope, to advance a particular
view, but *to draw the strict attention* of those who are able
to *investigate and judge the matter*, to *what must be a turning
point in the theory of electricity*; to a separation of two roads,
one only of which can be right . . .

And so again he discusses the possible refutations of his views. He discusses
the dark space and shows how impossible and unnatural is the opponents'
explanation of the glow. The current must be such, he says, that *each section
of it is similar to any other in the quantity of action that it conveys*, even though
the *kind* of action is "experimentally *convertible* at pleasure" (§ 1634). I need
not say, this is just the cause of conservation of force applied to currents.

Again he tries to criticize himself. He fails to do so. Then he reveals a little
more and I cannot resist quoting his expression:

1642. All these considerations, and many others, help
to confirm the conclusion, drawn over and over again, that the
current is an indivisible thing; an axis of power, in every part
of which both electric forces are present in equal amount (517.
1627). With conduction and electrolyzation, and even discharge
by spark, such a view will harmonize without hurting any of
*our preconceived notions*; but as relates to convection, a more
startling results appears, which must therefore be considered.

Current is a thing, an axis and still a thing—axis of power that should be
viewed as a whole, not as parts running along it. It is a line of electric forces
that, in fact, travel along it. Two charged bodies, he adds (§ 1643), moving
toward each other, are a current. (The lines of force become more dense; forces
move into concentration.)

Now here is the "startling" fact: there is nothing to hide behind now, as
two charged bodies can move *in vacuo*; the convection current thus created
can take place *in vacuo*; the line of discharge, being a line of force, surely

acts through contiguous particles if they are there. But they are inessential, they only transmit the force. If they are not there, *space itself* transmits the force. It would be easier for a twentieth-century reader had Faraday started here, speaking first of the polarization of empty space. Now we can see that it is not the current that causes the change of the field structure; *it is* the change itself, it is identical with it, with the transmission of electric force, no matter how. As the forces are distributed in space, the change must be through the medium, be it empty or nonempty. But this is now a consequence of the whole theory. After a further argument, he finds himself "very much tempted to indulge in a few speculations respecting the lateral action" of currents (§ 1658). He searched, and still searches, for that that will act on static electricity as magnets act on currents—to no avail; his kinematic intuition is at fault here. The next speculation happens to have been more successful:

> 1659. According to the beautiful theory of Ampère, the transverse force of a current may be represented by its attraction for a similar current and its repulsion of a contrary current. May not then the equivalent transverse force of static electricity be represented by that lateral tension or repulsion which the lines of inductive action appear to possess (1304.)? Then again, when current or discharge occurs between two bodies, previously under inductrical relations to each other, the lines of inductive force will weaken and fade away, and, as their lateral repulsive tension diminishes, will contract and ultimately disappear in the line of discharge. May not this be an effect identical with the attractions of similar currents? *i.e.*, may not the passage of static electricity into current electricity, and that of the lateral tension of the lines of inductive force into the lateral attraction of lines of similar discharge, have the same relation and dependences, and run parallel to each other?

Poynting said (*Philosophical Transactions* [1885], p. 277) that this speculation made him think of his theory of the flow of energy in space. The fundamental idea is extremely simple, no matter what problems it raises: if we connect the two plates of a condenser with a wire, it will suck the lines of force: we are back to the 1832 theory at last, where currents induced by creating and destroying currents are declared to be the same as currents created by moving magnets since conductors emit and swallow lines of force.

Next comes another little speculation that Maxwell employed: voltaelectric induction (creating and breaking a current) affects any conductor, including the one in which the current flows; this is self-induction. It ought to be discovered also in the electrolytic medium since the difference between conductor and insulator is merely a matter of degree (§ 1661).

Next comes an idea that Faraday himself later succeeded in carrying through. There must be some analogue between the medium's action on electric lines and on magnetic lines. In 1836 he saw that all matter must be magnetic. In 1838 he reports surprise at his failure to detect the relation between matter and magnetic lines. He still was looking for it. In 1845 he found it; but this belongs to the next period.

"But leaving these hypothetical notions respecting the nature of the lateral action out of sight" (§ 1666) the series ends upbeat: ". . . The great point of distinction and power (if it have any) in the theory is, the making of the dielectric of essential and specific importance, instead of leaving it as it were a mere accidental circumstance or the simple representative of space, having no more influence over the phenomena than the space occupied by it." This is not to say that space is merely passive, but it surely is an attempt rather to stress the point that the dielectric medium is not merely passive. The first period ends with the stress on a point that is partial, but on which he has more to say. This brings us to the fourteenth series, on the nature of electric force, mainly, and the last in the first volume and the first period of his research.

Again Faraday finds himself emphasizing his main point, much against his will. His theory is essentially a field theory. It can be reconciled with the bifluid theory by attributing two particles of electricity to one particle of matter, or even to the monofluid theory by attributing one particle of fluid to one side of each particle of matter. His concern is not with matter or matters but with configurations and transitions as wholes. Here, then, is his summary of his views.

1669. The theory assumes that all the *particles*, whether of insulating or conducting matter, are *as wholes conductors*.

1670. That not being polar in their normal state, they can become so by the influence of neighbouring charged particles, the polar state being developed at the instant, exactly as in an insulated conducting *mass* consisting of many particles.

1671. That the particles when polarized are in a forced state, and tend to return to their normal or natural condition.

1672. That being as wholes conductors, they can readily be charged, either *bodily* or *polarly*.

1673. That particles which being contiguous are also in the line of inductive action can communicate or transfer their polar forces one to another *more or less* readily.

1674. That those doing so less readily require the polar forces to be raised to a higher degree before this transference or communication takes place.

1675. That the *ready* communication of forces between contiguous particles constitutes *conduction*, and the *difficult* communication *insulation*; conductors and insulators being bodies whose particles naturally possess the property of communicating their respective forces easily or with difficulty; having these differences just as they have differences of any other natural property.

1676. That ordinary induction is the effect resulting from the action of matter charged with excited or free electricity upon insulating matter, tending to produce in it an equal amount of the contrary state.

1677. That it can do this only by polarizing the particles contiguous to it, which perform the same office to the next, and these again to those beyond; and that thus the action is propagated from the excited body to the next conducting mass, and there renders the contrary force evident in consequence of the effect of communication which supervenes in the conducting mass upon the polarization of the particles of that body (1675.).

1678. That therefore induction can only take place through or across insulators; that induction is insulation, it being the necessary consequence of the state of the particles and the mode in which the influence of electrical forces is transferred or transmitted through or across such insulating media.

Developing these thoughts, he shows again their similarity to Poisson's theory of the magnetic dipole, and ends up by saying that what he is *against* is the assumption of *free charge*: electricity is inductive force (§ 1684). Again, he endorses Poisson's mathematics, not his physics.

Next to theory come facts. He tried to discover connections between electric polarity and crystallization. He failed. "But as I think it of equal importance to show either that there is or is not such a relation I shall briefly describe the results" (§ 1689). In brief, it is again a lesson, a guidance to discovery. I do not know the history of this particular discovery, but as the effects are very small, very probably Faraday's method was not used in it: some radical improvement was necessary before the experiment was successful.

Next Faraday raises the problem whether it is the atom or the molecule that is polarized (§ 1699). It is the molecule, he answers (§ 1700). Elements, he says, sometimes insulate and are polarizable (sulphur) sometimes conduct (metals). Yet the insulating element in compounds will sometimes be a conductor, while the conducting element in compounds will sometimes insulate. The last case shows, he thinks, that the molecule is polarized, not its atoms. Electrolysis, of course, is another argument in favor of this view. This view, to repeat, is problematic; but Faraday pushes on.

Next he returns to experiments, with negative results again, attempting to find the magnetic analogue of the dielectric medium.

Next he tries to explain electric excitation, not very convincingly, I think. Next he tries to show that the electricity of the electric fish is not created from nothing, and he speculates on electrophysiology. The speculations were taken up by Du Bois-Reymond later on. Next he returns to the pile to argue that the contact theory assumes the creation of force, which is absurd.

This ends the first period of his research in electricity. The final two hundred pages, of November 1837 to June 1838, are most impressive in quantity, most rich in suggestion, and yet quite undisputably anticlimactic.


### Summary

The theories I have discussed thus far are refuted. The guiding ideas are varied. One is the identification of whatever you can identify, different electricities, electricity and matter, material forces, currents and the field changes, chemical action and chemical currents, conductors and nonconductors; try to see every situation as a whole.

Another guiding idea was the conservation and convertability, "experimentally at pleasure," of all forces.

Another, more concrete idea is that of a current as an axis of power able to transmit forces.

The last, still more definite idea is that the field of force in a medium polarizes its particles of matter.

In this way both discoveries and the development of theory were achieved. The lines of force curved themselves, became elastic, repelled each other, turned into lines of discharge through the favorable part of the medium. The dynamic picture of the discharging field is sketched. This is about all. Faraday was very self-restrained not to apply his theory to empty space. But the whole point of his philosophy of the medium is to apply to it the theory of the distribution of the forces in space, empty or not; this much he indicates, and on occasion says, and no more.

This, I feel, his contemporaries well realized, and they shrank from the new theory that threatened the whole of their framework. When ultimately they accepted his electrification of matter, they admitted that forces are distributed—but in the particles, they insisted. At the time Kelvin worked on this compromise, Faraday was destroying the whole distinction between space and matter. This view was not accepted. The distinction between space and matter was retained well into the twentieth century. But meanwhile some changes occurred. The discovery that electric waves filled space and the discovery of the electron changed the whole theory of contiguous particles, even though they established more firmly the view that electricity is a property of matter.

Much of what Faraday discussed, like the density of air in the glow and its relation to the tension of discharge, were problematic; they were not polarized particles discharge trains, nor were they mere convections. Thus the glow became a central problem of Lorentz's theory of the electron, and of the beginning of the present century in general. Faraday learned of the deflection in the glow tube when he was old. He tried in 1858 to refute his theory of the glow, but it was too late. The glow became a center of interest, as much of Faraday's researches of the first period, during the last quarter of the nineteenth century. They opened the problems of constitution of matter and opened the way to the *sub*atomic world. Not surprisingly, then, Faraday's studies on the electric conditions of matter were both refutations of views of his predecessors and openings of new problems that, he hoped, could be solved along the lines of his programs. But he himself could not do the whole job.

# 9 The Magnetization of Matter

## A Personal Interlude

Thus far we have reached the end of the first volume of *Experimental Researches in Electricity* and the year 1839; our next station is the beginning of the third volume of that work and the year 1845. In the meantime Faraday reached his fiftieth birthday, had his first nervous breakdown, wrote four more memoirs, a few notes, chiefly controversial, gave a few lectures, chiefly speculative, published one speculation and prepared the second volume of his *Researches* for the printer.

The chief symptoms of his first nervous breakdown were giddiness and forgetfulness. He suffered them in fits, and even as a chronic complaint of sorts, during the whole of his adult life. Its mode of attack was extreme revulsion and depression. There were no earlier warning signs. He had only one attack of what we would now call a subclinical depression when he was twenty-one. This was due to his inability, as a journeyman bookbinder, to devote any time at all to studies; and so it cannot count as anything expect a normal response to extreme strain. Concerning his breakdown in 1839, Silvanus P. Thompson quotes (*Michael Faraday*, pp. 222 ff.) the data—a letter from a doctor to a friend, an autobiographical fragment, a note by his wife. The doctor said, "He looks up to his work; but, in truth, he is not fit and if he is pressed he will suddenly break down." Mrs. Faraday's note concerns his interest in animals, their frequent visits to the London Zoo—"Michael was one of the earliest members of the Zoological Society"—and her wish that they cease living in the Royal Institution "with the continual calls upon his time and thought; but he always shrank from the notion." She did her best to amuse him in London, as he insisted on hanging around. Significantly, I think, he was amused by monkeys—they could make him laugh hysterically—

by acrobats, giants, and dwarfs, and by Punch and Judy (*Life and Letters*, 2: 114). And when things were bad indeed, she took him away.

Here is, finally, one of Faraday's own notes, reproduced by Thompson, preceded by the remark that Faraday complained bitterly that "the physicians did not understand his condition":

> Whereas, according to the declaration of that true man
> of the world, Talleyrand, the use of language is to conceal
> the thoughts; this is to declare in the present instance, when
> I say I am not able to bear much talking, it means really,
> and without any mistake, or equivocation, or oblique meaning,
> or implication, or subterfuge, or omission, that I am not able;
> being at present rather weak in the head, and able to work no
> more.

There is little need, in this post-Freudian age, to interpret Faraday's illness—it is so classic. Bence Jones says (*Life and Letters*, 2:126) of this period of illness, "His letters are free from the slightest sign of mental disease. His only illness was overwork, and his only remedy was rest." This is more a reflection on Victorian ignorance of psychology, of course, than on Faraday. Clearly, had Faraday been at all able to show in a letter a "sign of mental disease" he would have been a healthier man. Not that he gave no such signs; but that he gave them only at rare moments of despair and at once tried to wipe out all trace of their having occurred at all. Thompson reports that he was extremely composed and reserved, yet given to brief "hot flashes of temper" —especially when he faced open injustice. He made people love him or fear him—I suppose by such simple means as alternating between showing enormous patience and using enormous impatience to force them into quick decisions. Gladstone tells us that he expressed strong indignation and strong attachment—as I have said, he had a few close friends but hardly a circle of friends and acquaintances. Even in his relations with his wife all this is reflected. She first learned about him by reading an antifeminist poem of his and allegedly intended to face him merely in order to tease him; but the encounter proved emotionally charged, first with fear and hostility, very soon with the prospect of love and marriage. She adored him and dreaded him, feared for him and basked in his glory. He was publicly most courteous to her, and she gracefully appreciated this. He was punctual: even today the Friday Evening

Discourse in the Royal Institution, a social event with a tinge of Victorian pomp, begins ceremoniously as the clock at the center of the auditorium strikes once at nine o'clock and the doors burst open to allow the speaker to rush to the rostrum to begin his lecture. I do not think anyone ever declared this tradition, but so strong was Faraday's personality, his obsessive hard work, and his obsessive precision, that his ghost still hovers over the Royal Institution. Though he would burst in on time and charge the atmosphere at once, she, Mrs. Faraday, would appear late, at her leisure, and a bit lost. He would at once stop the show and with infinite tenderness welcome her and escort her to a seat in the front row. He had refused a knighthood, and perhaps felt that he had been unjust to her in depriving her of being called Lady Faraday. He once walked forty-five miles on a rainy day in order not to miss a Sunday with her.

The strong personality expressed itself with a strong image of the philosophical life, and the ideal was not realizable and in spots not even consistent. Was Talleyrand right or was he in error: should a gentleman and a philosopher be more frank than gentle or more gentle than frank? He was sick, he thought, because "his physicians did not understand his condition." This is not merely a depression plus a touch of paranoia, not only the justified black rage of helplessness that every patient is subject to when he fails in his plea with his doctors to take him seriously for a moment and believe him however tentatively.[1] Faraday was a man who, evidence abounds, could well conceal his thoughts, and who, my last quotation indicates, noticed that when Talleyrand's philosophy has its day, credibility is not much in evidence. It is not surprising that this preoccupied him before he decided to speculate in public.

1. I hate to defend doctors, who are often too narrow-minded to consider the possibility that the patient may be right; but the patient may be in error even when reporting his own experiences. See my "Privileged Access," *Inquiry*, 12 (1969). A glaring case is the following from Faraday to Schoenbein, 16 May 1843, *Correspondence*, p. 109, quoted by Williams, *Michael Faraday*, pp. 358–59, with no comment: "I must begin to write you a letter, though feeling, as I do, in the midst of one of my low, nervous attacks, with my memory so treacherous, that I cannot remember the beginning of a sentence to the end—hand disobedient to the will, that I cannot form the letters, bent with a certain crampness, so I hardly know whether I shall bring it to a close with consistency or not." This gem of a sentence is a grammatical and literary tour de force, with deep psychological insight, yet self-refuting.

This is not to say that since Faraday's sentence is self-refuting he did not suffer what he describes; rather, it may be said that he forced himself to achieve even minor accomplishments only with the greatest of efforts. His last letter to Schoenbein is similarly indicative: "Again and again I tear up my letters, for I write nonsense. I cannot spell or write a line continuously. Whether I shall recover—this confusion—do not know. I will not write any more. My love to you."

The second volume of *Experimental Researches in Electricity* covers the period between 1839 and 1844, his slack period. It contains his speculations and a few more memoirs—series fifteen to eighteen. These memoirs are chiefly expressions of his obsessive tidiness: they tie some loose ends, experimental and bibliographical, mainly from earlier series. They also repeat Faraday's plea to his opponents not to be so closed-minded as to ignore entirely the fact that he has discovered so many "experimental arguments" against them (the term is archaic, and taken from Boyle and Newton, but is used here [e.g., §§ 1799, 2010] in a new sense: negatively, not positively), leading to the conclusion that the opponents are "most unphilosophical" (§ 2053). Apart from these additional series there are the old papers of the 1820s, a few polemic notes, and the earliest speculations.

The third volume remains more frank and speculative than its predecessors, and is as confined to the magnetic conditions of matter as the first volume is to the electric conditions of matter. The second period of Faraday's research, and the third volume opens with the nineteenth series of November 1845; and with a bombshell, magneto-optics, the discovery that is still known as the Faraday effect. A great sufferer, Faraday looks like Nature's spoiled child. He got sick of his futile labors and would not reopen his show without a spectacular. So She let him have one. There is no doubt that the discovery was a spectacular and that he took it in this manner: he announced it to the public at what one may consider the world's first science press conference; the discovery was first published in a nonscientific magazine (the *Athenaeum*) and became the talk of the town.

## Magnetization of Light

Faraday's effect takes one or two paragraphs to describe. But now Faraday is an experienced hand, and he starts with a fancy title and a long preface. The fancy title "On the magnetization of light and the illumination of magnetic lines of force" had raised a brow at the time, so Faraday adds a long explanatory note: he expresses a view neither concerning the aether nor concerning light—since we know less about light than about lines of magnetic force, electric force, "or even of a line of gravitational force." This is reminiscent of the historian in a play by Ibsen who made light of his book since it only concerned the history of the past and he was in possession of a manuscript on the history of the future. Anyway, when speaking of the illumination of the lines of force, he says that he does not mean that they are luminous like lamps but illuminated "as the earth is illuminated by the sun, or the spider's web illuminated by the astronomer's lamp." All this explaining, of course, only increased the confusion, as Tyndall tells us (p. 98). But all this is just fun: it was good while it lasted, before Faraday was again depressed by the silence about all lines of force and headed for more nervous breakdowns.

Perhaps an explanation of the confusion Faraday caused is in order. After all, he said no more than that we know less about the aether and light than about all sorts of lines of force; and this, true or false, is hardly confusing. What was so confusing was what was so annoying or irritating, namely Faraday's use of a rather standard inductive mode of moralizing, and of launching subtle invectives, in so unexpected a manner and to such a surprising effect. It is, indeed, the fact that one reason why Faraday succeeded in creating a break from the inductive style was his unusual ability to misuse it, to follow its unwritten code to the last unwritten letter while violating its spirit. Perhaps the most charming example of this is his celebrated letter to *The Times*, which has nothing of course to do with science, though he was exercising his authority as a scientist.

His letter to *The Times* describes an experiment: he was on a boat going down the Thames and dropped pieces of paper into the water and measured the time it took them to disappear as a function of the opacity of the water that, together with the stench, was an indication of the dirtiness of the water. Soon *Punch* came out with a cartoon depicting Faraday giving his card to smudged Father Thames. The point of the inductive style was to let the facts talk for themselves, but here Faraday made a different use of them: the facts themselves were too well-known to want any description from a floating scientist; but they had failed to get across to the politicians who were too wary to legislate in the public interest in an era of *laissez-faire*. But Faraday recorded the facts as if to say his rage was too violent to record, so better record the facts themselves; the inductive style and the method of understatement, both so very English, merged in his hand.

But we must return to business. Thus far we have merely noted the lengthy footnote to the lengthy introduction. In it Faraday mentions his theory of unity and convertibility of all forces. He adds that his "strong persuasion extended to the *powers* of light" had led him a few times to search for mutual actions between electricity and light; even though the results were negative, he stuck to his view and now began to search for mutual relations between magnetism and light. He then defines magnetic and electric lines of force and diamagnetic (on which more later) matter. Then the experiment.

The effect is simple. A polarized light is light that vibrates in one given direction. Tourmaline, for instance, polarizes light by blocking all the rays but those that pass in a plane parallel to that in which its particles are arranged. A snake that moves with its body on the ground will pass under a low log, while a caterpillar with its humps will not. If we polarized light with one piece of tourmaline and look at it through another, it will pass unobstructed only when the particles of the second piece are parallel to the particles of the first. If we rotate one of the two pieces slightly, the light will dim, and when the rotation is at a right angle it will disappear. Now Faraday discovered that when lines of magnetic force pass parallel with the ray of light through matter, the light will disappear, to reappear only if the second piece is slightly rotated. The direction of the rotation and its magnitude will depend both on the matter and on the direction and intensity of the magnetism.

Faraday started his paper by explaining what he meant by lines of force. He showed how many simple tests he had devised to show that the lines have to be *parallel* to the polarized light. He himself was surprised at the simplicity of the results. This feeling he expressed in his letter to Herschel (R.S., MS.) of 13 November 1845 (after he had submitted his discovery to the Royal Society and before it was read):

> Several years ago I made similar experiments . . . but obtained
> nil results . . . Wartmann repeating them came to . . . similar
> conclusions. It was only *the very strongest conviction* that
> Light, Mag & Electricity must be connected that could have
> led me to resume the subject & persevere through much labour
> before I found the key.[2] *Now all is simplicity itself.*

His previous research, whether or not it agreed with the accepted theory of action at a distance, at least could be expressed in its language. This result can of course be described in part by reference to phenomena alone, by explaining in what position the magnet, the glass, the source of light, and the two polarizers should be placed in order to perceive it are. But no general statement

2. This sentence is quoted by Williams, *Michael Faraday*, p. 385.

of the discovery can be made except in Faraday's language.[3] The general fact can be expressed with great simplicity in his language: "The results briefly are these. If certain transparent substances be placed between the poles of a magnet that lines of power commonly called the *magnetic curve* pass through them. . . ."

The rest of this unfinished statement can be expressed in the accepted optical terminology, but not the idea of lines of force parallel to the light. Of course, theoretical import due to terminology should not be taken too seriously. But this was Faraday's point when attacking the current dogmatism. And those who took seriously theoretical import through terminology could not express Faraday's discovery as a general fact, though they were convinced it was indeed a general fact. We may here remember that Herschel was the one who strongly demanded in his *Preliminary Discourse to the Study of Natural Philosophy* of 1831 that scientists avoid theoretical import when describing facts. This impossibility of avoiding the "representative lines of force" surely was a great encouragement to Faraday. In the next paper, one month later (§ 2252), he introduces another concept—that of the magnetic FIELD.[4] He had, by the way, used the concept earlier, but never before in print.

It is hard to place the discovery in the history of thought. In general it has a very important place: here is a fact which can only be the result of the cooperation of matter, magnetism, and light; the compartmentalization of the studies of these phenomena was too evidently an impediment to any attempt to explain this discovery. Yet, in particular the discovery is, and still remains, rather singular. There is only one general fact directly connected with it, already tested by Faraday and confirmed only a few decades later, and that is the extension of the effect to metals. Being opaque, metals could not serve for the experiment as described, in which the ray passes through matter. But

3. This point was stressed by Maxwell in his article on Faraday in the *Britannica*: "Up to the present time the mathematicians who have rejected Faraday's method of stating his law [in terms of lines of force] as unworthy of the precision of their science [*sic!*], have never succeeded in devising an essentially different formula which shall fully express the phenomena without introducing hypotheses about mutual action of things which have no physical existence, such as elements of currents which flow out of nothing, then along a wire, and finally to sink into nothing again."

Maxwell had in mind Faraday's discovery of 1831. The point, however, was pressed on the public only in 1845.

4. The earliest quotation in the *Oxford English Dictionary* that contains the word "field" in its Faradayan meaning is Tyndall's at the end of 1863. Faraday's third volume of *Experimental Researches in Electricity* employs the word quite often from 1845 onward. Does this show that Faraday is not read?

metals reflect light, and when magnetized they effect the polarity of the light.

After Herschel heard about the great success of Faraday's magnetization of light, he had an explanation of it which, he wrote to Faraday, he wanted him to test. On the day Faraday finished writing his paper on diamagnetism (see the end of the 21st series), he answered Herschel. Even though he had reported on his failure to detect an electro-optic effect (Kerr's effect, § 2217), he asked Herschel to retain a sealed note containing his own plans to make further electro-optic experiments, to protect himself against slander (R.S., MS., 22 December 1845).[5]

> I shall make your experiment but in return I must request
> you to take care of the accompanying paper not opening it
> but doing with it as I may hereafter direct. I have certain
> views and amongst them two which if verified people might
> say were in some way derived from your suggestions. I do not
> think it likely your experiment will lead you to them,
> nevertheless least it should do so I wish to guard my own position
> by putting on sure record beforehand what are my expectations
> in these respects.

The scientific value of the exchange between Herschel and Faraday is nil. It reflects, however, the excitement and novelty; also the fear of new accusations—a fear dispelled by the "negative result" as reported in a letter dated 15 January 1846: "As to my paper in your hands I have worked upon both the thoughts contained in it as far as I can at present & must now lay them fallow to resume them when I have sun. So now if it will amuse you open read & burn the paper or if you prefer it rather send it back to me." That, of course, Herschel did (*Life and Letters*, 2:203). Faraday tried to return to electro-optics in 1853 and later (*Life and Letters*, 2:301–3), but he never had the chance to work with very strong sunlight. Anyway, the results are negative.

## The Magnetic Conditions of All Matter

In the same publication that includes the discovery of the magnetization of light Faraday provides some theoretical considerations that led him to a new

5. Quoted in part by Williams, *Michael Faraday*, p. 390.

discovery. This is a continuation of his revolutionary approach: he no longer hid ideas that lead to discovery.

Faraday tried repeatedly to magnetize what was considered nonmagnetic matter. He failed. From this he concluded, not that matter can be nonmagnetic, but only that "electric induction and electrolyzation show a vast superiority in the energy with which electric forces can act as compared to magnetic forces." Now he showed that "in another direction" magnetism is superior (§ 2223). The magnetic force acts not directly on light but through matter (§ 2224). Assuming matter to be a compound of forces (§ 2225)—no less!—we come to the conclusion that glass can interact somehow with a magnet (§ 2226). If magnetic force renders glass a magnet, it would be very interesting to look into a transparent magnet. Therefore glass has a *new magnetic force* (§ 2227). Now, if we accept Ampère's hypothesis of currents in the magnet, we may try to assume that glass and its like, which Faraday now terms "*diamagnetic*," have molecular currents like iron. Then we may assume that the magnetic field acts differently on the currents in the diamagnetic bodies than on the magnetic bodies. Ampère's hypothesis assumes that the external field produces currents in magnetic bodies.[6] Glass is affected similarly; its electricity is not yet rotated since magnets act on it less intensely; but its light, namely the light passing through it, does rotate (§ 2229). Hence, stronger magnetism may still be found to act on the glass (§ 2237). The next paper describes the magnet's effects on glass and on other bodies not containing iron—on diamagnetics.[7]

Faraday tried to find magnetic action on the same glass that under magnetic influence rotated light. An elongated bar of this glass, he found, tends to lie not along the lines of force, like an iron bar, but *across* them (as a compass it will point in the east-west direction). This may be explained by assuming *repulsion* to take place between glass and magnetic curves, instead of attraction as in the case of iron and the magnetic curves. But here he is thinking more in the mode of his opponents. He himself prefers to distinguish between the *magnetic* curves of iron and the *diamagnetic* curves of glass, and their interactions with the magnetic curves of the field or the medium.

6. Strangely, Faraday is here historically accurate but physically deliberately inaccurate— a prank of his, I suppose. Ampère did assume that in magnetization molecular currents are *produced*; Faraday showed him in error in 1831 and assumed the molecular currents to be *not* produced but *reoriented*, as in Poisson's old theory of magnetic dipoles. Faraday's attachment to Poisson's theory is very understandable.

7. Priority for the discovery of some diamagnetic substances goes to Becquerel. Faraday made it independently and showed that the effect is more general. In a footnote (p. 27) he expresses his surprise at the fact that Becquerel's work had not been taken up.

It is strange that diamagnetism, discovered over two millennia after magnetism, or *para*magnetism as Faraday now calls it, is the general case, and that paramagnetism is the exception. A few theories explained diamagnetism satisfactorily. They all assume that *all* matter is diamagnetic. This is not problematic, since iron can be both diamagnetic and paramagnetic, only more *para* than *dia*. This will ascribe to the same particle (of iron) both attractive and repulsive forces. This was the chief idea of Tyndall's program (see above, p. 185). But a satisfactory explanation of paramagnetism was not found until the advent of the new quantum mechanics, and in my opinion even the present explanation is not very satisfactory.

Faraday pursued the line of thought of a composite of attractive and repulsive forces—but with relation to magnecrystallic action, which comes later. For diamagnetism he offered mainly three explanations. Because of its simplicity I discuss first the explanation that he took up last, namely the possibility of repulsion being an Archimedes effect or buoyancy. Archimedes, we may remember, found that the *levity* of wood when in water is the result of the *stronger gravity* that water possesses. This also explains the buoyancy or *levity* of balloons in terms of gravity. Now the question is whether the *diamagnetic repulsion* of glass is not a consequence of the bigger *paramagnetic attraction* of air. No, says Faraday, since there exist diamagnetic gases in the atmosphere with which diamagnetic experiments can be repeated. But, argues Faraday, perhaps *empty space* is paramagnetic! This sounds perplexing. How can space, *empty* space, attract magnetic lines?

Again we see that such questions should not deter us from making the hypothesis that raises them. If the hypothesis is confirmed, we may try to explain it; but first we want to test it, assuming that it is testable, of course. If not, we may try to render it more testable—say we may try to contradict it, to create a competing hypothesis. Indeed, in this way Faraday's theory of the magnetism of space was refuted much later. As late as 1881 Helmholtz subscribed to it ("Faraday Lecture"), not noticing its "metaphysical" character. But he also seems not to have noticed that Faraday offered two additional theories to explain diamagnetism.

The theory that gained popularity at once is this: under the same conditions a paramagnetic body will be polarized in one direction and a diamagnetic body in the opposite direction (§ 2429). This can be explained in its turn in various ways. In Poisson's terms, the magnetic molecules in bismuth are oppositely polarized than those in iron. In Ampère's terms, currents are created in one kind and are stopped in the other kind of magnetic bodies (§ 2430).

Or, we can say, the molecular currents are usually (in diamagnetic bodies) directed in one way, and for some reasons, depending on the structure of paramagnetic bodies, in them the currents are directed in the opposite way. This is Weber's theory.

The third theory is the one that Faraday propagated: it is a field theory: diamagnetics repel or dilute lines of force and paramagnetics attract them or concentrate them. The homogeneous magnetic field ||||||| will be rendered ||||◻|||| if a paramagnetic body is in it, and || |◻||| if a diamagnetic body is placed in it. If the lines in the first figure above is of an *electric* field, then the second figure is that of the same field with a dielectric in it and the third is the same with a conductor in it.

The analogy here is almost complete. It is clear why Weber, and others, accepted the second hypothesis, namely that, under the same conditions, opposite polarities are created in para- and in diamagnetic bodies; they considered fields as fictions. In 1854, almost ten years after he proposed the hypothesis, Faraday refuted it by a priori reasons. The refutation is simple; it applies to any diamagnetic theory of action at a distance, whether Poissonian or Ampèrian or otherwise. It shows that there is a flaw in the argument that diamagnetics are polarized similarly to paramagnetics only in the opposite direction. Weber considered the case with one magnetic pole, say north, and one body acted upon. If the body is paramagnetic, its nearer pole will be south. Otherwise it will be north:

Now, says Faraday (§ 3310), consider the three bodies together. The diamagnet that is repelled by the magnet is also supposed to be repelled by the paramagnet; but the figure shows that now it is attracted to it. Moreover, take only the magnet and the diamagnetic body; according to both Poisson and Ampère, its particles are polarized. We see immediately the mistake: the north pole of each particle is attracted to the *north* pole of the large magnet and *also* to the *south* pole of its neighbor. This shows that we need *four* magnetic fluids or *two kinds of electric currents* to retain the idea of diamagnetic and paramagnetic polarity. The present theory of magnetization avoids Faraday's arguments, both by being field theory and by assuming indeed that paramagnetism is entirely different from diamagnetism. Ampère's hypothesis came to explain paramagnetism (since he did not know of diamagnetism); it is nowadays employed to explain diamagnetism. The direction of the molecular current thus is reversed today as compared with Ampère's days.

## Atmospheric Magnetism

When Faraday discovered that he had overlooked the diamagnetism of flames, it grieved him. That he should have forgotten to connect his diamagnetic research with such a beautiful thing! "I . . . scarcely know how I could have failed to observe the effect years ago," he said later. He could now show that various gases are diamagnetic—though more so when hot. He further discovered the important and very strange fact that oxygen is *para*magnetic. The most important fact about the magnetism of oxygen, Faraday thought, was that it lost its magnetism when heated—just like iron. He soon came to think that with such a vast amount of a paramagnetic substance in the atmosphere, whose magnetism so depends on the weather, atmospheric variations cannot fail to show their influence on the compass. He conjectured that this is the cause of the variations of the earth's magnetism that bothered philosophers and navigators alike ever since Gilbert's theory of earth's fixed magnetism was refuted.

The details of his discussions on this are extended over a hundred pages. The main point about them is this: whether the accepted theory is in principle applicable to the phenomena or not, his theory of atmospheric magnetism was in practice inexpressible in accepted terminology because of the vastness of the problem. Ampère had no scruples about employing Faraday's ideas of 1821 when he learned that they are more easily applicable to experiment than his own; yet later on, physicists were afraid to accept Faraday's suggestion to employ lines of force—even as a mere tool. In 1850, therefore, Faraday's theory of atmospheric magnetism came as a real surprise. People had no idea of the sheer expressive force of his ideas. Characteristic, I think, is Herschel's reaction to Faraday's work, as privately expressed in his letter of 12 March 1851 (copy, R.S.): "Your speculations on the diurnal and annual variations as referable to the magnetization of oxygen took me quite by surprise. I had no idea you had gone so far into the matter. I find them difficult to follow from habitual use of as totally different a mode of 'envisaging' the magnetic force."

Faraday's theory is strikingly similar to Galileo's theory of the tides. Both tried to apply a new principle to an old and very difficult problem. Both had poor means to cope with very unstable phenomena. Galileo's theory was discussed by many; Faraday's, for all I know, only by Tyndall. Here is Tyndall's comment (p. 144):

> . . . Humboldt, in Berlin, [said] "Tell Faraday that I entirely agree with him, and that he has, in my opinion, completely explained the variation of the declination." Eminent men have since informed me that Humboldt was hasty in expressing this opinion. In fact, Faraday's memoirs on atmospheric magnetism lost much of their force—perhaps too much— through the important discovery of the relation of the variation of the declination to the number of the solar spots. But I agree with him and M. Edmond Becquerel . . . in thinking, that a body so magnetic as oxygen, swathing the earth, and subject to variations of temperature, diurnal and annual, must affect the manifestations of terrestrial magnetism. . . . But Faraday's writings on this subject are so voluminous, and the theoretic points are so novel and intricate, that I shall postpone the complete analysis of these researches to a time when I can lay hold of them more completely than my other duties allow me to do now.

There is a letter from Faraday to de la Rive on this research (*Life and Letters*, 2:258); it starts with magnetic lines of force, continues with the magnetic properties of oxygen, and ends with conclusions about earth's magnetism. Much as the force of the explanation has been lost, to echo Tyndall, its mode of expression became standard. Studies of earth's magnetism were— still are—rather esoteric, and it is hard to say how much Faraday's triumph in this field effected his victory globally; also it is hard to say when exactly the local triumph was effected: as noted already, Ampère was ready to use Faraday's ideas when studying earth's magnetism, even in the 1820s; had he lived longer, or were there more open-minded people like himself around, Faraday might have suffered less heartbreak.

### Magnecrystallic Action

Magnetic action on crystals was discovered when "anomalies" in diamagnetic action were investigated. ("Anomaly," as Faraday observed later, is only the result of an error in the theory that cannot explain it as normal.) The discovery is that in a magnetic field a crystal tends to resume a certain position. The action is neither attraction nor repulsion but one tending toward equilibrium, reached when the magnetic axis of the crystal is parallel to the lines of force. The explanation that was later forwarded is not difficult. Upon Ampère's hypothesis, plus the generally received hypothesis that in crystals the molecules are *ordered* in space, it would be almost self-suggesting that the molecules are *also polarized* in a given direction, that the electric currents' polarity is ordered in the crystal just as the particles are ordered in it, that crystals are not only the location order of the particles but also the *polarity order* of them. From this it follows, within Faraday's framework, that the crystals order themselves in the magnetic fields. The interesting point begins when we try to *explain* crystallism by electromagnetic assumptions.

The significance of the discovery (for which partial priority goes to Plücker[8]) is that it is another weakening of the action-at-a-distance theory of magnetism. An attempt to restore it was made, as usual, by Faraday himself. His idea was taken up by Knoblauch and Tyndall a few years later. As Faraday admitted when he published the third volume of his *Researches*, their theory was satisfactory. Tyndall later declared his theory proven. Faraday's many alternative suggestions with no action at a distance were hardly taken up, though Kelvin's work should be noted. Later on, powerful mathematical theories with tensorial addenda to Maxwell's equations have rendered the whole controversy ancient history.

## Magnetic Philosophy

Following magnetocrystallic action and the theory of atmospheric magnetism comes the first paper in which Faraday returns to magnetoelectric induction (28th series). He makes another effort to explain. From his earliest experiments of 1831, he says twenty years later, "I have had to think and speak of lines of magnetic force" as representing the forces in both quantity and direction. The necessity to use these concepts (he gives reference to magneto-optics) "had led me to believe that the time has arrived" to explain the idea "very clearly" and present it to examination (§ 3070).

I do not think that it was noticed that in his first paper he makes quantitative determinations. The experiments alluded to are comparative experiments

8. Plücker discovered the phenomena in transparent crystals only. Faraday said, "2836. The beautiful researches of Plücker . . . cannot have been forgotten, and I hope that my own experiments . . . are remembered in conjunction with his. . . ."

with Arago's machine, which involve not a little calculation. But, with one exception, Faraday never presented calculations, only results. This made people wonder. Whewell said that he was a "natural mathematician." Helmholtz said (Faraday Lecture): "... it is in the highest degree astonishing to see what a large number of general theorems, the mathematical deduction of which requires the highest powers of mathematical analysis, he found, by a kind of intuition, with the security of instinct, without the help of a single mathematical formula ..."

In his late memoirs Faraday presents his method of calculations, and so the above awed and mystified descriptions of them are somewhat embarrassing. He breaks his deductions into small simple tests; he shows that he has a simple technique of calculation. Yet he was not understood, and his results surprised people. Maxwell was the first who said that he found in Faraday's works a *mathematical* theory that he only translated into a symbolic language. In his opening to his *Treatize* he said bluntly, "I perceived that his method of conceiving the phenomena was also a mathematical one, though not exhibited in the conventional form of mathematical symbols ... I ... translated what I considered to be Faraday's ideas into a mathematical form ..." Apart from the excessive humility, there is much truth in Maxwell's claim. I do not know why "$2 \times 2 = 4$" impresses people more than "twice two equals four"; but so it is. Faraday hated mathematical symbolism. His view was that you should calculate in your own way and give to the public an outline of your calculation in *ordinary* language to enable each person to repeat the calculation for himself and in his own way. I do not know how, with his deep aversion to symbolism, he succeeded in scrutinizing so many mathematical works of his time; but he made it clear in his writings that, once he got the idea, he translated it into his own language and proved the point to his own satisfaction.

It is quite obvious that he was thoroughly familiar with Poissoin's theory and that he knew how to apply it to his discovery of dielectricity—he gave a specific outline of how to do it; Mossotti and Kelvin did it. In a letter to Schoenbein written in his old age, Farady says even chemical symbols gave him trouble and prevented him from fully understanding Schoenbein's later papers. In a letter to Tyndall a similar sentiment is expressed, regarding a paper by Tyndall. In a letter to Maxwell he expresses his admiration for the latter's ability to translate mathematical results into a language comprehensible to the experimenter. And Maxwell, the mathemetical genius, always retained the feeling that there is an immense virtue in the ability to translate mathematical results into ordinary language.

No doubt there is a limit to this, since symbolism used intelligently is only a means for mathematical reasoning, and it is the reasoning, not the symbolism, that gets intricate; the symbolism should only aid us in mastering the intricacy. There is little doubt, for example, that in some sense Faraday used laboratory lools such as condensers and magnets as symbols in his thinking,[9] that his mental block against symbols cost him a lot of energy. There is also little doubt, let me add, that he made a virtue of his necessity. Yet it is not always easy to say where mathematical ideas yield to mathematical symbolism. In retrospect we can look at Faraday's ideas and Maxwell's ideas with a certain freedom from the fact that the one used lines of force where the other used tubes of force vectors, and surfaces of equal vectors (equipotential surfaces). Yet we know that certain differences between the two are deeply linked to notations or sets of symbols used at the time—the symbols used are often organically linked with the ideas they express, even though later efforts are made to free mathematics from its orthographic chains.

Let us elaborate on this with our own example of the difference between Faraday's and Maxwell's language. But let us not enter a discussion of the difference between Maxwell's and Faraday's ideas—except to indicate briefly that the difference was partly but not entirely a matter of mathematics. There is, first, the matter of different versions of Maxwell's theory—not all of which could possibly be identical with Faraday's theory, since they differed from each other. In general, however, as Faraday spoke consistently of lines of force and Maxwell spoke consistently of the (equipotential) surfaces that are perpendicular to the lines of force, we can ask how much these two modes are equivalent to each other. A tube of force of unit strength will cut a larger area of the equipotential surface in the weaker field than in the stronger field since the lines are less concentrated there. In the vectorial presentation, the strength of the field is presented by the length of the force vector. These two presentations are equivalent, as was shown by Maxwell. But I wish now to point out

9. In this, too, Faraday operated intuitively, and for this, too, he may be called "a mathematician of high order," as Maxwell called him. The idea, a generalization of the calculation machine, has meanwhile become rather well-known. See H. M. Poynter (ed.), *A Palimpsest on the Electronic Analog Art* (George A. Philbrick Researches Inc., Dedham, Mass., 1965); first paper by Philbrick and Poynter, "The Electronic Analog Computer as a Lab Tool." Of course, the Monte Carlo method of assessing distributions empirically instead of deductively (when deduction is difficult) also belongs to this class. Roughly, the intriguing fact about it is that seemingly the effect stands as a model for the theory that describes it; thus seemingly (but not really) canceling all error in theory by repetition (of the error). See also Maxwell's *Treatise*, §§ 594, 404.

the difference: the vector presentation involves the vector theory that includes three major theorems, of Gauss, of Green, and of Stokes. Faraday proved the analogues to the theorems of Gauss (§ 3088) and of Stokes (§ 3073) in his own system. There is no room in his theory for an analogue of Green's theorem, at least not in a general form. In this respect the framework to his theory is much poorer and less restrictive. Faraday has, quite accidentally, a slight advantage over Maxwell. The field theory in Maxwell's presentation is less adequate than in Faraday's because the magnetic force cannot be presented as a vector in the strict sense of the word (it is called a pseudovector), but it can be adequately presented by a surface. But this point was very minor before Einstein, Minkowski, and von Laue. And it could not be brought about without the use of highly sophisticated geometrical ideas developed by various writers from Riemann onward.

Faraday's theory, viewed as purely mathematical, is much inferior to the works of Riemann, his younger contemporary, with which he was of course utterly unacquainted. As to the method of work, while most of the mathematicians of Faraday's days usually worked by trying to deduce one theorem from another, in the main he used within the constricted realm of his theory the method of approximation by variation. He tried to imagine or assume a slight variation of the situation or of the process, calculate the results, and deduce from it conclusions independent of the variation itself. (He used this method in mechanics, too; see *Life and Letters*, 2:341–44.) But Faraday never considered his theory as purely mathematical. He viewed both the field and the variation technique as physical. And of course he never bothered to look for causal explanation of the variation technique.

All these factors were not clear at the time. Faraday's system not having an analogue of Green's theorem has both advantages and disadvantages that I cannot discuss. Its having something like tubes of force rather than vectors of force and equipotential surfaces only recently proved fruitful in light of the fact that the magnetic force is not a vector but an antisymmetric tensor that could be presented as a directed surface-element and was so presented by von Laue and by Weyl and other twentieth-century mathematical physicists. Only recently J. A. Schouten used this fact in physics in order to exploit results open to Faraday's but not to Maxwell's treatment.[10] All this could hardly be

10. See J. A. Schouten, *Tensor Analysis for Physicists* (Oxford, 1949), and E. J. Post, section 6, "The Faraday-Schouten Geometric Images for Electromagnetic Fields in Space," in his contribution to M. Bunge's *Delaware Seminar in the Foundations of Physics* (New York, 1967).

envisaged before; indeed the invention of the vector and tensor notations, long after Maxwell's death, helped to clear matters in a way not accessible beforehand.

Faraday's use of lines of force and of small variations were soon forgotten, and revived independently by modern plasma physicists. Partly this is so because in plasma physics ions strongly interact with lines of force, partly because of the problems of plasma technology that concern stability, i.e., the influence of small variations on the system at large. This, within an inner logic, revived a problem that was forgotten entirely and that no writer on Faraday save L. Pearce Williams has ever mentioned. It was of vital importance for Faraday to discover, and all his life he tried to discover, whether a cylindrical magnet rotating on its axis of symmetry affects the field by its rotation. Maxwell's theory leaves this question open. Plasma physics became very concerned with it; and so, in our century, we have, by some freak accident, come nearer to Faraday than Maxwell in *some* sense, though, of course, to revive Faraday's ideas seriously and as a whole is sheer madness.

From his first memoir Faraday groped toward an idea that he never fully expressed concerning a state of polarization called the electrotonic state. He introduced the term a few times and took it back. We do not quite know what he wanted the term to mean; perhaps when the image became clearer, the term was used more sparingly; the image, if the word "image" is right, was of a polarized space that, of course, has as a first approximation the properties of ordinary space filled with ordinary things. What he wanted, then, was to develop a theory of pure fields without matter, in order to *explain* matter. He tried to perceive the magnetoelectric induction of space. As usual, he proceeded in steps. He first tried the idea of magnetic induction in the dielectric; but he could not observe it. It is at this point that he reintroduced the electrotonic state (§ 3172). He tried to show that the current is possible in the metals just because of their high conductivity. (The current under the same condition, he showed, is merely a linear function of the conductivity of the different metals.) If we formulate this slightly more precisely, and remember that the current for Faraday is the change in the whole field and not confined to the conductor, we see how near Faraday's theory of electrotonicity comes to Maxwell's idea that in *empty space* (genuinely empty, or filled with aether) the *induced magnetism* is *a function of the change of the electric field*. This is Maxwell's great idea of the "*displacement current*," the current of the field itself, the change of the electric field. In his first paper, "On Faraday's Lines of Force" of 1856, Maxwell formulated more precisely Faraday's ideas. He assumed, counter to Faraday's ideas, that the magnetic induction is only dependent on the actual current in the conductor. He arrived mathematically at the result that this theory can only be valid for *closed* currents (not, for instance, for the discharge of a condenser) and that magnetic action in such cases moves with infinite velocity, that the lines of force are rigidly tied to the moving magnet. This was a wonderful success. He published in fact a false theory knowing it to be false, or valid only as a first approximation.[11] This helped to find a better, more precise presentation of Faraday's vague ideas. As it happened, Maxwell himself took the next step. It really is miraculous how the slight change, the addition of the idea of "*displacement current*," the assumption that the magnetic induction depends also on the mere change of the electric tension *in* space, or *of* the space itself, or of the *field*, made the whole difference. Maxwell symmetrized the magnetic induction with electric induction. Faraday's electric induction is a "*magnetic displacement*," he assumed that the electric force depends on the change of the magnetic *field*; and Maxwell now added that the same action takes place in the opposite way, as an "electric displacement." I do not wish to belittle Maxwell but to show the similarity of his ideas in expressions that could be linked to Faraday's, which were put vaguely. I wish to show both where similarity lies and the two points at which it is dissimilar in respect to magnetic waves and the medium. For, where most historians stress dissimilarity I find similarity, but I also find other dissimilarities that were overlooked. Maxwell ascribed the new element, the "displacement current," the dependence of magnetic induction on the field, as the property of the *aetherial* medium, the mechanical model. Consequently the similarity between Maxwell's correction, his "*electric displacement*," and Faraday's was overlooked. Maxwell's first theory was traditionally taken literally as a translation of Faraday's ideas into mathematical language, and Maxwell's second theory, the correction with the "displacement," was then taken to be his own. I consider *both* theories to be in one way entirely original creations of Maxwell's and in another way a continuation of Faraday's lines of thoughts.

Maxwell's great and most significant deviation from Faraday was never noticed, to my knowledge. While Faraday considered light to be a magnetic wave, Maxwell showed that a magnetic wave would die out too soon and would not be of the strength of light. Light for him was not magnetic but *electromagnetic*. A magnetic wave, according to Faraday's idea, even though Faraday

11. The classic example is Niels Bohr's model of the atom of 1913; I do not know whether Maxwell influenced Bohr in this respect, but indirectly I suppose he did.

did not notice this, should cause an electric wave, and the electric wave causes a magnetic wave according to Maxwell's correction. In brief, the wave does not die out soon because the change of the magnetic field causes a momentary electric change, while on return to its previous state the electric force strengthens the magnetic wave again. The two waves of forces support each other, in a kind of bootstrap operation. (For Faraday, we remember, electric waves were currents and magnetic waves light. See p. 228, above.)

Faraday's theory only vaguely indicated how things stood; due to the imprecision of his theory, Faraday himself failed to notice some significant details. Faraday presented many detailed suggestions that Maxwell had to sift and decide which to take up and get the results that he and Faraday had desired. In Maxwell's final theory, which contained a more precise version of *some* of Faraday's ideas, the desired results follow clearly, together with other results that are *not* in Faraday's theory. (The most important of those results is that the velocity of the electromagnetic wave is that of light.)

I now come to the medium. If we mean by "medium" matter, like dielectric, then surely neither Faraday nor Maxwell thought of the field as confined to the medium, since it can dwell in empty space. If by "medium" we mean empty space, space void of matter, then both assumed it to act—only Maxwell filled it with invisible fluids, with the aether, since really empty space, he thought, cannot act. All that Faraday wanted is that electricity and magnetism should not be confined to the charged bodies or the magnets. Whether space itself be filled with aether or not was secondary in his view—especially since he was confident that any aether would be only a temporary stopgap.

A passage from Boltzmann illustrates, I think, that the difficulty was to think of the medium, to abandon the polar bodies (electrically charged or magnetic); the question whether the medium is the aether or empty space was, indeed, secondary. Here Boltzmann's remark (*Nature* [1895], p. 413): "It is curious to see that in Germany, where till lately the theory of *action at a distance* was much more cultivated than in Newton's native land itself, where Maxwell's theory of electricity was not accepted, because it does not *start* from quite a precise [*sic!*] hypothesis, at present every special theory is old fashioned . . ."

Faraday's idea was that precision could come later, and perhaps, if we wish, the model may come still later; "but I always tried to be very critical on myself before I gave everybody else the opportunity . . . Still the old views are so untenable *as a whole*, that I am clear they must be wrong, whatever is right" (*Life and Letters* 2:362).

## Electrogravity

"It was almost with a feeling of awe that I went to work, for if the hope should prove well founded, how great and mighty and sublime in its hitherto unchangeable character is the force I am trying to deal with, and how large may be a new domain of knowledge that may be opened up to the mind of man." So wrote Faraday in his diary (5:156) after a day's work without results. He never got positive results, and he never gave up hope. The older he became, the less successful he was in experimenting and the more general and interesting became his arguments against received opinion (including his unsuccessful experiments). His ideas were taken up by Kelvin and Maxwell. Kelvin was too tied to his Cartesian or semi-Cartesian idea of the model, and produced a theory of little interest. Maxwell arrived at a definite conclusion: a field theory that accepts Newton's law as rigorously true breaks down because of the field's infinite energy. He declared that he gave up the research. "As I am unable to understand in what way a medium can possess such properties [as infinite energy], I cannot go any further in this direction in searching for the cause of gravitation." Faraday showed another direction—the assumption that gravity takes *time* to propagate—and in a letter to Maxwell he showed another way out. But Maxwell did not choose another direction and dropped the subject for a while. He never returned to it (he died young), and so it is perhaps only just to explain what his brief remarks amount to. Faraday had argued that the field theories are incompatible with the accepted theory of gravity acting at a distance. Maxwell, in publishing his negative results, however briefly and without fuss, only expressed a tacit agreement with one of the most revolutionary of Faraday's thoughts.

Faraday started to reject Newton's theory of gravity shyly and slowly; he was led by his general field theory—his theory of convertibility of all forces. When discussing this point, Tyndall entirely agrees (p. 168): gravitational energy can indeed be transformed into any energy since it can be transformed through *motion*. But Faraday's whole point, his grand generalization, that which he viewed as the light of his whole studies and searches, was that *any force can directly transform to any other force*. He made it quite clear that transforming gravity into electricity through motion was neither problematic nor the whole story.

Let us, then, turn to the problem as Faraday saw it. We may do so either by attempting to create a competing theory to the accepted one or by refuting it directly. The first mode of attack was adopted by Einstein—and others since.

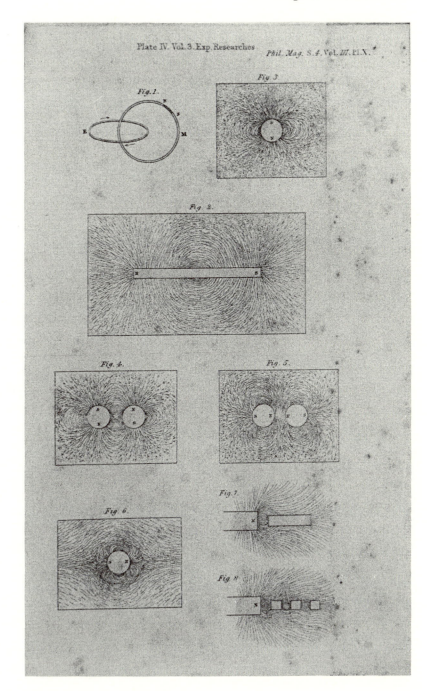

The second was Faraday's. If unification is possible, he thought, then we must be able to find the electric effects of gravity on earth. This is *a priori* an almost hopeless task, in view of the small magnitude of gravity relative to electricity. This fact was discovered by Faraday. By rubbing a small dielectric we accumulate enough force to raise a small piece of paper, to counteract the action of the huge mass of earth on that piece of paper. Therefore, Faraday's exeriments are by no means conclusive. They should be repeated with much more accuracy—much more than was available at the time. Stokes rejected Faraday's very last paper, which was on electrogravity. His argument was that the results were negative. The editors of Stokes's published letters remark that they were of little value anyhow, since he experimented by throwing bodies from a very low tower. Big towers would not do either, and Faraday himself suspected so. He merely tried to arouse interest—in the only manner he could, namely with negative results. By now we can perform the experiments with lasers and Mössbauer's effect; and get positive results, of course, though (as usual) not exactly those expected by Faraday.

According to Newton's theory, only mass and distance are responsible for gravity. Now heavy mass cannot be annihilated, since it equals the inert mass. And inert mass cannot be annihilated, since it is an essential property of matter. (Incidentally, this is true even according to present-day theories, since energy, to which matter can be transformed, also has mass or inertia.) Faraday thought that he could find circumstances in which the *acceleration* of a rolling body is *less* than predicted, the rest of the force turning into electricity. This was a shot in the dark, but he was used to shots in the dark, hoping for one hit in several thousand misses.

The snag of the matter is that while electricity is a dual force, gravity is not; and problems of symmetry arise. Faraday first thought (§ 2704) that, in order to restore symmetry, there may occur currents in two bodies approaching in opposite directions. This is not reasonable as it stands: it is not tenable that this is a universal law, and we need some more general rule for restoring symmetry. Indeed, Faraday later thought that perhaps in the presence of, say, a metallic tower this might happen. But this raises new problems, especially in view of the small magnitude of gravity. Faraday thought and experimented simultaneously and here his thought is underdeveloped. He even considered the possibility of *one* electricity evolving, but he was very skeptical on this (*Life and Letters*, 2:413). As it happens, this does not restore the symmetry. The problem troubled Einstein in the same manner, and for thirty years. Probably his solution, generalized relativity, is not satisfactory either. It is not surprising, then, that Faraday could not offer any interesting specific idea here.

Faraday's general idea, however, was a part of his whole philosophy—it was not merely to unite electricity and gravity. His theory of conservation and conversion of force implies both a gravitational field theory—since the force of gravity cannot *vary* at the distance, it must be there all the time, whether it acts or not—and a convertibility to any other force in a direct manner. The idea of forces filling space and not acting, as in the case of a single body in the universe, was strongly rejected by his contemporaries as a metaphysical supposition that assumes much and explains nothing.

This must be admitted. But the admission need not go against Faraday; it may go against the idea that strong assumptions that explain little are unwanted—against Ockham's razor so-called. This idea—Ockham's razor—is, without doubt, so central to philosophy, methodology, science, or what have you that the result of Faraday's stand is not surprising: he was now openly courting hostility. Since early adolescence he had posed as a gentleman, avoided controversy, and kept away from bitterness—as much as he could. And then, past his sixtieth birthday and in spite of onsetting senility, he became, by his own or by accepted standards, a cantankerous old man. He got engaged in somewhat bitter correspondence, especially when crossing swords with the Astronomer Royal, the mouthpiece of the English scientific establishment.

His acrimony, I am afraid, cannot be dismissed as unjustified. His criticisms were for decades dismissed offhand; his proposals were sneered at as not up to scratch. Now, as he admitted, often enough they really were not up to scratch. But half-baked ideas are better than none. The question is, then, did the Astronomer Royal have none? Faraday's criticism, in other words, was it devastating? It is hard to say. In retrospect, when his half-baked ideas are available to us fully baked in their Einsteinian version, when we are in full possession of all the arguments by now sufficiently worked out, we can easily find it in ourselves to say, yes, Faraday's criticisms are quite devastating. At the time I do not know how matters could have been judged; conjecturing about variations on history is not unpermissible, but it is no easy matter either. All we can say is, by the accepted standards, which were much too high, no doubt Faraday's criticisms were devastating. Also, by the accepted admiration of science and of Newton, which were too high as well, judgment may go the other way.

Let us agree that things were unclear at the time. Why, then, all the personal bitterness? Faraday struggled all his life to be recognized as a thinker.

They offered him all the honors he could wish for, and a few more that he rejected (knighthood, in particular, as well as the rectorship of the University of London, the presidency of the Royal Society, and that of the Royal Institution). Every time he pushed for recognition as a thinker, it seems, they forged a new medal to give him as a consolation prize. They do look as if they felt quite guilty about him—not only his friends like Grove, de la Rive, and Tyndall, but also editors, secretaries of learned societies, and their like. Yet their ideologists, the spokesmen of the establishment, were self-righteously and pigheadedly adamant and would not budge a hairbreadth; they would not admit even the possibility that he was a thinker because they would not admit even the possibility that his criticism was valid. Here they were—to use Faraday's idiom—quite "unphilosophical."

It was the scientific establishment, then, that took it equally personally. It was as important, say, for the Astronomer Royal personally to ignore Faraday as it was for Faraday to be recognized by the Astronomer Royal. There was a personal need on one side to defend Newton's theory of gravity as above the slightest suspicion of any need for the slightest alteration or face-lift. It was a matter of personal faith. Faraday's personal faith was not only in the need for change but also in a community of "philosophical men" able to admit it. It is no accident that the Astronomer Royal and Faraday did not address their letters to each other; they addressed them to a mutual friend who was a clergyman with a good scientific background. I wish on no one a clash with any scientific establishment; they are all alike. (See Oliver Heaviside, *Electric Papers*, 1:x.)

Faraday's views were half-baked, and his criticism and suggestions were general; as replacements for such a fully baked idea as Newtonianism, the Astronomer Royal felt they could not be recognized; Faraday felt they could and should be recognized if the scientific community were to abide by its acknowledged standards. Faraday bet all on its abidance by these—from adolescence the thing that mattered to him was to belong to a truly philosophical community. He won in the end, but the tension of the waiting was too painful, and so he died utterly senile. He paid heavily for his ignorance of the fact that the truly philosophical does not court any establishment. (Einstein was unhappy even about Galileo's politics for science.)

Faraday recommended two specific corrections to Newton's theory; one, that gravity should interact with other forces. The other, that it should not act at a distance but take time. Both points were incorporated in Einstein's general theory of relativity of 1916; in 1919 Eddington observed the interaction of gravity and light waves. Gravitational forces traveling in time are still problematic within Einstein's theory.

Why should force travel in time? Does it follow from the law of conservation of force that force propagates in time? Faraday's view on time is definite: "I do not know any state the acquiring of which does not need time," he says (*Experimental Researches in Electricity*, 3:466): The question is whether it is necessary. Reasoning intuitively it must be so. If force can move infinitely rapidly in space (as Newton's theory implies), then there is no point to speak of the identity of it, to say nothing of what remains there to be conserved. This argument Faraday expanded in detail, especially in his correspondence.

How strong is this argument I cannot tell. We need not be deterred from intuitive arguments, but we must beware of relying on them too much. With an almost unnoticeable change of the usage of a word, we may arrive at a different conclusion. But although Faraday forwarded hardly more than intuitive arguments, Maxwell really did show that Newton's dynamics must be thrown overboard altogether.

Maxwell showed that timeless propagation of action is incompatible with the field theory on the basis of the law of conservation of energy. Now, arguing against L. V. Lorenz, who assumed propagating (retarded) potentials, he showed that this assumption leads to perpetual motion. Assume two balls tied to a stick attracting each other. We now push them to the right along the line on which the stick lies. It follows that the right-hand body is *less* attracted to the left-hand body and the left-hand body *more* to the right because the forces move *in time*. The whole thing will be pushed to the right, then, with an ever-increasing velocity. Now this is very puzzling: in Maxwell's system itself this argument is valid too: he attacked a system in which potentials are propagated in time since that means that forces propagate in time, but his theory implies too that forces propagate in time. Maxwell escaped this criticism by rejecting retarded potentials and instead assuming the existence of a *medium*, which is a sort of *absolute space*, where potentials are at rest.

This is not to say that Maxwell needed the aether for this reason alone. Electromagnetic theory has mechanical implications, and these may be different if motions were considered from different viewpoints (inertial systems) and if Newtonian mechanics were accepted. In Faraday's theory of the magnetically induced current, for example, there is no difference between the case where the magnet moves and the wire rests and vice versa; and, of course, mechanical considerations do signify here, since currents and work are interchangeable. This is why, between Faraday and Einstein, thinkers took it for granted that the case of the moving wire differs from the case of the moving magnet. The symmetry was reestablished by Einstein in 1905, after he had reformed mechanics. Faraday and Einstein had no use for the aether, but most of their intermediaries were aetherists. What forced them to accept the aether was not electricity but mechanics. As Einstein put this point (in his scientific autobiography), Maxwell's equations "can be grasped formally in a satisfactory fashion only by way of the special theory of relativity." What could not be satisfactorily grasped within special relativity, then, was Newtonian gravity. There is an inner logic to the development of physics from Faraday to Einstein; Faraday merely sensed some of its aspects, and Maxwell a bit more.

And so we come to Faraday's view of gravity. Here is a letter from Maxwell to Faraday about the problem, written on 9 November 1857 when he was still hopeful (R. Appelyard, *Tribute to Faraday* [London, 1931], p. 112; Williams, *Michael Faraday*, pp. 511–13; italics in the original):

> We have had streams of hooks and eyes flying around
> magnets, and even pictures of them so beset, but nothing is
> clearer than your description of all sources of force keeping
> up a state of energy in all that surrounds them, which state
> by its own increase or diminution measures the work done by
> any change in the system. You seem to see the lines of force
> curving round obstacles and driving plumb at conductors and
> swerving towards certain directions in crystals, and carrying
> with them everywhere the same amount of attractive power
> spread wider or denser as the lines widen or contract.
>
> You have also seen that the great mystery is not how like
> bodies repel and unlike attract but how like bodies attract
> (by gravitation). But if you can get over that difficulty, either
> by making gravity the residual of the two electricities or by
> simply admitting it, then your line of force can "weave a
> web across the sky" [Newton was said to have cleaned the
> webs] and lead the stars in their courses without any necessarily
> immediate connection with the objects of their attraction.
>
> The lines of force from the sun spread out from him
> and when they come near a planet *curve out from it*, so that
> every planet diverts a number depending on its mass from
> their course and substitutes a system of its own so as to become
> something like a comet, *if lines of force were visible* . . .

Now conceive every one of these lines (which never interferes but proceeds from the sun and planet to infinity) to have a *pushing* force instead of a *pulling* one, and then sun and planet will be pushed together with a force which comes out as it ought proportional to the product of the masses and the inverse square of the distance.

The difference between this case and that of the dipolar forces is, that instead of each body catching the lines of force from rest all the lines keep as clear of the other bodies as they can and go off to the infinite sphere against which I have supposed them to push.

Here then we have conservation of energy (actual and potential) . . . and besides this we have conservation of "lines of force" as their number and total strength for *every* body always sends out a number proportional to its own mass, and the pushing effect of each is the same. All that is altered when bodies approach is the direction in which these lines push . . .

I think this charming letter gives us a slight glimpse of the fantastic optimism of the last century. We have here everything to please everybody: lines of force, push, conservation—everything. Only, we know, the program did not work. Faraday's reply is interesting as an ingenious suggestion presented as a reading of Maxwell's letter (*Life and Letters*, 2:392): ". . . The idea that we may possibly have to connect *repulsion* with the lines of gravitation-force (which is going far beyond anything my mind would venture on at present, except in private cogitation), shows how far we *may* have to depart from the view I oppose [italics Faraday's]." The idea was later tried by Einstein (his lambda). That Faraday would think about it only in private shows that he never was as frank and open as Einstein was. How right he was to exercise caution to the last is hard to know how to judge. We are lucky that we do not face such problems today, at least not to that extent.

## Conclusion

The second period of Faraday's *Experimental Researches* is much easier to follow than his first. His principle becomes explicit and much easier to apply, his ideas become clearer and much simpler, his work becomes more precise, and he has no such great obstacles as the electric current.

The older he became the more interested he was in principles: his experiments were scantier and of much stronger bearing. Toward the end of his life he worked on gravity, on currents (the glow tubes), and his last experiment was on magnetizing the source of light (the Zeeman effect), which he could not observe due to lack of a strong spectroscope that, he had (rightly) hoped, would show a change of color.

He started to see a new movement of followers—hesitant, not always understanding, but with good will, and inspired by his work. The wall of isolation was slowly crumbling. Here is an interesting quotation from the biography of his first follower, Kelvin, written by a close associate, largely from the horse's mouth (S. P. Thompson, *Life of William Thomson* [London, 1910], p. 19):

> In the circle of University acquaintances in Glasgow was one
> David Thomson, a cousin of the great Faraday. . . . [He] took over
> the duties of Professor Meikelham's chair from 1842 to 1845,
> during the latter's illness. He subsequently held the chair
> of Natural Philosophy at Aberdeen . . . By him William Thomson
> was, as he himself expressed it "INOCULATED WITH FARADAY
> FIRE." He indoctrinated the youthful student into Faraday's
> *then heterodox notions of electric action in a medium.* Hitherto
> the doctrines taught him respecting electricity and magnetism
> had been on the then accepted lines of *Newtonian forces acting
> at a distance*, with all the weight of Poisson and Laplace to
> support the analytic theory. Of the Boscovichian theory of atoms
> as centres of force acting at a distance he had heard from
> Nichol. BUT now David Thompson inculcated the *Faraday
> conception of electric and magnetic forces acting along curved
> lines in the medium, and the further possibility of a screening
> of electric forces by the interposition of a conducting sheet.*
> At first, William Thomson rejected these notions thinking them
> *incompatible with first principles*, and argued eagerly against
> Faraday's views. Ultimately he was convinced, and ever
> afterwards retained the most sincere admiration for Faraday and
> his work.

Plate III. Vol. 3. Expl Researches

Phil. Trans. MDCCXLII. Plate IX. p.158.

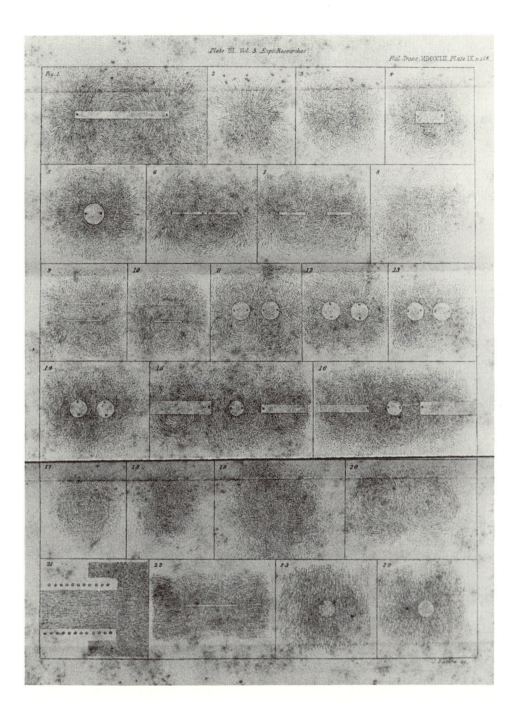

The end of the story, the story of the rise of Faraday's school, of the success of Maxwell's theory and its spread, and the rise of the theory of relativity —all this is a long story that will be written by others. Here I am content to present Kelvin's summary of it, sketchy and biased and distorting and even incongruous as it is. It was published in the preface to the English edition of Hertz's *Electric Waves*, and republished in S. P. Thompson's *Michael Faraday* (p. 284):

> The long struggle of the first half of the eighteenth century was not merely on the question of a medium to serve for gravific mechanism, but on the correctness of the Newtonian law of gravitation as a matter of fact however explained. The corresponding controversy in the nineteenth century was very short, and it soon became obvious that Faraday's idea of the transmission of electric force by a medium not only did not violate Coulomb's law of relation between force and distance, but that, if real, it must give a thorough explanation of that law. Nevertheless, after Faraday's discovery of the different specific inductive capacities of different insulators, twenty years passed before it was generally accepted in continental Europe. But before his death, in 1867, he had succeeded in inspiring the rising generation of the scientific world with something approaching to faith that electric force is transmitted by a medium called ether, of which, as had been believed by the whole scientific world for forty years, light and radiant heat are transverse vibrations. Faraday himself did not rest with this theory of electricity alone. The very last time I saw him at work at the Royal Institution was in an underground cellar, which he had chosen for freedom from disturbance; and he was arranging experiments to test the time of propagation of magnetic force from an electromagnet through a distance of many yards of air to a fine steel needle, polished to reflect light; but no result came from those experiments. About the same time, or soon after, certainly not long before the end of his working time, he was engaged (I believe at the Shot Tower, near Waterloo Bridge, on the Surrey side) in efforts to discover relations between gravity and magnetism, which also led to no result.

Kelvin's eulogy is partly an expression of what he found impressive and admirable in Faraday, and partly what he had hoped others might find impressive and admirable in Faraday. His claim that around 1860 Faraday's views were in some sense accepted on the Continent is a slight exaggeration. Even in England, where Faraday's views were popular earlier than on the Continent, it was not known how far and wide Faraday's influence was.

S. P. Thompson, who quotes Kelvin's assessment approvingly, became interested in Faraday and wrote his life, as a result of realizing this (and perhaps also because his granduncle was Phillips, one of Faraday's few personal friends). Here is the story of Thompson's findings.[12]

> With regards to the resources made at this time [1878] a rather curious occurrence took place in connection with a paper on "Some Magnetic Figures made by Means of Iron Filings," which Thompson had shown at the Physical Society, and which had been apparently accepted as a new piece of research. However, afterwards, Professor Guthrie admitted in conversation that these were not new to him [as] three or four years [earlier] Professor Barrett of Dublin had shown him some similar figures, but that he did not claim them as new and advising him to ask Professor Barrett what literature there was on the matter.
>
> Before receiving this advice, Thompson found that his electromagnetic figures had already been shown by Faraday from whose researches Professor Barrett also had got them. He wrote: "I am surprised, not that I did not know of their existence in Faraday's book, but that no one of the members of the Physical Society knew . . ."

Even Faraday's followers in the Physical Society, who used his lines of force regularly, were ignorant of their debt to him; a professor in Dublin knew, but that was the exception. How all this came about is incredible: it was a new atmosphere that Faraday had created. There is a story about the old Faraday walking down the street, saying a kind hello to children, and of these children running around the block to say hello again to him. This is

12. *Silvanus Phillips Thompson, His Life and Letters*, by Jane S. and Helen G. Thompson, London, 1920, pp. 43–44.

known, of course, because some of these children later became scientists. How deeply they were influenced by Faraday, they never knew—particularly as he was unread by them and their contemporaries.

How deep was Faraday's influence can be seen in the popular myth that in the early nineteenth century the British were empiricists and the Continental a priorists. This myth has survived to this day. At the turn of the century it was still popular; early in the century it was repeated by various writers on the Continent, reputable and otherwise. At the same time, Fitzgerald (of the Lorenz-Fitzgerald contraction), in a review of a Continental book in the *Philosophical Magazine*, wrote that obviously the English national character is theoretical and the Continental one is empiricist. This view reflects a transitory state of affairs as far as popular mythology is concerned. It also reflects the tacit influence of Faraday in his own country.

How the revolution started by Faraday—more precisely by Boscovich (who dared present Newton's theory as a mere approximation) and Kant (who presented space as filled with forces in varying degrees of fullness)—got going is a most interesting question. Against it worked not only a conspiracy of silence but also taboos against publishing speculations and controversial opinions in the scientific press. To a large extent Faraday adhered to these taboos to the end. This is why his lecture notes in places are more revealing than his published papers. They are more revealing not only as historical documents but also as instruments with which history was forged. What Jeffreys' bibliography shows most clearly is that Faraday lectured incessantly; and, as we know, superbly. Apart from thirty years of regular lectures in the Royal Institution and of twenty years of regular lectures in the Royal Naval Academy, he instituted the Friday Evening Discourses and turned the Christmas Juvenile Lectures into an event of unusual magnitude. It is doubtless that Kelvin and Maxwell played a crucial role in the success of the revolution and in the shaping of it this way rather than any other. Yet, doubtless, they were not isolated, thanks to Faraday's incessant work, and to his peculiar style—scientific as well as personal.

# 10 Epilogue

### Physics and Metaphysics

The world view that lies behind a scientific program, in fact behind any scientific project, is metaphysical. Antimetaphysics is as old as Bacon's influence, that is to say, as old as the Royal Society. There is much to say in favor of antimetaphysics on the condition that it is not taken too seriously. But never was the antimetaphysical tendency taken so literally as it is today. The Royal Society's official creed, its metaphysical world view, was first Cartesian and later Newtonian. The struggle between the two trends, the Cartesian and the Newtonian trend, ended with Coulomb's abolition of the electric effluvia. Fluids took the place of effluvia everywhere. In the Newtonian camp some Cartesian maneuvers took place—always unsuccessfully. Some inviduals were heretics in every part of the Newtonian era. But even the most brilliant heretics, Kant and Boscovich, had practically no influence on the course of events—except through a chain leading to Faraday, who started a one-man struggle on a large scale. His campaign was followed by a few individuals and his seeds of heresy soon grew and provoked the attempt to overthrow Newtonianism altogether.

In a brisk process the outcome proved most unusual. First came Einstein's operationalism that he later so much regretted—his so-called definition of simultaneity. Next came the confusion due to the contradiction between two unsatisfactory theories, the wave and the corpuscle theories of light. To many this conflict seems to have proved the fertility of irrationalism (rather than of rational disagreement). An eminent quantum physicist has said that he does not mind contradictions if they enable him to make predictions. Niels Bohr's interpretation of quantum theory endorses—up to a point—each of the two conflicting views. Bohr emphasized so much reality's refusal to obey our mechanical picture that one may suspect that mechanism was his ideal; and with no mechanism, it looks as if he preferred to have no picture of the universe at all. Or rather, he argued that we can have no picture of the world, meaning "mechanical picture."

All this, the definition of simultaneity, the wave-corpuscle problem, and Bohr's disillusionment, contributed to the new antimetaphysical fashion. Physical theory, we are told, is no picture of reality but a tool for prediction. So now there is no world view and no program.

A few people, Einstein, Schrödinger, De Broglie, Bohm, Vigier, and Landé, have tried to present a world view and a program—each in his own way. As yet they have raised no public interest. This is due partly, at least, to the severe defects of these views—particularly of the determinism all but Landé share. Today physicists declare often enough that they are not interested in comprehension, in pictures of the universe. They surely have pictures, but they take them for granted and are not critically interested in them. The pictures are complexes of naïve realism and scientific theories, which although officially denied the status of pictures of reality, are still pictures of reality, true or false ones.

The result is undesirable—not because antimetaphysics prevails while naïve realism is the tacitly accepted metaphysics, but rather because existing world views are not subject to public criticism. The official creed is that there is no official creed and therefore everybody agrees with everybody else, save some heretics who are left to Heisenberg to refute. Consequently there are no overall scientific programs, rather science breaks up into more and more specialisms. Each is expert in his own branch, and he determines what is important, what research project is more promising, and so on. All this is not objectionable in itself, but some may regret it—namely those who are more interested in comprehension and in speculations, such as Alexandre Koyré.

Doubtless, the history of science shows how science has rendered this or that metaphysical view unimportant. Likewise the same history may show that a metaphysical view may have played a role in its time, and this is what Koyré tried to show all his life. Metaphysical views are not as refutable as scientific views. But some of them, the more important of them, are criticizable and therefore may be surpassed. If we are not capable of being critical toward a metaphysical doctrine, then metaphysics may stagnate and *become* uninteresting. If however, we *can* be critical, we *may* develop interesting new metaphysical theories.[1]

1. For a detailed discussion of this view see my "The Nature of Scientific Problems and Their Roots in Metaphysics" in M. Bunge (ed.), *The Critical Approach, Essays in Honor of Karl Popper* (New York, 1964), and in my *The Continuing Revolution* (New York, 1968).

### Epilogue

The fact that nineteenth-century metaphysical views were abandoned has left a metaphysical vacuum. Old problems became obsolete, and professional philosophers dare not touch upon physical problems. Once things were different and classical philosophy was deeply rooted in classical natural science. The urgent problem of both physics and metaphysics nowadays is how to re-establish a little closer contact.

### Futurism in Physics

Often one meets such a historical statement as "when $A$ introduced his new idea, he was ridiculed, but later he was proved right." Usually, if we confine ourselves now to the history of science, a brief examination would show that still later $A$ was proved mistaken, though his early detractors were in worse error; anyway, let us not argue this point here. We assume now that $A$ was right, leaving aside the problem of proof. The statement that $A$ was ridiculed or confronted with some kind of opposition or criticism is historically true for many cases. But the *reasons* of the opponents to $A$, who were proved so wrong, or the *reasons* of the party that lost are seldom recorded.[2] Sometimes, most of the critics of the new idea had indeed no *reason* at all, they were irrationalists. But this is, I contend, at best the exception to the rule. As a rule the opponents whom historians censure had some reason to oppose the new idea, even when the views they defended were much inferior to the views they were attacking. Their reasons are not recorded by historians of science, and this is a lacuna.

The tacit assumptions of those who ignore the *reasons* of the opponents to the right new view are two: (a) the opponent to the truth cannot be rational, he cannot have valid arguments; (b) he criticized the true view because he cherished his beloved prejudice. Assume for the moment that these two assumptions are generally true. It follows that the most advisable method of science is to avoid arguing with one's opponent. Nothing remains then to do about it but to stick to one's inner conviction with self-righteousness, and wait for the verdict of the future. But this is a very risky game: for every new view that was later "proved right," scores of other new views were proposed that contradict it. And at least all but one of these inventors of new ideas were admittedly proved wrong; but how?

2. See my *Towards an Historiography of Science* for this and for other points of this section.

The irrational faith in the verdict of the future is dangerous. It leads to fear to criticize lest the future is on the side of the view we wish to criticize, lest we be declared by future historians of science to be among those who backed the wrong horse.

The suggestions to avoid these obstacles are not very important. He who loves the truth will examine critically any view that interests him and he can criticize; and he will disregard the reward or punishment of posterity. But those who place these obstacles, the inductivist historians of science, may perhaps be seen as those who back the wrong horse, irrationalism, or the dead horse, inductivism.

Future generations may possess the whole truth and be able to tell which among us today will have been proved right. We cannot do so. We cannot present the history of science reasonably except as the history of *arguments*; we may benefit if we realize that many of those who were proved wrong were very able thinkers and critics, and good scientists. We may, here and there, make a historical statement like "Tyndall was prejudiced," and try to explain our reasons for this statement. But the knowledge that Newtonianism is false is no argument for the view, which I accept on other grounds, that he was prejudiced. Other "conservative" scientists like Dalton and Ampère were surely not prejudiced. It is not enough now to write histories of science merely in order to show that $B$ and $C$ and $D$ were in error and conclude that they were prejudiced. We may learn more from $B$'s and $C$'s *arguments* against $A$ than from the proof that they were prejudiced. Otherwise better not mention them at all, just as we do not mention the names of the many enemies of science through the ages. Prejudices are less important than arguments; the history of science is not a chronology of confirmations of Bacon's doctrine of prejudice and of infallible truths but a history of rational arguments for and against views mostly now defunct.

Temperamentally, and being critical of much of contemporary physics, I tend to sympathize with the heretic, with the rebel. My present study has made me modify my view. It is not rebellious feelings and readiness to become heretics that count. Nor is a conservative feeling or the desire to be orthodox important one way or another. What matters is not even the conflict between heretic and orthodox—only the rationality of the conflict between the two. Besides, what is orthodoxy and what is heresy, one simply cannot decide except by employing social criteria that are not much relevant to science. In the final analysis there are two components to Faraday's struggle, a just one, the defense of the minority viewpoint and its right for a hearing, and an irrelevant one, concerning the unphilosophicalness of the Royal Society and its like. Let me echo Einstein and Shaw and Popper here: we need neither heresy nor orthodoxy, neither the right nor the prejudiced—we want differences of opinion and a rational argument. It is much less important to note that of the two parties, *A* or *B*, one belongs to the majority or holds the older view or both. The main thing is how well he argues against his opponent and whether his opponent can learn from his criticism. Back to Socrates then.

The claim that there exists a vast unanimity of scientists is either false or an indication of some danger of stagnation. It is not the future that proves us right or wrong, not even all the scientists of the whole future of mankind. It is we who may progress—and by arguing: there is no other known way.

Those who would rescue futurism at least as the doctrine of Faraday's period may be interested to note, first, that Faraday himself was no futurist. Not only was he far from hoping that history is the final court of appeal. He once, perhaps under the influence of the surroundings, wrote to Matteucci anxious to defend his priority that time will sort things out, correctly and unalterably; and then he crossed out this remark (*Life and Letters*, 2:320). He was a conservative in science no less than in politics: again and again we find him a rebel despite himself, not an avant-gardist of any sort. For my part I find both of the following documents, both private, so conservative that I am almost uncomfortable about them. The first is a letter to Sir John Herschel (R.S., MS, 10 November 1832):

> When your work on the study of Natural Philosophy came out I read it as all others did with delight. I took it as a school book for philosophers and I feel that it has made me a better reasoner and even experimenter and has altogether heightened my character and made me if I may be permitted to say so a better philosopher.
>
> In my last investigations I continually endeavoured to think of that book and to reason and investigate according to the principles there laid down.

This is, no doubt, a sincere fan letter. It concerns a very apologetic defense of science as certainty based on as strict Baconian canons as possible; its thesis, unstated, is that, though Newton's optical theory has been overthrown, there was not the slightest reason to suspect that Newton's theory of gravity may have the same fate since it had been amply demonstrated.[3] I do not know what to make of Faraday's letter. All I can do is remind the reader that in the early 1830s Faraday flirted again with the idea that all "doubtful knowledge" can become either knowledge—i.e., demonstrated—or be overthrown.

The last document showing Faraday's deep-seated conservatism is from his *Diary* (6:330, 18 September 1854):

> 13443 Might write a useful paper at the present time—starting strongly and in a way of tests those points which may serve as settlers between my theory or hypothesis and the former ones—asking for answers upon the old theory and showing the answers from the new one.

> 13444 The hypothesis is not so much mine as one renewed from old times. Look at Euler's letters and what he says.

What this means is that Faraday's medium theory has a respectable Cartesian ancestry, which is much more important than his dismissal of the aether from the medium. I cannot see merit in this position; I only have to make it clear that this is Faraday's position; he never intended to be a rebel.

One more example of Faraday's conservatism may exist, but I wish first to warn my reader against taking it too seriously. It is always questionable to use private documents in evidence: they do not carry the weight of a deliberate public pronouncement. The two passages just quoted are somewhat weightier perhaps than a mere passing thought, since Faraday's relations with Herschel, as we had occasion to notice, were friendly but formal, and since his diary was not a note book but a carefully prepared document. Yet the following highly conservative—nearly casuistic—extract is one that I certainly consider unqualified as evidence; at most it may testify to a certain mood that Faraday was in on a rare occasion—when relaxed and confidential, as he was when writing a rare private letter to Matteucci, whom he considered small fry both as an intellect and as a characrer but an engaging and charming one at that, almost an image of the repressed, somewhat irresponsible, almost carefree imp that was always there within Faraday himself. The letter, of 2 November 1855, was published by Bence Jones; I know of no comment on it, although it

---

3. See my "Sir John Herschel's philosophy of success," in Russell McCormmach (ed.), *Historical Studies in Physical Science* 1 (Philadelphia, 1969). See also Faraday's praise of Herschel in his Priestley celebration talk, *Phil. Mag.*, 2, 1833, p. 391.

discusses the deepest question that ever beset Faraday: were the physical lines of force the deepest layer of reality? (So, at least, I read Faraday.) Here it is, with Faraday's own emphasis:

> I go with Newton when he speaks of the *physical lines of gravitational forces* (3305 n.), and leave that part of the subject for the consideration of my readers.

Now, what Newton says and Faraday quotes in § 3305 is concerning the cause or agent of gravity that Newton says must be there; "but whether this agent be material or immaterial," i.e., God's sensorium, adds Newton, "I have left to the considerations of my reader." The agony that Faraday felt must at times have been unbearable. At least at such moments, I suggest, Faraday was willing to clutch a conservative straw.

## A Portrait of Faraday

What we see in a man is largely what we are ready to see in him. And so, whatever else we see in Faraday, we see an investigator, a student of nature. As his friend Dumas put it, in his obituary, "There was nothing dramatic in the life of Faraday." It is strange that one who rose from the slums to become a grand old man should strike Dumas as lacking in drama. It is not that he had not met him except in his days of glory; he was a young upstart himself when he met Faraday, and he saw very well how Davy was humiliating him. "We admired Davy, but we loved Faraday," was his unforgettable verdict (Thompson, *Michael Faraday*, p. 20). Dumas evidently knew some men of science whose lives and whose appearances were dramatic. And he judged Faraday to have been rather domestic.

This was not a matter of devotion to science alone, but also a domesticated attitude even toward extracurricular activities, which he undertook in enormous quantities. His correspondence with his wife alone is quite sufficient to draw attention to him, not to mention his other correspondence, his journals, his lecture notes, his notes on work for the Admiralty, his public service in various commissions, his public service as an inventor who never drew patents out of principle, his help to academies, museums, lighthouses, educational institutions of all sorts, his functions as an elder in his church, including visits to the sick.

What would strike us today about Faraday's character, I think, is first the very wide range, of his emotional and intellectual responses, and second the intensity with which he responded to his environment. Later we would notice that he could not respond except intensely. He learned to behave like a light-hearted fellow, but he did this intensely too—charming people, playing tricks like a conjurer, being extravagantly chivalrous to all the ladies and strongly attached to all the children. Certainly he was never pompous, and he had a tremendous sense of fun; for instance, when he was mistaken for a porter he played the part to perfection.

Faraday's extreme sensitivity, his pride, his self-irritation—even with such trifles as the slightly excessive length of his nose—these would come to our notice next. (His portraits conceal the length of his nose; he disliked being photographed; his sensitivity to smells was proverbial.) There is no doubt that his correctness cost him much effort, that it interacted in a vicious circle with his touchiness. When he took the lid off he boiled excessively hard. Alternatively, sometimes his tension would become intolerable—and he would drop it all and come up with a marvelous new idea, deep and beautiful, just befitting the occasion. His emotional richness and his intellectual richness, each by itself could have annihilated him; but to an extent they protected him from each other.

All this—Faraday's strong personality, his wide range and depth of emotional and intellectual faculties—impressive as it is, does not go deep enough. In the final analysis it is a person's ideal, what he stands for, that characterizes him as banal, or exceptional, or in-between like most of us. What was so peculiar to Faraday, I think, was his image of the philosophical man and his hope of attaining personal salvation, peace of mind, by joining a community of philosophic men. As Davy noticed at once, it was an aspiration too naïve to require criticism; as Davy failed to notice, Faraday's strong personality and immense ability helped him turn this aspiration into a metaphysical commitment of sorts. To be sure the transformation did not take place overnight. It started as an ambition of a rather pathetic youngster in the employ of a rather pathetic refugee who had a bookbinding shop in the outskirts of London, less than a couple of miles from the newly founded, somewhat adventurous, Royal Institution. The ambition began to turn into an ideal for no better reason, perhaps, than that young man Faraday was as stubborn as a mule, and rather than notice that his dream was a fairy tale from the *Arabian Nights* he decided to make it true. He always believed that experiment saved him from confusing fact with fiction; this was the fiction that kept him going:

somehow all those who lived around him who failed to see the facts, who were dogmatists, were in a sense unreal to him, a part of a bad dream. It is no wonder that he often doubted his sense of reality—we all come to that when we notice how unreal are most people around us. What is real, then, in the last analysis, is the dream, says Jorge-Luis Borges. In Faraday's case it was the dream of the philosophic men and their tranquillity and liberalmindness that was the most real thing. Deep down, Faraday was the last representative of the Age of Reason and as such the link between the classical and the new Enlightenment. But his religious sectarianism and his political conservatism made him a nineteenth-century man. In these respects he was behind—not as well-rounded as—his predecessors of the seventeenth and eighteenth centuries, and he evidently gave up hope of catching up with them—a circumstance that encouraged him to specialize and concentrate more intensely on his science. Yet his idea of the community of philosophic men had a romantic tinge to it as well. Much as Faraday helped reform the scientific community and its customs, he also contributed significantly to its professionalization and to its readjustment to a new equilibrium—better than the old one by far, but stagnant too. We can be proud of having implemented much of his teaching, in physics and in the traditions of the republic of learning. What impresses me about him is not what he achieved but his struggle for improvement, with its defects and with its admirable humanity.

# Bibliography

Aepinus, Franz Ulrich Theodor

1756        Mémoire concernant quelques nouvelles expériences électrique
            remarquables. In *Histoire de l'Académie Royale des Science et
            Belles Lettres*, pp. 105–21. Berlin.

1759        *Tentamen Theoriae Electricitatis et Magnetismi*. Saint Petersburg:
            Typis Academiae Scientiarum.

Agassi, Joseph

1954        The confusion between physics and metaphysics in standard stories
            of science. In *Ithaca, 1952*, ed. Henry Guerlac, 1:231–38, 249–50.
            Paris.

1961        An Unpublished Paper by The Young Faraday. *Isis* 52:87–90.

1963        *Toward an Historiography of Science, History and Theory*. Supple-
            ment 2. The Hague: Mouton. Facsimile reprint, 1967. Middletown,
            Conn.: Wesleyan Univ. Press.

1964        The nature of scientific problems and their roots in metaphysics.
            In *The Critical Approach to Science and Philosophy: Essays in
            Honor of Karl R. Popper*, ed. Mario Bunge, pp. 189–211. New
            York: Free Press.

1968        *The Continuing Revolution: A History of Physics From the Greeks
            to Einstein*. New York: McGraw-Hill.

1969a       Leibniz's place in the history of physics. *J. History of Ideas* 30:
            331–44.

1969b       Unity and diversity in science. In *Boston Studies in the Philosophy
            of Science*, eds. R. S. Cohen and M. W. Wartofsky, pp. 463–527.
            Dordrecht: Ridell.

1969*c*        Sir John Herschel's philosophy of success. In *Historical Studies in the Physical Sciences*, ed. Russell McCormmach, pp. 1–36. Philadelphia: Univ. of Pennsylvania Press.

Alembic Club Reprints

1932        Prout's hypothesis. No. 20. Edinburgh.

Ampère, André-Marie

1820        De l'áction mutuelle de deux courants électriques. *Ann. Chim. Phy.* 15:59–76.

1821        Notes of the communications which he made to the Academy of Sciences. *Phil. Mag.* 57:47–49.

1826        *Théorie des phénomènes électro-dynamiques, uniquement de dérite de l'expérience.* Paris.

1936        *Correspondence du Grand Ampère*, publiée par L. de Launay de l'Académie des Sciences, avec le concours de l'Académie des Sciences (Fondation Loutreuil) et du Ministère de l'Éducation Nationale, par de Société des Amis d'André-Marie Ampère. 3 vols. Paris: Gauthier-Villars.

Appleyard, Rollo

1931        *A Tribute to Faraday*. London: Constable.

Babbage, Charles

1830        *Reflections on the decline of science in England.* London: R. Clay.

Bacon, Francis

1857        *The Works of Francis Bacon, Lord of Verulam, Viscount of Saint Albans, and Lord High Chancellor of England*, ed. James Spedding, Robert Leslie Ellis, and Douglas Denon Heath. 15 vols. London.

Barlow, Peter

1825        On the Laws of electromagnetic action. . . . *Edin. Phil. J.* 12: 105–11.

Barrett, W. F.

1827        Review of John H. Gladstone, Michael Faraday. *Nature* 6:412.

Beccaria, Giambattista

1770        *A treatise upon artificial electricity*, in which are given solutions of a number of interesting electric phenomena, hitherto unexplained. To which is added an essay on the mild and slow electricity which prevails in the atmosphere during severe weather. Translated from the Italian. London.

1793        *Dell' electricismo opera del p. Giambattista Beccaria delle scuole pie con molte note nuovamente illustrate.* 2 vols. Macerata.

Becker, Carl L.
1932        *The Heavenly City of the Eighteenth Century Philosophers*. New Haven: Yale Univ. Press.

Bence Jones, Henry
1870        *The life and letters of Faraday*. 2 vols. London and Philadelphia.
1871        *The Royal Institution: its founders and its first professors*. London.

Biot, Jean Baptiste
1820        Note sue le magnétisme de la pile de Volta. *Ann. Chim. Phys.* 15: 222–74.
1824        *Precise élémentaire de physique expérimentale.* . . . 2 vols. 3d ed. Paris. *See* John Farrar for a selection translated and published in 1826.
1858        *Mélange scientifique et littéraire*. 3 vols. Paris.

Boas, Marie
1952        The establishment of the mechanical philosophy. *Osiris* 10:412–541.

Boltzmann, Ludwig
1895        On certain questions of the theory of gases. *Nature* 51:413–15.

Boscovich, Roger Joseph
1759        *Theoria naturalis philosophiae redacta ad unicam legem virium in natura existentium*. Vienna. Translated as *A theory of natural philosophy* by J. M. Child. Chicago and London, 1922. Paperback reprint, Cambridge, Mass.: M.I.T. Press, 1966. *See also* L. L. Whyte.

Boyle, Robert
1744        *The works of the honourable Robert Boyle in five volumes* . . . , ed. Thomas Birch. London. Second ed., in six volumes. London, 1772.

Bragg, William Henry
1931        Michael Faraday. Broadcast National Lectures No. 8. London: B.B.C. Reprinted in *Scientific Monthly* 33:481–99.
1931        Commemoration oration. In The Royal Institution Faraday Celebration. London.
1926        The influence of learned societies on the development of England. Birmingham and Midland Institute Presidential Address. Birmingham.
1941        *The story of electromagnetism*. London: G. Bell.

Bromberger, Sylvain
1963        A theory about the theory of theory and about the theory of

theories. In *Philosophy of Science: The Delaware Seminar*, ed. B. Baumrin, 2:79–105. New York and London.

Brewster, David

1830    *The Edinburgh encyclopedia*, conducted by D. Brewster, etc. Edinburgh.

1831    *The life of Sir Isaac Newton*. London: John Murray.

1855    *Memoirs on the life, writings, and discoveries of Sir Isaac Newton.* 2 vols. Reprinted 1860, 1875. Edinburgh: Constable.

1837    A treatise on magnetism. Under this heading in 7th ed. *Encyclopaedia Britannica*. Edinburgh: Black.

Buber, Martin

1923, 1970  *I and Thou.* A new translation by Walter Kaufmann, New York: Scribner.

Čapek, Milič

1967    Dynamism. In *The Encyclopedia of Philosophy*, ed. P. Edwards, 2:444–47. New York: MacMillan and Free Press.

Carnap, Rudolf

1922    *Der Raum: Ein Beitrag zur Wissenschaftlehre*. Berlin.

1935    *Philosophy and logical syntax.* London: Kegan Paul.

Cavendish, Henry

1879    *The electrical researches of the Honourable Henry Cavendish, F.R.S.* Written between 1771 and 1781, edited from the original manuscripts in the possession of the Duke of Devonshire, K.G., by J. Clerk Maxwell. Cambridge: Cambridge University Press. Second ed., revised by J. Larmor, 1921.

Chemical Society of London

1928    *The Faraday Lectures*, London. 1869–1928.

Cohen, I. Bernard

1956    *Franklin and Newton:* An inquiry into speculative Newtonian experimental science and Franklin's work in electricity as an example thereof. Philadelphia: American Philosophical Society.

Coulomb, Charles Augustin de

1785–88  Mémoirs sur l'électricité et magnétisme. In *Mémoirs de l'Académie des Sciences* 1:569–77; 2:578–611; 3:612–38; 4:67–77; 5:421–67; 6:617–705. Reprinted 1884 in *Collection de mémoires relatifs à la physique.* 1: *Mémoires de Charles Augustin de Coulomb.* Paris: Gauthier-Villars.

Dalton, John
1808        *A new system of chemical philosophy*. Part I. Manchester and London.

Davy, Humphry
1839–40     *The collected works of Sir Humphry Davy, Bart*. Edited by his brother John Davy. 9 vols. London: Smith, Elder. *For biographies see* Charles Babbage, John Davy, A. J. Paris, and T. E. Thorpe.

Davy, John
1836        *Memoirs of the life of Sir Humphry Davy*. 2 vols. London: Smith, Elder.
1858        *Fragmentary remains, literary and scientific, of Sir Humphry Davy* . . . with a sketch of his life, and selections from his correspondence. London: John Churchill.

Delametherie, J. C.
1798        On the system of forces. In *Phil. Mag.* 2:277–82.

De la Rive, Auguste
1854–58     *Traité d'éléctricité théorique et applique*. 3 vols. Paris.
1853–58     *A Treatise on Electricity in theory and practice*, translated from the French by C. V. Walker. London: Longman.
1867        Notice sur Michael Faraday, sa vie et ses travaux. In *Archive des Science, de la Bibliothèque Universelle* 30:131–176. Reprinted 1867, Geneva. English translation 1867 in *Phil. Mag.* 34:409–36 and *Annual Report of the Smithsonian Inst. for 1867*, Washington 1867, pp. 227–45.

Dibner, Bern
1962        *Oersted and the discovery of electromagnetism*. New York and London: Blaisdell.

D'Israeli, Isaac
1858–59     *Works*, ed. Benjamin Disraeli. 4 vols. London.

Dumas, J. B. S.
1874        *Eloge Historique D'Arthur-Auguste de la Rive*. Read at a public meeting of the Institut de France, Académie des Sciences, 28 December 1874. Paris. *See also* Chemical Society of London.

Einstein, Albert
1905        Elektrodynamik bewegter Körper. In *Annalen der Physik* 17:891–921. English translation 1923 by W. Perrett and G. B. Jeffrey in *The principle of relativity, a collection of original memoirs*, ed.

H. A. Lorenz. London: Methuen. See also *The principle of relativity*, original papers by A. Einstein and H. Minkowski, trans. M. N. Saha and S. N. Bose, with a historical introduction by P. C. Mahalanobis. Calcutta: University of Calcutta Press, 1920.

1929    The new field theory, trans. L. L. Whyte. London: *The Times*, February 1929. Quoted in full in Observatory (1930) 52:82–87, 114–18.

1934    *The world as I see it*. New York: Covici Friede.

1949    Autobiographical Notes. In *Albert Einstein: Philosopher-Scientist*, ed. Paul Arthur Schilpp, pp. 1–96. Evanston, Ill.

1950    *The meaning of relativity, including the generalized theory of gravitation*. 3d ed. Princeton: Princeton Univ. Press.

1950    *Out of my later years*. New York: Philosophical Library. *See also* Max Jammer.

**Euler, Leonhard**

1802    *Letters of Euler on different subjects in physics and philosophy*. Addressed to a German princess. Trans. Henry Hunter. 2 vols. London. American ed. 1833. New York: Harper.

**Eve, A. S., and C. H. Creasey**

1945    *Life and work of John Tyndall*. With a chapter on Tyndall as a Mountaineer by Lord Schuster and a preface by Granville Proby. London: Macmillan.

**Faraday, Michael**

1817    Some observations on the means of obtaining knowledge and on the facilities afforded by the Constitution of the City Philosophical Society. Read to the body of members, at 53 Dorset Street, Salisbury Square, 19 February 1817. London: Effingham Wilson.

1821–22    Historical sketch of electromagnetism. In *Annals of Philosophy* 2:195–200, 274–90, 3:107–21.

1827–29    *Chemical manipulation*; being instructions to students in chemistry, on the methods of performing experiments of demonstration or of research, with accuracy and success. 2d ed. 1830, 3d ed. 1842. London.

1833    Address delivered at the commemoration of the centenary of the birth of Mr. Priestley. In *Phil. Mag.* 2:390–91.

1839–55    *Experimental researches in electricity*. Reprinted from *Phil. Trans. 1831–32*. With other electrical papers ... 3 vols. London: Taylor and Francis.

1853    The subject matter of a course of six lectures on the non-metallic elements. Delivered before members of The Royal Institution, in the Spring and Summer of 1852. Arranged, by permission, from the lecturer's notes, lent for the occasion by J. Soffern. To which is appended, remarks on the quality and tendencies of chemical philosophy, on allotropism, and ozone. . . . London.

1855    Magnetic remarks. In *Phil. Mag.* 9:253–55.

1856    Experimental researches in electricity, series 30, *Phil. Trans. 1856*, pp. 159–80.

1859    *Experimental Researches in Chemistry and physics.* Reprinted from *Phil. Trans.of 1821–57*, London: Taylor and Francis.

1860    *A course of six lectures on the various forces of matter and their relation to each other.* Delivered before a juvenile auditory at the Royal Institution of Great Britain during the Christmas holiday of 1859–60. ed. William Crookes. London and Glasgow.

1861    *A course of six lectures on the chemical history of a candle: to which is added a lecture on platinum*, ed. William Crookes. Delivered before a juvenile auditory at the Royal Institution of Great Britain during the Christmas holidays of 1860–61. London: Griffin, Bohn.

1899    *The letters of Faraday and Schoenbein, 1836–1862.* With notes, comments, and references to contemporary letters. eds. George W. A. Kahlbaum and Francis V. Darbishire. London, Basle.

1932–36    *Faraday's diary* . . . , ed. Thomas Martin. Seven volumes plus index. London.

Farrar, John

1826    *Elements of electricity, magnetism, and electromagnetism embracing the late discoveries and improvements, digested into the form of a treatise, being the second part of a course of natural philosophy, complete for the use of students of the university of Cambridge, New England.* Hilliard: Boston.

Franklin, Benjamin

1941    *Franklin's experiments, a new edition of Franklin's experiments and observations on electricity*, ed. I. Bernard Cohen with a critical and historical introduction. Cambridge, Mass.: Harvard Univ. Press.

1962    *Autobiography*, ed. Lewis Leavy. New York: Collier.

FitzGerald, George Francis

1896    Review of Ostwald's "Emancipation from scientific materialism,"

*Nature*, 53:441–2, reprinted in his scientific writings. 1902 London: Longmans, Green, pp. 387–91.

Fulton, John F.

1931    "The rise of the experimental method: Bacon and the Royal Society of London." In *Yale J. Biol. and Med.* 3:299–320.

1932    "Robert Boyle and his influence on thought in the seventeenth century." In *Isis* 18:77–102.

Gilbert, William

1893    (of Colchester, physician of London), *On the loadstone and magnetic bodies, and on the great magnet the earth, a new physiology demonstrated with many arguments and experiments*, trans. by P. F. Mottaley. New York: Wiley.

Gladstone, John Hall

1872    *Michael Faraday*, 2d ed. 1873; paper reprint. Macmillan: London.

Gray, Stephen

1731–32    "Letters . . . concerning electricity." In *Phil. Trans.* 37:18–44, 227–30, 285–90, 397–407.

Green, George

1903    *An essay on the application of mathematical analysis to the theories of electricity and magnetism, Nottingham, 1828*. Reprinted in Mathematical papers of the late George Green, ed. N. M. Ferrers Libraire Scientifique. Paris: A. Hermann.

Grove, Sir William

1865    *Correlation of physical forces: being the substance of a course of lectures delivered in the London Institution in the year 1843, London, 1846*. A few (revised) editions, including the following: Grove *et al*. The correlation and conservation of force. New York: Appleton.

Hadamard, Jacques

1945    *An essay on the psychology of invention in the mathematical field*. Princeton: Princeton Univ. Press. Dover paperback.

Hadfield, Sir Robert Abbott

1931    *Faraday and his metallurgical researches, with special reference to their bearing on the development of alloy steels*. London: Chapman and Hall.

H[agenbach], J.

1872    Notice of Christian Frederick Schoenbein, in *Annual Report of the Smithsonian Institute for 1868*. Washington, pp. 185–92.

Heaviside, Oliver

1950    *Electromagnetic theory*, 3 volumes, The Electrician, London, 1893, 1899, 1912. New York: Dover one-volume edition.

1892    *Electrical papers*, 2 volumes. Macmillan

Helmholtz, Hermann von

1853    *On the conservation of force, Scientific memoirs selected from the transactions of foreign academies of science; natural philosophy*. Eds. Tyndall and Francis, London: Taylor and Francis. *See also* Grove *et al.*

1870    Faraday as a discoverer. In *Nature* 2:51–52. Preface to German edition of Tyndall. *See also* Chemical Society of London.

Herschel, Sir John F. W.

1831    *Preliminary discourse of the study of natural philosophy*. Cabinet Encyclopedia, conducted by Dionysius Lardner assisted by eminent literary men. London and Philadelphia. New ed. 1833. Facsimile reprint, Johnson reprints, London, 1967.

1843    View on science and general education, ed. V. A. Huber, *The English Universities*. London: William Picering, pp. 645–48.

Hertz, Heinrich

1893    *Electric waves, being researches on the propagation of electric action with finite velocity through space*. Trans. D. E. Jones, with a preface by Lord Kelvin. New York: Macmillan; Dover edition, 1962.

1896    *Miscellaneous Papers*. Translated by D. E. Jones and G. A. Schott, with an introduction by Phillipp Lenard. New York: MacMillan.

Hoff, Jacobus Henricus van't

1967    *Imagination in science* (inaugural lecture, 1878). Trans. into English, with notes. A general introduction by George F. Springer. Molecular biology, biochemistry, and biophysics series. New York: Springer-Verlag.

Jammer, Max

1954    *Concepts of space, the history of theories of space in physics*. Foreword by Albert Einstein. Cambridge, Mass.: Harvard Univ. Press.

Johnston, William E.

1857    *England as it is . . . in the middle of the 19th century*. 2 volumes. London: John Murray.

Joule, James P.
1884        *Scientific papers*, London.

Kant, Immanuel
1883        *Kant's Prolegomena and Metaphysicae foundations natural science*. Trans. with a biography and introduction by Ernest Belfort Bax. London: George Bell.

1888        *Vom Ubergange von den metaphysischen Anfangsgrunden der Naturwissenschaft zur Physik*, ed. A. Krause. Frankfurt.

1900        *Kant's cosmology as in his essay on the retardation of the rotation of the earth and his natural history and theory of the heaven*, with an introduction, appendices . . . , ed. and trans. W. Hastie. Glasgow: Maclehose.

1929        *Critique of pure reason*, trans. Norman Kemp Smith. London: Macmillan; New York and Toronto, 1965.

1929        *Kant's inaugural dissertation and early writings on space*, trans. John Handyside. Chicago.

Kelvin, Lord. *See* Thomson, Sir William

Koyré, Alexandre
1965        *Newtonian Studies*. Chicago: Univ. of Chicago Press. Paper edition, 1968.

1968        *Metaphysics and measurement*. Cambridge, Mass.: Harvard Univ. Press.

de Kruiff, Paul
1926        *The microbe hunters*. New York: Harcourt, Brace; Pocket Book edition, 1940, and innumerable reprints.

Kuhn, Thomas S.
1957        "Energy conservation as a simultaneous discovery," ed. Marshal Clagett. *Critical problems in the history of science, Proceedings of the Institute for the History of Science at the University of Wisconsin*, 1–11 September. Madison: University of Wisc. Press, 1959, pp. 321–56.

Larmor, Joseph
1937        *Origins of Clerk Maxwell's electric ideas: as described in familiar letters to William Thomson*, Cambridge Univ. Press.

1938        "Faraday on electromagnetic propagation." In *Nature* 141:36–37.

Lakatos, Imre
1965        Changes in the problem of inductive logic, ed. I. Lakatos, *Problems of inductive logic, Proceedings of the International Colloquium in*

the *Philosophy of Science*, London, in three volumes. Amsterdam, 1968, pp. 315–417.

Levere, T. H.
1968    Faraday, matter, and rational theology—reflections on an unpublished manuscript. *Brit. J. Hist. Sci.* 4:95–107.

Liebig, Justus von
1863    *Induction and Deduction*, Munich.
1863    Bacon as a natural philosopher, *Macmillan's Magazine*, 237–49 and 8:258–67.
1944    Letters to Faraday of 31 August 1832, *The Times*, 19 December.

Lodge, Sir Oliver
1889    *Modern views on electricity*. London New York: Macmillan.
1914    Presidential address to the British Association. *Brit. Assoc. Report*, 1913.

Mach, E.
1911    *History and roots of the principle of conservation of energy*. Trans. Phillip E. B. Jourdain. Chicago/London: Open Court.

MacLeod, Roy M.
1969    Science and government in Victorian England: light house illumination and the Board of Trade, 1866–1886. In *Isis* 60:91–103.

Manuel, Frank Edward
1951    *The Age of Reason*. Ithaca: Cornel Univ. Press.
1963    *Sir Isaac Newton, Historian*. Cambridge: Harvard Univ. Press.
1968    *A Portrait of Isaac Newton*. Cambridge: Harvard University Press.

Marcet, Jane
1806    *Conversations on Chemistry, in which the elements of that science are familiarly explained, and illustrated by experiments.* Two volumes. Sixteenth edition, two volumes, London, 1853.

Martin, Thomas
1934    *Michael Faraday*. London.

Maxwell, James Clerk
1873    *A treatise on electricity and magnetism*, two volumes. Oxford: Clarendon Press. Third edition, 1891; Dover reprint, 1954.
1890    *Scientific papers*, ed. W. D. Niven, two volumes, Cambridge Univ. Press. Reprint in one volume, New York: Dover. *See also* Larmor.

McGuire, J. E.
1966    "Intellectual History or Scientific Biography?" (a review of L. P.

Williams's *Michael Faraday*). In *History of Science*, ed. A. C. Crombie and M. Hoskins, 5:140–44, Oxford.

Meadows, Denis
1954    *Obedient Men: an autobiography*. London and New York: Appleton, Longmans, S. J. R. Saunders.

Merton, Robert King
1957    *Social theory and social structure. Toward the codification of theory and research*. Revised edition. Glencoe, Ill.: Free Press.
1957    "Priorities in scientific discovery." In *Am. Soc. Rev.* 22:635–59.
1968    "The Matthew effect in science." *Science*, 5 January 1968, 159:56–63.

Meyerson, Emile
1930    *Identity and reality*, trans. Kate Loewenberg. London: George Allen and Unwin. Dover reprint, 1962.

Moll, Gerrit (or Gerard)
1831, 1833 *On the alleged decline of science in England*, by A. Foreigner (ed. M. Faraday). London: Boosey.
        Letter to Faraday. See Agassi (ed.), An Unpublished Paper . . . .

Mottelay, Paul F.
1933, 1935 *Bibliographical history of electricity and magnetism*, chronologically arranged. With an introduction by S. P. Thompson. London and Philadelphia.

Munro, John
1890    *Pioneers of electricity*. London and Chicago.

Newton, Sir Isaac
1796    *Four letters to Dr. Bentley; containing some arguments in proof of a deity*. London. This is also published in various works and editions, including some editions of Bentley's sermons (Boyle lectures).

Oersted, Hans Christian
1820    *Experimenta circa effectum conflictus electrici in acum magneticam*, Hafnia, 21 July. 4 pages, privately published. English translation is titled differently: Experiments on the effect of a current of electricity on the magnetic needle. In Thomson's *Annals of Philosophy* 16:273–276, and in Dibner's *Oersted*.
1852    *The soul in nature with supplementary contributions*, trans. Leonora and Joanna B. Horner. London: Henry G. Bohr. Johnson's Reprint, 1970.
1920    *Naturvidenskabelige skrifter, Scientific papers*. Collected works in

the language of their publication with two essays by the ed. Kirstine Meyer. Copenhagen.

Ohm, Georg Simon
1827    *Die galvanische Kette mathematische bearbeitet*, Berlin. English translation, 1841, *The galvanic circuit investigated mathematically*, trans. W. Francis. In Taylor, *Scientific Memoirs*, Vol. 2. Reprinted with a preface by the editor, T. D. Lockwood. New York: Van Nostrand, 1891. Determination of the law in accordance with which metals conduct contact electricity, together with an outline of a theory of the voltair apparatus and of Schweigger's Multiplier. In Nies H. de Vanrey Heathcote, A translation of the papers in which Ohm first announced his law of the galvanic circuit, prefaced by some account of the work of his predecessors. In *Science Progress*, 1931.

Olson, Richard
1969    "The reception of Boscovich's ideas in Scotland." In *Isis* 60:91–103.

O'Rahilley, Alfred
1938    *Electromagnetics.* London: Macmillan; Dover reprint.

Ostwald, Friedric Wilhelm
1909    *Grosse Männer*, Leipzig.
1924    *Michael Faraday, eine psychographische Studie* . . . Zurich. *See also* Chemical Society, London.

Paris, John Ayrton
1831    *The life of Sir Humphry Davy*. London: Colburn and Bentley, both a one-volume edition and a two-volume edition.

Peacock, George
1855    *Life of Thomas Young*. London: Murray.

Philbrick, George A., and H. M. Poynter
1965    "The electronic analog computer as a lab tool," ed. H. M. Poynter. In *A palimpsest on the electronic analog art*, printed by George A. Philbrick Researchers, Inc., Dedham, Mass., pp. 4–10.

Philo Veritatis (pseudonym)
1819    *Three minutes' commentary on the mistakes of Dr. Young in his observations on Sir R. Phillips' theory of proximate causes of material phenomena.* London.

Planck, Max
1949    *Scientific autobiography and other papers*. With a memorial

address by Max von Laue, trans. Frank Gaynor. New York: Philosophical Library.

Poisson, Siméon Denis

1811    *Mémoires sur la distribution de l'électricité à la surface des corps conducteurs*, Memoires de l'Institut, Paris, pp. 1–92, 163–274.

1842    *A treatise of mechanics*, translated from the French and elucidated with explanatory notes by H. H. Harte. Two volumes, London. 1958.

Polanyi, Michael

1932    Theories of adsorption of gases, *Trans. Faraday Society*, 28:316–33.

1958    *Personal knowledge; towards a post-critical philosophy*. London: Routledge and Kegan Paul; Chicago: University of Chicago Press; New York: Harper Torchbook edition, 1964.

1969    *Knowing and being*. Ed. Marjorie Grene. Chicago: University of Chicago Press.

Popper, Sir Karl R.

1945, 1952    *The open society and its enemies*, in 2 volumes. London: Routledge and Kegan Paul; Princeton: Princeton Univ. Press, one-volume edition 1952. 4th revised edition, 1960. Reprint, Harper Torchbook edition.

1958    *The poverty of historicism*. London. Reprint, Harper Torchbook edition.

1959    *The logic of scientific discovery*, London and New York. Reprint, Harper Torchbook edition.

1962, 1963    *Conjectures and refutations*, London and New York. Reprint, Harper Torchbook edition.

Post, E. J.

1967    "General covariance in electromagnetism," ed. Mario Bunge. In *Delaware seminar in the foundations of physics*. New York: Springer-Verlag.

Poynter, H. M. *See* Philbrick, George A.

Poynting, John Henry

1920    *Collected scientific papers*. Cambridge: Cambridge Univ. Press. and J. J. Thomson,

1902    *A textbook of physics* 1, *Properties of matter*, London. Eleventh edition, London 1927.

Priestley, Joseph
1767        *The history and present state of electricity, with original experi-
            ments*. London. Third edition, 2 volumes, London 1775.
Raumer, Frederick von
1836        *England in 1835*. Philadelphia.
Rayleigh, Lord
1942, 1963  *The life of Sir J. J. Thomson*. Cambridge: Cambridge Univ. Press.
Riguad, Stephen Peter
1841        *Correspondence of scientific men of the seventeenth century, including
            letters of Barrow, Flamsteed, Wallis, and Newton*, printed from the
            originals in the collection of the Right Honourable the Earle of
            Macclesfield, 2 vols. Oxford University Press.
Roget, Peter Mark
1829        *Four treatises on electricity, on galvanism, on magnetism, on
            electro-magnetism*, Society for the Diffusion of Useful Knowledge,
            Library of Useful Knowledge, Natural Philosophy. London.
Schagrin, Morton
1963        The resistance to Ohm's Law. In *Am. J. Phys.* 31:536–47.
Schouten, J. A.
1949        *Tensor Analysis for physicists*, Oxford.
Snow, A. J.
1926        *Matter and gravity in Newton's physical philosophy. A study in the
            natural philosophy of Newton's time*. London: Oxford Univ. Press.
Snow, C. P.
1963        *The two cultures: and a second look*. An expanded version of the two
            cultures and the scientific revolutions. Cambridge University Press.
            New York: New American Library.
1967        *Variety of Men*. New York: Scribner.
Stephen, Sir Leslie (ed.)
1885        *Dictionary of National Biography*. London: Smith, Elder.
Stewart, Balfour
1890        *The conservation of energy*. International Science Series, New
            York: Appleton.
Stimson, Dorothy
1948        *Scientists and amateurs. A history of the Royal Society*. New York:
            Schumann.
Sturgeon, William
1850        *Scientific researches, experimental and theoretical, in electricity,*

*magnetism, galvanism, electro-magnetism, and electro-chemistry*. London and Barry.

Synge, J. L.

1970　Some reassessments (review of C. Truesdale's Essays in the history of mechanics). In *Science* 168 (17 April) 354.

Tait, P. G.

1860　*Position and prospect of physical science*. Edinburgh.

1876*a*　Force. In *Nature* 14:459–63.

1876*b*　Note appended to his translation of F. Mohr's View of the nature of heat. In *Phil. Mag.* 2:110–14. *See also* Thomson and Tait.

Thomson, Silvanus Phillips

1898　*Michael Faraday. His life and work*. London: Cassell; reprinted, 1901.

1910　*Life of William Thomson, Baron Kelvin of Largs*, two vols. London: Macmillan.

Thompson, Jane S. and Helen G.

1920　*Silvanus P. Thompson, his life and letters*. London.

Thomson, Joseph John

1885　Om some applications of dynamical principles to physical phenomena. In the *Philosophical Transactions of the Royal Society of London*, Vol. 176, 307–42.

1893　*Recent researches in electricity and magnetism*. Intended as a sequel to Professor Clerk-Maxwell's Treatise on electricity and magnetism. Oxford: Clarendon Press.

1904, 1905　*Electricity and matter*. New Haven, Cambridge, and New York.

1907　*The corpuscular theory of matter*. London: Constable.

Thomson, Thomas

1830　*History of Chemistry*, 2 vols. London.

Thomson, Sir William

1872　*Reprints of papers on electricity and magnetism*. London, 2d ed., 1884.

1882–1911　*Mathematical and physical papers ... collected from different scientific periodicals, from May 1841 to the present time (vols. 4–6 arranged and revised by Sir Joseph Larmor)*, six vols. Cambridge University Press.

1904　Baltimore lectures on molecular dynamics and the wave theory of light. London: Clay.

Thomson, William, and Tait, Peter Guthrie

1867        *Treatise on natural philosophy*. Vol. I. Oxford; new ed., Cambridge, 1879–83.

1873        *Elements of natural philosophy, Part I*. Oxford; 2d ed., Cambridge, 1879.

Thorpe, T. E.

1896        *Humphry Davy, poet and philosopher*, London.

Tyndall, John

1855        On the existence of a magnetic medium in space. In *Phil. Mag.* 9:205–9.

1868, 1870 *Faraday as a discoverer*. London: Longmans, Green; reprinted, 1894; 1898.

1870*a*      *Notes of a course of nine lectures on light delivered at the* R.I.G.B. 8 April–3 June 1869, Longmans, Green.

1870*b*      *Notes of a course of seven lectures on electrical phenomena and theories, delivered at the R.I.G.B., 28 April–9 June 1870*. London: Longmans, Green.

1871        *Fragments of science for unscientific people*: a series of detached essays, lectures, and reviews. London: Longmans. 10th impression, 1899.

1873        *Six lectures delivered in America in 1872–73*. London: Longmans, Green; 4th ed., 1885. New York: Appleton.

1876        *Lessons in electricity at the Royal Institution 1875–1876*. London: Longmans, Green; 3d ed., 1882.

1891, 1892 *New fragments of science*. London: Longmans, Green.

Watson, James D. *See also* Eve and Creasy.

1968        *The double helix; a personal account of the discovery of the structure of DNA*. New York: Atheneum.

Watts, Isaac

1753        *Works*. London: Jennings and Doddridge; other editions, 1800, 1810–11, 1812, 1813.

Weyl, Herman

1931        *The theory of groups and quantum mechanics*, trans. from the second revised German edition by H. P. Robertson. London: Methuen.

Whewell, William

1837, 1857 *History of the inductive sciences: from the earliest to the present time*, 3 vols. London: Parker and son; 3d edition with additions,

New York: Appleton, 1860. Whewell's works are available in Johnson Reprints.

1858    *Noveum organum renovatum.* Being the second part of the philosophy of the inductive sciences. Third edition with large additions. London: Parker and Son.

1860    *On the philosophy of discovery*, chapters historical and critical; including the completion of the third edition of the philosophy of the inductive sciences. London: Parker and Son.

Whitehead, Alfred North

1920    *The concept of nature.* Tarner Lectures, delivered in Trinity College, November 1919. Cambridge Univ. Press.

1922    *The principle of relativity with application to physical science.* Cambridge Univ. Press.

1929    *Process and reality.* An essay in cosmology. Gifford Lectures, 1927–28. Cambridge Univ. Press.

Whittaker, Sir Edmund T.

1910–1953 *A history of theories of aether and electricity.* 1: the classical theories. Revised and enlarged edition, 1951; 2: *The modern theories, 1900–1926*, 1953. London, Edinburgh, Toronto, New York: Thomas Nelson and Sons.

Whyte, Lancelot Law

1961    *Roger Joseph Boscovich.* New York: Humanities Press.

Williams, L. Pearce

1965    *Michael Faraday: a biography.* London: Chapman. New York: Basic Books.

1967    Some doubts on Faraday's authorship of "On Argument." In *Isis* 53:389–91.

Young, Thomas

1807    *A course of lectures on natural philosophy and the mechanical arts*, 2 vols. London: Johnson.

1855    *Miscellaneous works of the late Thomas Young*, 3 vols.; ed. George Peacock. London: Murray. *See also* Peacock.

# Name Index

# Name Index

Core, George, 39
Cotes, Roger, 109
Coulomb, Charles Augustin de, 40, 114, 115, 146, 234, 265–67, 270–72, 274, 321, 324
Crooke, Sir Thomas W. F., 10

Dalton, John, 37, 85, 118, 119, 185–87, 215, 218–25, 234, 252, 253, 255, 256, 274–78, 327
Darbishire, Francis V., 11
Davy, Sir Humphry, 1, 2, 12, 15–29, 33–43, 67, 77, 90, 91, 117, 118, 120–23, 127, 145, 147, 152, 165, 169, 195, 205, 211, 213, 220, 234, 244, 263, 330, 331
Davy, Dr. John, 118, 120, 123, 147
Delametherie, J. C., 28, 90
De la Rive. *See* Rive
Democritus, 44, 90, 110
Descartes, René, 44, 67, 87, 90, 114, 115, 154, 178, 205, 312, 324, 329
Dewey, John, 153
Dibner, Bern, 45
Disraeli, Isaac, 119
Döbereiner, Johann Wolfgang, 251
Doureen, D. I., 41
DuBois-Reymond, Emil, 290
Dufay, Charles François, 277
Duhem, Pierre, 129, 158, 198
Dulong, Pierre Louis, 251
Dumas, Jean Baptiste, 173, 330

Eddington, Sir Arthur Stanley, 8, 144, 166, 316
Edison, Thomas Alva, 200
Einstein, Albert, vii, x, 4, 5, 7, 8, 16, 24, 43, 50, 65, 78, 85, 88, 105, 126, 144, 148, 166, 167, 176, 194, 201, 208, 211, 225, 229, 232, 308, 312, 314, 315, 316, 317, 318, 319, 324, 325, 328
Epinus. *See* Aepinus
Euclid, viii, 232
Euler, Leonhard, 80, 154, 329

Faraday, Sarah, x, 21, 292–94, 330
Fitzgerald, George Francis, 323
Fourier, Jean Baptiste Joseph, Baron, 223
Franklin, Benjamin, 12, 16, 40, 84, 114, 163, 244, 277

Fresnel, Augustin Jean, 65, 75, 212
Freud, Sigmund, x, 293

Galileo, 88, 148, 153, 303, 316
Gassiot, John Peter, 35
Gauss, Karl Friedrich, 110–12, 115, 308
Geiger, Hans, 283
Gilbert, Dr. William, 243, 303
Gladstone, John, 11, 37, 102, 166, 170, 175, 198–200, 293
Goethe, 125
Gogh, Vincent van, 34
Goudsmit, S., 165
Gray, Stephen, 235, 243, 244
Green, George, 308
Grotthuss, Frieherr Theodor von, 281
Grove, Sir William Robert, 27, 35, 65, 66, 75–77, 154, 156, 207, 211, 316
Guthrie, Frederick, 322

Hadamard, Jacques, 41
Hadfield, Sir Robert Abbott, 20, 33
Hamilton, Sir William Rowan, 94, 204, 205
Hansteen, Christian, 199
Hare, Dr. Robert, 67, 147, 149
Harris, Sir William Snow, 35
Haydn, Franz Joseph, x, 34
Heaviside, Oliver, 8, 114, 115, 316
Hegel, Georg Wilhelm Friedrich, 90
Heisenberg, Werner, 158, 325
Helmholtz, Hermann Ludwig Ferdinand von, viii, 68, 113, 129, 140, 146, 154, 191–200, 207, 256, 301, 306
Henry, Joseph, 260
Herapath, John, 67
Herschel, Sir John Frederick William, 22, 35, 36, 70, 72, 133, 174, 297–99, 303, 328, 329
Hertz, Heinrich Rudolf, 68, 108, 113, 115, 154, 208, 321
Higgins, William, 118
Hobbes, Thomas, 119
Hoff, Jacobus Henricus van't, 126
Hooke, Robert, 63, 119, 125, 145
Humboldt, Alexander Freiherr von, 37, 304

Ibsen, Henrik, 295

Jacobi, Karl Gustav Jacob, 67

# Subject Index